M000266148

Paul Long, Sarah Lawrey and Victoria Ellis

Cambridge International AS and A Level

IT

Coursebook

CAMBRIDGE
UNIVERSITY PRESS

CAMBRIDGE
UNIVERSITY PRESS

University Printing House, Cambridge CB2 8BS, United Kingdom

One Liberty Plaza, 20th Floor, New York, NY 10006, USA

477 Williamstown Road, Port Melbourne, VIC 3207, Australia

4843/24, 2nd Floor, Ansari Road, Daryaganj, Delhi – 110002, India

79 Anson Road, #06–04/06, Singapore 079906

Cambridge University Press is part of the University of Cambridge.

It furthers the University's mission by disseminating knowledge in the pursuit of education, learning and research at the highest international levels of excellence.

Information on this title: www.cambridge.org

© Cambridge University Press 2016

This publication is in copyright. Subject to statutory exception and to the provisions of relevant collective licensing agreements, no reproduction of any part may take place without the written permission of Cambridge University Press.

First published 2016

20 19 18 17 16 15 14 13 12 11 10 9 8 7 6 5 4

Printed in Dubai by Oriental Press

A catalogue record for this publication is available from the British Library

ISBN 978-1-107-57724-4 Paperback with CD-ROM

Cambridge University Press has no responsibility for the persistence or accuracy of URLs for external or third-party internet websites referred to in this publication, and does not guarantee that any content on such websites is, or will remain, accurate or appropriate. Information regarding prices, travel timetables, and other factual information given in this work is correct at the time of first printing but Cambridge University Press does not guarantee the accuracy of such information thereafter.

....

NOTICE TO TEACHERS IN THE UK
It is illegal to reproduce any part of this work in material form (including photocopying and electronic storage) except under the following circumstances:
(i)   where you are abiding by a licence granted to your school or institution by the Copyright Licensing Agency;
(ii)   where no such licence exists, or where you wish to exceed the terms of a licence, and you have gained the written permission of Cambridge University Press;
(iii)   where you are allowed to reproduce without permission under the provisions of Chapter 3 of the Copyright, Designs and Patents Act 1988, which covers, for example, the reproduction of short passages within certain types of educational anthology and reproduction for the purposes of setting examination questions.

....

All questions and answers provided have been written by the authors. In examinations, the way marks are awarded may be different.

Throughout this book we have used specific brand names to illustrate points in examples. Please note that the examples used do not constitute an exhaustive list, and other brand names are available and should be considered.

Content

AS

A2

Learning objectives

By the end of this chapter, you will be able to:

- define the differences between data, information and knowledge
- define static and dynamic data
- compare static information sources with dynamic information sources
- define direct and indirect data sources
- understand the advantages and disadvantages of gathering data from direct and indirect data sources
- understand how the accuracy, relevance, age, level of detail and completeness of information can affect its quality
- describe the coding of data and discuss its advantages and disadvantages
- evaluate the need to encode data and analyse different methods for encoding data
- define encryption and describe different methods of encryption
- evaluate the need for encryption and how it can be used to protect data
- discuss encryption protocols
- define validation and analyse a range of validation methods
- define verification and analyse verification methods
- explain the need for both validation and verification
- define proof reading

KEY TERMS

Data: raw numbers, letters, symbols, sounds or images without meaning

Information: data with context and meaning

Knowledge: information to which human experience has been applied

Key Terms
— clear and straightforward explanations are provided for the most important words in each topic..

DISCUSSION POINT

Some people get a little confused with dynamic data because they think it can be any data that changes at any time. For example, some people think that any website includes dynamic data. However, if you look at http://www.bbc.co.uk/contact the information on this page is mainly static with links to other pages. Although it can be changed, it can only be done by changing the actual data on the page, whereas dynamic data changes because the original source has changed. If you look at www.bbc.co.uk/click, you will see that most of the information on this page is sourced from programme schedules and programme information which will be stored in another database – this makes it dynamic data because it will update when a new programme has been shown.

Extension activities and Discussion points
— additional lesson activities.

Learning Objectives
— set the scene of each chapter, help with navigation through the book and give a reminder of what's important about each topic.

TASK

Look at the BBC website www.bbc.co.uk – identify which data is static and which data is dynamic (updates automatically).

Task
— exercises for the student to test their knowledge and understanding.

QUESTION

A company creates websites using style sheets.

1. Identify one item of data that will be used by the company.
2. Describe how this item of data can become information.
3. Describe the term knowledge.

Questions
— supporting questions that the student should be able to answer to demonstrate understanding at this level..

Remember

JavaScript is a programming language that can be used to add interactivity to web pages. Its code can be integrated into a HTML file to: create buttons, create text boxes, change content etc. It can be integrated with a range of other web-based programming languages such as PHP. JavaScript is often use with HTML forms, where it can validate data or perform actions such as when a button is pressed.

Remember
— these are pieces of vital information to remind you about key facts and highlight important points.

TIP

Take a blank notepad and draw a shape in the bottom right-hand corner, then draw the same shape but in a slightly different position on the next page. Repeat this on a number of pages. You can then create a basic animation by flicking through the page of the book.

Tip
— quick suggestions to help you to understand important concepts.

EXAMPLE

The confectionary shop could use various indirect sources including:

- giving out a survey to customers who have purchased sweets from the other shops (the price was given to the customer for the purpose of selling the sweet which may have been a different date or may have been discounted)

- looking at till receipts from the shop (the price was printed on the till receipt for the purpose of providing proof of purchase, not for identifying prices)

Examples
— offer students contextualised explanation of critical points

Review Questions

1   Give an example of data (**1**).

2   Describe the term knowledge (**1**).

A news and sports website includes both static and dynamic data.

3   a   Compare static and dynamic data (**4**).

   b   Identify and describe two factors that affect the quality of information on the website (**4**).

   c   Give an example of coded data related to the news and sports website (**1**).

The website streams news and sports videos.

   d   Explain why the video is compressed when it is encoded (**2**).

   e   Identify three factors that will affect the size of a video file (**1**).

   f   Identify and describe two factors that affect the file size of images on the website (**4**).

Users can pay for premium services on the website using their credit card.

4   a   Explain why the website uses https at the beginning of the website address instead of http (**4**).

   b   Describe symmetric encryption (**1**).

The journalists working for the website encrypt their emails.

   c   Describe how asymmetric encryption is used with emails (**2**).

When the users subscribe to premium features, they have to choose a password.

   d   Describe how verification can be used when entering the password (**1**).

There is a form on the website that can be used to submit news stories. When data is entered onto the form, it is validated.

5   a   Describe the purpose of validation (**1**).

   b   Using an example related to submitting a news story, identify and describe one method of validation (**3**).

Review Questions
— final set of questions to test student comprehension and to give any extension tasks.

This full-colour, illustrated textbook has been written by experienced authors specifically for the Cambridge International AS and A Level Information Technology syllabus (9626).

The qualification replaces A-Level Applied ICT. The new syllabus develops a broad range of IT skills. Throughout the book there are examples of IT in practice, tasks for students to complete, discussion points or extension exercises to provoke further thought and discussion and questions that will test students' knowledge and understanding. Whenever a task is presented, we would encourage students to carry it out before progressing further.

The syllabus defines three assessment objectives: AO1 Recall, select and communicate knowledge and understanding of IT, AO2 Apply knowledge, understanding and skills to produce IT-based solutions and AO3 Analyse, evaluate, make reasoned judgements and present conclusions. Each chapter defines a set of learning objectives which closely match these assessment objectives and a series of key concepts (hardware and software, network, the internet, system life cycle, new technologies) recur throughout the syllabus. This coursebook has been written to reflect these, in particular in the following chapters: the impact of information technology (Chapter 12); hardware and software (Chapter 2); network (Chapter 13); the internet (Chapters 4 and 19); system life cycle (Chapter 15); new technologies (Chapter 11). It is not necessary to work through the book in order from start to finish.

The content of the syllabus is geared towards current practice and practical applications of computers in everyday life. To reflect this, the practical elements of the book are not concerned with, for example, providing step-by-step advice on how to use particular software, but rather with helping students to discover what is available and have the confidence to apply their knowledge to different types of software. This will help to prepare students for the many different aspects of using computers that they will encounter in life, and not just for an exam.

Chapter 1
Data, information, knowledge and processing

Learning objectives

By the end of this chapter, you will be able to:

- define the differences between data, information and knowledge
- define static and dynamic data
- compare static information sources with dynamic information sources
- define direct and indirect data sources
- understand the advantages and disadvantages of gathering data from direct and indirect data sources
- understand how the accuracy, relevance, age, level of detail and completeness of information can affect its quality
- describe the coding of data and discuss its advantages and disadvantages
- evaluate the need to encode data and analyse different methods for encoding data
- define encryption and describe different methods of encryption
- evaluate the need for encryption and how it can be used to protect data
- discuss encryption protocols
- define validation and analyse a range of validation methods
- define verification and analyse verification methods
- explain the need for both validation and verification
- define proof reading

1.01 Data, information and knowledge

KEY TERMS

Data: raw numbers, letters, symbols, sounds or images without meaning

Information: data with context and meaning

Knowledge: information to which human experience has been applied

Data

Data is raw numbers, letters, symbols, sounds or images with no meaning.

EXAMPLE

P952BR

@bbcclick

359

23557.99

Figure 1.01 - Example of raw data.

The data P952BR could have several meanings. It could possibly be:

- a product code
- a postal / ZIP code
- a car registration number.

As it is not known what the data means, it is meaningless.

DISCUSSION POINT

When answering a question such as 'Give one item of data', do not try to explain what the data means because it then becomes **information**. Just give the raw numbers, letters, symbols or image.

Information

When data items are given context and meaning, they become information. A person reading the information will then know what it means.

Data is given context by identifying what sort of data it is. This still does not make it information but it is a step on the way to it becoming information as shown in the next example.

EXAMPLE

Data	Context	Comment
P952BR	A product code	This is a product code but it is still not known what it is a product code for so it is still data.
@bbcclick	A Twitter handle	This is an address used for Twitter but it is not information unless it is known to be a Twitter handle or used within Twitter software. It's also not known whose address it is.
359	Price in Pakistani Rupees	This is a currency value but it is not known what the price is for, so it is still data.

For the data to become information, it needs to be given meaning. Information is useful because it means something.

EXAMPLE

Data	Context	Meaning
P952BR	A product code	A product code for a can of noodles.
@bbcclick	A Twitter handle	The Twitter address for the BBC's weekly technology show, *Click*, which is worth watching on BBC World News and BBC2 to keep up to date with technology.
359	Price in Pakistani rupees	The price of a mobile phone cover.

Knowledge

Knowledge is basically what a person knows. This is known as their knowledge base. A knowledge base gets larger over time as a person gains experience or learning. Knowledge requires a person to understand what information is, based on their experience and knowledge base. Crown Prince Salman was appointed Crown Prince of Saudi Arabia on 18 June 2012. This is information. Knowing that he had been Crown Prince for 2 years on 1 August 2014 is knowledge. Knowledge allows data to be interpreted. In computing terms, knowledge is also what a machine knows through the use of a knowledge base consisting of rules and facts, often found in knowledge-based systems, modelling and simulation software.

EXAMPLE

Information	Knowledge
100km/h is the speed limit on expressways in Pakistan.	Travelling at 120km/h on expressways in Pakistan is illegal.
Figure 1.02 - A red traffic light.	A red traffic light means a car should stop.
359 Pakistani rupees is the price of a mobile phone cover.	The price of a mobile phone cover is more expensive than a cup of coffee.

QUESTIONS

A company creates websites using style sheets.

1. Identify one item of data that will be used by the company.
2. Describe how this item of data can become information.
3. Describe the term knowledge.

1.02 Sources of data

🔑 **KEY TERMS**

Static data: data that does not normally change

Dynamic data: data that changes automatically without user intervention

Direct data source: data that is collected for the purpose for which it will be used

Indirect data source: data that was collected for a different purpose (secondary source)

Static data

Figure 1.03 - A good example of static data.

Static means 'still'. It is data that does not normally change. **Static data** is either fixed or has to be changed manually by editing a document.

EXAMPLE

- title of a web page
- magazines
- CD-ROMs
- column headings for a football league table (e.g. P, W, D, L, F, A, GD)
- instructions on a data entry screen.

Dynamic data

Dynamic means 'moving'. It is data that updates as a result of the source data changing. **Dynamic data** is updated automatically without user intervention.

3

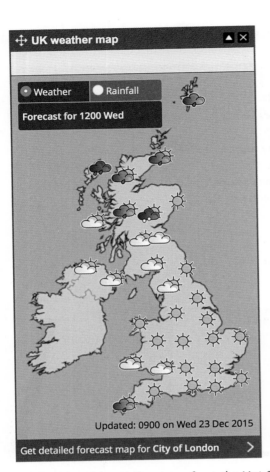

Figure 1.04 - This weather map, from the Met Office website, is an example of dynamic data.

Static information sources compared with dynamic information sources

Static information source	Dynamic information source
The information does not change on a regular basis.	Information is updated automatically when the original data changes.
The information can go out of date quickly because it is not designed to be changed on a regular basis.	It is most likely to be up to date as it changes automatically based on the source data.
The information can be viewed offline because live data is not required.	An internet or network connection to the source data is required, which can be costly and can also be slow in remote areas.
It is more likely to be accurate because time will have been taken to check the information being published, as it will be available for a long period of time.	The data may have been produced very quickly and so may contain errors.

Table 1.01 - Static and dynamic information sources.

EXAMPLE

- live sports results on a website (when a goal is scored, the scores will update on the website)
- news feeds on a mobile phone app (when the news is changed in the main database, the news feed will be updated on the phone)
- availability of tickets for a concert (when somebody books a ticket, the ticket is no longer available)
- product prices for a till/point of sale (if a price is reduced or increased in the database, this new price will be used the next time the barcode is scanned)
- train expected arrival times (these will update automatically based on the train's position)
- profit for a product in a spreadsheet (profit = price – cost so when either the price or cost changes, then the profit changes too)

DISCUSSION POINT

Some people get a little confused by dynamic data because they think it can be any data that changes at any time. For example, some people think that any website includes dynamic data. However, if you look at www.aljazeera.com/contactus, the information on this page is mainly static, with links to other pages. Although it can be changed, it can only be done by changing the actual data on the page, whereas dynamic data changes because the original source has changed. If you look at www.aljazeera.com/programmes, you will see that most of the information on this page is sourced from programme schedules and programme information, which will be stored in another database. This makes it dynamic data because it will update when a new programme is scheduled.

TASK

Look at the Al Jazeera website www.aljazeera.com and identify which data is static and which data is dynamic (updates automatically).

Direct data source

Figure 1.05 - Direct data source.

Data collected from a **direct data source** (primary source) must be used for the same purpose for which it was collected. It is often the case that the data will have been collected or requested by the person who intends to use the data. The data must not already exist for another purpose though. When collecting the data, the person collecting should know for what purpose they intend to use the data.

EXAMPLE

A sports shop wants to find out what other shops are charging for trainers. There are various direct sources that this data can be collected from. These could include:

- visiting the other shops and noting down the prices
- visiting the other shops' websites and noting down the prices
- carrying out a survey of other shop owners to ask their prices (although they are unlikely to want to give these).

Indirect data source

Figure 1.06 - Indirect data source.

Data collected from an **indirect data source** (secondary source) already existed for another purpose. Although it can still be collected by the person who intends to use it, it was often collected by a different person or organisation.

EXAMPLE

The sports shop could use various indirect sources to find out what other shops are charging for trainers including:

- carrying out a survey of customers who have purchased trainers from the other shops (the price was originally given to the customer for the purpose of selling the trainers which may have been given on a different date to when it is now being used or it may have been discounted at the time)
- looking at till receipts from the shop (the price is printed on the till receipt for the purpose of providing proof of purchase, not for identifying prices).

TASK

Which of the following are direct data sources and which are indirect data sources?

Data	Reason collected	Reason used
Names and email addresses of members of a political party	To record their membership and to be able to contact them.	To contact members by email to see if they will donate some money.
Employee attendance dates and times	To identify when employees attended work and to calculate their wages.	To allow a police officer to check an employee's alibi if a crime has been committed.
Flight times and prices from airline websites	To compare the prices and times for a trip to Florida.	To decide the best flight to use for a trip to Florida.
Names, ages and addresses of people	For a national census.	To allow a marketing company to find out which areas have the highest population of children.
Weather measurements from a weather station	To record the current weather.	To show the current temperature and rainfall on a website.

5

DISCUSSION POINT

Remember that direct data is usually used by the person that collected it and for the purpose they collected it. However, it's also possible for a person to collect data from an indirect (secondary) source. For example, if a journalist is writing a news article and bases his story on existing news articles, then he has used indirect sources rather than interviewing the people involved in the original story.

Advantages and disadvantages of gathering data from direct and indirect data sources

The general rule is that data collected directly for the purpose for which it is intended is more likely to be accurate and relevant than data that is obtained from existing data (indirect source).

Direct data source	Indirect data source
The data will be relevant because what is needed has been collected.	Additional data that is not required will exist that may take time to sort through and some data that is required may not exist.
The original source is known and so can be trusted.	The original source may not be known and so it can't be assumed that it is reliable.
It can take a long time to gather original data rather than use data that already exists.	The data is immediately available.
A large sample of statistical data can be difficult to collect for one-off purposes.	If statistical analysis is required, then there are more likely to be large samples available.
The data is likely to be up to date because it has been collected recently.	Data may be out of date because it was collected at a different time.
Bias can be eliminated by asking specific questions.	Original data may be biased due to its source.
The data can be collected and presented in the format required.	The data is unlikely to be in the format required, which may make extracting the data difficult.

Table 1.02 - Direct and indirect data sources.

QUESTIONS

The spreadsheet below is used to calculate the area of a driveway.

	A	B	C
1	**Area calculator**		
2	Length =	3	m
3	Width =	5	m
4	Area =	15	m²

Figure 1.07 - Part of a spreadsheet.

4 Identify one item of data that is static.

5 Identify one item of data that is dynamic.

The builder using the spreadsheet needs to know the length and width of a driveway for a customer.

6 Identify one direct source the builder could use to find the length and width.

7 Identify one indirect source the builder could use to find the length and width.

8 Give one advantage of using the direct source instead of the indirect source to find the length and width.

1.03 Quality of information

The quality of information is determined by a number of attributes.

Accuracy

Information that is inaccurate is clearly not good enough. Data must be accurate in order to be considered of good quality. Imagine being told that you need to check in at the airport 45 minutes before the flight leaves, so you turn up at 18:10 for a 19:05 flight only to find that you were actually supposed to check in one hour early.

EXAMPLE

Examples of inaccurate information include:

- decimal point in the wrong place, for example $90.30 instead of $903.00 could suggest a product is much cheaper than it really is

- misspelling such as 'stair' instead of 'stare', where words have completely different meanings

- misplaced characters, such as a licence plate of BW9EP3T instead of BW93PET.

Relevance

Information must be relevant to its purpose. Having additional information that is not required means that the user has to search through the data to find what is actually required.

> **EXAMPLE**
>
> Examples of irrelevant information include:
>
> - being given a bus timetable when you want to catch a train
> - being told the rental price of a car when you want to buy the car
> - a user guide for a mobile phone that includes instructions on how to assemble a plug.

Age

Information must be up to date in order to be useful. Old information is likely to be out of date and therefore no longer useful. When using indirect data sources, always check when the information was produced.

> **EXAMPLE**
>
> Examples of out of date information include:
>
> - the number of residents in a town based on a census from 2011, but 500 new homes have been built in the town since then
> - a rugby score that has not been updated for 5 minutes during which time a player scored.

Level of detail

There needs to be the right amount of information for it to be good quality. It's possible to have either too little or too much information provided. If there is too much information, then it can be difficult to find the exact information required. If there is not enough information, then it is not possible to use it correctly.

> **EXAMPLE**
>
> A person orders a pizza. They ask for a large pepperoni to be delivered. They forgot to say what type of base they wanted and where it should be delivered to. The pizza company does not have enough information to fulfil the order.
>
> A traveller needs to catch a train from Bhopal to Kacheguda. They phone up to find out the time of departure and arrival, but they have to listen to all the times of the stations in between before they get the arrival time at Kacheguda.

Completeness

All information that is required must be provided in order for it to be of good quality. Not having all the information required means it cannot be used properly.

> **EXAMPLE**
>
> A person has booked their car in for a service over the phone. The mechanic tells them the name of the street but doesn't give the building number.

> **TASK**
>
> Look at the invitation below.
>
> Come and Celbrate
> # Emmanuel's Bithday
> 11:00–1:30pm
>
>
>
> 18 Main Street
>
> RSVP
>
> There will be a magician. The magician was born on March 1st 1978 in Queen Elizabeth hospital in Birmingham.
>
> **Figure 1.08 - Birthday party invitation.**
>
> Describe how accuracy, relevance, level of detail and completeness affect the quality of information in the invitation.

8

QUESTIONS

9 Identify three factors that could affect the quality of information.

10 Describe how the age of information could affect the quality of information within a user guide for a mobile phone.

1.04 Coding, encoding and encrypting data

KEY TERMS

Coding: representing data by assigning a code to it for classification or identification

Encoding: storing data in a specific format

Encryption: scrambling data so it cannot be understood without a decryption key to make it unreadable if intercepted

SSL: Secure Sockets Layer

TLS: Transport Layer Security

HTTPS: hypertext transfer protocol secure

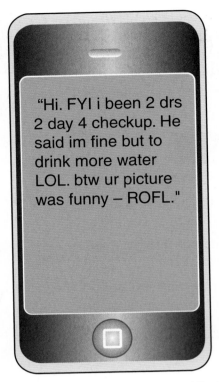

"Hi. FYI i been 2 drs 2 day 4 checkup. He said im fine but to drink more water LOL. btw ur picture was funny – ROFL."

Figure 1.09 - Text message on a mobile phone.

Coding data

You are probably very familiar with **coding** data already. When you send a text message or instant message you probably code your data. You might use codes like:

- LOL = laugh out loud
- ROFL = roll on floor laughing
- FYI = for your information
- BTW = by the way
- 2 = to
- 4 = for
- BRB = be right back.

In a similar way, data stored on a computer can be coded. Coding is the process of representing data by assigning a code to it for classification or identification.

Often genders are coded as M for male and F for female. Clothing can be coded by the type, size and colour:

- DR = dress
- 2XL = extra extra large
- BL = blue
- DR2XLBL = a dress in size extra extra large and colour blue.

EXAMPLE

Using numbers for international dialling codes:

- 44 = Great Britain
- 33 = France
- 49 = Germany
- 34 = Spain
- 93 = Afghanistan
- 971 = United Arab Emirates
- 81 = Japan

Using abbreviations for international vehicle registration plates:

- GB = Great Britain
- F = France
- D = Germany (Deutschland)
- E = Spain (España)
- AFG = Afghanistan
- UAE = United Arab Emirates
- J = Japan

Advantages and disadvantages of coding data

There are a number of reasons for coding data. In the examples used above, it would take a long time to use all the letters of a country to dial a telephone number and there would not be enough space on the rear of a car to display the full country name.

The advantages of coding data can be summarised as shown in Table 1.03.

Presentation	Data can be presented in small spaces, such as on labels or when listing large amounts of data.
Storage	Less storage space is required because less characters are used to store the data.
Speed of input	Data can be input more quickly because only a few numbers or letters need to be input instead of whole words or phrases.
Processing	Processors can process data more quickly because they only have to process the coded data instead of the whole word or phrase.
Validation	It's possible to validate data by checking it is a particular length or within a certain range or matching other rules. For example, an international vehicle registration code must be a maximum of three letters and not contain any numbers or symbols.
Confidentiality	Sometimes data can be coded so that it only makes sense to people who know what the codes mean.
Consistency	If the correct codes are used then data will be input consistently without spelling errors, making it easier to be searched or summarised.

Table 1.03 - Advantages of coding.

DISCUSSION POINT

Can you see problems that might occur when these numbers and letters are used in codes?

0 or o or O

l or L or l or i

Z or 2

7 or 1

The disadvantages of coding can be summarised as shown in Table 1.04.

Limited codes	There may not be enough codes available to use, meaning that more letters or numbers need to be added. For example, with international vehicle registration codes, E is already used for Spain and so Egypt has to use ET and Ecuador has to use EC. Now that Egypt has taken ET, Ethiopia can't use it and so has to use ETH.
Interpretation	Codes may be difficult to interpret. For example, with international vehicle registration codes, somebody might look at ET and assume it is Ethiopia or look at S and assume it is Spain. It's even more difficult when considering international dialling codes that are represented by numbers.
Similarity	Some letters and numbers can be difficult to distinguish such as O and 0 or Z and 2, especially if handwritten. With codes, it's difficult to guess what the value might be and so mistakes can occur. At least with words it's possible to guess what the badly written letter might be.
Efficiency	If a user inputting codes does not know what code to use, then they will not be able to enter the data efficiently. Instead they will have to look up the code.
Missing information	It's possible that some information gets lost during the process of coding. For example, if devices on a network are coded as L for laptop, P for printer, D for desktop computer and M for mobile phone, then information about whether or not the mobile phone or laptop is touch screen is lost.

Table 1.04 - Disadvantages of coding.

9

TASK

Create a coding system for clothing that includes the type of clothing, size, colour and other information that you think is relevant. Show it to a friend. Can they interpret the code efficiently? Did you have any duplicate codes? Do you think the sizes would be understood by potential customers?

TASK

Create a coding system for the names of people in your class. Show it to a friend. Can they interpret the code efficiently? Did you have any duplicate codes?

Encoding data

When data is **encoded**, it is stored in a specific format. Computers do not recognise text, sound and images in the same way we do. Computers use binary digits which are 1s and 0s. One means on and zero means off. A typical binary number would look like this: 11011010. Therefore, data needs to be encoded into a format which the computer understands. Codecs are programs that are used to encode data for images, audio and video. The codecs are also needed to read the data.

Text

Text is encoded as a number that is then represented by a binary number. A common encoding method is ASCII (American Standard Code for Information Interchange). ASCII consists of 256 codes from 0 to 255. Here is a subset of the ASCII code table:

Character	Decimal number	Binary number
@	64	01000000
A	65	01000001
B	66	1000010
C	67	1000011
a	97	01100001
b	98	01100010
c	99	01100011

Table 1.05 - ASCII code table.

There are other encoding methods, too, such as extended ASCII which allows for more characters to be used, particularly for international languages. Other encoding methods include Unicode and EBCDIC but you don't need to learn about these.

TASK

Visit the website www.ascii-code.com and look at the ASCII code table. What sentence does the following ASCII code represent?

084 104 101 032 098 105 103 032 098
097 100 032 119 111 108 102 033

Visit the website www.unicode.org/charts or www.unicode-table.com.

Choose a language script and then choose a short sentence (less than ten words). Encode your sentence into UNICODE. Now show the Unicode to a friend and see if they can convert it back into the original sentence.

Images

Encoding is also used to store images. At the most basic level, images are encoded as bitmaps. A Microsoft Windows bitmap includes the following data when encoding an image (this is not the complete list):

- width of bitmap
- height of bitmap
- bit count which represents number of colours:
  - 1 = monochrome
  - 4 = 16 colours
  - 8 = 256 colours
  - 16 = 65 536 colours
  - 24 = 16 million colours
- compression type (no compression, eight-bit run-length encoding or four-bit run-length encoding)
- horizontal resolution in pixels per metre
- vertical resolution in pixels per metre
- raster data (the actual shape of the image in pixels).

For the raster data, we will assume a monochrome image (black and white). Each bit will represent either a black or white pixel. A byte consists of eight bits and so will represent eight pixels. The encoding starts from the bottom left of the image, works to the right-hand side and then up to the next row and again from left to right.

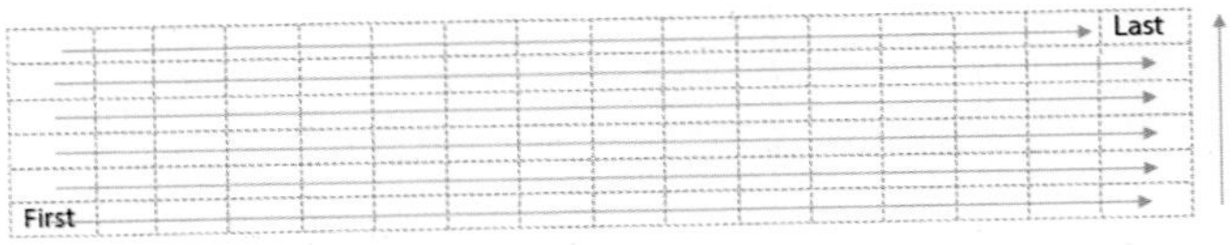

Figure 1.10 - Empty raster grid.

As the image gets bigger, it takes up a lot of storage space. Therefore a method called run-length encoding (RLE) can be used to reduce the amount of storage space that is used. This is known as compression. RLE takes consecutive values and combines them together. At a basic level, the image above has ten black pixels in a row. Instead of storing ten separate pixels, RLE would store the quantity and colour, for example ten × black or ten × 1111.

Sometimes when files are compressed, they use lossy compression, which means some of the original data is removed and the quality is reduced. For example, Figure 1.11 shows how the quality of an image can be reduced if lossy compression is used.

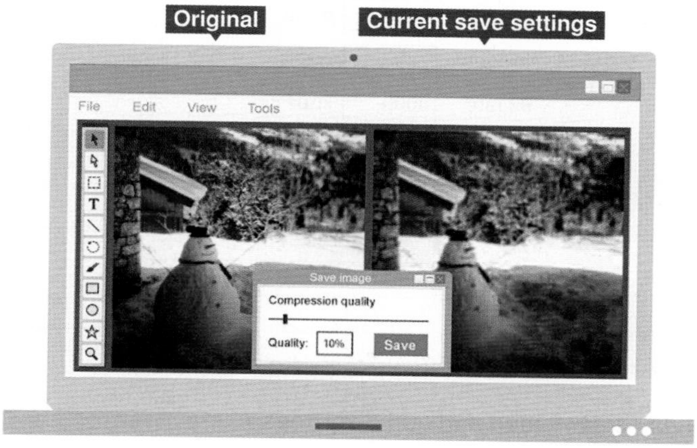

Figure 1.11 - Lossy compression.

TASK

Images can be encoded into a variety of different file types. Find out what the purpose of each of the following file types is:

- JPEG/JPG (Joint Photographic Experts Group)
- GIF (Graphics Interchange Format)
- PNG (Portable Network Graphics)
- SVG (Scalable Vector Graphics)

Sound

When sound is encoded, the sample rate, bit depth and bit rate are stored. When sound is recorded, it is converted from its original analogue format into a digital format, which is broken down into thousands of samples per second.

The sample rate, also known as the frequency, is the number of audio samples per second. The higher the

sample rate, the higher the quality of the music, but also the more storage that is required. Each sample is stored as binary data. The sample rate is measured in hertz (Hz). Typically, music on a CD will use a sample rate of 44.1 kHz (kilohertz) whereas a simple telephone call would find 8 kHz sufficient.

The bit depth is the number of bits (1s and 0s) used for each sound clip. A higher bit depth will give a higher quality sound. CDs use a bit depth of 16 which means 16 bits (0s and 1s) are used. 16 bits gives 65 536 combinations of binary storage.

The bit rate is the number of bits that are processed every second. It is measured in kilobits per second (kbps). The bit rate is calculated using this calculation:

$$\text{bit rate} = \text{sample rate} \times \text{bit depth} \times \text{number of channels}$$

EXAMPLE

A CD sound file has a sample rate of 44.1 kHz (44 100 Hz), a bit depth of 16 bits and two channels (left and right for stereo).

$$\text{bit rate} = 44\,100 \times 16 \times 2 = 1\,411\,200\text{ bps} = 1.4\text{ mbps}$$
(megabits per second)

That means that 1.4 megabits are required to store every second of audio. Therefore, we can multiply the bit rate by the number of seconds to find the file size. So for a 3 minute 30 second audio file (210 seconds):

$$\text{file size (in bits)} = 1\,411\,200 \times 210 = 296\,352\,000$$
(296 megabits)

There are eight bits in a byte and we use bytes to measure storage, so the file size in bits is divided by eight:

$$\text{file size (in bytes)} = 296\,352,\,000 \div 8 = 37\,044\,000$$
$$\text{megabytes} = 37\text{ MB (megabytes)}$$

TASK

Calculate the file size of a sound file with the following properties:

- sample rate = 8 000 bps
- bit depth = 16
- channels = 1

The encoding method above does not compress the file and a typical storage format is WAV (Waveform Audio File Format), which is used on PCs. However, music files are often compressed to allow for efficient streaming across the internet and to enable lots of music files to be stored on a single storage medium. Compression reduces the file size.

There are two types of compression: lossy compression and lossless compression. Lossless compression reduces the file size without losing any quality, but it can only reduce the file size by about 50%.

Lossy compression reduces the file size by reducing the bit rate, which means that some of the quality is lost. Most human ears won't be able to detect the loss in quality, but an experienced musician would notice. When compressing an audio file, it is possible to choose the bit rate. A bit rate of 128 kbps is equivalent to what would be heard on the radio.

EXAMPLE

A CD file originally has a bit rate of 1.4 Mbps (1 411 200 bps). This is reduced to 128 kbps (128 000 kbps). The original file size was 37 MB. To calculate the change in file size, divide by the original bit rate and multiply by the new bit rate.

$$\text{Compressed file size} = 37 \div 1\,411\,200 \times 128\,000$$
$$= 3.36\,\text{MB}.$$

In this example, the file size has been reduced to approximately 10% of the original size.

Video

When video is encoded it needs to store images as well as sound. Images are stored as frames. A standard quality video would normally have 24 frames per second (fps). High definition (HD) uses 50 fps and 60 fps. The higher the number of frames per second, the more storage that is required, but the higher quality the video will be.

The size of the image is also important. A HD video will have an image size of 1920 pixels wide and 1080 pixels high. The higher the image size, the more storage that is required. Other common resolutions include:

- 7680 × 4320 (8K / ultra high definition)
- 3840 × 2160 (4K / ultra high definition)

- 1024 × 768 (Extended Graphics Array (XGA) – often used with digital projectors)
- 1280 × 720 (Wide Extended Graphics Array (WXGA) – wide screen)
- 800 × 600 (Super Video Graphics Array (SVGA))
- 480 × 320 (useful for mobile phones where the screen is smaller and internet bandwidth could be low).

The bit rate for videos combines both the audio and frames that need to be processed every second. The bit rate is the number of bits that need to be processed every second. A higher frame rate requires a higher bit rate.

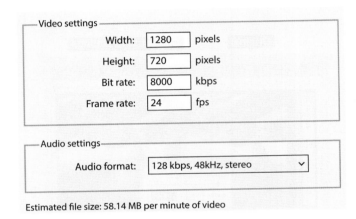

Estimated file size: 58.14 MB per minute of video

Figure 1.12 - Video and audio settings.

A one hour, eight-bit HD video with 24 fps would require 334 GB (gigabytes) of storage. This would be far too much data to download or even broadcast. Therefore, compression is required. Compression usually involves reducing the:

- resolution
- image size or
- bit rate.

These all result in lossy compression. A common lossy compression format is MP4, which is a codec created by MPEG (Moving Pictures Expert Group). There are also lossless compression methods such as digital video (DV).

TASK

Edit a short video using video editing software. Try saving it with different resolutions, different frame rates and different audio formats. Compare the file sizes of each video file that is created.

Advantages and disadvantages of encoding data

Data has to be encoded in order to be stored and processed by a computer system. It is essential that data is encoded into binary digits (1s and 0s).

One purpose of encoding data is often to reduce the file size. The advantages of reducing the file size include:

- enabling real-time streaming of music and video over restricted bandwidth (e.g. home broadband, mobile broadband)
- reducing the time taken to download files
- faster downloading of websites with images, music or video
- enabling more music and video to be stored on CDs, DVDs, flash memory and other storage media.

Another purpose of encoding is to enable different formats to be used. The advantages of different formats for images include:

- formats such as PNG and GIF enabling transparent backgrounds
- formats such as GIF allowing animated images
- formats such as JPG allowing a very large colour depth, meaning that the image will be of high quality
- formats such as bitmap image file (BMP) including all the original uncompressed data so that the image is of the highest possible quality and can be manipulated
- formats that are designed for specific software such as Paint Shop Pro and Photoshop containing layers which allow for various adjustments to be made to the image and being able to enable or remove those layers
- vector formats such as SVG storing the shapes rather than the pixels so that graphics can be enlarged and reduced without loss of quality due to pixelation.

The main disadvantage of encoding data is the variety of encoding methods, resulting in a large variety of file types. Problems include:

- the required codecs may not be installed and so a file cannot be saved in the desired format
- the necessary codecs must be installed, in order to open an encoded file
- not all software is capable of opening different file types
- some hardware such as music and video players only play files encoded in certain formats (for example, a CD player may only be able to play MP3 files but not

Audio Interchange File Format (AIFF) or Advanced Audio Coding (AAC) audio files)

- quality of images, sound and videos is lost when files are compressed using lossy compression
- text that has been encoded using ASCII or UNICODE needs to be decoded using the correct format when it is opened. If some international characters have been included using UNICODE and the file is opened as an ASCII file, then the international characters will not be recognised.

TASK

Compare the file types that can be opened and saved using different graphics software packages.

Encryption

One specific type of encoding is **encryption**. This is when data is scrambled so that it cannot be understood. The purpose of encryption is to make the data difficult or impossible to read if it is accessed by an unauthorised user. Data can be encrypted when it is stored on disks or other storage media, or it can be encrypted when it is sent across a network such as a local area network or the internet. Accessing encrypted data legitimately is known as decryption.

Caesar cipher

A cipher is a secret way of writing. In other words it is a code. Ciphers are used to convert a message into an encrypted message. It is a special type of algorithm which defines the set of rules to follow to encrypt a message. Roman Emperor Julius Caesar created the Caesar cipher so that he could communicate in secret with his generals.

The Caesar cipher is sometimes known as a shift cipher because it selects replacement letters by shifting along the alphabet.

EXAMPLE

In this example the alphabet is to be shifted by three (+3) letters so that A = D, B = E and so on:

Original	A	B	C	D	E	F	G	H	I	J	K	L	M	N	O	P	Q	R	S	T	U	V	W	X	Y	Z
Encrypted	D	E	F	G	H	I	J	K	L	M	N	O	P	Q	R	S	T	U	V	W	X	Y	Z	A	B	C

So to encrypt the word 'Hello', we would use:

H = K, E = H, L = O, O = R

which gives KHOOR.

!

DISCUSSION POINT

Figure 1.13 - The Enigma machine.

The Germans used encrypted messages during World War II using the Enigma machine. An operator would type in a message and then scramble it by using three to five notched wheels. The recipient would need to know the exact settings of the wheels in order to decipher the message. There were 159×10^{18} possible combinations.

Encrypted messages from the Lorenz cipher machine led to the development of the world's first electric programmable computer, Colossus, which helped British code breakers read encrypted German messages.

The first major encryption algorithm for computers was the Data Encryption Standard (DES) used in the 1970s. It used a 56-bit (1s and 0s) key. This offered 70×10^{15} possible combinations, but the development of computers meant that it eventually became possible to 'crack' the code. This was replaced by the Advanced Encryption Standard (AES) which uses up to 256-bit keys. This can offer 300×10^{11} possible combinations.

TASK

1 Using the Caesar cipher +3 example above, write an encrypted message to a friend. Ask your friend to decipher it.

2 Choose how many letters you are going to shift by and write another encrypted message to a friend. Don't tell your friend how many letters you shifted by. Your friend should try to decipher the code by working out which letters appear most commonly.

3 See www.math.uic.edu/CryptoClubProject/CCpacket. pdf to create a cipher wheel and use it to encrypt and decrypt messages.

Symmetric encryption

This is the oldest method of encryption. It requires both the sender and recipient to possess the secret encryption and decryption key. With symmetric encryption, the secret key needs to be sent to the recipient. This could be done at a separate time, but it still has to be transmitted whether by post or over the internet and it could be intercepted.

Figure 1.14 - Symmetric encryption.

Asymmetric encryption

Asymmetric encryption is also known as public-key cryptography. Asymmetric encryption overcomes the problem of symmetric encryption keys being intercepted by using a pair of keys. This will include a public key which is available to anybody wanting to send data, and a private key that is known only to the recipient. They key is the algorithm required to encrypt and decrypt the data.

The process works like this:

Figure 1.15 - Asymmetric encryption.

In the next example, Tomasz sends a message to Helene. Tomasz encrypts the message using Helene's public key. Helene receives the encrypted message and decrypts it using her private key.

This method requires a lot more processing than symmetric encryption and so it takes longer to decrypt the data.

In order to find a public key, digital certificates are required which identify the user or server and provide the public key. A digital certificate is unique to each user or server. A digital certificate usually includes:

- organisation name
- organisation that issued the certificate
- user's email address
- user's country
- user's public key.

Tomasz

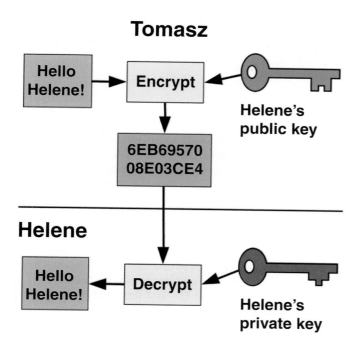

Figure 1.16 - Asymmetric encryption example.

When encrypted data is required by a recipient, the computer will request the digital certificate from the sender. The public key can be found within the digital certificate.

Asymmetric encryption is used for **Secure Sockets Layer (SSL)** which is the security method used for secure websites. **Transport Layer Security (TLS)** has superseded SSL but they are both often referred to as SSL. Once SSL has established an authenticated session, the client and server will create symmetric keys for faster secure communication.

> **TASK**
> Watch the video about SSL at
> http://info.ssl.com/article.aspx?id=10241.

Hard disk

Disk encryption will encrypt every single bit of data stored on a disk. This is different to encrypting single files. In order to access any file on the disk, the encryption key will be required. This type of encryption is not limited to disks and can be used on other storage media such as backup tapes and Universal Serial Bus (USB) flash memory. It is particularly important that USB flash memory and backup tapes are encrypted because these are portable storage media and so are susceptible to being lost or stolen. If the whole medium is encrypted, then anybody trying

to access the data will not be able to understand it. The data is usually accessed by entering a password or using a fingerprint to unlock the encryption.

HTTPS

Normal web pages that are not encrypted are fetched and transmitted using Hypertext Transfer Protocol (HTTP). Anybody who intercepts web pages or data being sent over HTTP would be able to read the contents of the web page or the data. This is particularly a problem when sending sensitive data, such as credit card information or usernames and passwords.

Hypertext Transfer Protocol Secure (**HTTPS**) is the encryption standard used for secure web pages. It uses Secure Sockets Layer (SSL) or Transport Layer Security (TLS) to encrypt and decrypt pages and information sent and received by web users. This is the encryption method that is used by banks when a user logs onto online banking. A secure web page can be spotted by its address beginning with https:// and in addition some browsers display a small padlock.

Figure 1.17 - The 's' after 'http' and the padlock indicate that this is a secure website.

When a browser requests a secure page, it will check the digital certificate to ensure that it is trusted, valid and that the certificate is related to the site from which it is coming. The browser then uses the public key to encrypt a new symmetric key that is sent to the web server. The browser and web server can then communicate using a symmetric encryption key, which is much faster than asymmetric encryption.

> **EXAMPLE**
>
> The web browser requests the certificate from the web server.
>
>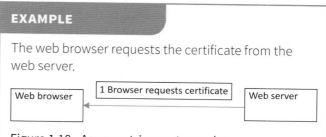
>
> Figure 1.18 - Asymmetric cryptography.
>
> The web browser then uses the web server's public key to encrypt a new symmetric key and sends that encrypted symmetric key to the web server. The

15

web server uses its own private key to decrypt the new symmetric key.

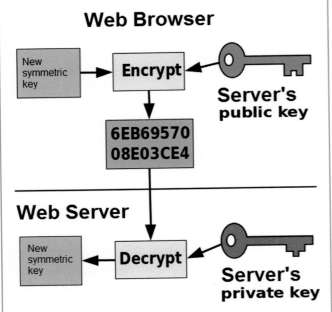

Figure 1.19 - Secure website identification.

The browser and web server now communicate using the same symmetric key.

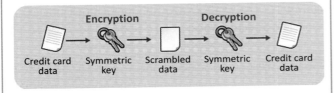

Figure 1.20 - Symmetric encryption.

Email

Email encryption uses asymmetric encryption. This means that recipients of emails must have the private key that matches the public key used to encrypt the original email. In order for this to work, both the sender and recipient need to send each other a digitally signed message that will add the person's digital certificate to the contact for that person. Encrypting an email will also encrypt any attachments.

How encryption protects data

Encryption only scrambles the data so that if it is found, it cannot be understood. It does not stop the data from being intercepted, stolen or lost. However, with strong

256-bit AES encryption it is virtually impossible for somebody to decrypt the data and so it is effectively protected from prying eyes.

DISCUSSION POINT

Most Wi-Fi access points and Wi-Fi routers use encryption. This serves two purposes. The first is to only allow people who know the 'key' (usually a password) to access the network, so that any unauthorised users cannot gain access. The second is to encrypt the data, so that it cannot be understood by somebody 'snooping' on the Wi-Fi network.

Wi-Fi networks are particularly susceptible to 'snooping' because no wires are required to connect to the network. It is possible to sit in a car outside somebody's house and see the Wi-Fi network. The 'key' stops that person from accessing the network and also stops that person from understanding the data that is moving around the network.

Did you know that if you access a public Wi-Fi hotspot that is 'open' and therefore not encrypted that anybody with the right software can see what you are sending over the network, including your emails? This applies to laptops, tablets and mobile phones or any other device using public Wi-Fi.

QUESTIONS

11 Give two reasons for encoding data.

12 Explain why encoding is necessary for text.

13 Identify two factors that affect the size of a sound file.

14 Decipher the following text that has been encrypted using the Caesar cipher with a shift of +4.

AIPP HSRI

1.05 Checking the accuracy of data

KEY TERMS

Validation: the process of checking data matches acceptable rules

Verification: ensuring data entered into the system matches the original source

Proof reading: checking information manually

Validation

Validation takes place when data is input into a computer system. The purpose is to ensure the data is sensible and conforms to defined rules. A railway season ticket will have an expiry date. The season ticket is valid until it expires. Once it expires it is invalid. The rule here is that the date the season ticket is used must be before its expiry date.

When data is validated, if it conforms to the rules then it will be accepted. If it does not conform to the rules, then it will be rejected and an error message will be presented. Validation does not ensure that data is correct.

TASK

Create a flow chart to describe the process of validation. You should include the following:

- Start
- End
- Input of data
- Error message
- Data accepted
- Data rejected
- Validation decision

There are a variety of different validation checks that can be used to check whether data is acceptable. These different checks are the different types of rules that are used.

Presence check

A presence check is used to ensure that data is entered. If data is entered, then it is accepted. If data is not entered, then the user will be presented with an error message asking them to enter data.

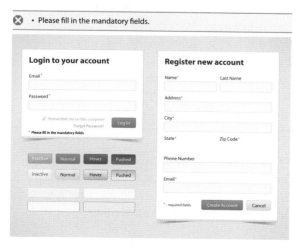

Figure 1.21 - Required data on a website.

EXAMPLE

When filling in a 'contact us' form on a website, it is essential that an email address is entered. The following would be valid if only a presence check is carried out:

- a
- a@b
- a@bc.d
- @
- 372823

Notice that none of these are correct but they pass the rule that data must be present.

Range check

A range check ensures that data is within a defined range. A limit check has a single boundary. This could be the highest possible value or the lowest possible value. A range check includes two boundaries, which would be the lower boundary and the upper boundary. The following symbols are used when comparing with a boundary:

$>$ greater than

$<$ less than

$>=$ greater than or equal to

$<=$ less than or equal to

EXAMPLE

An opinion poll is taken and asks for the respondent's age. The respondents have to be at least 18 years old. The lower boundary is 18. There is no upper boundary, so this is a limit check. This could be written as:

$$Age >= 18$$

Letters representing grades for an exam are entered. Only the letters A–E are valid grades. The grade must be less than F. The upper boundary is E. There is no lower boundary, so this is a limit check. This could be written as:

$$Grade < F$$

The number of students in a class must be between 5 and 28. The lower boundary is 5 and the upper boundary is 28, so this is a range check. This could be written as:

$$Number\ of\ students >= 5\ and <= 28$$

17

Data that is within the boundaries is valid. Data that is outside the boundaries is invalid. Data that is valid and within the boundaries is not necessarily correct. A grade of C could be entered when a grade A should have been entered. C is valid but incorrect.

Type check

A type check ensures that data must be of a defined data type.

> **EXAMPLE**
>
> - If an age is entered, it must be an integer.
> - If a grade is entered, it must be text with no numbers.
> - If a price is entered, it must be numerical.
> - If a date of birth is entered, it must be a date.

Data that is of the correct data type is valid. Data that is valid and of the correct data type is not necessarily correct. A date of birth of 28/12/2087 could be entered. The date is valid because it is a date data type, but it is clearly incorrect.

Length check

A length check ensures data is of a defined length or within a range of lengths.

> **EXAMPLE**
>
> - A password must be at least six characters long.
> - A grade must be exactly one character long.
> - A product code must be at least four characters and no more than six characters.

Data that is of the allowed length is not necessarily correct. For example, a valid date might require six digits. A date of 2ndFeb would be a valid length because it contains six characters, but it would not be correct because it does not follow the required format.

Format check

A format check ensures data matches a defined format. It is sometimes known as a picture check and the data has to follow a pattern.

> **EXAMPLE**
>
> An email address must include an @ symbol preceded by at least one character and followed by other characters. The following data would be valid:
>
> - john@bldef.co
> - a@b.dek
> - fdc@jb
>
> A student ID must be four numbers followed by two letters. The following data would be valid:
>
> - 3827BD
> - 1111AA

Data that matches the pattern is valid. Data that is valid and of the defined format is not necessarily correct. An email address of fdc@jb meets the rules above but is clearly incorrect.

Lookup check

A lookup check tests to see if data exists in a list. It is similar to referential integrity in Chapter 9, but uses a list defined within the validation rule.

> **EXAMPLE**
>
> When asking a user for their gender, they can respond with 'Male' or 'Female'. A lookup validation rule would check to see that the values are within this list. Students taking a qualification could be issued grades of pass, merit and distinction. When inputting the data, a validation rule could check that only 'X', 'P', 'M' or 'D' are entered ('X' would be for fail).

Consistency check

A consistency check compares data in one field with data in another field that already exists within a record, to see whether both are consistent with each other.

19

EXAMPLE

When entering the gender of 'M' or 'F', a consistency check will prevent 'F' from being entered if the title is 'Mr' and will prevent 'M' from being entered if the title is 'Mrs' or 'Miss'.

When entering data about dispatching products, it would not be possible to mark an item as being dispatched until after it has been packaged.

Check digit

A check digit is a number (or letter) that is added to the end of an identification number being input. It is a form of redundancy check because the check digit is redundant (not needed for the identification number, but just used for validation). When the identification number is first created, an algorithm (a series of calculations) is performed on it to generate a check digit. When the identification number is input, the same algorithm is performed on it. The result of the algorithm should match the check digit. If it matches, then the data is valid. If it does not match then the data is invalid.

Original identification number = 20392
Algorithm is performed on 20392
Check digit = 4

Data including check digit = 203924

Valid Example
Identification number including check digit is entered into the computer: 203924
Algorithm is performed on 20392
Result of algorithm = 4

Result of algorithm (4) is compared with check digit that was entered (4).
They match.
Data is valid.

Invalid Example
Identification number including check digit is entered into the computer: 205924
Algorithm is performed on 20592
Result of algorithm = 7

Result of algorithm(7) is compared with check digit that was entered (4).
They do not match.
Data is invalid.

Figure 1.22 - Valid and invalid check digit calculations.

There are a variety of calculations that can be performed to determine what the check digit should be. The important thing is that the same calculation used to create the check digit in the first place should be used to confirm the check digit when the identification number is input.

EXAMPLE

Figure 1.23 - Unique Product Code check digit.

The Unique Product Code (UPC) check digit is used with 13 digit barcodes. It is the last digit shown on a barcode. The algorithm for calculating the check digit is:

1 Add all the digits in even numbered positions together.

2 Multiply the result (1) above by 3.

3 Add all the digits in odd numbered positions together.

4 Add results (2) and (3) together.

5 Divide the result (4) above by 10.

6 Calculate the remainder (modulo 10) of result (5) above.

7 Subtract (6) above from 10.

Valid example

In this example, the International Standard Book Number (ISBN) is 978095734041-1 where the last 1 is the check digit. To calculate the check digit, the following algorithm is performed on the ISBN (excluding check digit):

1 Add all the digits in even numbered positions together (9**78**0**95**7**34**0**41**) : $7 + 0 + 5 + 3 + 0 + 1 = \mathbf{16}$.

2 Multiply result (1) above by 3: $16 \times 3 = \mathbf{48}$.

3 Add all the digits in odd numbered positions together (**9**7**8**09**5**7**3**4**04**1) : $9 + 8 + 9 + 7 + 4 + 4 = \mathbf{41}$.

4 Add results (2) and (3) together: $48 + 41 = \mathbf{89}$.

5 Divide the result (4) above by 10: $89 \div 10 = \mathbf{8.9}$.

6 Calculate the remainder (modulo 10) of result (5) above: 89 MOD 10 = **9**.

7 Subtract (6) above from 10: 10 - 9 = **1**.

The result of the algorithm is 1.

Invalid example

In this example, the ISBN has been entered incorrectly as two numbers have been transposed (7 and 3) accidentally: 978095**37**4041-1.

1 Add all the digits in even numbered positions together (9**7**80**9**5**3**74**0**41) : 7 + 0 + 5 + 7 + 0 + 1 = **20**.

2 Multiply result (1) above by 3: 20 × 3 = **60**.

3 Add all the digits in odd numbered positions together (**9**78**0**95**3**74**0**41) : 9 + 8 + 9 + 3 + 4 + 4 = **37**.

4 Add results (2) and (3) together: 60 + 37 = **97**.

5 Divide the result (4) above by 10: 97 ÷ 10 = **9.7**.

6 Calculate the remainder (modulo 10) of result (5) above: 97 MOD 10 = **7**.

7 Subtract (6) above from 10: 10-7 = **3**.

The result of the algorithm is 3. The result 3 is compared with the check digit of 1 that was entered. They do not match. The ISBN entered is invalid.

TASK

Use the website www.upcdatabase.com/checkdigit.asp to generate check digits for product codes.

DISCUSSION POINT

The usual algorithm for UPCs is to multiply the odd digits by 3 rather than the even digits. It is only for 13 character barcodes that the even digits are multiplied by 3.

Find out how to calculate a check digit for 10 digit barcodes.

Verification

Verification is the process of checking that the data entered into the computer system matches the original source.

Visual checking

A method of verification can be for the user to visually check that the data entered matches the original source. This can be done by reading the data displayed on screen and comparing it with the original data. If the data matches, then it has passed the verification process. If it does not match, then it has failed the verification process and needs to be re-entered. Visual checking does not ensure that the data entered is correct. If the original data is wrong, then the verification process may still pass. For example, if the intended data is ABCD but ABC is on the source document, then ABC will be entered into the computer and verified, but it should have been ABCD in the first place.

Double data entry

Another method of verification is to input data into the computer system twice. The two items of data are compared by the computer system and if they match, then they are verified. If there are any differences, then one of the inputs must have been incorrect.

EXAMPLE

When changing a password, most systems will ask the user to enter the new password twice. This is because it is critical that the password is entered correctly in order that the user can gain access to the system in the future. If the new passwords match, then the password will be changed. If the new passwords don't match, then one of the passwords must have been entered incorrectly.

It is still possible to pass double entry verification and for the data to be incorrect. If the data is entered incorrectly twice, then the two values may match. For example, if the CAPS key is left on by mistake then both entries would match.

The need for both validation and verification

As you will have seen in the two sections above, it is possible to enter valid data that is still incorrect. It is also possible to verify incorrect data. By using both validation and verification, the chances of entering incorrect data are reduced. If data that is incorrect passes a validation check, then the verification check is likely to spot the error.

EXAMPLE

The validation rule is that a person's gender must be a single letter. N is entered. This passes the validation check but is clearly incorrect. When verified using double entry, the user enters N first followed by M the second time. The verification process has identified the error.

However, it is still possible that the user could enter N twice and both the validation and verification processes would fail.

Proof reading

Proof reading is the process of checking information. For example, when this book was written it was checked for spelling errors, grammar errors, formatting and accuracy. Proof reading can take place for a document or when data is input. When proof reading a document, it is best to have a proof reader who is different from the original author of the document, as they will be able to check the work objectively and identify errors. However, it is also possible for the original author to proof read their own document, but they may not notice some of their own errors. When data is input, it is usually proof read by the person inputting the data.

TASK

Check the information below by proof reading it.

I were walking along the road yesterday wen I spotted a dog without a lead I called the dog but it did not respond. the dog ran away;

QUESTIONS

15 Describe the purpose of verification.

16 Identify three methods of validation.

17 Explain using examples why validation and verification do not ensure data is correct.

1.06 Summary

Information has context and meaning so a person knows what it means. The quality of information can be affected by the accuracy, relevance, age, level of detail and completeness of the information. Proof reading is the process of checking information.

Data are raw numbers, letters, symbols, sounds or images without meaning. Knowledge allows data to be interpreted and is based on rules and facts. Static data does not normally change. Dynamic data updates as a result of the source data changing. Data collected from a direct data source (primary source) must be used for the same purpose for which it was collected. Data collected from an indirect source (secondary source) already existed for another purpose.

Coding is the process of representing data by assigning a code to it for classification or identification. Encoding is the process of storing data in a specific format. Encryption is when data is scrambled so that it cannot be understood.

Validation ensures that data is sensible and allowed. Validation checks include a presence check, range check, type check, length check, format check and check digit. Verification is the process of checking data has been transferred correctly. Verification can be done visually or by double data entry.

Review questions

1 Give an example of data. [1]

2 Describe the term knowledge. [1]

A news and sports website includes both static and dynamic data.

3a Compare static and dynamic data. [4]

3b Identify and describe two factors that affect the quality of information on the website. [4]

3c Give an example of coded data related to the news and sports website. [1]

The website streams news and sports videos.

3d Explain why the video is compressed when it is encoded. [2]

3e Identify three factors that will affect the size of a video file. [1]

3f Identify and describe two factors that affect the file size of images on the website. [4]

Users can pay for premium services on the website using their credit card.

4a Explain why the website uses https at the beginning of the website address instead of http. [4]

4b Describe symmetric encryption. [1]

The journalists working for the website encrypt their emails.

4c Describe how asymmetric encryption is used with emails. [2]

When the users subscribe to premium features, they have to choose a password.

4d Describe how verification can be used when entering the password. [1]

There is a form on the website that can be used to submit news stories. When data is entered onto the form, it is validated.

5a Describe the purpose of validation. [1]

5b Using an example related to submitting a news story, identify and describe one method of validation. [3]

Chapter 2
Hardware and software

Learning objectives

By the end of this chapter, you will be able to:

- define hardware
- evaluate internal and external hardware devices
- explain the purpose of and evaluate storage devices
- explain the purpose of input and output devices
- evaluate input, storage and output devices for a given task
- define software
- evaluate different types of software
- explain the purpose of system software
- evaluate application software
- evaluate user interfaces
- evaluate mental models
- describe utility software
- compare custom-written and off-the-shelf software
- describe and evaluate a compiler and interpreter

2.01 Hardware

KEY TERMS

Hardware: a physical component of a computer system

Device: a hardware component of a computer system consisting of electronic components

Output device: a device used to communicate data or information from a computer system

Storage device: a device used to store data onto a storage medium

Input device: a device that allows data to be entered into a computer system

Storage medium: the medium on which data is stored

Volatile: data is lost when there is no power

Non-volatile: data remains when there is no power

Hardware

Remember

An item of **hardware** is a physical component that forms part of a computer system. Items of hardware are often known as **devices** because they comprise electronic components. Hardware devices can be internal to the computer system (such as the central processing unit, memory or motherboard) or they can be external to the computer system (such as the monitor, keyboard or mouse).

Hardware is categorised into input, output and storage devices. **Input devices** allow data to be sent to a computer (e.g. keyboard). **Output devices** allow the communication of data/information from a computer (e.g. monitor). **Storage devices** store data onto a **storage medium** so that it can be used at a later time.

Internal hardware devices
Central processing unit

Figure 2.01 - A central processing unit.

Remember

The central processing unit (CPU) is the brain of a computer. It is the part of the computer that carries out calculations, executes instructions and processes data. It includes the arithmetic logic unit (ALU) and control unit (CU).

The ALU performs calculations and logical operations. The CU runs the fetch–execute cycle which fetches instructions from memory and executes them.

Input data is taken from input devices (such as a keyboard) or storage and processed by the CPU, which produces output data that can be stored or sent to an output device (such as a monitor).

CPUs usually consist of multiple cores. Each core is a separate processor, so a quad-core CPU has four processors. Processors are measured by the number of instructions they can process per second (hertz). A 3 GHz (gigahertz) processor can process up to 3 billion instructions per second.

Motherboard

Figure 2.02 - A motherboard.

Remember

The motherboard is a printed circuit board (PCB) which connects the main components of a computer. Some of these components may be an integral part of the motherboard. Such components can include Universal Serial Bus (USB) ports, a network port and an integrated graphics card. A motherboard will always include the main bus which is used to transfer data between hardware components.

Other hardware components can be connected directly to the motherboard, including random access memory (RAM), the CPU and expansion cards. Expansion cards offer additional functionality, such as enhanced graphics processing and additional USB ports.

Random access memory

> **Remember**
> Random access memory (RAM) is memory that is used to store currently active programs and data. The more RAM that is available to the computer, the more data and programs can be used at the same time.

This is particularly important in multitasking environments, when several programs may be open at the same time.

When the RAM becomes full, programs or data that are no longer active will be removed to make space for new programs or data. If the RAM becomes full and there are no inactive programs or data to remove, then an area of secondary storage (e.g. hard disc drive (HDD) or solid state drive (SSD)) known as virtual memory is used to expand the amount of memory available to the CPU. Virtual memory is very slow because secondary storage access times are thousands of times slower than RAM access times.

RAM is **volatile**, which means the content of the memory is lost if there is no power to the RAM. When you are using a computer and experience a power cut, this is why the data you are currently using is lost unless it has recently been saved to secondary storage.

Read only memory

Read only memory (ROM) is memory that, once it has been written to, can no longer be changed. It is permanent and it is **non-volatile**, which means that when there is no power to the computer, the contents of the ROM will be retained. This is because it is powered by a small long-life battery.

> **TIP**
> In a computer, there is usually some ROM that stores the instructions to boot (start) the computer.

ROM is also used in small devices such as calculators where there is only one program or set of instructions.

> **TASK**
> Find out what is the purpose of programmable read only memory (PROM) and erasable programmable read only memory (EPROM).

Graphics card

A graphics card is also known as a video card, display adapter or graphics adapter. It is a printed circuit board that connects to one of the motherboard's expansion slots. Its purpose is to generate the signals needed to display the output image from the computer. Often the graphics adapter is integrated into the motherboard and does not require a separate card. However, by using a separate card, the graphics performance can be improved as a separate processor can be used for graphics (a graphics processing unit).

Figure 2.03 - A graphics card.

Graphics cards include a variety of options for output. Standard video graphics array (VGA) output to a monitor is achieved through the RGB port which transmits red, green and blue signals to the monitor in an analogue format. High definition display is achieved through a high-definition multimedia interface (HDMI) port. Another option is Digital Video Interface (DVI) which supports high resolution displays using digital signals.

Sound card

The purpose of a sound card is to generate the signals needed to output sound from the computer to a speaker or set of speakers. It is often an integrated part of the motherboard and will include a single output for audio (green socket), a single input for a microphone (red socket)

25

and a single input for line level devices (blue socket). If higher quality or surround sound is required, then it is usually necessary to have a separate sound card which connects to one of the motherboard's expansion slots. This will enable multiple outputs for front, rear, centre and sub-woofer speakers.

Hard disk drive

A hard disk drive (HDD) is the most common form of secondary storage for a computer due to its relatively low cost per MB (megabyte). In 2015, hard disk drives could store up to 8 TB (terabytes) of data with access speeds of 6 GB/s. The hard disk drive consists of two main parts: the device that is the electronics which store the data, and the disk that is the medium onto which the data is stored. The device (or drive) includes a read-write head which sits at the end of an access arm and magnetises sectors on the disk (platter).

Figure 2.04 - A hard disk.

There is usually more than one platter and therefore there will be several read-write heads for each side of each platter as shown in Figure 2.05. Each platter will have tracks and each track will be split into sectors. The tracks that are in the same position on each platter form a cylinder. Wherever possible, a computer will attempt to store data on a single cylinder as this requires the least access arm movement and the access arm is the slowest part of the hard disk.

Data stored on a hard disk is non-volatile. This means that when the computer is turned off and there is no power then the data will still be safely stored on the hard disc. Hard discs can be internally connected to the computer using a Serial Advanced Technology

Attachment (SATA) or Integrated Drive Electronics (IDE) cable.

Figure 2.05 - Multiple platters.

> **DISCUSSION POINT**
> Do you know where the phrase 'my computer has crashed' comes from? It relates to when the read-write head crashes into a platter and causes damage to the hard disk, meaning that data and programs can no longer be retrieved.

Solid state drive

A solid state drive (SSD) is another secondary storage device that is non-volatile. However, there are no moving parts and the data is stored onto flash memory. It is also not necessary to store data in the same cylinder in order to maximise access speed as the data can be stored anywhere on the flash memory and access speeds will not be affected. SSDs are also non-magnetic and so are not susceptible to damage from to close, strong magnetic fields.

In 2015, SSDs could store up to 8 TB, but due to the newer technology were far more expensive than HDDs and were more common in capacities of 128, 256 or 512 GB. SSDs have access speeds of around 400–600 MBps (two to three times faster than a HDD). This means they are used in higher performance computers. A frequent compromise between speed, capacity and price is to have a smaller SSD to store the operating system and software (for speed of access) and use a larger HDD to store data. SSDs also require a lot less power than HDDs and so are preferred in laptop and tablet computers.

TASK

Have a look at the inside of an old computer. Identify each of the main components that can be seen on the motherboard, the hardware devices that are connected to it and any available connection ports.

External hardware devices

Cloud

Cloud computing is a term that refers to anything where computing services are hosted over the internet and not in the same physical location as the computer being used. Data is stored on banks of servers that are accessed remotely. The physical devices that store the data are owned by a hosting company rather than the person or organisation using the data.

When data is stored in the cloud, the hosting company takes all responsibility for storing the data, managing the data, securing the data and backing up the data, so that people or organisations no longer have to be concerned with this. As the data is stored remotely, it also means that it can be accessed at any time in any place, so people do not have to be sitting at a specific computer or within an organisation to access that data.

EXAMPLE

Examples of cloud storage for personal use include:

- OneDrive
- Google Drive
- Dropbox
- Box

The downside is that it takes longer to access the data as access times are limited by the bandwidth available to the hosting company and other users who may be accessing data on the same servers at the same time. It can also be quite costly to store large amounts of data on cloud storage.

Some cloud storage options allow synchronisation to a computer, so the cloud acts as a backup to the data stored on the computer. It also means that when accessing the data from the allocated computer, access times will be faster than accessing from cloud storage.

Monitor

Although not an essential part of every computer system, a monitor is certainly an essential part of most computer systems as it enables the user to visualise the output. It is connected to the computer using one of the ports on a graphics card. Monitor sizes are measured diagonally and, apart from some very old 'legacy' monitors, they now have flat screens which minimalise the amount of desk space that is used and they are light enough to be mounted on a wall or a desk using a bracket or on a shelf.

A monitor will be limited by its resolution. This is the number of pixels it can display and is measured horizontally by vertically. For example, a high definition (HD) monitor can display 1920 x 1080 pixels. Some monitors also include a touch interface (known as a touch screen), which means that the user can select items by directly interacting with the display on the screen. These are often integrated into tablet computers and mobile phones.

Keyboard

Figure 2.06 - A Chinese keyboard.

A keyboard consists of a number of buttons which are used to input text or to control parts of an interface. Its main limitation is the number of keys available. With a Roman alphabet, this isn't too much of a problem because the alphabet only contains 26 letters and ten digits. However, some alphabets, such as Arabic or Chinese contain many more characters and so combinations of keys have to be used.

A keyboard can be connected to a computer using a USB port, by wireless Bluetooth or by other wireless technology. Keyboards vary in style and shape, and ergonomic keyboards are available to provide more comfort and protection for the user from repetitive strain injury (RSI).

Mouse

A mouse is a pointing device which allows objects to be selected and manipulated on the screen. The mouse controls a pointer which is displayed on the screen. When the mouse is moved, the pointer moves and objects such as menus can be selected on the screen using one of the mouse buttons. Like a keyboard, a mouse can be connected using a USB port, by wireless Bluetooth or by other wireless technology.

Printer

A printer produces a hard copy (printout) from a computer usually onto paper. A simplex printer can print on a single side of paper, whereas a printer with a duplex unit can print on both sides of each sheet of paper. Some printers include additional functions such as a scanner.

Laser printer

A laser printer negatively charges a cylindrical drum which then attracts electrically charged toner (powdered ink). The toner is then heated so that it melts onto the paper.

Inkjet printer

Cartridges full of ink in four different colours (black, cyan, magenta, yellow) are used to 'squirt' ink onto the paper to form the required printout.

Dot matrix printer

Before laser and inkjet printers, dot matrix printers were commonplace. They are a type of impact printer which means that the printout is achieved by hitting the paper and the operation is very noisy. This is done by a set of pins being driven onto a ribbon which then transfers its ink to the paper. The main advantage of dot matrix printers is that they can print on duplicate and triplicate paper (carbon copies) due to the impact. They are also very robust printers and so last for a long time.

Plotter

In the 1990s, a plotter used to 'plot' lines onto large sheets of paper by moving the paper backwards and forwards and drawing using pens to create vector drawings. Today, plotters are inkjet printers designed to be used with large sheets of paper, typically A2, A1 and A0. If only black and white printouts are required, then light-emitting diode (LED) plotters are much faster and have cheaper running costs than inkjet plotters.

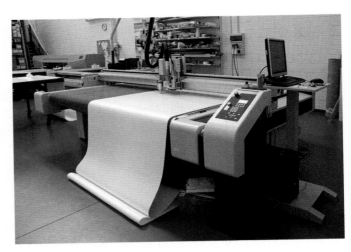

Figure 2.07 - Modern inkjet plotter.

Speakers

Speakers are used to provide sound output from a computer. These can be as simple as a pair of stereo speakers or full surround sound.

> **TASK**
>
> Find out the difference between mono sound, stereo sound, 5.1 surround sound, 6.1 surround sound and 7.1 surround sound.

Camera

A camera can be used to capture still or moving images (movies). When connected to the computer, the images or movies can be transferred from the camera to the computer's storage. The images can then be viewed on screen, manipulated and shared. A digital still camera is optimised for capturing still images but usually has the capability of capturing movies too, whereas a digital video camera is optimised for capturing movies but can also capture still images.

Webcam

A webcam is a camera that is connected to the computer for the purpose of capturing still or moving images while using the computer. It will not be as high quality as a dedicated digital camera or digital video camera. It will usually have an integrated microphone for capturing sound. Its main purpose is for users to engage in online video chat or video conferences. They can also be used as security cameras.

	Laser	Inkjet	Dot matrix	Plotter
Typical printing speed	The laser printer is the fastest of all printers, with some industrial models reaching 200 pages per minute (ppm) and office printers achieving around 50 ppm.	Standard inkjet printers can usually print around 15–20 ppm in black and white, but colour speeds are a bit slower.	Very slow compared with other printers.	The time per page to print is quite slow because a much larger area needs to be covered.
Typical purchase cost	A laser printer is typically twice the cost of an inkjet printer with similar features.	Inkjet printers are the cheapest of all printers available, but they vary depending on the features that are included.	These used to be very cheap, but are now more expensive than an inkjet printer because they are not mass produced.	Plotters are the most expensive type of printer due to their physical size and the need to cope with large sheets of paper.
Typical running cost	Although toner cartridges are more expensive than inkjet cartridges, they last a lot longer and so the cost per page is less than other printers.	Inkjet cartridges vary in price and 'compatible' versions can be purchased more cheaply than original manufacturer versions.	Very low as the ink ribbon lasts for a long time.	The running costs are the same as inkjet printers, but of course per page costs are higher because the page sizes are larger. LED plotters have cheaper running costs than inkjet plotters.
Colour	Most are monochrome but colour laser printers are available.	Almost all inkjet printers can print in colour.	It is very rare to find a dot matrix printer that uses coloured ribbons.	Plotters can print in colour.
Quality	The highest quality of all printers due to the way it melts toner and attracts it to the page.	A reasonably good quality, but ink can show through thin paper and smudges can occur.	Quality is usually poor due to the bitmapped nature of printing characters.	Same issues as inkjet printers, but if pens are used then the quality of line drawings is high.
Typical uses	Letters, bulk printing, general office and home printing.	Photographs, charts, small maps, general office and home printing.	Invoices or receipts requiring duplicate or triplicate paper, automated teller machines (ATMs), point of sale systems, data logging, hot and dusty environments.	Architectural drawings, large maps, canvas prints and signs.

Table 2.01 - Different types of printer.

Scanner

A scanner is used to capture two dimensional (2D) documents in the form of an image. They perform a similar function to a digital camera but are specifically designed to take close-up images of 2D documents. Flat-bed scanners can capture a full-colour image and save the image as a file on the computer's storage. If the image contains lots of text, then it is possible to run optical character recognition (OCR) to recognise the text. Some flat-bed scanners include an automatic document feeder (ADF) that enables documents with multiple pages to be scanned in one operation.

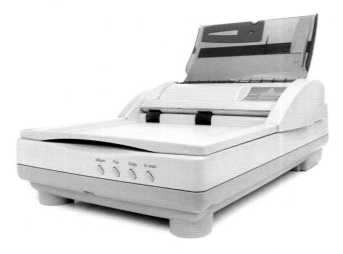

Figure 2.08 - Flat-bed scanner with an ADF.

Optical character reader

An optical character reader (OCR) is a device that enables characters on a document to be identified and understood by the computer as letters, numbers, characters and words. This isn't really a device in itself, but is a scanner combined with software that performs optical character recognition (also OCR). The picture of the document is analysed and characters are recognised by the software and turned into a document so that the text can be searched or edited.

Magnetic ink character reader

Figure 2.09 Checkbook with magnetic ink.

Magnetic ink is used to print numbers at the bottom of checks. The numbers are printed using the MICR E-13B or CMC-7 font. The ink contains iron oxide which means that it is easily detected when using a magnetic ink character reader (MICR) and the characters can be understood. It is important that mistakes aren't made and so MICR provides a much better level of accuracy than OCR.

Optical mark reader

An optical mark reader (OMR) detects the marks that are made on a multiple choice document such as a multiple choice answer paper for an examination. A scanner-like device is used to reflect a beam of light onto the marked sheet and detect where the marks have been made. Software is then used to translate the position of the mark to the information that it represents. OMR devices are only really suitable for multiple choice responses as they cannot interpret letters that form words.

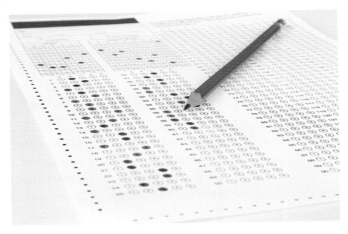

Figure 2.10 - Multiple choice OMR exam paper.

Barcode reader

A barcode reader is used to detect the width of lines and gaps that form a barcode. A laser beam is shone onto the barcode and a photodiode is used to measure the amount of light that is reflected back. Black lines will not reflect any light but white gaps will. A barcode represents letters and numbers which usually identify something, such as a book or other product. The barcode scanner usually includes its own hardcoded circuitry so that it can send the letters and numbers directly to the computer without the need for additional software.

DISCUSSION POINT

Barcodes are limited in terms of the amount of data that can be stored, which is why quick response (QR) codes are now being used for items of data beyond a string of letters and numbers.

Pen drive

A pen drive is a nickname for a USB flash drive. It is a small data storage device about the size of a thumb which stores data on flash memory and includes an integrated USB interface. The USB interface means that the flash drive is recognisable on all computers with a USB port and therefore data can be transported easily between computers. Flash memory is very fast and so the limiting factor is the speed of the USB port. As a flash drive does not have any moving parts it is safe to transport, although its size means that it can be easily lost. It also does not rely on magnetising and therefore is not susceptible to damage if it comes in contact with a strong magnetic field.

Portable hard disk drive

Hard disk drives were introduced earlier in this chapter. As well as an internal HDD, it is possible to have an external HDD. An external HDD can be connected to the computer using a USB or External Serial Advanced Technology Attachment (eSATA) port. An external HDD can store a lot more data than a USB flash drive, but it is more susceptible to damage due to it having moving parts and its vulnerability to strong magnetic fields.

Blu-ray disc drive

A Blu-ray disc is an optical storage medium. It is the same size and shape as a compact disc (CD) and digital versatile disc (DVD). The Blu-ray disc was introduced because it can store HD video and therefore a whole film can be stored on the Blu-ray disc. A single layer Blu-ray disc can store 25 GB of data and a dual-layer Blu-ray disc can store 50 GB of data. This compares to a DVD which can store 4.7 GB of data and a CD which can store 700 MB of data (or 80 minutes of audio).

A Blu-ray disc drive is required to read data from or write data to a Blu-ray disc. It uses lasers to read data that has been written in 'pits'. A basic Blu-ray disc drive can read data at 4.5 MB/s, whereas a 16× Blu-ray drive can read data at 72 MB/s. This is much slower than a HDD but the discs are very cheap to purchase compared with a whole HDD.

A standard Blu-ray disc is read only and used to distribute HD movies. However, it is possible to buy recordable (Blu-ray) discs that can be written to once and are useful for archive and backup purposes, or rewritable (Blu-ray) discs which can be rewritten to and erased making them useful for both backup and data transfer purposes.

DISCUSSION POINT

Find out about the next advancement in optical storage, the holographic versatile disc (HVD).

Memory card

A memory card is flash memory on a small card. They are typically used in digital cameras, digital video cameras and mobile phones. They take up very little space so are well suited to fitting into a small device, as well as being portable so that data can be transferred to a computer. There are many different formats of cards, but most devices favour Secure Digital (SD) and microSD cards. MicroSD cards are only 15 × 11 × 0.7 mm in size.

TASK

Categorise each of the internal and external hardware devices into input, output and storage devices.

Storage devices

Remember

The main purpose of a storage device is to store data or software that can be used by a computer. A storage device is known as secondary storage, which is non-volatile and so data is not lost when the computer is turned off.

There are many reasons why a user may want to save data to secondary storage:

- when creating a document, a user is likely to want to make changes to that document in the future and therefore it is necessary to save it to secondary storage
- the user may want somebody else to edit or read the document and so it will be saved to secondary storage to allow the person to do that
- users are likely to want to keep documents for archive purposes so they can be referred to in the future

- when using a database, each new record or change to a record will be saved to the database in secondary storage
- the user may want to back up the data so that a spare copy is available.

Other reasons for secondary storage include:

- each program will be stored on secondary storage ready to be loaded into RAM when the program is opened
- the computer will use secondary storage to save a virtual memory file which extends the amount of RAM available, albeit making the virtual part of the memory very slow.

Magnetic tape drive

Magnetic tape is used for backing up and archiving data. Data is stored serially which means one item after another. The tape is wound through the tape drive and as it winds through data is written to it. The low cost and high capacity of tapes makes them ideal for backing up and archiving data because the data is simply stored in a sequential manner.

When retrieving data, it does take a while to find the data that is required because the tape has to be wound to the exact position where the data is stored. This makes it unsuitable for everyday use. Backups and archives are not intended for everyday use. If data does need to be restored from backup, it may take a while but it is at least available when needed. If the whole of a computer's secondary storage needs to be restored, then this can be done by reading the tape sequentially.

Tapes are ideal for backing up the whole of secondary storage for a computer or server because they can hold several terabytes (TB) of data. In 2014, Sony developed a tape capable of storing 185 TB of data.

TASK

Find out how the grandfather–father–son backup rotation system works using magnetic tapes. How many tapes would be needed if the monthly backups were kept for three months at a time?

Optical

Optical storage was introduced earlier in this chapter under the heading Blu-ray. In 2015, there were three main types of optical storage.

	Compact disc (CD)	Digital versatile disc (DVD)	Blu-ray disc
Capacity	700 MB	4.7 GB	25 GB (single layer)
Original purpose	Music	Films	HD films

Table 2.02 - Types of optical storage.

In addition to distributing music and films, optical storage has been a popular medium to distribute software due to the low cost of each disc, the fact that read-only versions of each disc exist and the low cost of posting them. Using recordable and rewriteable versions of optical discs makes them suitable for backups and archives. It is quicker to restore a single file from an optical disc backup rather than a tape backup because the file can be accessed directly rather than having to read through a whole tape. This also makes optical discs more suitable for archived data because files can be found quickly. The capacity of optical discs is much less than tapes, which means they are only suitable for backing up a selection of files rather than the whole of secondary storage.

Hard disk drive

HDDs were introduced earlier in this chapter. Their principal purpose is to act as the main secondary storage device for a computer. Data and programs are stored on the HDD so that they can be accessed as and when required. External HDDs can also be used to back up data (although this is an expensive way of doing it) or to transfer data to another computer. Moving parts within a HDD make it vulnerable to damage if dropped.

Solid state drive

SSDs were introduced earlier in this chapter. Similar to a HDD, a SSD can store the data and programs that are used by a computer. SSDs are faster than HDDs, but also more expensive. SSDs require less power than a HDD so they are often used in tablet computers and high-end laptops to extend the battery life. Storing the operating system and programs that are used most on a SSD instead of a HDD will significantly improve the performance of a computer.

TASK

Compare the prices of SSDs and HDDs. Work out an approximate cost per megabyte (MB) for each.

	Hard disk	Solid state	Cloud	Pen Drive
Cost of purchase	The cheapest cost per MB for everyday storage (e.g. $0.06 per GB).	More expensive per MB than a hard disk (e.g. $0.10 per GB).	Usually a subscription charge that varies depending on supplier.	Designed for portability and so cost per MB varies depending on size.
Running cost / power consumption	Requires constant supply of electricity when the disk is spinning but if not in use can be temporarily turned off. Moving parts mean that it may fail in the future.	Does not require constant source of power as only needed when in use.	Running costs are included within a subscription charge.	Power only required when in use. Portability means that they may get damaged and need replacing.
Speed of access	Depends on SATA connection used.	Up to 30% faster access speed than hard disk.	Depends on broadband bandwidth of user and that offered by supplier.	Depends on whether using USB 2 or USB 3 ports. USB 3 offers faster data transfer than USB 2.
Interoperability	If internal, can only be used in device connected to unless moved permanently, but if external can be used in any device with a USB port.	If internal, can only be used in device connected to unless moved permanently, but if external can be used in any device with a USB port.	Can log on from any device including mobile devices.	Can be connected to any device with a USB port.
Typical use	In a desktop computer.	Laptop and tablet computers.	Collaboration with other users, backups, sharing of files and general storage.	For transferring data between devices.

Table 2.03 - Comparing storage devices.

TASK

Complete a table similar to that shown in Table 2.03 for memory cards, magnetic tape drives and Blu-ray disc drives.

Input and output devices

TIP

Input devices allow data to be sent to a computer (e.g. keyboard). Output devices allow the communication of data/information from a computer (e.g. monitor). When data is input into a computer, it is processed and then either output from the computer or stored for later use as shown in Figure 2.11 and is known as an input–process–output–storage (IPOS) diagram.

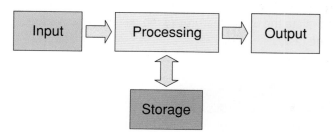

Figure 2.11 - IPOS diagram.

Data that has been stored can also be processed and then output from the computer.

EXAMPLE

Multiple choice answers from an examination are scanned using an OMR and the answers for each student are stored. Once all the answers have been

33

scanned, the stored answers are checked and the marks calculated for each student. The marks are printed out.

Figure 2.12 shows this process.

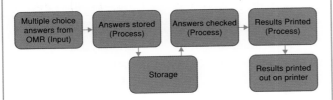

Figure 2.12 - Multiple choice IPOS diagram.

Evaluate different input, storage or output devices for a given task

Based on your understanding of a variety of input, storage and output devices, you will now need to evaluate the suitability of a device for a given task. When evaluating, you need to consider both the reasons why the device would be suitable and also the reasons why the device would not be suitable. You should then make a conclusion. In real life, this is what you would do to advise somebody which device they should use.

You could also be asked to evaluate the use of a given device for a given task. In this situation, you would only need to give positive reasons why that device would be suitable.

When analysing and evaluating, you should consider which features of the device make it suitable for the specific task that has been presented to you. To do this, you will need to identify the important aspects of the task and relate the useful features of the device to each aspect of the task.

EXAMPLE

Question: A school needs to back up data from its servers every day and keep the backup data off site. Evaluate the use of an external hard disc drive for this task.

The first thing you should do is identify the important aspects of the scenario that will give you clues as to whether the external HDD is suitable or not:

A **school** needs to back up data from its **servers** every day and keep the **backup** data **off site**. Evaluate the use of an external hard drive for this task.

It may be important to know who or what needs the device and you should refer to the **school** in your answer:

- It's important to know the data is being backed up from **servers** because this tells you that a large capacity will be required.

- Knowing the data is a **backup** means you know immediate access to the data is not essential.

- The fact that data has to be kept **off site** is essential because this means the device used must be able to be moved away from the school.

Here is an example of how the question could be answered:

Answer: An external HDD is lightweight and portable meaning that it will be easy for the **school** to take the **backup off site**.

As the HDD contains moving parts, the heads could crash causing data to be lost when transporting it **off site**.

The HDD will have a reasonably large capacity which could be around 8 TB. This may be enough to store all of the data from a small **school**'s **server**, but a larger **school** would require more than one external HDD.

As it is a **school**, some of the data being backed up is likely to be personal data which must be kept secure according to the Data Protection Act. When taking the data **off site**, it is possible that it could be lost or stolen due to its size. However, encryption could be used to make the data unreadable if it was lost or stolen.

Storing the backup on a single external HDD means that it would have to come back to the school each day, which defeats the object of keeping it off site. Therefore, several external HDDs would be required to ensure that there is always a backup **off site** and this could become very expensive.

In conclusion, although the external HDD can be taken off site, I would suggest that it is not suitable due to the cost of multiple drives and because the capacity may not be sufficient. Using tapes would be more cost-effective and would overcome the cost issue.

Note how the answer makes reference to the scenario and links to the features of an external HDD.

TASK

Analyse and discuss the use of the following devices for each scenario given. Remember that you only need to give positive reasons.

Device	Scenario
Plotter	An architect is preparing drawings for a new house that is to be built. Different colours will be used to identify electricity, water and gas services.
Digital camera	An employee travels regularly as part of her job. She is required to keep a record of expenses and to email copies of all receipts to the finance department.
Pen drive	A church records the preacher's talk each week. The computer that is used is not connected to the internet, but the talk needs to be uploaded to a website after the church service.

Turn your answers into evaluations by also looking at reasons why each device would not be suitable for each task and give a conclusion.

QUESTIONS

1   Define the term hardware.
2   Describe the role of the central processing unit (CPU).
3   Describe the role of a graphics card.
4   Contrast random access memory (RAM) and a storage device.
5   Compare and contrast a digital camera to a scanner.
6   Evaluate the suitability of an optical mark reader (OMR) and an optical character reader (OCR) for marking exam papers.

2.02 System, application and user interface

KEY TERMS

Software: programs which give instructions to the computer

User interface: communication between the user and the computer system

TIP

Software is also known as programs, such as word processing, spreadsheet, anti-malware or operating system. Each program consists of programming code which gives instructions to the computer in order to carry out a task. The code that is passed to the hardware is in binary format which consists of instructions in the form of lots of ones and zeros (e.g. 101011101110).

System software

Programs that are designed to maintain or operate the computer system are known as system software. The software that operates the computer hardware is known as the operating system. Programs that are used to maintain a computer system (e.g. anti-malware software) are known as utility software.

Operating systems

Remember

An operating system manages the hardware within a computer system. When a computer is turned on and after the Basic Input/Output System (BIOS) has loaded, the operating system is the first piece of software that will load. It sits between hardware and applications software and manages any communication between the two.

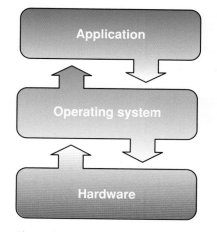

Figure 2.13 - Operating system.

An operating system manages hardware by carrying out tasks such as:

*   allocating memory to software
*   sending data and instructions to output devices
*   responding to input devices such as when a key is pressed
*   opening and closing files on storage devices
*   giving each running task a fair share of processor time
*   sending error messages or status messages to applications or users
*   dealing with user logons and security.

TASK

Microsoft Windows is an example of an operating system. Find at least two other operating systems used by desktop computers and at least three operating systems used by mobile phones or tablets.

35

Device drivers

While the operating system can manage the general instructions to deal with hardware such as displaying graphics on a screen, it requires the use of device drivers to deal with specific makes and models of hardware. A device driver is the software that comes with an external hardware component and sends customised instructions to that specific component. By using common device drivers, software applications are able to issue generic commands such as 'print' to the operating system without having to know the different instructions required for every different make and model of external hardware components.

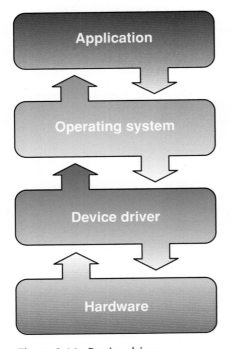

Figure 2.14 - Device driver.

Utilities

Utilities are part of system software. They are designed to perform functions which maintain the computer system. Utilities are discussed later in this chapter.

Compilers

A compiler translates a program written in a high-level programming language into machine code which a computer can understand. The file containing the machine code is known as an executable file because it can be executed by the processor. It can also be referred to as the object file. The original high-level programming language file is known as the source file.

When a program is compiled, the whole source code is translated into the executable file at once and can then

be distributed to resellers, customers and individual computers. As it is in an executable format, it can only run on operating systems for which the compiler has translated it. For example, programs that have been compiled for Windows will not work on Linux unless they are compiled again for Linux. The same situation exists with mobile phone and tablet operating systems.

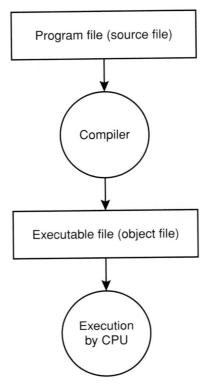

Figure 2.15 - Compiler diagram.

Interpreters

Interpreters also translate a program written in a high-level programming language into machine code, but use a different method. Instead of translating the whole source code at once, it is translated one line at a time. This can be less efficient than a compiler because it takes time to do the translating as the program is being executed and also because statements within programming loops (e.g. FOR, REPEAT, WHILE) have to be analysed each time round.

Interpreters are often used to translate macros or application-based script languages (e.g. Visual Basic for Applications), which can be particularly useful when a document needs to be opened on a variety of operating systems. Interpreters are also used when testing programs so that parts of the program can be executed without having to compile the whole program.

DISCUSSION POINT

Java uses both a compiler and an interpreter. The original Java source code (files with a .java extension) is compiled into Java bytecode (files with a .class extension) which is an intermediate code. In order that the Java program can work on any operating system, a Java Virtual Machine installed on the computer is used to interpret the bytecode at the time of execution.

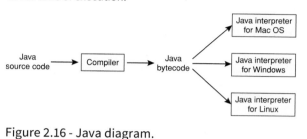

Figure 2.16 - Java diagram.

Linkers

Computer programs often consist of several modules (parts) of programming code. Each module carries out a specified task within the program. Each module will have been compiled into a separate object file. The function of a linker (also known as a link editor) is to combine the object files together to form a single executable file. In addition to the modules used, the program may make reference to a common library. A common library contains code for common tasks that can be used in more than one program, such as mathematical functions, memory management, open and save dialogues, progress bars and input/output. The linker is able to link modules from a library file into the executable file, too.

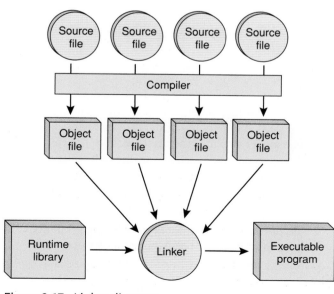

Figure 2.17 - Linker diagram.

Not all modules are always needed and a linker is able to select which modules will form part of the executable file.

Application software

Programs that are intended for productivity or to carry out a task for the user are known as application software. Examples include word processor, games, web browser and graphics software. On a mobile phone or tablet, this type of software is usually referred to as an app.

You are likely to be asked to analyse or evaluate the use of a particular piece of software for a given task. You will need to look at the details of the task and relate appropriate features of the software that are likely to help solve parts of the task. You will also need to consider whether there are other software options available, consider how they could be used to complete the task and then provide a conclusion.

When making reference to software always use the name of the type of software (e.g. word processor) rather than a trade name (e.g. Microsoft Word).

Word processing

TIP
The function of a word processor is to primarily process words.

It is therefore appropriate for tasks such as:

- writing a letter
- producing a report
- producing coursework
- creating a menu
- mail merging
- writing a book.

Features of word processing software include:

- tables
- headers and footers
- footnotes and endnotes
- sections
- formatting text
- styles
- spellchecker
- bullets and automatic numbering
- automatic contents page
- tracking changes
- frames for images
- text alignment

- text wrap
- indentation and tabs.

TASK

If you are unfamiliar with any of the features above, then find out about them and try using them. A website that may help you with this is www.teach-ict.com/videohome.htm or the official Microsoft video tutorials on Microsoft's Office support site.

EXAMPLE

Question: Give reasons for the use of word processing software for creating a menu for a restaurant.

Think of the features you would expect to find on a menu and how it might be produced. Then relate them to the features of word processing software that could be used to create the menu.

Answer: Alignment could be used to centre the name of the restaurant and the word 'Menu' at the top of the page.

The name of the restaurant could be formatted using a different font in a larger size to the rest of the text and in a different colour.

Frames could be used to include images of each dish on the menu.

Text wrap could be used so that text wraps around the images of each dish.

Automated numbering could be used to give each dish a number that can be used when ordering.

The spellchecker could be used to ensure that all descriptions of the dishes have been spelt correctly.

Footnotes could be used to identify dishes which contain nuts or are vegetarian options.

Styles could be used so that subheadings are kept consistent by applying a style rather than manually formatting each subheading.

TASK

Give reasons for the use of word processing software for writing a book.

Spreadsheet

	A	B	C
1	Starting distance	Ending distance	Distance travelled
2	20,035	19,829	=A2–B2
3			

Figure 2.18 - Spreadsheet formula.

	A	B	C
1	Starting distance	Ending distance	Distance travelled
2	20,035	19,829	206
3			

Figure 2.19 - Spreadsheet calculation.

Spreadsheet software is used mainly for performing calculations and modelling. Spreadsheets are often used for financial and statistical information. Spreadsheets work on the basis of input–process–output whereby data is input, then formulae and functions process that data to generate an output. When input data changes, the output data automatically changes because the formulae and functions are automatically recalculated. This allows users to experiment with values and ask 'What-if' questions such as 'What will happen if we try to sell another 10 000 cars this month?'

Spreadsheets contain cells which form the intersection of rows and columns. In Figure 2.19, cell C2 contains the value 206.

TASK

CD 2.01 Lease pricing model

Open CD 2.01 Lease pricing model.xlsx and experiment with changing the input values in the yellow cells in the Pricing Model spreadsheet. This spreadsheet calculates the total cost of a hire car based upon different variables including the list price and carbon dioxide (CO_2) emissions of the vehicle.

1 Watch what happens to the total cost of the lease when you adjust the input values.

2 Compose a list of at least three 'What-if' questions that could be asked using this spreadsheet model.

You will learn more about spreadsheets in Chapter 8.

Database management systems

Remember

Database management systems (DBMS) are used for viewing and editing data within a database. A database is a structured collection of data in the form of tables which are related to each other. For example, an invoicing database would include tables for customer, products, orders and order-lines (orders for each product).

A DBMS can provide features including:

- data entry screens / forms for inputting data
- filters and queries for selecting data that meets specified criteria
- reports for displaying information in an easily readable format
- graphs for analysing data
- security features so that users can only access the parts of the database they have been authorised to access
- relationships to link related tables.

You will learn more about databases in Chapter 9.

Graphics manipulation software

TIP

As its name suggests, graphics manipulation software is designed to manipulate graphics. This can be either bitmap graphics or vector graphics.

The features included in graphics manipulation software vary depending upon the complexity of the software.

Features for both bitmap and graphics manipulation software can include:

- drawing shapes
- changing the canvas size
- resizing the image
- adding layers
- adding text to an image
- selecting a colour based on picking an existing colour.

Features for bitmap graphics manipulation software can include:

- filling an area with a colour
- moving part of the image
- resizing part of the image
- erasing parts of an image

- cloning parts of an image
- softening (blurring) and sharpening an image.

Features for vector graphics manipulation software can include:

- filling a shape with colour
- changing features of the border of a shape such as thickness and colour
- combining shapes together into a group
- moving a shape or group of shapes
- resizing a shape or group of shapes
- aligning objects.

Using graphics manipulation software requires a lot of skill and advanced features are usually more appropriate for serious artists.

You will learn more about graphics manipulation in Chapter 16.

TASK

Investigate the features available in Paint.NET, IrfanView and CorelDRAW.

Photo editing software

Remember

Photo editing software is a specific type of graphics manipulation software that is focused on editing photographs. This can be used by professional photographers and enthusiasts to enhance photographs or by people at home to make minor changes.

Features of photo editing software include:

- cropping parts of the photo
- adjusting the brightness or contrast
- resizing the canvas
- removing red eye
- changing the colour balance
- cloning parts of the photo
- identifying common areas of an image (e.g. background) using a 'magic wand' tool
- applying effects such as black and white or sepia
- softening (blurring) and sharpening a photo.

Photo editing software requires a large amount of RAM and complex operations can use up a lot of processing time.

Video editing software

Remember
When videos are recorded, they are known as 'raw' video files (footage). There are many enhancements that can be made to a raw video file and this is where video editing software comes in useful.

Features of video editing software include:

- importing or capturing raw video
- clipping the beginning and end of a video
- clipping sections within a video
- adding titles to the beginning or credits at the end
- overlaying videos with text or images
- speeding up or slowing down footage
- rotating footage
- using more than one video track
- transitioning between clips (e.g. fade)
- add backing music, narration or other sound
- using picture-in-picture to show two video clips at once.

Video editing software does have some downsides and these include:

- using up a lot of processing time
- requiring a large amount of RAM
- importing raw video files can take a long time
- encoding the final video takes a very long time.

You will learn more about video editing in Chapter 10.

Communications software

Remember
Communications software can cover a range of tasks including instant messaging, audio conferencing, video conferencing and email.

Instant messaging software allows a user to communicate with another user by sending text-based messages which are instantly sent and received. This can be a slow form of communication because of the need for typing, but some people prefer it to having a real conversation.

Audio conferencing allows users to speak and listen to each other in a similar way to a telephone call. The main difference is that more than two people can be included in the conference. This is usually achieved with voice over internet protocol (VOIP). A popular example is Skype. Making conference calls over the internet is usually free of charge but it does require every participant to be logged on at the

same time. During an audio conference it can be difficult to know whose turn it is to speak. Video conferencing expands upon audio conferencing by including real-time video of the people involved in the conference.

Email clients provide users with a larger range of features than webmail and enable emails to be read and composed while offline. This can be useful when no fixed internet connection is available and 3G/4G coverage is poor or non-existent.

Features of email clients include:

- address book of contacts
- ability to send and receive emails
- signatures
- prioritising of emails
- delaying delivery of emails
- delivery and read receipts
- rules that can be applied to email messages (e.g. moving messages that contain a specific subject to a specific folder)
- using more than one email account at once
- adding attachments to messages
- digital signatures and encrypted messages
- integration with a calendar
- inviting contacts to a meeting in the calendar and receiving responses.

TASK
If you are unfamiliar with any of the features above, then find out more about them. There are several freeware email clients that you could download and use.

Web authoring software

Remember
Web authoring software is used for the creation and editing of websites.

There are now many online content management systems and other tools that are used to create and update websites, but some web developers sometimes prefer to use offline web authoring software such as Dreamweaver.

Web authoring software can be very complex to use because of the vast number of configurations available for web pages, which is why using an online tool like www.wix.com enables people with little experience of websites to create a site quickly, although it can be difficult to customise it to exact requirements. Web authoring software gives the most flexibility and websites can be configured exactly as required.

Features of web authoring software include:

- common navigation bar
- ability to publish individual files or sites to a web server
- preview of web pages
- viewing and editing in either what you see is what you get (WYSIWYG) view or Hypertext Markup Language (HTML) code view or a mixture of both
- adding basic HTML features such as tables, horizontal lines and headings
- management of a web page's metadata
- designing templates that can be applied to all pages
- interactive features such as interactive buttons
- forms and form fields
- validation of form fields.

Control and measuring software

Remember

Control software is used for controlling devices that are not part of the computer system. Measuring software is used to measure values in the real world.

EXAMPLE

An automated house would require control software to turn lights on and off, open a garage door, turn on the heating, open blinds and sound a burglar alarm. The measuring aspect of the software would measure the level of light and time of day and turn on the lights when appropriate. It would also detect whether security sensors were triggered before sounding the burglar alarm. Heating would only be turned on based on the measurement of the current temperature.

Control and measuring software is used in a wide variety of situations including automated features of cars (e.g. automatic windscreen wipers), science experiments, weather stations, pollution management and traffic lights.

Measuring software will measure values from sensors including:

- pressure (amount of pressure applied)
- moisture
- temperature

- wind speed
- distance (measured by lasers)
- pH (acid/alkaline) levels.

Control software will control devices such as:

- lights
- motors (e.g. to make windscreen wipers move)
- speakers/sirens
- heating.

Apps

An app is another name for a program. It is a piece of software that can run on a desktop computer, over the internet, on a tablet computer or on a mobile phone. The most common reference to 'apps' is when referring to software that is designed to work on mobile devices such as tablets or mobile phones. In this case, apps are optimised to work with touch screen interfaces and smaller screens. They will provide essential features that can be carried out using the limited interface of mobile devices, but often lack more complex features due to the need for more processing power or accurate input devices such as a mouse and keyboard.

Apps are also available over the internet and usually exist within web pages. For example, webmail is an app that allows a user to manage their emails. Other examples include online games, online office software (e.g. Office 365), content management systems, online banking and online shopping.

Applets

An applet is a small program that is designed to carry out a specific task. An applet cannot run on its own but must be executed from within another piece of software. Applets are often known as add-ins, add-ons or extensions. They can carry out additional tasks that the original software is not capable of doing or they can simplify tasks within the original software.

TASK

Explore some of the extensions available to Google Chrome and add-ins available to Microsoft Excel.

Evaluate application software for a given task

Based on your understanding of a variety of software applications, you will now need to evaluate the suitability of a software application for a given task. When evaluating, you need to consider both the reasons why the application would be suitable and also the reasons why the application would not be suitable. You should then make a conclusion. In real life, this is what you would do to advise somebody which application they should use.

You could also be asked to give reasons for the use of a given application for a given task. In this situation, you would only need to give positive reasons why that application would be suitable.

When analysing and evaluating, you should consider which features of the application make it suitable for the specific task that has been presented to you. To do this, you will need to identify the important aspects of the task and relate the useful features of the application to each aspect of the task.

42

EXAMPLE

Question: Evaluate and discuss the use of spreadsheet software for deciding what the best tariff is for a customer to use for a mobile phone.

Start by identifying the important parts of the question that you will relate to in your answer. These should include **tariff, customer** and **mobile phone**. Then consider what data might be used in this spreadsheet model and relate features of a spreadsheet to that data.

Answer: Spreadsheet software will enable the **customer** to experiment with different variables (inputs), such as the purchase cost of the **mobile phone**, number of minutes they normally use and the amount of data needed.

Formulae and functions can be used to calculate each **tariff,** including the total cost over the period of the contract.

Graphs could be used to compare the cost of buying a **mobile phone** up front with a SIM-only **tariff** and buying a **tariff** which includes a **mobile phone**.

A separate worksheet can be used to store a table of **tariffs** and another worksheet for the **customer** interface.

TASK

A supermarket needs to decide how best to use the space within the shop. More space should be allocated to profitable items. Give reasons for the use of spreadsheet software to assist with deciding how much space to allocate to each type of product.

EXAMPLE

Introduction: A warehouse company needs to keep accurate records of how many of each product is currently in stock and to where each product has been delivered. It also needs to know when new stock is due to arrive and ensure that stock levels do not fall too low.

Question: Evaluate the use of a database management system (DBMS) for this task.

Start by identifying the important parts of the question that you will relate to in your answer. These should include **warehouse, records, products, stock** and **stock levels**. Then consider what data might be used in this database and relate features of a DBMS to how that data might be used. You should also consider the problems with using a DBMS or other software that would be appropriate.

Answer: A DBMS will be able to relate data stored in tables for **products, deliveries**, destinations and sources. For example, a foreign key of ProductID in the delivery table could relate to a primary key of ProductID in the product table.

A query could be created in a DBMS to find all the **stock** where **stock levels** are low so that more **stock** can be ordered. This would be achieved by using criteria to compare the current stock level with a field that stores the minimum stock level that should be maintained. If the current stock level falls below the minimum stock level, then the product will be included in a re-order query.

A DBMS could produce graphs to show how much stock has been delivered by the **warehouse** to each destination. For each record in the destination table, the number of products that have been delivered to that destination would be counted.

However, spreadsheets can also be used to create graphs of the **stock** and the graphs can be customised in more detail when using a spreadsheet such as deciding on axis titles, grouping destinations based on their geographical location and choosing the intervals to display on axes.

Databases can be very complex to set up whereas a spreadsheet could be set up quickly with worksheets for **products**, destinations and **deliveries**. Databases require tables, field types, field lengths, primary keys, foreign keys, relationships, queries and reports all to be set up following a very clearly defined structure.

Conclusion: Although the spreadsheet would be simpler to set up, it would not be able to easily manage the complex relationships needed for **stock** control and **deliveries** and so a DBMS would be appropriate for the **warehouse** in this case.

TASK

Give reasons for the use of the following applications for each scenario given. Remember that you only need to give positive reasons.

Application	Scenario
Word processor	A charity sends out monthly newsletters. They require a standard layout that will be used every month and they would like each newsletter to be addressed personally to their supporters.
Web authoring software	A primary school wants to create a website that can be updated regularly. It must include a navigation bar with links to each page and a contact form, as well as general information about the school.
Video editing software	A church records the preacher's talk each week including the video. There are three cameras used in total plus a microphone for the preacher.

Turn your answers into evaluations by also looking at reasons why each application would not be suitable for each task and giving a conclusion.

Different types of user interface

An interface is the boundary between two systems. A **user interface** is the boundary between the user and the computer system. A user interface represents the communication between a user and the computer system. This communication can take many forms.

Command line interface

A command line interface (CLI) allows a user to enter text commands to which the computer system will respond. The computer system will respond by producing results in a text format.

EXAMPLE

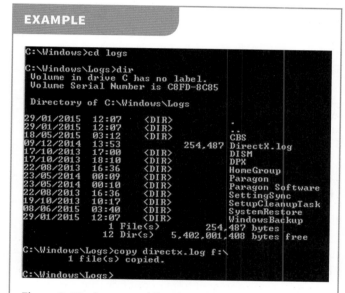

Figure 2.20 - Command line interface.

In this example, the user has changed the directory (folder) to the logs directory ('cd logs'). Then the user has requested a listing of the directory ('dir'). Finally the user copies the file directx.log to the root directory of the f drive ('copy directx.log f:\'). The user gets a confirmation message that one file has been copied. The only prompt that the user gets is information about which directory is currently active ('C:\Windows\Logs>')

CLIs use very little memory so they are useful in old systems or for maintenance of very small systems/devices (e.g. engine management systems). They are also useful for technical users who need to carry out complex operations which cannot be performed using more user-friendly interfaces. However, CLIs can be difficult to learn and use because users have to learn and remember all the commands, and errors are easily made when entering those commands.

43

Graphical user interface

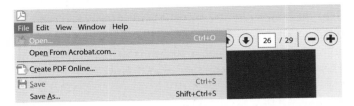

Figure 2.21 - Graphical user interface.

The most common type of interface that we use is a graphical user interface (GUI). GUIs are found on desktop computers, tablet computers, mobile phones, televisions, set-top boxes, photocopiers and some in-car entertainment systems.

GUIs can include some or all of the elements shown in Table 2.04.

Windows	An area of the screen devoted to a specific task, for example a software application, a file within a software application or a print dialog box.
Icons	An image that is used to represent a program, file or task. The icon can be selected to open the program, file or task.
Menus	Menus are words on the screen which represent a list of options that can be expanded into further sub-menus.
Pointers	This is the method of representing movement from a pointing device such as a mouse or the human finger on a touch screen. The pointer is also used to select and manipulate objects on the screen.

Table 2.04 - Graphical user interface elements.

The acronym WIMP is commonly used to remember these elements.

Complex GUIs require a lot of memory to operate, but simpler GUIs can be used where memory is limited. Although CLIs don't require much memory, simple GUIs can be used instead of a CLI in small systems such as embedded systems. It is commonplace to find simple web-based GUIs for the maintenance of devices such as routers, switches and printers.

GUIs are intuitive to use which means they are easy to learn because commands are represented by pictures and menus provide options that can be selected. However, they can be restrictive for some technical users who need to carry out unusual tasks.

Dialogue interface

A dialogue interface refers to using the spoken word to communicate with a computer system. A user can give commands using their voice and the computer system can respond by carrying out an action or with further information using a synthesised voice.

Figure 2.22 - Dialogue interface.

Dialogue interfaces are very popular with mobile devices, including mobile phones and in-car entertainment systems. Some cars will accept commands such as 'Temperature 20' or 'Call John Smith at home'. Mobile phones will accept commands and questions such as 'What is the time in Islamabad?' or 'Give me directions to get home'. Some automated telephone systems will recognise voice, too, so that the user doesn't have to use the dial pad to input information.

A big advantage of dialogue interfaces is that no hands are required, which makes them suitable for use in cars or when holding a telephone. In many circumstances, words can be spoken by a user more quickly than a user can type them. There is no need for a physical interface with dialogue interfaces , so they are suitable for systems such as home automation where voice commands can be given from anywhere to control equipment such as lights, entertainment systems and curtains. With entertainment systems such as televisions, the user does not have to find a remote control to use and anybody in the room can give the command to increase the volume or change the channel.

The main problem with this type of interface is the computer system's ability to recognise the spoken word. Many things can make it difficult for the computer to understand, including accents, different voices, stammers and background noise (e.g. a car's engine). Dialogue interfaces also require the user to know what commands are understood by the computer system as otherwise the system will not know how to respond. Some dialogue interfaces will give prompts telling the user from which options they can choose. Systems are not intelligent enough to simply understand requests in any format that the user chooses.

Gesture-based interface

Gesture-based interfaces will recognise human motion. This could include tracking eyes and lips, identifying hand signals or monitoring whole body movement.

There are many applications of gesture-based interfaces, including gaming, which have led to the development of other gesture-based interfaces. The original Nintendo Wii enabled gamers to move their hands while holding a remote controller and that movement would be mimicked in games such as ten pin bowling and boxing. Microsoft's Xbox took this a stage further and was able to track whole body movement without any devices being held or worn by the user. This enabled gamers to fully engage with a game using their whole body, so boxing could now become kick-boxing and ten pin bowling could include a run-up.

Many computer systems, including mobile devices, are now starting to accept hand gestures as a way of controlling objects on screen. For example, a swipe of the hand across a screen may close a program, while pinching fingers together in front of a screen may zoom out on an image. This can avoid greasy screens and could help with infection control in hospitals and specifically in operating theatres.

Gestures can be an essential form of interaction for some disabled users who cannot use conventional input devices. A person who has no control from the neck downwards could control a computer system with their eyes because the computer can track the movement of each eye.

One of the biggest problems with gesture interfaces is accuracy. In order for a gesture interface to be effective, it needs to accurately interpret the movements made by the human user. Tracking individual fingers, arms, eyeballs and legs requires highly accurate cameras or sensors. This is why many virtual reality applications still use sensors attached to various parts of the body in order to improve accuracy. It can also be very difficult to control a pointer when a finger is in mid-air rather than when firmly fixed to a touch screen or holding a mouse.

Colour, layout, font size, quantity of information and controls in user interface design

When designing a user interface, it is very important to ensure that it is accessible and efficient for the user. Therefore the colour, layout, font size, quantity of information and controls need to be considered when designing the interface.

Colour

Text must be legible. This means using a light font on a dark background or a dark font on a light background. For example, black text on a white background works well, but black text on a grey background is very difficult to read. It's also important to avoid using foreground and background colours that clash, such as red and green which are indistinguishable to people who are colour blind. The focus must be on accessibility rather than making an interface look pretty. If an interface is difficult to read due to clashing colours, then it will take the user longer to complete tasks.

If an organisation has a house style then the corporate colours should be used within the interface so that it looks as if it belongs to the organisation. Users expect hyperlinks to be in blue and so blue should be used rather than another colour. Users expect green to mean 'go' or 'good' and so confirmation buttons and 'OK' buttons could use green, whereas 'cancel' and 'no' buttons could be red. It is important that text is also used so that colour blind users can access the interface too. Colour can also be used to highlight information such as an important message or instruction.

Layout

Careful consideration should be given to the layout of information, icons and inputs on a screen. Similar information, icons or inputs should be grouped together. For example, icons that perform a formatting function should all be next to each other and inputs about contact details should be together. There should be sufficient space separating objects on the screen so that the user can identify those objects clearly, but at the same time it's important to try to fit all related objects on the screen together.

Prompts for text boxes or other inputs should always be just above or to the left of those inputs when working with languages that read from left to right. Similarly, text should be left aligned, numbers right aligned and decimals aligned on the decimal point. Instructions should always be at the beginning of a form or just before each input, whereas confirmation and cancel buttons should be at the end of a form.

Essential information should always be displayed in a prominent position. Additional information such as detailed help can be available through a hyperlink or pop-up message, but should not use up valuable space on the main interface.

Font size

The standard size of font for reading is 11 or 12 points which is legible for most users. This should be used wherever possible, with titles in slightly larger fonts. It is important that the font size is consistent throughout the interface so that it does not confuse users. A larger font size should be used for young children. One of the biggest problems with interfaces is that they can vary based on the size of screen and so what looks good on a desktop monitor may not look good on a mobile phone. It's therefore important to test the interface on a variety of screen sizes to see what happens to the legibility. Fonts that are too large take up too much space on screen meaning that not all information can be seen at once, whereas fonts which are too small make reading difficult and so slow down productivity. If all the required information cannot fit on one screen, then the information should be separated into more than one page.

Quantity of information

If too much information is provided to a user, then this can cause information overload and may mean that much of it is ignored. A user can typically remember seven items of information, so you should try to keep this as a maximum number of icons or inputs that are grouped together. If necessary, more than one page/screen of information should be used with forward and backward buttons.

Controls

Controls are used on forms. Table 2.05 shows some of the controls that are available to a user.

Mental models

A mental model is a person's understanding of how something works. That understanding may be different for different people depending on the different experiences each person has had in life and the assumptions they make about how something works.

> **EXAMPLE**
>
> A person understands that a professional soccer player in a top league earns a lot of money. They therefore may assume that all sportsmen in the top leagues get paid a lot of money. But it may be that cricket players and bowls players get paid a lot less.

When it comes to designing an interface, the person is the user. The user has their own understanding of how a computer system and its interface works and will make their own assumptions based on their own experience. The more experience a user has had with a computer, the more easily they will learn new interfaces and new systems. But it is not just their computer experiences that matter. Life experiences are also important.

> **EXAMPLE**
>
> A mental model of how to access a paper document may be something like:
>
> 1 Find the appropriate filing cabinet.
>
> 2 Find the appropriate folder from the folders stored in alphabetical order.
>
> 3 Look through the folder until the document is found.
>
> This concept has therefore been used for accessing documents on a computer system:
>
> 1 Find the appropriate storage area (e.g. My Documents, My Pictures, Shared Documents).
>
> 2 Find the appropriate folder (usually stored in alphabetical order but this can be changed).
>
> 3 Look through the folder until the document (file) is found (the order is dependent on the user's preference, which is how a paper folder would work, too).

Control	Description	Example
Labels	Labels are used as prompts or instructions to enter data. They are text and cannot be edited by the user.	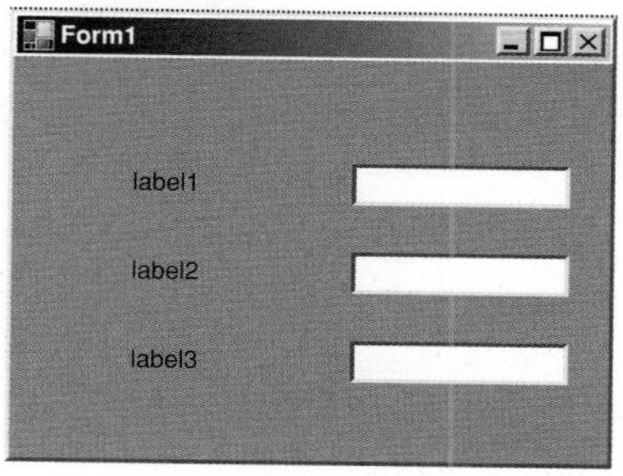 Figure 2.23 - Label.
Text boxes	Text boxes are an area where the user can enter text such as their surname or credit card number. Errors can easily be made by the user when entering data into a text box, such as spelling things incorrectly.	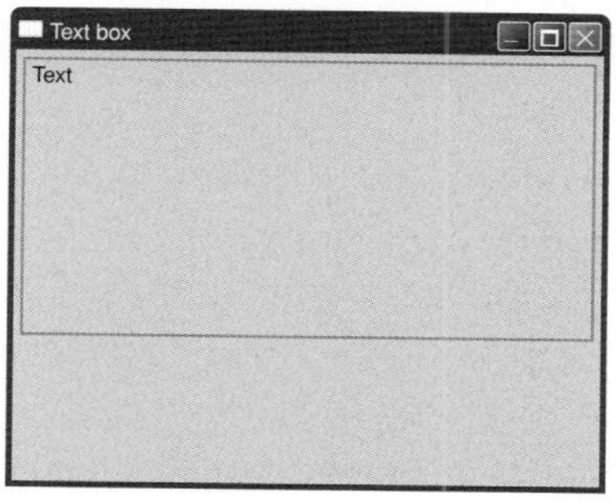 Figure 2.24 - Text box.
Tick boxes	Tick boxes (also known as check boxes) allow the user to select from a set of options. The user can choose as many options that apply. For example, when printing, a user can choose to collate documents and to print on both sides.	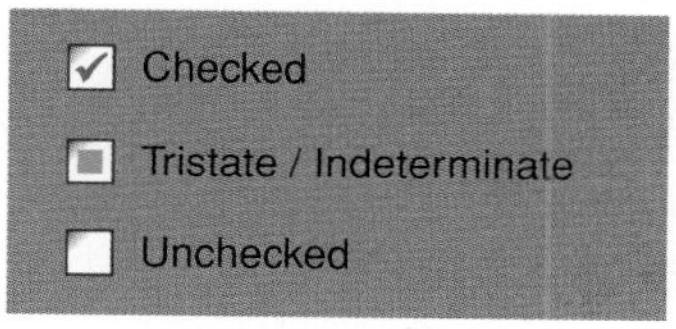 Figure 2.25 - Tick box.
Option buttons	Option buttons (also known as radio buttons) differ from tick boxes in that only one option in a group can be selected at once.	 Figure 2.26 - Option button.
Drop-down boxes	Drop-down boxes allow a user to select from a list that appears when the drop-down box appears on screen. Only one option can be chosen. The user can usually start typing the option so that it is found more quickly. Drop-down boxes are more appropriate than option buttons when there are a large number of options to choose from, as the drop-down box doesn't take up as much space on the screen.	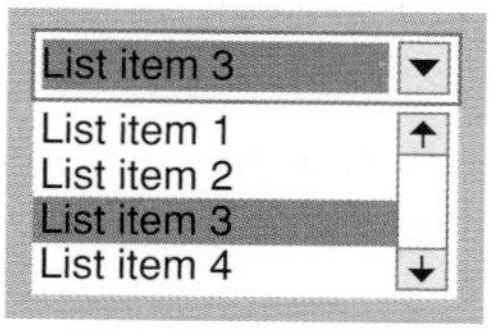 Figure 2.27 - Drop-down box.
Buttons	Buttons can be used to navigate through an interface (forwards and backwards), to confirm that inputs have been completed, to clear inputs, to gain help and to access any other area of an interface.	 Figure 2.28 - Confirm button.

Table 2.05 - Form controls.

Figure 2.29 - Badly designed input screen.

48

TASK

Criticise the input screen in Figure 2.29 and suggest improvements that could be made.

If interfaces can be designed to be similar to the user's mental model, then it will reduce the amount of time it takes a user to learn how to use the interface because they will already understand some of the key concepts. Interfaces should reflect the preconceived ideas of the majority of users, but at the same time allow options for different users to follow different routes. These options could include menus, icons, shortcut keys and command words. The same task can be achieved in more than one way, which fits with each user's mental model. Some users may prefer to click on the B icon to make text bold whereas other users may prefer to use the shortcut Ctrl+B.

EXAMPLE

Examples of matching the user's mental model:

- magnifying glass for zoom
- envelope for email
- recycle bin
- cut, copy and paste.

Sometimes it is not appropriate to follow the user's mental model of the real world because it would make an interface inefficient. For example, when searching for information in a text book, a student would turn to the index and then look through the index until they found the topic they were wanted. Then the student would turn to the page that is listed in the index.

With a computer interface, this process can be improved by using a search option whereby the student can enter the topic they are searching for into a text box and the computer will respond with some suggestions of where to find that information. This is not part of the user's mental model of the real world, but helps to make an interface more efficient than the real world.

QUESTIONS

7 Describe the difference between system software and application software.

8 Identify two functions of an operating system.

9 Evaluate the use of word processing and web authoring software for the development of a website.

10 Describe the purpose of an applet.

11 Explain how colour should be used when designing a user interface.

2.03 Utility software

KEY TERMS

Utility software: software that performs some sort of maintenance on the computer system

Operating system: software that manages the hardware within a computer system

Remember

Utility software is system software that performs some sort of maintenance on the computer system. Utility software does not include the **operating system**, but an operating system may come pre-installed with some utility software.

The roles of different utility software

Anti-virus

Anti-virus software is sometimes referred to as anti-malware software as it deals with other threats such as adware and spyware as well as viruses. It has two main functions. The first is an anti-virus monitor that is continually monitoring the system for viruses and malware. If the anti-virus monitor detects any unusual behaviour or tell-tale signs of viruses or malware then it will prevent them from being executed so they cannot cause damage to files or programs. The second function is to check for viruses or malware that may already be on a system. This is usually known as scanning the system. If anything is found then the user will usually be given the option to disinfect the affected area, put it into quarantine or ignore it. Ignoring it is very dangerous because it means the virus or malware will be executed and may have unexpected results. Disinfecting is the safest option as it completely removes the threat from the system, but it does mean that any data or program that had been affected would be deleted. The compromise is to put the affected area into quarantine. This is a safe area where the virus or malware cannot be executed, but the data or program remains isolated until it can be checked more thoroughly.

Backup

Backup utilities create a second copy of data and programs that are in storage. A backup utility can be executed by the user, in which case the backup takes place when the user asks it to, or it can be scheduled to execute at a predetermined time so that the backup takes place automatically. The user is usually able to select which folders and files will be backed up and can usually decide where the backup will be stored.

Data compression

Data compression utilities will reduce the original size of files so that they use up less storage space. This can be achieved on a file-by-file basis or for a set of files or even a set of folders. It will be slower to open the compressed file, but as it is smaller it will use up less storage and can be transferred from one location to another more quickly.

Disc defragmentation

As a hard disc gets used, files are kept together in storage on the same cylinder or adjacent cylinders. As files grow in size, they use up more space on the disc and this may no longer be on the same or adjacent cylinder. The problem with this is that when opening the file, the access arm of the hard disc drive has to keep moving to different locations which makes opening the file a slow process.

When files are deleted, gaps are left on the disc. When all the cylinders have been used, the only space to store files is within the gaps. If the gaps are not big enough, then files have to be split across gaps, meaning that they become defragmented.

EXAMPLE

In Figure 2.30, files have been neatly stored on the disc with file A, followed by file B, then file C.

Figure 2.30 - Non-fragmented files.

The next diagram shows how each of the files has got bigger. First of all file A got bigger with an extra two sectors, then a new file D was added, then file B got bigger by a sector, then file A again by a sector and finally file C.

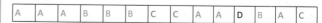

Figure 2.31 - Fragmented files.

The files are fragmented and so they need to be defragmented as in Figure 2.32.

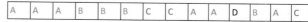

Figure 2.32 - Defragmented files.

EXAMPLE

In Figure 2.33, files Q and S have been deleted.

Figure 2.33 - Non-fragmented files.

A new file U needs to be stored but it requires four sectors. It could end up being stored as in Figure 2.34.

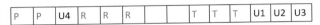

Figure 2.34 - Fragmented files.

Defragmentation can solve this problem by temporarily moving U4, moving all of R next to P, moving all of T next to R and then moving all of U next to each other, as shown in Figure 2.35.

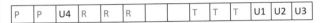

Figure 2.35 - Defragmented files.

A defragmentation utility will reorganise all the files so that each file is contiguous (kept together). It will do this by moving fragmented parts of files and small files to free space on the disc and creating space on whole cylinders or adjacent cylinders. It will then move the defragmented files to a place where the whole file is kept together. This can significantly improve the performance of a computer system, especially if program files have become fragmented and can be defragmented.

TASK

CD 2.02 FragmentationDefragmentation

Open CD 2.02 FragmentationDefragmentation.

In the grid, each colour represents a file, and each cell represents an item.

- The red file is originally stored as items 1 to 7.
- The blue file is then stored as items 1 to 4.
- Additional items 8 to 10 are added to the red file, which are fragmented from the red file items 1 to 7.
- The green file is then stored as items 1 to 3.
- The cyan file is then stored as items 1 to 5.
- Additional items 4 to 5 are added to the blue file, which are fragmented from the blue file items 1 to 3.

- Additional items 4 to 5 are added to the green file, which are fragmented from the green file items 1 to 3.
- The orange file is then stored as items 1 to 7.
- The blue file is then deleted.

Now watch what happens as the purple file is added as items 1 to 2 where the blue file used to be and the green file items 6 to 8 are added in a fragmented manner.

Finally, watch how the file is defragmented by moving files into blank spaces and then reorganising them so each file is kept together.

Formatting

When a disc is prepared for first time use, it needs to be formatted. Formatting is the process of organising the tracks on the disc into sectors. Each sector is where data will be stored. A used disc can also be formatted, in which case all data will be lost and the tracks prepared again as if the disc was being used for the first time.

File copying

Files can be copied using features within an operating system's own interface. However, this can be slow and options are limited. File-copying utilities enable users to have more control over which files are copied and how they are copied. For example, a user may only want to copy word processing documents that are within a series of folders and they may want all the files to be copied to a single folder on the destination storage. It is also possible to synchronise files across multiple storage locations or even multiple computer systems, so that when a change is made to a file in one location, it will then be updated in all other locations.

Deleting

Some files become locked by an operating system and it becomes almost impossible to delete them. Deleting utilities can overcome this problem by deleting locked files and folders. When files are deleted using normal deletion methods, the data is still on the disc although the user can't see it. Therefore another function of deleting utilities is being able to delete files permanently so that they cannot be restored or accessed. Some deletion utilities will remove temporary files that are no longer needed by the computer system, or files that are no longer used but haven't been deleted when a program has been uninstalled or a user profile removed.

QUESTIONS

12 List two utilities.
13 Describe the role of anti-virus software.

2.04 Custom-written versus off-the-shelf software

KEY TERMS

Custom-written: software that is written especially to meet the requirements of a client

Off-the-shelf: general purpose software available to a large market

When a client requires a software solution that will carry out a specific purpose that is unique to their organisation, they will ask for the software to be written for them. This is known as **custom-written** software because it is customised to the needs of the client and will meet the requirements of the client.

When software already exists and is purchased online or from a shop, it is known as **off-the-shelf** software. The software will have been written for a general purpose that is likely to be useful to a large market. Anybody can purchase the software for a specified price.

QUESTIONS

14 Describe off-the-shelf software.
15 Describe two drawbacks of custom-written software.

2.05 Compilers and interpreters

KEY TERMS

Compiler: translates high-level programming language into an executable file in machine code

Interpreter: translates high-level programming language into machine code, one line of source code at a time

Custom-written software	Off-the-shelf software
The entire development cost of custom-written software is met by the client for whom it is written, which makes it very expensive.	The development cost of off-the-shelf software is spread between all the customers who purchase it at a specified price, which means the cost is much lower.
Custom-written software takes a long time to develop, so the client will have to wait before being able to use the software.	Off-the-shelf software is immediately available, so the customer can start using it straight away.
The requirements of the client can be met precisely with no additional features that are not necessary.	Some tasks that the customer needs to carry out may not be possible and there will be lots of features that the customer never uses.
The developers of the software will ensure that the software is compatible with the hardware, software and data used by the client.	The software may not be compatible with existing hardware, software and data used by the customer.
As the software will not have been used before, apart from testing, it is likely that bugs will be found within the software as it gets used by the client.	The software will have been used by thousands of customers and bugs will have been identified and fixed, and patches will be released as more bugs are found so that the software runs as expected.
The client will have access to support from the company that developed the software.	Customers will be able to get support from a wide range of sources including telephone support, discussion forums and online training.

Table 2.06 - Custom-written software versus off-the-shelf software.

Compilers were introduced earlier in this chapter.

Interpreters were introduced earlier in this chapter.

Compiler and interpreter differences

Compiler	Interpreter
Translates source code into object code all at once in advance of execution.	Translates source code into object code one line at a time.
Compiled object code will only work on the operating system it has been compiled for.	Source code can be translated into object code for more than one operating system.
Object code is ready to be executed without delay.	Object code has to be generated, so additional time is added to the execution time.
Compiling can take a long time, which is not appropriate for on-the-fly testing.	Only the required code needs to be interpreted, so this is efficient for on-the-fly testing.

Table 2.07 - Compiler and interpreter differences.

QUESTIONS

16 Describe the function of a compiler.

17 Describe two advantages of an interpreter over a compiler.

2.06 Summary

Hardware devices are the physical components of a computer. Internal hardware includes the CPU, motherboard, RAM, ROM, graphics card, sound card, hard disc drive and solid state drive. External hardware components include a monitor, keyboard, mouse, printer, camera, webcam, scanner, OCR, MICR, OMR, barcode reader, flash memory drive, portable hard disc drive, Blu-ray disc drive and memory card. Input devices allow data to be sent to a computer and output devices allow the communication of data/information from a computer.

Software are programs that run on the hardware. System software includes operating systems, device drivers, utilities, compilers, interpreters and linkers. Application software includes word processing, spreadsheets, database management systems, graphics manipulation, photo editing, video editing, communications, web authoring, control and measuring, apps and applets. Utility software can include anti-virus/anti-malware, backup, data compression, disc defragmentation, formatting, file copying and deleting. Off-the-shelf software is software that already exists and can be purchased online or from a shop and custom-written software is written especially for an organisation to meet their specific requirements.

Different user interfaces include a command line interface, graphical user interface, dialogue interface and gesture-based interface. When designing a user interface, the following should be considered: colour, layout, font size, quantity of information and controls.

Review questions

Geraldine has purchased a new computer. It includes a motherboard, CPU and RAM.

1 a Describe the purpose of a motherboard. [1]

1 b Some of the data needs to be available when the computer is turned off. Identify a suitable device that will fulfil this function. [1]

1 c Explain why Geraldine will need a graphics card. [2]

Geraldine has been advised that she should keep a backup of the data stored on her computer.

2 Give reasons for the use of cloud storage for this purpose. [4]

A local council with over 500 employees and several servers backs up its data using magnetic tape.

3 Explain why magnetic tape is used for this backup. [6]

The council carries out regular surveys of residents.

4 Explain why an optical mark reader (OMR) would be appropriate for inputting the results of the surveys. [4]

The council needs some new software for waste management that will link in with their website where residents can log problems such as missed collections.

5 Evaluate the use of a custom-written software solution for this purpose. [6]

The council uses video editing software to prepare public information videos.

6 a Identify two features of video editing software. [2]

6 b Give two examples of how the council could use those two features. [2]

Chapter 3
Monitoring and control

Learning objectives

By the end of this chapter, you will be able to:

- identify a range of different sensors
- describe how sensors are used in monitoring and control technologies
- evaluate using monitoring and control technologies in everyday life

3.01 Sensors

KEY TERMS

Sensor: a device that records data about the surrounding physical environment

Input device: a device that allows data to be entered into a computer system

Analogue: this is the smooth stream of data that we process on a daily basis

Microprocessor: an integrated circuit used in monitoring and control technologies

Actuator: this is a type of motor that controls a mechanism or system

Infrared: a wave of light emitted by an object that is invisible to the naked human eye

Microwave: an electromagnetic wave of energy

Piezoresistance: a specific level of electrical charge that is linked to a specific level of resistance or pressure

Humidity: the amount of water in the atmosphere

Photoresistor: a light controlled resistor

A **sensor** is an **input device** that records data about the surrounding physical environment. The sensor inputs this data into a computer system to be processed. Once the data has been processed, if necessary, an output can be triggered as a response.

TIP

Sensors can automatically enter data into a computer system, removing the need for a human to manually enter the data. They can be very beneficial as it can increase the accuracy of the data by removing the possibility of human error.

Using sensors can also be very beneficial in environments that could be harmful and dangerous for a human, for example in a nuclear plant to detect radiation levels, or inside an active volcano to detect changes in activity.

Monitoring and control technologies make use of many different sensors. Monitoring technologies use sensors to monitor an environment, often collecting data about the environment.

Remember

Control technologies use sensors to automatically control elements of a system, or a whole system, by using the data from them to trigger an action or event.

The basic concept behind most monitoring and control systems is very similar. They will normally go through the following steps:

- The sensor will constantly monitor the surrounding environment
- The data readings from the sensor will normally be **analogue**. Therefore, they will be converted to a digital signal for a computer system to process. This is done by an analogue to digital converter
- The digital signal is then sent to a **microprocessor**. The microprocessor processes the value and compares it to a pre-set value or range of values
- If the value is outside the acceptable range, the microprocessor will send a signal to an **actuator** to trigger any action that needs to be taken.

A real-life example of a control technology in operation would be an automated street light. This may include the following stages:

- A light sensor will constantly monitor the level of light present in the surrounding environment.
- The analogue data from the reading will be converted to a digital value by an analogue to digital converter.
- The digital signal is sent to a microprocessor and the microprocessor will compare the value to a pre-set range.
- If the value is outside the pre-set range, the microprocessor sends a signal to an actuator that will trigger the action to turn the street light on or off.
- The whole process will then be repeated.

We can represent this as a flowchart:

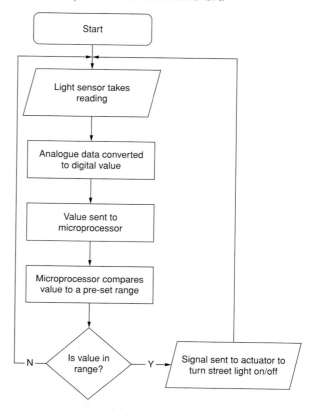

55

This is an example of a control system at work. It is a control system as an action is triggered to control an element of the system as a result of the monitoring that is taking place. A monitoring system outputs results in a different way. Rather than an action being triggered, the results of the readings taken from the monitoring can be output in the form of graphs or charts. This allows the readings to be compared and any patterns or trends to be identified. This information can then be used to inform any future decision making.

Monitoring systems can be used in scientific experiments. The experiments are often left to run for periods of time, with a monitoring system taking readings at regular intervals. The readings are then output and can be analysed. This kind of technology removes then need for a human to regularly take the readings. This means that the readings can be taken over long periods of time and can often be more accurate if taken by a system.

There are a range of different sensors that we need to be able to define. We also need to describe how they are used in monitoring and control technologies and evaluate using these technologies in our everyday lives.

Motion sensors

A motion sensor detects movement. It can do this either passively or actively. A passive motion sensor reads the energy in its surrounding environment and detects changes caused by movement. An active motion sensor emits energy into the surrounding environment to detect any movement. An example of a passive motion sensor is a passive **infrared** sensor. This is a sensor that detects the presence of infrared energy if it appears in its surrounding environment. An example of an active motion sensor is a **microwave** sensor. This is a sensor that emits microwaves and detects the changes in the reflection it receives back when bouncing off nearby objects.

Passive infrared sensors are commonly used in security systems. These sensors are normally wall mounted in the corner of a room. As an intruder walks in front of a sensor, the sensor detects the infrared energy emitted by the intruder. The detection of infrared energy by the sensor can then trigger an alarm to sound.

Active motion sensors can also be used in security systems. A microwave sensor continuously emits microwaves into a room. As an intruder walks through the microwaves, they will be reflected back much more quickly to the sensor and it will detect the change. This change in reflection of the microwaves can then cause an alarm to sound.

Motion sensors are not error proof and can sometimes cause a false alarm to sound.

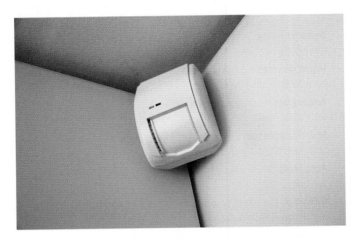

Figure 3.01 - Passive infrared sensor in a security system.

TASK

Find out how passive and active motion sensors can be combined to create a security system that is less prone to error.

Motion sensors can be used in lots of other monitoring and control systems. These include:

- CCTV systems, to manoeuvre the camera to the direction of motion that is detected
- opening and closing automatic doors
- automatically turning lights on or off in a room when a person enters or leaves
- automatically turning water taps on or off
- automated barriers in a car park.

Figure 3.02 - CCTV security cameras.

Figure 3.03 - A car park barrier.

DISCUSSION POINT

By using motion detectors in various ways a business can be made more environmentally friendly. Using motion sensors, a business can make sure that lights are only turned on when a person is working in a room and they can also make sure that no water is left running. Why could this be important to a business?

Pressure sensors

A pressure sensor measures pressure, normally of a liquid or a gas. The measure of pressure is based upon the force it takes to stop a liquid or gas from expanding.

Most modern pressure sensors use a principal called **piezoresistance**. In piezoresistance, a specific level of pressure is linked to a specific level of charge through a substance. If a change in the level of charge is detected, this is interpreted as a change in pressure. Pressure sensors can be used in things such as pipes to measure the flow of liquid or gas through them, to make sure they do not flow too quickly.

Pressure sensors can be used in many different monitoring and control technologies. These include:

- The vehicle industry. They are used to form part of the safety system of a vehicle. Pressure sensors are used to monitor the oil and coolant in the vehicle. They are used to regulate the power given to the engine based on the pressure placed on the accelerator and brake. The airbag safety system also uses pressure sensors. The air bags will be triggered to inflate when a high amount of pressure is applied to certain parts of the vehicle.

- Chemical and nuclear plants. They are used to monitor and control the flow of gases and liquids in industrial plants. This means that substances that are being transported in the plant, or any chemical reactions that are carried out, are done extremely safely. This makes sure that a high level of safety is maintained in the industrial plant at all times.
- Aviation and marine industry. They are used to monitor and control the atmosphere within an aeroplane or submarine. This is to make sure that the correct breathing conditions are maintained.
- Touch screens. A touch screen that uses pressure sensors is built up of multiple layers. When pressure is applied to the top layer of the screen it is pushed into the bottom layer of the screen, creating a connection that generates an electrical signal. This electrical signal informs the device of the location where the pressure has been applied to the screen.

DISCUSSION POINT

Pressure sensors are used extensively in industrial plants. How would safety change within the plant if pressure sensors could not be used and why does this make them important?

TASK

Find out how pressure sensors are used in traffic control systems.

Figure 3.04 - A nuclear plant.

Figure 3.05 - A submarine cockpit.

Moisture and humidity sensors

Humidity sensors monitor and measure the humidity that is in the air. To monitor the humidity they measure both the moisture and temperature in the air. The percentage of moisture present in the air at a certain temperature is expressed as the level of humidity. Humidity sensors normally use capacitive measurement. This type of measurement uses two electrical conductors that have a non-conductive film separating them. Moisture collects on the film and changes the level of voltage between the electrical conductors. The measurement of the change in voltage is converted into a measurement of humidity.

Humidity sensors can be used both in the home and the workplace to monitor and control humidity levels, including:

- Wine cellars. The humidity level in the atmosphere of a wine cellar is very important. Too much or too little humidity can cause the wine to spoil. The humidity level needs to be kept at a constant and correct level in order to keep the wine at its best.
- Meteorological stations. They are used to help monitor and predict weather conditions by measuring humidity levels.
- Controlling allergies. An atmosphere that is high in humidity can encourage the growth of bacteria and mould. This can trigger allergies. Humidity sensors can be used to monitor and control the level of humidity in a room.
- Manufacturing. In the manufacturing of many products the level of moisture in the atmosphere is very important. If humidity is too high or too low it could adversely affect the product.

- Agriculture and farming. Humidity and moisture sensors can be used to grow and farm crops in the best conditions possible. By monitoring and controlling the conditions in which the crops are grown, the most perfect conditions can be created, producing the best crops. The level of moisture in the soil can be kept constant to help the crops grow.

Temperature sensors

Temperature sensors monitor and measure the temperature of an environment. They do this by measuring how much heat is present. Temperature sensors are used in a great number of control systems, many of them in our home appliances. These include:

- Washing machine and dishwasher. A temperature sensor is used in a washing machine and a dishwasher to measure the temperature of the water. A microprocessor in the washing machine or dishwasher will receive the data sent by the temperature sensor and can trigger an action to heat up or cool down the water if necessary.
- Dryer. A temperature sensor is used in a dryer to measure the temperature of the hot air flowing into the dryer. A microprocessor in the dryer will receive the data sent by the temperature sensor and can trigger an action to heat up or cool down the air if necessary.
- Refrigerator and freezer. A temperature sensor is used in a refrigerator or freezer to measure the ambient temperature inside. A microprocessor in the refrigerator or freezer will receive the data sent by the temperature sensor and can trigger an action to heat up or cool down the air if necessary.

TASK

Can you think of any other appliances in your home that may use a temperature sensor as part of a monitoring and control system?

Light sensors

Light sensors monitor and measure light. There are different types of light sensor and they measure light in different ways. The most common type of light sensor is a **photoresistor**. This type of light sensor will change its resistance when light shines on and is normally used to measure the intensity of light. This is important in

58

devices such as digital cameras or street lights. The camera can adjust the level of flash needed depending on the level of light currently detected by the light sensor. A street light can detect when it gets dark enough to need to switch the light on.

Figure 3.06 - A digital camera.

Light sensors can be used in many different devices including barcode scanners, display screens, automated lighting systems and smartphones.

TASK

Research at least two other types of sensor and explain how they can be used in a monitoring and control system.

Sensors are used in a wide variety of monitoring and control systems. These systems are part of our everyday lives, from helping us cross the road safely, to making sure our clothes are washed properly. The use of sensors in computer systems can benefit us greatly. This remove the need for a human to monitor and measure an environment as this can be done continuously by the sensor. This can leave us to get on with other tasks that we need to complete. It can also mean that the monitoring and measuring is more accurate.

For a human to complete a repeated action, for example taking a reading over and over for long periods of time, can be very arduous and it may prove difficult to maintain accuracy. A computer system that has a sensor that can perform this role is able to run for long periods of time, with a high level of accuracy. This level of accuracy

can make a system more reliable than one operated by humans.

By using a sensor or a number of sensors in a monitoring or control system, multiple readings can be taken in quick succession. It would require people to perform the same function, and so these people can be made available to perform other tasks. The computer system will make decisions based on the data it is given. It will act logically on these decisions in the way it has been programmed. This can be beneficial as the decisions made and actions taken will be consistent. If a human performed the same decision-making process, external factors may affect the decision they make, for example how tired they are. This could cause inconsistency in the decision-making process and actions taken. This can sometimes be a disadvantage and a computer system may not be able to react to an unexpected event that a human would be able to assess and make a decision about.

Remember

A computer system using sensors can operate 24 hours a day, 365 days a year, meaning that monitoring can be done on a continual basis. It can also remove the possibility of human error in the measurements.

Sensors are also extremely beneficial for use in environments that are dangerous to humans. This means that we can be kept safe yet dangerous environments can still be monitored. Also, computers can process data much more quickly and respond faster to any necessary actions than a human, so a dangerous environment can be monitored and controlled more effectively.

There is always a risk involved in using computer systems in monitoring and control. The system is electronic and if a power failure occurs, the system will not operate. If the system is controlling a crucial process, this could have a detrimental effect. This could also happen with a simple system malfunction.

3.02 Summary

A sensor is an input device that records data about the surrounding physical environment. Sensors are used in monitoring and control technologies. They monitor the surrounding environment and trigger any events that need to occur to control a process.

A monitoring system uses sensors to take readings and mostly outputs them in graphs and charts, or a simple print out. A control system uses sensors to take readings and an action can be triggered if a reading is, for example, outside an acceptable range.

There are a wide range of sensors used in monitoring and control systems. These include motion sensors, pressure sensors, moisture and humidity sensors, temperature sensors and light sensors. There are a number of other sensors that you may have researched including sound sensors and gas sensors.

The use of monitoring and control systems can be very beneficial. They can keep us safe from the need to monitor dangerous environments and they can carry out monitoring on a more continuous basis, as well as having a higher degree of accuracy.

Review questions

1. Define the term sensor. [2]
2. Describe two types of sensor that can be used in a security system. [4]
3. Explain two benefits of using sensors to monitor the environment in a nuclear plant. [4]
4. Evaluate the use of monitoring and control systems in household appliances. [6]
5. Explain how a monitoring and control system could be used to create an environmentally friendly office building. [4]

Chapter 4
E-safety and health and safety

Learning objectives

By the end of this chapter you will be able to:

- explain why e-safety is necessary and why data should be kept confidential
- describe how personal data can be gathered by unauthorised persons and how we can protect against this
- describe a number of malware issues
- describe potential health and safety issues relating to using computers

4.01 Introduction

The use of IT is increasing all the time, making awareness of e-safety and health and safety vitally important. E-safety is concerned with protecting personal data to avoid online exploitation either by bullying or identity theft. It is also associated with protecting software against malware issues. Health and safety is concerned with protecting both the person using the IT from physical harm, and protecting the computer itself.

4.02 E-safety

KEY TERMS

Confidential: needs to be kept secret

Legitimate: genuine and a real document

Malicious code: code that is intended to harm a computer

Remember

Personal data is extremely valuable and a lot of harm can be done to someone if their personal data is used against them. It is therefore vital that it is kept **confidential**.

A person should be very careful about revealing their personal data, such as their bank details, medical records, their salary, and sometimes sensitive data, such as their political opinions. Revealing personal data could lead to criminal activity, such as identity theft. It can also lead to more personal matters and could be used for something as severe as blackmail or bullying. By revealing personal data you are providing a person with the potential ability to harm you in some way. Therefore it is best done only when safeguards are in place to make sure that your personal data is secure and protected.

We are taught from a young age how to keep ourselves safe in our daily lives. However, when we are online, we often do not worry about our safety as much. We feel that the internet provides us with a lot of freedom, but it also creates many risks. We often do not recognise these risks as we somehow seem to feel safer online than in the world outside. Many people that use the internet are genuine, but it is quite simple to hide your identity online and some people exploit this. Therefore, in the same way we learn about how to keep ourselves safe when we leave the house, we should learn to keep ourselves safe online.

There are a number of simple measures we can take to improve our e-safety:

- only use websites that are recommended by a trusted source, for example, a teacher or a parent
- use a search engine that has a filter to remove inappropriate content
- do not open any email attachments from a sender you do not recognise
- be very cautious when providing personal data
- be cautious about any pictures or opinions that you post or send to people
- do not become friends on social networking sites with people you do not know
- never arrange face-to-face meetings with a person that you meet online
- make sure you set all the privacy controls that are available on social media accounts
- report and block any unwanted user
- use a nickname or pseudonym when using the internet for entertainment, for example, playing games.

Revealing personal data online can lead to cyberbullying. This is most prominent amongst young people. Cyberbullying is using the internet and mobile devices for bullying. Social networking and messaging facilities are most commonly used in cyberbullying. A person may reveal information about their interests or their opinions and another person may choose to bully them based on that information. Therefore, we should be very careful about the data we post and make sure that we do not allow people to see data that we wouldn't want them to know.

One big issue with cyberbullying is that any malicious things that are posted can be seen by many people and in certain cases may go viral. This is another reason why it is better to keep your personal information and close feelings to yourself. There is less potential for people to exploit these if they are not posted for them to use. If people do post false or malicious rumours about you online, you should report this behaviour to the authorities e.g. the police. This kind of behaviour is often classed as harassment and is normally a criminal offence.

There are ways that you can keep yourself safer online when using social networking sites, for example:

- If another person posts anything abusive about you online, you can report this behaviour and they could face criminal prosecution. Similarly, if you post anything online that is abusive about another person you could face criminal proceedings. Even if the abuse is from an anonymous source, it is easy to trace from where the messages or images have been sent.

- Make sure that the passwords you have set on your social networking accounts are strong. This means they should be unusual and contain a mixture of numbers, punctuation and letters (both lower case and capitals) if possible. If someone else posts something abusive using your account, it is difficult to prove that it was not you who did it. For this reason, make sure you sign out of your account when you are not using it. This will prevent a person picking up your phone or using your personal computer (PC) and gaining access to your account.

- Think twice before you post anything online. Once you have posted it you cannot take it back again. Even if you delete it, the social networking site will still have

record of it and will still own the data or image you have posted.

Revealing personal data can lead to identity theft or fraud. A person stealing your identity is able to steal your money, borrow money in your name, and even commit crimes using your identity. This may result in you being left without any money or savings but, even worse, may result in false imprisonment for crimes you did not commit. It is therefore extremely important to keep any personal data safe to avoid such consequences.

As our personal data is very valuable, some individuals will go to great measures to try and obtain it. There are four main methods that unauthorised persons will exploit to collect your personal data. These are phishing, pharming, smishing and vishing.

PayPal

Problem with your account, rectify now to prevent deactivation!

Dear PayPal User,

Your PayPal account has generated some critical errors on our system. If this problem is not corrected, we will be forced to shut down your account. You are required to correct this problem immediately to prevent your account from being deactivated.

During our verification procedures we encountered a technical problem caused by the fact that we could not verify the information that you provided during registration. Most of your data in our database were encrypted to an unreadable format and could not be recovered due to system errors. Because of this, your account will not be able to function properly and will lead to account de-activation. We urgently ask you to re-submit your information so that we could fully verify your identify, otherwise your PayPal account will be shut down until you pass verification process.

> **Click here to rectify your account problem immediately**

Verification of your Identity will further protect your account against possible breach of security. We urgently ask you to follow the link above to correct this problem as soon as you have read this message. Your PayPal account security is our concern. We are very sorry for the inconveniences this might have caused you.

Thank you for using PayPal!
The PayPal Team

Figure 4.01 - An example of a phishing email claiming to be from PayPal.

Phishing

Remember
Phishing is when an unauthorised person attempts to gather personal data, such as passwords and credit card details, by disguising themselves as a trustworthy person or organisation.

Phishing is normally carried out via electronic communication, such as email. The email will look **legitimate** and will normally encourage a person to click on a link in the email. When the link is clicked it will take the user to a website that will ask them for their personal details. This will be a fake website and the personal details will then be stolen and used in criminal activity.

Phishing emails will usually contain text that will express the need for urgent attention to a matter, for example asking a user to cancel a subscription to a service or they will be charged, or to verify their identity to clear up a possible security attack on their account. Phishing can also be an email simply asking for banking details.

Phishing gets its name from the reference to fishing for a person's data using bait (the legitimate looking email). 'Ph' replaced the 'f' in reference to a name given to early hackers known as breaks. Phishing has been around since 1995, but it didn't become an issue until about ten years later.

There are measures that can be taken to protect against phishing:
- Users should make sure that they are cautious when clicking any links in an email.
- Users should question whether they know the sender of the email and only open links from known senders.
- Users should check the URL that they are being linked to, to see if it is legitimate. This can be done by hovering over the link and looking to see if the address is the real address of the site, for example www.paypal.com would be legitimate but www.paipal.com would be identified as fake because of the spelling mistake.
- Another thing that should raise suspicion is any spelling or grammatical errors in the email content.

Pharming

Remember
Pharming is another method of collecting personal data. A hacker will install **malicious code** onto a person's computer or server. When a user types in a web address they will be redirected to a fraudulent, but legitimate looking, replica website, without their consent.

The user will continue using the website as they normally would, unaware of the redirection, and enter their personal details that will then be stolen.

A particularly big case of pharming occurred in 2004, when a German teenager hijacked eBay's domain and redirected thousands of eBay users to a fraudulent site.

There are measures that can be taken to protect against pharming:
- Users should check if the website looks the same as when they last visited it.
- Users should look for the padlock security symbol used to signify the HTTPS, showing that the website is secure, before entering any personal and financial details.
- Users should run regular scans of their computer with anti-virus software that is designed to detect pharming programs.

Smishing

Remember
Smishing is short for SMS phishing. It is similar to phishing, but it is carried out using SMS text messaging rather than email.

An SMS text message is sent to a user that will ask them to telephone a number or click on a link. When that number is telephoned, the person receiving the call will attempt to get personal details from the caller. The caller could also be charged a great deal of money for the call. When a link is clicked malware is downloaded onto the user's phone. The malware can be used to collect the user's data to commit identity fraud and theft. It can also make the device part of a bot network. At a later stage the device could then be used to launch a denial of service attack. The link could also take the user to a legitimate looking website, as it does in phishing, and cause the user to give away their personal details.

Smishing will often entice a user into telephoning a number or clicking the link by advising them of a profitable gain they will receive if they do so, for example a voucher or a gift card that will give them money off a product or service.

Remember
The use of smishing is rising. This may be because people seem less suspicious about a message they receive on their phone, rather than their computer.

Most major web browsers have built in phishing protection that can help to alert a user to a possible phishing issue. Mobile phones are not equipped in the same way.

There are measures that can be taken to protect against smishing:

- Users should be very cautious in telephoning any numbers they are sent in an SMS message.
- Users should be very cautious when clicking on any links in messages.
- Users should not install any applications from senders they do not know.
- If a user receives a suspicious message from someone they do know, they should check with the person that they have actually sent that message.
- Users should be wary of numbers that do not look like usual mobile numbers, such as '5000'.
- Users can add security software to their mobile to help detect any malware.

Dear Walmart shopper,
Congratulations you have
just won a $1000 Walmart
Gift Card. Click here to
claim your gift.
www.WmartClick.com
(cancel: reply STOP)

Figure 4.02 - An example of a smishing message claiming to be from Walmart.

Vishing

Remember
Vishing is short for voice phishing. It is the act of using a telephone call to try and scam a user into giving their personal data. The scammer will usually pretend that they are a legitimate business calling the person.

The person who is vishing will either say they are alerting the victim to an issue with their account, or advising the victim of a profitable gain. They will often ask the victim subtle questions to get the personal data they want.

One tactic vishers will sometimes resort to, is that when the victim become a little suspicious and wants to call their bank to check if the call is legitimate, the scammer will not hang up when the victim tries to call their bank. The victim

will then pick up the telephone to call their bank, but the line is actually still being held by the scammer. The victim thinks they have called their bank, but it is still the scammer, and the victim gives them their personal details, thinking they are giving them to their bank.

Unfortunately, it is often the elderly and the vulnerable that are targeted for vishing.

There are measures that can be taken to protect against vishing:

- People should exercise caution when any institution contacts them, especially when they ask for personal details. If in doubt hang up and call them back on a number that is known.
- People should never give out any personal details regarding a security issue with their account. A bank will prevent any kind of attack on an account without needing assistance from the account holder.

DISCUSSION POINT
Many banks will not take responsibility, and are not held responsible by the authorities, for vishing scams. This is because the victim gives their personal data for the account to be accessed, so the money is not directly stolen. Do you think it is right that the banks are not responsible for refunding the money?

Remember
Malware is a computer program that is designed to damage or disrupt a computer system and the files that are stored on it.

Malware can take many forms and we are going to look at a number of them.

Trojan horse

A Trojan horse is a malicious computer program that disguises itself as another application, such as a game or a utility program. When the application is run, the Trojan horse will act as a computer virus would, deleting and corrupting files in the computer system.

The term Trojan horse comes from Greek mythology. A wooden horse was given as a peace offering to the people of the city of Troy. The Trojan horse was in fact a container that held a number of Greek soldiers who, when night fell, climbed out of the Trojan horse, opened the city to the rest of the soldiers who were able to conquer the city of Troy.

A malware Trojan horse works in a similar way. It looks harmless, like an application that would be desirable, but it hides a malicious program.

Worms

A computer worm is a small computer program that uses computer networks and finds security holes to replicate itself. They can exploit a security hole in a piece of software or operating system. While replicating they will often clog up network bandwidth and can make things run slowly.

There have been a number of famous computer worms One of these was called Code Red. Code Red occurred in 2001 and managed to replicate itself over 250 000 times in several hours. It scanned the internet for Windows servers, exploiting a security hole in ones that did not have a Microsoft security patch installed. Each time it found a vulnerable server, it replicated itself onto the server and then set off to find the next one. All the servers that were affected then launched an attack on the domain for the White House, www.whitehouse.gov.

Spyware

Spyware covers quite a broad range of malware. The term refers to any technology that is used to gather data about a person without their knowledge. It is most commonly used to track the movements of people online. A common type of spyware is a key logger. This is a piece of software that records the key presses from a keyboard and will allow the person who installed it to gather personal data about the victim.

Adware

Adware is short for advertising-supported software. In its most basic form, it is simply a software program that is used to display adverts that are targeted at the user. It can analyse the websites the user visits and will target them with advertising of a similar nature. Many program developers will justify the inclusion of adware in their product by claiming that it will generate revenue for them, keeping the cost of the product lower.

Adware as malware will present adverts when a user is browsing the web that are often shown constantly. They are normally in the form of popups or windows that cannot be closed. They will mostly just be irritating.

In certain circumstances, adware can be bundled in with legitimate software downloads. This means that you may end up with the software on your computer without actually asking to download it. This can happen when the software is being downloaded, as you may be given the chance to customise what is downloaded. For example, there may be a hidden option to download a task or search bar that is added into your current internet browser. You can customise the download and uncheck the box so that you do not get the adware, but if you do not know to do this you may download it unknowingly. Once downloaded, the adware can prove difficult to delete. It may not act maliciously, but will often serve as a method of advertising for the company, or try to get you to use their search function.

Rootkit

A rootkit is a computer program that enables a person to gain administrator access to a victim's computer. It normally gets installed because a victim's password is cracked. The person installing it can then use the access to stop the computer recognising that the rootkit is there, so the victim will not know that someone else has complete access to their computer system. Other malware can then be concealed on the computer to cause harm.

Malicious bots

A bot is an application that is automated and used to carry out simple and repetitive tasks. These are normally tasks that a human would find mundane and time-consuming. Bots can be used for very productive reasons, but they can also be used as a form of malware.

Malicious bots are used by cybercriminals in a variety of ways:

- SPAM bots are used to bombard people's email inbox with SPAM emails.
- Zombie bots are used to create a bot network. The bot will lay dormant on a computer until an attack is launched. The computer will then be connected with lots of other computers that have been compromised by zombie bots to launch a large-scale attack on an organisation.
- Chatter bots will pretend to be humans on sites such as social networking and dating sites.

Ransomware

Ransomware is a type of malware that restricts a user's access to their computer system and files. The ransomware will normally demand that the user pays

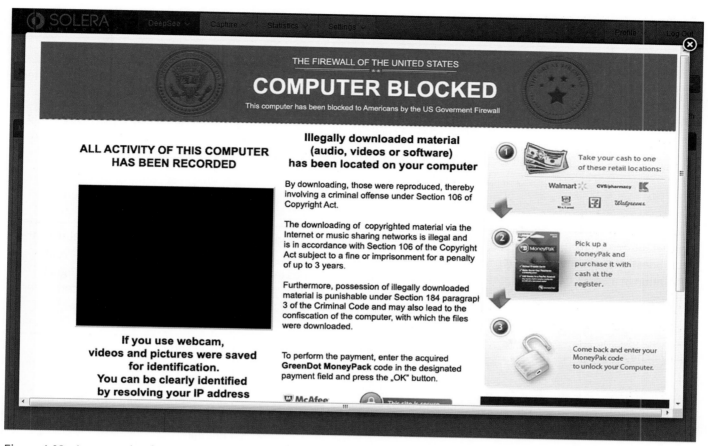

Figure 4.03 - An example of a ransomware message claiming to be from the US Government.

a ransom in order to regain access to their computer system. Some ransomware programs will completely lock a user's system and some will encrypt all of the files on their system in a way that renders them useless. Ransomware will normally try to enter a system in a similar way to a Trojan horse.

The message or ransom with which the user is presented will often imitate a law enforcement agency. It will falsely claim that the system has been used for illegal activity and that a ransom must be paid to regain access to the system.

How can malware be avoided?

Remember

Malware can be very difficult to remove from a computer system. It can often take numerous scans from anti-virus software, as well as the use of various malware removal programs, depending on the type of malware infecting the system.

There are a number of measures that can be taken to avoid malware:

- A user should never open a program unless they know it is legitimate.
- A user should have a firewall in place that is monitoring their internet traffic.
- A user should regularly run an anti-virus check and malware detection software on their computer system, to detect the presence of any malware. Any anti-virus or malware detection program should be kept up to date in order to detect newly developed malware.
- A user should not open any attachments to emails from unknown users.
- A user should use open Wi-Fi points with extreme caution as anybody could be connected to them.

4.03 Health and safety

As well as the e-safety issues that can occur when using a computer system, there are also health and safety issues to be aware of. A computer user should understand what the risks are, how they are caused and what they can do to prevent them occurring.

What potential health issues could arise?

Health issue	Cause	Prevention
Repetitive strain injury is pain, numbness or weakness that occurs in the hands, arms, shoulders and neck.	It is caused by repetitive movements and actions. For example, continuous and repeated clicking of a mouse or pressing of keys on a keyboard. This can often be triggered by poor posture.	A good posture should be maintained when using the computer. A user should also try to avoid doing the same action repeatedly without taking regular breaks. A wrist rest can also be used to support a user's wrists when working.
Carpal tunnel syndrome is pain, numbness or sometimes a tingling sensation in a user's hands and fingers.	It is caused by the compression of a major nerve in the hand that passes over the carpal bones in the hand. This happens because of repetitive and continual movements.	Prevention is similar to repetitive strain injury, where a user should avoid repeated actions and take regular breaks when working on a computer.
Back ache and muscle spasms.	These are caused by poor posture when working on a computer, and from sitting in the same position for long periods of time.	A user should sit on an adjustable chair to make sure that they are sitting at the correct height for their desk and computer system. A chair that has added back support will also be helpful.
Eye strain that causes sore, tired eyes and sometimes blurred vision.	This is caused by looking at a monitor for long periods of time.	Monitors can be purchased that have settings that help avoid eye strain. A user should also make sure they regularly look away from the screen and focus on a point far away from where they are. A user should also make sure they are sitting at the correct distance from their monitor when using it.
Deep vein thrombosis is when blood clots occur, normally in a user's legs.	This is normally caused by sitting in a chair that puts pressure on the back of a user's legs, mostly behind their knees.	A user should regularly stand and move around when using a computer for long periods of time.
Fatigue is when a user feels very tired and lethargic. Fatigue can often occur alongside stress.	This can be caused by overworking for continuous periods on work requires a lot of mental application.	Working for shorter periods of time and taking regular breaks when working can reduce levels of stress and fatigue.

Table 4.01 - Potential health risks associated with using IT.

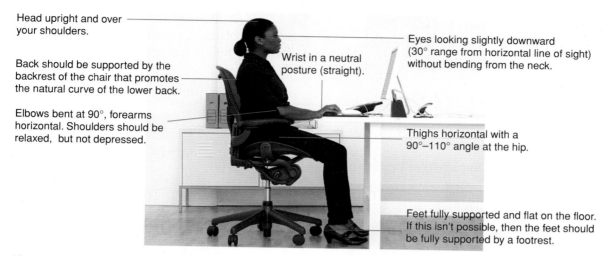

Head upright and over your shoulders.

Eyes looking slightly downward (30° range from horizontal line of sight) without bending from the neck.

Wrist in a neutral posture (straight).

Back should be supported by the backrest of the chair that promotes the natural curve of the lower back.

Elbows bent at 90°, forearms horizontal. Shoulders should be relaxed, but not depressed.

Thighs horizontal with a 90°–110° angle at the hip.

Feet fully supported and flat on the floor. If this isn't possible, then the feet should be fully supported by a footrest.

Figure 4.04 - An example of correct posture at a computer.

What potential safety issues could arise?

Safety issue	Prevention
Fire can occur when computers overheat. This could also happen because of an overloaded plug socket.	A computer should be used in a room that is fairly cool and well ventilated. If a number of computers are in a room it is advisable that the room has air conditioning to keep it cool. In case of a fire occuring, a CO_2 fire extinguisher should be in any room that has a computer. Plug sockets should not have too many devices plugged into them, especially devices that require a lot of power.
There can be trailing wires, especially when plug sockets are not near to computer systems. A person could trip over these wires.	Make sure wires are secured in some way, such as by a cable management system that will clip all cables together and make them less of a risk.
Spilt drinks can cause a computer to short and when food is trapped in a keyboard it can cause difficulties in using the computer, or even start a fire.	Eating and drinking at a computer should be avoided where possible.

Electric shock can occur if a user touches wires. It can also occur if wires are worn or haven't been checked.	Caution should be taken when handling any electrical wires. All wires should repaired if they look worn and should have regular electrical checks.
Electric shock can also occur if liquids are spilt on an electrical device, especially a loose connection.	Liquids should be kept away from electrical devices.

Table 4.02 - Potential safety risks associated with using IT.

4.04 Summary

Personal data is very valuable and precious and for that reason should be kept confidential and safe. It is important that a person knows how to keep themselves safe when online so that they are not exploited or have their personal data stolen.

There are a number of ways that personal data can be collected, including phishing, pharming, smishing and vishing. There are also a number of malware issues a person can encounter when online, including Trojan horses, worms, spyware, adware, rootkit, malicious bots and ransomware.

A user should be very cautious when providing any personal data online. They should only do this when they are certain that the receiver is completely legitimate. A user should make

69

sure they are cautious about any attachments or applications they open, and any links they click. They should not open any of these if they are not from a known user.

As well as e-safety issues when using a computer, there are also a number of health and safety issues. A user should understand how to prevent these from occurring.

Review questions

1   Explain the difference between phishing and pharming. [6]

2   Describe the term ransomware. [2]

3   Describe the term malicious bot. [3]

4   Discuss the need to keep personal data confidential. [6]

5   Describe two health issues relating to using a computer and suggest how each can be prevented. [4]

6   Describe two safety issues relating to using a computer and suggest how each can be prevented. [4]

Chapter 5
The digital divide

Learning objectives

By the end of this chapter you will understand:

- what is meant by the digital divide
- what causes the digital divide, including diff erences in technology and areas of society
- what can be done to reduce the digital divide

5.01 What is the digital divide?

KEY TERMS

Demographic: a particular section of a population

Economic: relating to a country in terms of their production and consumption of goods and services

Broadband: a method of faster data transmission that can carry several channels of data at once

Infrastructure: the physical structures that are needed for a service or operation

Ecommerce: business that is conducted electronically

Bandwidth: the amount of data that can be transmitted at one time

The term digital divide was first popularised in the 1990s. It describes the technology divide (or gap) between countries, **demographic** groups and **economic** areas. It is a technical, social and economic issue, which covers the difference in availability and use of modern technology. The divide that people experience can depend on many aspects, such as age, status and location.

Remember

Many people believe that the digital divide refers merely to internet access, but it can refer to access to several forms of modern technology, including telephones, television, personal computers (PCs) and the internet.

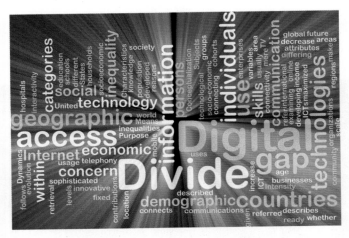

Figure 5.01 - Terms connected to the digital divide.

All countries experience a digital divide at one level or another. At a national level, the digital divide describes the difference between those in the population who have regular access to modern technology, and those who have the necessary skills to make good use of the technology. At an international level, the digital divide describes the difference between developed and developing countries.

5.02 What can cause a digital divide?

There are many factors that can create a digital divide and they can do this for a great number of reasons.

City versus rural areas

A person's geographical location can have an effect on their access to technology services. One location aspect that can affect this is whether they live in a city or a rural area.

Access to high-speed internet services can differ greatly between city and rural areas. The availability of **broadband** services is expanding in most countries, but not at the same rate for those who live in rural areas, compared to those who live in cities.

People who live in cities have much greater access to high-speed broadband. This mainly occurs for two reasons:

- The **infrastructure** needed is mostly in place and just needs to be improved or expanded in order to provide high-speed broadband services. Therefore, the cost implications are not as great, as the current infrastructure can be used.
- The concentration of people, and therefore potential customers, in a city is far greater. Therefore, there is a greater chance of quickly recuperating the costs of building the infrastructure needed for the high-speed access.

People who live in rural areas have less access to high-speed broadband. This is mainly because the infrastructure is not in place to provide the high-speed access, therefore the cost of building the required infrastructure would be very expensive. As the concentration of people living in a rural area is much less than in a city, the amount of potential customers is far fewer. This means that it would take a lot longer, if ever, to recuperate the costs of building the infrastructure. For this reason, many broadband companies do not look to provide high-speed access to people in the countryside.

This means that the experience of using the internet, in terms of speed, differs greatly between a user in a city and a user in a rural area. Because of this people living in rural areas may find that they are not able to use internet services such as film and television streaming because they cannot get an internet connection that will support it. Even if they are able to get a connection that will support streaming, they may be limited to standard, rather than high definition, quality, as this would be the only capability of the connection.

Another service that can be affected depending on a person's location is access to mobile telephone internet services. Their location will determine whether their connection is 3G or 4G, or if they can get any connection at all.

2G technology allowed people to make telephone calls and send text messages, but accessing the internet was very slow and cumbersome. The invention of the 3G network made it possible for users to access the internet with their mobile telephone at a reasonable speed. The development of 4G has made internet access using mobile devices much quicker. The 'G' refers to the generation of network presently available. The availability of 4G and also 3G will depend on whether a person lives in a city or a rural location.

Remember

The availability and speed of the different networks again depends on infrastructure. A frequency band is used to provide network coverage. The strength and speed of coverage will often depend on how close together the network masts are, with those closer together providing better coverage at a greater speed.

In a city, network masts will tend to be close together, but in smaller towns and villages they may be much further apart. Many rural areas do not have access to the 4G network, and sometimes have little access to the 3G network. This greatly limits the internet services that can be used with a mobile telephone.

More versus less industrially developed areas

The parts of the world that have greater access to modern technology are the USA, Europe and northern Asia. These areas mostly consist of developed countries. Areas where access is more restricted are in some parts of Africa, India and south Asia. These are areas that consist of countries that are less industrially developed. This is possibly because the less developed countries are having to use their financial resources to provide more important services and do not have the funds available to concentrate on the development of their technology services. The start-up costs for these countries to build the infrastructure would be very great. This could put them at both a competitive and economic disadvantage. They may not have the ability to trade using modern technologies and therefore cannot access the same customer and supplier base as businesses in developed countries. It may also affect the level of education that can be provided as there may be a wealth of information unavailable to them that is accessed using the internet. This can have an impact on both the education and the skill level of people in those countries and prevent them from competing on an international level.

Socio-economic groups

The rich/poor digital divide can also occur in more developed countries. Richer people are able to afford access to high-speed internet connections and expensive advances in technology. The poorer members of society may not be able to afford access to these services and levels of technology. This can have an impact on their level of education and **ecommerce**, essentially creating a greater divide. A great number of companies are moving their business to the internet and new businesses are being developed that operate using only the internet. There is a wealth of information available to users of the internet and a vast social network exists. The inability to access the internet creates a significant divide between rich and poor people and between countries across the world.

TIP

A great number of companies are moving their business to the internet and new businesses are developing that operate using only the internet.

High versus low performing technologies

A digital divide can also occur between people who have higher and lower performing technologies. Those who are able to afford mobile devices with high performance capabilities may be able to enjoy a better experience than those who have lower performing technologies.

73

They may be able to watch movies and stream music without interference and at a much higher quality than those with technologies that do not have the processing power to handle the high level of **bandwidth** needed for this.

TIP
An increased level of experience when using technology may lead to a better lifestyle for those who can afford high performance technologies.

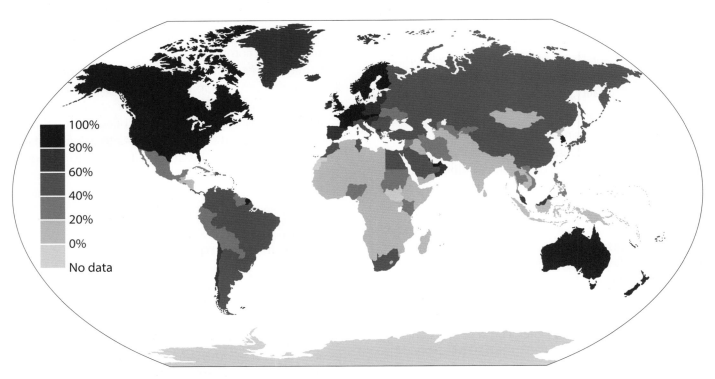

Figure 5.02 - Internet users in 2012 as a percentage of the country's population.

DISCUSSION POINT
Find out about the digital divide that occurs in your country. What could be done to decrease this level of divide?

EXAMPLE

The digital divide in the United Kingdom (UK)
The UK enjoys modern digital communication networks. As of 2014, commercial mobile networks claimed to provide telephone and 3G internet access to 99% of the population, and 4G services to 41%. Additionally, a report by the UK's telecommunications regulator, Ofcom, revealed that 78% of the country's population had access to broadband with speeds of at least 30 Mbps, with 82% of households having a wired internet connection.

The use of modern technology in the UK is widespread and wide-ranging. Devices such as PCs, laptops, tablets and smartphones are used throughout industry, education, government, military, police and fire services. Ecommerce is common, with 1 in 4 people shopping online at least once per week. In 2014 the value of goods purchased online exceeded $100 billion.

Schools, colleges and universities enjoy modern technology, with broadband internet connections, wireless coverage, laptops and tablet devices. The country's National Health Service makes extensive use of these facilities to provide fast and accurate health assessments and diagnoses. Additionally, many hospitals and clinics provide information on websites about their quality of care and allow out-patients to book appointments online.

However, the digital divide exists in the UK and in several ways. For example:

- In 2015 the country's Office for National Statistics (ONS) reported that 11% (5.9 million) of the country's adult population had never used the internet. Many of these adults were aged 75 and over. In the same year the Royal Geographical Society reported that 39% of people without internet access were aged 65 or over.

- The ONS found that only 68% of adults with physical impairments were recent internet users, compared with 92% of those who were not disabled. Sometimes this was due to a lack of, suitable facilities being available, such as a braille keyboard for a visually impaired user.

- The UK suffers a divide caused by the cost of services. Although mobile network coverage is extensive, many mobile phone payment packages are broken down into call usage and data usage. Less wealthy people often cannot afford large data costs, and so their internet access is restricted. Similarly, broadband access is priced according to speed and usage. People with limited financial resources can only afford slower broadband speeds and restricted data use, which also limits access to the internet. The Royal Geographical Society found that 49% of the population with little or no internet access belong to the lowest UK socio-economic groups.

- In 2013 a report by the British Computing Society found that less than 16% of people working as IT specialists were women. However, ICT usage between men and women was found to be roughly equal in some areas, such as online shopping and banking.

- The UK government has committed to bringing fast broadband access to 95% of the country by 2017. However, many users in rural areas will still not have broadband access by then.

- 70% of people living in provided accommodation have no internet access, and 38% of people not online are also unemployed.

The digital divide causes many problems for the UK, both as a country and for its population:

- Many organisations are moving their facilities online. For example, banks have closed branches, preferring to offer online and telephone banking instead. Those in the population who do not have access to suitable technology will find themselves increasingly isolated from these necessary day-to-day services.

- Many goods and services are cheaper online. It has been estimated that those households that cannot afford internet access also pay $560 a year more for everyday items than those who shop online.

- For people with no, or limited, access to technology, it is often harder to find employment in the modern world.

- Access to modern technology can help with a person's education. Those people without access may feel they miss out on opportunities to learn or practise skills.

EXAMPLE

The digital divide in South Africa
South Africa is a good example of a country that is trying to decrease the digital divide. In 1995, a mere 0.7% 100 000 half space of the country's population had internet access and modern technologies. South Africa is a very complex society, with some areas and socio-economic groups far worse off than others. In recent years the country has experienced great internal turmoil and social change, but is now growing in stability.

Between 2000 and 2003, the government funded a drive to place computers in schools. However, despite large uptake, still only around 40% of schools have computers, with less than one-third of schools using computers for teaching and learning.

In 2010 it was estimated that 24% of the population had internet access. By 2014, that percentage rose to just under 49%, around 25 million people, as South Africans have embraced the benefits of being online. The digital divide has fallen dramatically, but mainly because of growth in some areas of the country. The challenge for South Africa is to extend this usage into those areas that have lagged behind in development.

EXAMPLE

The digital divide in Singapore

Singapore is a developed country that has some of the fastest broadband connections in the world, with more than half a million homes receiving connections with a minimum of 100 Mbps. Over 86% of households have a computer, and ICT and Computer Science is considered an important part of education.

Singapore still does experience a digital divide. The country benefits from having a government that recognises the difficulties the digital divide brings and is working on initiatives to help reduce the divide. Subsidy programmes have allowed students to purchase computers for their homes at a far cheaper price than normal. The subsidies also extend to broadband connection. However, subsidised connections are limited to 1 Mbps, far slower than that enjoyed by many other households, creating a divide.

Another factor, like many other developed countries, is that Singapore has an aging population. As a result, government initiatives have seen plans put in place to provide medical care at home through the use of technology. Retirement villages are being built incorporating technology. Sensors can monitor a patient's health and doctors can take advantage of the high-speed broadband to make video conference calls to check in and look over the elderly, who find travel to a clinic difficult.

Additionally, initiatives have seen many public buildings, such as libraries and community centres, offering free internet access to the elderly in the hope of encouraging them to get online. The country sees the internet as integral to economic and social success and is striving to reduce the gap for all its population.

wealth rather than those who do not. For example, in 2013, 3.7 million smart watches were sold. By 2014, sales had risen to 6.8 million. Virtually all these sales were in developed countries. In 2015, Apple made its smart watch available to customers in just nine countries: Australia, Canada, China, France, Germany, Hong Kong, Japan, the United Kingdom and the United States. The populations of developing nations tend to get left behind when new technologies emerge, although the divide lessens as these technologies become more widespread and less costly.

Access to technology, or often a lack of it, is one of the biggest contributors to the digital divide. Having a digital device that is connected to the internet allows access to educational resources, ecommerce, online banking and entertainment, amongst other things. Many people who do have access are being encouraged to allow their older technologies to be refurbished and given to those who currently have no access.

For those who do not understand how to use the technologies available, there are courses being run in many areas to help people learn the skills needed. There are also many countries that are funding community teaching programs, especially for those in poorer areas.

In less developed countries there is a drive to set up cybercafes to make technologies available to communities and increase their chance of a better education and access to facilities such as ecommerce.

The digital divide will exist in many different ways for a long time yet but each initiative that is put into place will help to close that divide a piece at a time. There is hope that this will eliminate a culture of digital divide and create a culture of digital inclusion.

TASK

Plan a letter that could be sent to a government official about the digital divide in your country. Make at least two suggestions about how the gap could be closed.

5.03 The future

The digital divide tends to increase when new technologies become available. Younger generations tend to embrace technology more quickly than older generations. As new technology is usually initially expensive, it is taken up more quickly by those who have

5.04 Summary

The digital divide is the technology divide between countries, demographic groups and economic areas. It is a technical, social and economic issue about the availability and use of modern technologies. It refers to more than just the internet and can include technologies such as telephones, televisions, PCs and the internet.

The digital divide can occur for many reasons, including a person's age, status and location. There are many things that can be affected by the digital divide, including a person's access to ecommerce, their education, employment opportunities and entertainment experiences.

A divide can occur between countries that are more developed and those that are less developed, between people who live in cities and those that live in rural areas, between different socio-economic groups and amongst those that have higher and lower performing technologies.

Review questions

1 Describe the term 'digital divide'. [3]
2 Discuss the impact of the digital divide on countries that are less developed. [8]
3 Describe two strategies that could be put in place to reduce the digital divide. [4]

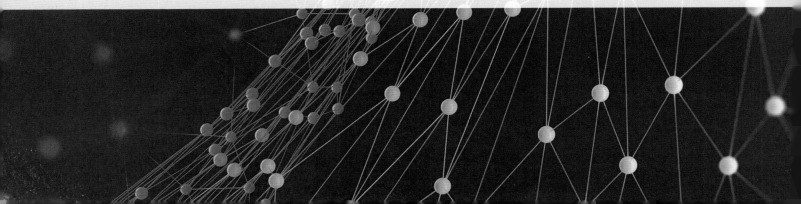

Chapter 6
Using networks

Learning objectives

By the end of this chapter, you will be able to:

- understand the advantages and disadvantages of networking computers
- be able to describe the characteristics and purpose of different types of networks, such as LAN, WAN, VPN, client–server, peer-to-peer, intranets, extranets and the internet
- be able to define the terms internet and World Wide Web and discuss the difference between the two
- be able to discuss the benefits and drawbacks of using the internet
- understand how the internet is used for communication
- be able to discuss the advantages and disadvantages of mobile networks
- understand how to set up a video and a web conference and describe how they use networks
- be able to describe how data is transmitted in a video conference
- understand the impact of video conferencing on our lives

6.01 Networking computers

KEY TERMS

Network: a set of computers and devices connected together so they can communicate and share resources

Network architecture: the design of a network

A single computer is known as a stand-alone computer. Up until the 1990s, computers in homes and organisations were largely stand-alone devices. Today, many computers are connected together.

TIP

When we connect stand-alone computers together we create a network.

The first instance of computers being linked together was in 1969 with the Advanced Research Projects Agency Network (ARPANET). Universities connected computers together with the intention of being able to communicate and share resources. This network was the predecessor to the internet.

Networking computers has a number of advantages and disadvantages.

The advantages of networking computers will mostly outweigh the disadvantages. This is why we choose to network computers together.

Remember

The way a network is designed is called its architecture. A **network's architecture** can be described by its geographical and physical nature, and by how data is stored and accessed on it.

Local area networks (LANs) and wide area networks (WANs)

KEY TERMS

Local area network (LAN): a network that covers a small geographical area

Wide area network (WAN): a network that covers a large geographical area

We can describe a network by its geographical and physical architecture. This creates two categories of network:

- **local area network (LAN)**
- **wide area network (WAN).**

Advantages	Disadvantages
Users can share their data with other users on the network.	Setting up a larger network can be expensive, especially if the network requires cabling, several servers, switches and wireless access points. The staffing costs to maintain a network can also be expensive.
Users can access their data from different computers on the network.	Networks can have security risks. Many users' data may be accessed if an unauthorised user gains access to a networked file server.
File servers can be used to store data in a central location. This makes it easier to keep the data secure and to create a back-up copy.	Viruses could easily spread from one networked computer to another, if a network is not sufficiently protected.
Application servers can be used to store software in a central location. This can often reduce software costs as a site licence could be purchased, if available. A software site licence is generally cheaper than individual licences. This also means that software updates would only need to be run on the server.	A whole network could fail if one element of the network fails. This will depend on how the network is structured.
Communications can be sent from one computer to another.	A high amount of network traffic may cause a network to run slowly and cause frustrating delays.
Printers can be shared. This means that a number of users can share resources in a company or home, rather than requiring their own.	
An internet connection can be shared, allowing each user on the network to access the internet.	

Table 6.01 - Advantages and disadvantages of a network.

79

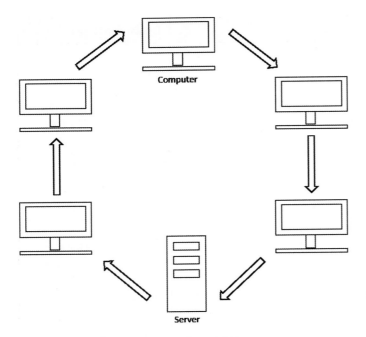

Figure 6.01 - A basic structure for a LAN.

A LAN is a network that is restricted to a small geographical area. LANs are usually found in homes, schools, universities and small businesses.

A WAN is a network that covers a larger geographical area. A WAN may be contained within a country or can spread across several countries. Organisations such as banks, police forces and hospitals use WANs to share data. The internet is a global WAN. Several LANs can be connected together to form a WAN. A business that has several

different branches often operate their networks this way.

The use of a LAN and a WAN can be compared using several different factors.

The terms LAN and WAN describe the geographical architecture of a network and how it is physically structured. They do not describe how data is stored and accessed. The two architectures for storing and accessing data on a network are:

- client–server
- peer-to-peer.

Client–server and peer-to-peer networks

KEY TERMS

Server: a computer on a network which provides resources that can be used by client devices

Client: a computer that is connected to a server

Peer: a computer in a network that is not connected to a server and does not control another computer

A client–server network uses a dedicated computer to store data, manage resources and control user access. This computer is known as a **server**. The server acts as a central point on the network that other computers connect to. A computer that connects to the server to access the data and resources it manages is known as a **client**.

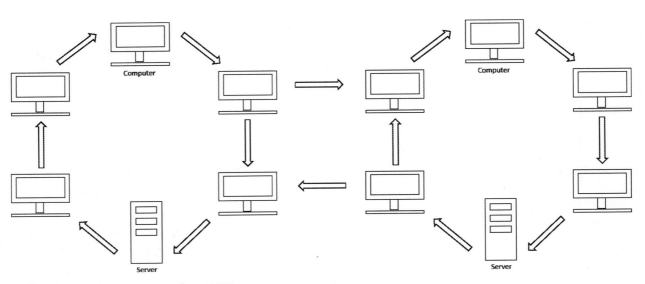

Figure 6.02 - A basic structure for a WAN.

Factors	Local area network	Wide area network
Data transfer rates	Can have up to 1 Gb per second.	Often restricted to less than 200 Mb per second.
Data transmission errors	Fewer errors as data packets are sent over short distances.	Greater chance of error as packets are sent over longer distances.
Connection method	Restricted to within a small location. Copper wire, fibre optic cable or radio waves are mostly used.	Expanded to a wider location. Copper wire, fibre optic cable or microwaves are mostly used. They can often use public telephone network systems, leased lines, transmission towers and satellite communication.
Security	Comparatively high as security can be easier to implement over a smaller number of devices and connections.	Comparatively low as security is difficult to implement across a higher number of devices and connections.
Ownership	Mostly owned by individuals or individual organisations.	Elements of the network often use communication infrastructures owned by others.

Table 6.02 - Comparison of a LAN and a WAN.

Network servers handle a variety of functions, including:

- storing a database of usernames and passwords to control user access
- data storage
- security
- assigning levels of access that determine what resources a user may access
- monitoring network traffic
- hosting of shared applications
- managing an internet connection
- scheduling and running back-ups
- email services
- printing jobs on network printers
- domain name services.

A client–server network will usually have at least one server and several clients. A network may have more than one server, each one dedicated to handling a specific function. For example, one server may handle user access, while another may handle data storage. This often occurs in larger networks where a server has to service many clients at the same time. Spreading the load across several servers helps to keep the network running efficiently.

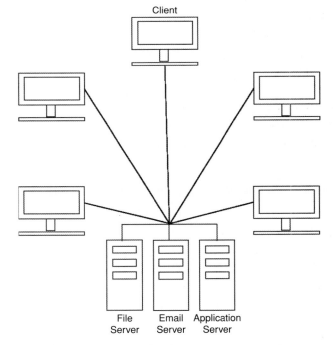

Figure 6.03 - Example of a client–server network.

A peer-to-peer network has no central server to manage the network. Each computer on the network shares its data and resources with all the others. No computer has control over another. Each computer is known as a **peer**.

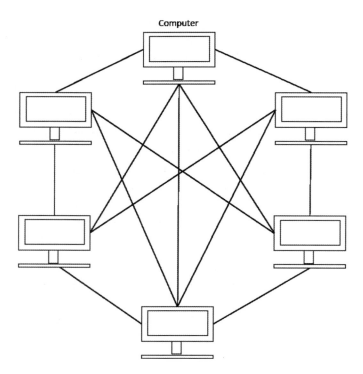

Computer

Figure 6.04 - Example of a peer-to-peer network.

On a peer-to-peer network, users store data on their own computer, but may allow other users access to it. Alternatively, they may choose to keep their data private. Individual peers may provide resources that others do not. For example, a peer may have a printer attached to it and other peers may print to that printer.

Table 6.03 shows a comparison of the architecture of a client–server and a peer-to-peer network.

Client–server network	Peer-to-peer network
A dedicated computer controls the network.	No individual computer controls the network.
Centralised database of users, usernames and passwords.	No centralised database.
Centralised data storage.	Data is stored on individual computers.
Centralised back-ups.	Relies on users remembering to back-up individual computers.
Suited to large networks with many computers.	Suited to small networks with few computers.

Table 6.03 - Comparison of client–server and peer-to-peer networks.

Each type of architecture has its advantages and disadvantages. Peer-to-peer networks are often cheaper to install and maintain than client–server networks. Client–server networks can be expensive to purchase and often require trained staff to maintain them.

Advantages of a client–server network	Disadvantages of a client–server network
Centralised database of users, usernames and passwords provides login security.	Expensive to set up and maintain.
User data is kept private.	Failure of a central server may make the whole network fail.
Levels of access can be applied to resources.	Requires specialist technical staff to maintain.
Users do not have to worry about security as a network manager maintains the network.	
Users do not have to make backups as back-ups are centralised and handled by the network manager.	
On larger networks several servers can be used for different functions to maintain network efficiency.	

Table 6.04 - Advantages and disadvantages of a client–server network.

Each type of network is used in many different ways, for example:

- Banks use client–server architecture to provide online banking services. When a device (such as a personal computer (PC), tablet or smartphone) connects to the bank through the internet, the device becomes a client. The bank's servers handle the client and provide access to online banking facilities.
- Companies use servers to host websites. Client computers access the web pages they contain.

82

- On-demand television and film providers have servers that stream content to client devices.
- Many peer-to-peer networks exist over the internet that allow users to share music, images and videos. Each peer has some content and allows other users access to it.

Advantages of a peer-to-peer network	Disadvantages of a peer-to-peer network
Cheap to set up and maintain. Does not require expensive servers.	No centralised database of users, usernames and passwords, making it harder to maintain security.
Failure of an individual peer only removes access to the resources and data which that peer handles. The rest of the network remains unaffected.	Users have to worry about making backups as no centralised backup service exists.
Does not require specialist technical staff to maintain.	The more computers there are on a peer-to-peer network, the slower it will run.

Table 6.05 - Advantages and disadvantages of a peer-to-peer network.

Virtual private networks (VPN)

KEY TERMS

Tunnelling protocol: a tunnel between two points on a network that is governed by a set of rules

Encryption: scrambling data so it cannot be understood without a decryption key, to make it unreadable if intercepted

Companies or organisations may want to allow users to access a network, often a LAN, from a remote location. They will need to use external resources to create this connection. The external resources will not be owned or maintained by the owner of the LAN, which can make access to the LAN network much less secure. This can be of great concern to the owner of the LAN and the users who want to remotely access it.

The issue of security can be overcome by implementing a virtual private network (VPN).

Remember

A VPN is a method of allowing a remote computer to connect securely to a private network using external resources.

Once connected to the VPN, the remote computer then has secure access to the LAN's resources, just as if it were directly connected to the LAN.

Security is implemented through the use of **tunnelling protocols** and **encryption**. For example, the secure shell (SSH) tunnel protocol uses encryption to securely transmit unencrypted data packets across an unsafe network.

To connect to a VPN, a user remotely logs on to the network. Once the user's identity has been authenticated, the VPN's tunnelling protocol sets up an encrypted link to the user's computer. Data can then be transmitted securely.

Remember

VPNs are often used by organisations to provide LAN access to travelling employees, employees who telework and users that want to access LAN resources at home. Users who want to securely access data on a home computer when they are away can also use a VPN.

There are several advantages and disadvantages for an organisation using VPNs as shown in Table 6.06.

TASK

Find out what kind of network you have in your school or home. What is the structure of it and how does it store data?

Does your school or home network have any servers? If it does, what are they used for?

Intranets and extranets

An intranet is a privately owned network that uses internet technologies, for example web pages, for internal use within an organisation. Web pages hold organisations' information such as news, events, historical data and commonly used documents. Email and instant messaging can also be used for internal communication. Training videos or corporate messages can be streamed and watched by employees.

Advantages of a VPN	Disadvantages of a VPN
VPNs maintain a high level of security for data transmission over the internet.	Performance of the VPN may be outside the control of the organisation. It is dependent on the external resources that are used.
VPNs use external resources. Organisations that use VPNs can save money as they do not need to purchase or implement secure, dedicated connections, called leased lines, for users who want to access the network.	A certain amount of technical expertise is required to set up and maintain VPNs. The cost of this expertise must be factored in when deciding whether to implement a VPN.
The cost of maintaining the external resources is covered by someone else.	
Adding extra clients costs very little as the network is virtual.	

Table 6.06 - Advantages and disadvantages of a VPN.

Intranets usually use client–server architecture. They often use several servers. A web server hosts the intranet's web pages, while an email server handles email communication. Another server will handle user accounts and access.

Many organisations now use an intranet. For example, schools use a virtual learning environment (VLE) to provide teaching and learning resources to students. The VLE is an intranet.

Remember
Intranets are used to increase efficiency because all information is stored centrally and can be easily accessed.

Additionally, unlike when browsing the internet, only information relevant to the organisation is available. An intranet is for internal use only. This increases security and confidentiality as only users within the organisation can access information on the intranet.

There may be times when an organisation will want to allow users that are currently external to the organisation

to access information on its intranet. It can do this by using an extranet. An extranet is an intranet that has been opened up to allow external user access. Extranets use VPNs to allow an external user to securely access the information on them.

Extranets usually only allow certain information to be accessed. For example:

- A school's VLE may allow parents to access their child's marks, attendance data and reports.
- A doctor's surgery may be able to access a local hospital's extranet to make an appointment for a patient.
- A company may provide tracking information on deliveries it is making to customers.

Access to an extranet is normally available through the organisation's website. A user logs in using an email address and password that will notify the extranet that the user is an authorised external user.

6.02 The internet

KEY TERMS

Packet switching: data that is broken down into packets is sent through different routes and reassembled by the recipient

TCP/IP: a communication protocol used by the internet

Internet service provider (ISP): A company that provides access to the internet

Remember
The internet is a global network made up of interconnected networks and individual computers. This global network allows users to access online facilities such as electronic communication, information sharing, data storage, banking, video and music streaming and social networking.

The beginnings of the internet were quite different from how it is now. In the 1950s and 1960s, the United States government formed several organisations whose purpose was to develop new technology. One organisation was the Advanced Research Projects Agency (ARPA). As projects developed, employees at ARPA became frustrated at the lack of computing power available to them. At the time, only a handful of powerful computers were available across the country. These were often at locations far away

Figure 6.05 - The internet connects the world.

from the researchers who needed them. The invention of **packet switching** allowed the creation of computer networks. Taking advantage of this communication breakthrough, ARPA created ARPANET, a network of computers that could share data and computing power.

The 1970s saw the introduction of the protocol, **TCP/IP**. This allowed separate networks to connect to each other, forming the basis for the internet. The term 'internet' originates from 'inter-network', meaning a network that was formed from the joining of networks.

The 1990s saw a huge increase in the size of the internet and its purpose, as many commercial, educational and home users took advantage of the facilities available online. Today, the number of users and devices on the internet runs into billions. It has become like a backbone, the purpose of which is to allow communication and sharing of data on a global scale.

Characteristics of the internet

Any device connected to the internet forms part of the internet. To connect to the internet we need to use an **internet service provider (ISP)**. ISPs use public telephone systems, underwater cables, microwave transmissions via satellites and radio waves to provide connections.

Data and information is held and distributed by content providers. A content provider is an organisation, group or company that offers content on web pages, for example text, images, sound and video, or web-based services, for example streaming media, gaming, shopping and electronic communication.

Although many of the computers connected to the internet can act as a server, most act as clients. The majority of data is held on web servers that are accessed by individual computers.

The widespread nature of the internet means that it has no centralised control. No one company or organisation runs or has authority over the internet, although various independent organisations control aspects of it:

- The Internet Corporation for Assigned Names and Numbers (ICANN) regulates domain names and their suffixes, such as .com, .co.uk, .in, .sa, .ae and .cn.
- The Internet Engineering Task Force (IEFT) devises and administers internet standards, such as protocols that govern communication.
- The World Wide Web Consortium (W3C) attempts to enforce agreement from organisations to adopt new standards.
- Telecommunications companies own the infrastructure that the internet uses for communication.

Remember
The lack of authority means that the information the internet carries is of mixed value. Information can be useful and correct, it can also be inaccurate, out of date or completely incorrect. Some information is deliberately designed to mislead.

85

The internet is constantly changing and evolving. For example:

- Every day, newly bought devices connect to it.
- The internet is expanding geographically as remote regions are connected through the installation of cables or through satellite communication.
- The data it holds constantly changes as organisations add, edit and delete data from their websites, and social networking users add and remove data.
- Newer technologies allow the range of facilities to expand. For example, the introduction of broadband connections has encouraged the growth of internet–based, on-demand television services.

The huge scale and size of the internet means that using it has many benefits and drawbacks for organisations, businesses and individuals.

DISCUSSION POINT
What would your life be like if you did not have the internet? What would be different? Would it be better or worse?

Benefits of using the internet	Drawbacks of using the internet
Information. A vast range of information is available on virtually any topic.	Incorrect information. Anyone can publish information on the internet. This means that some of the information available is inaccurate, out of date, incomplete or simply incorrect.
Global audience. The internet is worldwide, therefore contributors have a global audience.	Unsavoury behaviour. One serious problem with the internet is that it allows people to interact anonymously with other people. Users are unsure with whom they are really communicating. This means that people can make up fake identities in order to cyberbully, intimidate, steal and commit abuse.
Immediate transmission of information. Users can send messages immediately across the world. Postings on news sites and social media can be seen immediately by an audience.	Hacking. Some users may use the internet to attempt to gain access to other users' computers. This is often in an attempt to steal personal data or to crash websites. Protection against hacking can be expensive to an organisation.
Immediate availability of services. Users can quickly access services such as to bank online, book medical appointments, pay bills and book tickets for transport and for leisure.	Viruses. An organisation or individual will need to protect their computer against viruses. A virus is malicious software installed on a computer without consent or knowledge. Removal of a virus can be a difficult job.
International ecommerce. Users have access to online shops 24 hours a day and products from all over the world. Companies can also market products to consumers nationally and internationally.	Identity theft through phishing and pharming. Phishing uses fake emails pretending to be from an organisation. Phishing emails deceive users into giving their personal data by tricking them into following a link to a fake website. The website asks them to enter personal details. Once gathered, this data is used for criminal activities. Pharming works in a similar way. When users attempt to visit a known website, they are instead directed to a fake website that looks just like the real one. The cost of identity theft to individuals and businesses can be enormous.
Entertainment. Products such as software, music, films and books can be purchased and immediately downloaded. Users can play online games, or join in multiplayer games over the internet.	Unsuitable material. The free nature of the internet means that unsuitable content is present, such as pornography, graphic violence, promotion of terrorism, torture and physical and written abuse. Social networking allows anyone to publicly abuse friends, colleagues, celebrity figures and people in the news, often with little consequence to the offender.
Free education. Many free online tutorials and educational resources are available to help people learn new skills or knowledge.	Spamming. The ease of communication means that anyone can generate and transmit unwanted emails to millions of users. It is estimated that 69% of emails sent in 2014 were spam.
Social networking. The internet allows families, friends, organisations and businesses to regularly communicate, share and engage in social activities.	Online addiction. Some people have difficulty separating virtual environments from reality. Others find virtual worlds, such as those in massively multiplayer online role-playing games (MMORPGs) more alluring and comforting than the real world. They feel safer and happier in these environments than they do in real life. This can lead to social isolation and insecurity.
Up-to-date news. News stories on the internet can be read as soon as they are published.	

Table 6.07 - Benefits and drawbacks of using the internet.

Benefits of using the internet	Drawbacks of using the internet
Reduction in costs to businesses and organisations. Marketing over the internet, especially through social media, can be extremely cheap compared with traditional advertising and promotional methods.	
Feedback. The internet has allowed companies and organisations to easily gain feedback on products and services through rating systems, comments, online surveys and 'likes' on social media.	
Big data. The nature of the internet allows vast amounts of data to be collected by organisations. User behaviour on websites can be monitored, such as the type of products a person buys, or what information searches they make. Social networking sites collect data on what news items are trending, and what users like and dislike. Apps on smartphones collect data about online habits and behaviour. All of this collected data can be analysed by researchers or sold to businesses for marketing purposes.	
New communication applications. The internet allows communication applications that previously were not possible. For example, home security cameras can be monitored while the householder is away from home. Central heating can be remotely switched on or off from a smartphone app.	

Table 6.07 - Benefits and drawbacks of using the internet. (*cont.*)

87

6.03 The World Wide Web

 KEY TERMS

Hyperlink: a link that can be clicked to locate to another place in a document, or a different document entirely

Web browser: a software application for retrieving and presenting information on the World Wide Web

The term 'internet' describes the physical, global network of computers. The internet does not actually contain any information. It is a physical infrastructure.

The World Wide Web is an information system comprising documents, images, videos and sounds. It uses the internet as its base. Users access this information through websites and web pages, which are accessed through the use of a **web browser**.

The concept of the World Wide Web was developed by Tim Berners-Lee in 1989 when he worked for CERN.

Berners-Lee proposed a system for a more efficient communication system for CERN that allowed documents on an information system to be accessed via **hyperlinks**. He realised that any document could be accessed by a hyperlink, whether it is a text document, an image or a sound clip. In 1990 Berners-Lee and Robert Cailliau published a proposal to build a World Wide Web of hypertext-linked documents that could be viewed by a browser. Documents would be stored on servers, with users' computers acting as clients. From this proposal the World Wide Web was born and in 1991 it became available to the public.

Today the World Wide Web is the basis for, among other things, national and international information sharing, banking, shopping, on-demand television broadcasting and social networking. It has billions of users, including businesses, organisations, governments, schools, colleges, universities and domestic users.

6.04 Communication using the internet

The internet is for communication. It allows users to communicate in several ways, including:

- instant messaging (IM)
- voice over IP (VOIP)
- news services.

Instant messaging (IM) is a form of communication that allows real-time text transmission over a network, often the internet. Depending on the type of IM service, messages are either transmitted once a message is composed and sent by the user, or transmitted character by character as the user types. Some services allow files to be transferred and conversations to be saved.

IM is now a feature of many social networking sites, allowing users to chat online instead of posting messages on their profile page. Many organisations see IM as a valuable tool for customer interaction, for example support helplines. This can be especially useful where a support technician needs to give instructions to a customer. The customer can read (and reread) and follow the instructions in their own time.

Users of IM often see it as an equivalent or alternative to text messaging used on smartphones. They make use of text speak (where common words and expressions are abbreviated), for example LOL (laughing out loud), and emoticons to reduce typing and speed up replies.

An example of an IM service is the private messaging system available on Facebook. Users can send messages to each other privately as well as posting on each other's profile.

Voice over IP (VOIP) technologies allow users to have voice communications, just as if they were using a telephone system. Instead of using an analogue telephone transmission, the user's voice is recorded by the computer and transmitted digitally to the recipient. The VOIP system can work internally across a network, or externally by making use of the internet to carry the data transmission.

VOIP has advantages over traditional analogue telephone systems. When the system is run by using an organisation's LAN, calls within the organisation will be free. Extra VOIP phones can be added to a network, simply by connecting a new phone to a network point or by adding it to a wireless network. However, if a network is experiencing heavy traffic, voices can become garbled, distorted or missing altogether.

An example of a VOIP service is Skype. Users can make calls using the Skype application on the internet.

News services are organisations that collect and broadcast news stories for subscribers. Users can sign up for news alerts using a smartphone application. Some services allow news stories to be filtered out so that only news that covers topics a user is interested in is sent to their smartphone. Others broadcast headline news to subscribers.

An example of a news service is Google News. Users can subscribe and receive news stories on a daily basis, often in the categories of their choice.

All of these services are available because of packet switching technology.

Figure 6.06 - Many social networking services now offer an instant messaging feature.

Figure 6.07 - Users can subscribe to news services to receive news stories in the category of their choice.

6.05 Mobile networks

KEY TERM

Cell: the geographical area covered by a radio transmitter

Remember

A mobile network is a wireless WAN that uses radio to transmit and receive communications from portable devices, such as smartphones. Mobile networks now cover a considerable amount of the inhabited areas of world.

Mobile networks are broken down into small areas called **cells**. At the heart of each cell is a radio base station that transmits and receives messages. The base stations connect to public telecommunications services allowing access to the internet.

Cells vary in size:

- picocells cover an area of less than 200 metres
- microcells cover an area up to 2 kilometres
- macrocells cover larger regions.

There have been several generations of mobile networks, each providing faster access speeds and greater reliability:

- 1G networks. These were the first generation mobile networks that used analogue signals. These networks were largely limited to voice and text message communications.
- 2G networks. The second generation mobile networks switched from analogue to digital transmission, improving signal quality. 2G networks were able to connect with each other, allowing a phone to use other networks.
- 3G networks. Third generation networks increased data transmission speeds up to 2 Mbps, allowing internet access, video transmission and online gaming.
- 4G networks. Fourth generation networks are the current, latest generation of mobile network technology. In theory, they allow data transmission speeds of up to 1 Gbps, allowing greater use of video streaming facilities.

Mobile networks have their advantages and disadvantages.

Mobile networks have grown hugely in popularity, with many users now accessing the internet through 3G or

Advantages of mobile networks	Disadvantages of mobile networks
Mobile networks have enabled users to communicate with others and access the internet while on the move, often through the use of smartphones.	Quality of reception can vary and can be poor towards the edge of a cell, leading to interrupted or delayed transmissions.
Breaking the network down into cells allows for lower power radio transmitters to be used, bringing energy and cost savings.	The use of frequency must be carefully planned to avoid interference between cells.
There are only so many radio frequencies that can be used for mobile communications. These frequencies can be split among neighbouring cells, and reused in more distant cells, thereby increasing the number of communications that can take place at the same time.	
Larger geographical areas can be covered than by using a single transmitter. Even high power transmitters are limited in range. By using several, low power transmitters a wider area can be covered.	
The use of multiple transmitters means the network is more robust. Failure of one base station only affects one cell, leaving other areas of the network unaffected.	

Table 6.08 - Advantages and disadvantages of mobile networks.

4G connections. The rapid growth in use of social media networks has led to many people checking profiles and sending posts frequently during the day, often via a mobile network.

TASK

Find out what further developments are in progress for mobile networks.

6.06 Video and web conferencing

One form of communication that is slowly gaining in popularity is video conferencing. Video conferencing allows users to see and hear each other as they talk. Web conferencing is a similar communication medium. However, whereas video conferencing allows two-way communication, web conferencing traditionally allowed one-way communication. A user would broadcast a video to many watching users, for example a company delivering a training session or a university lecturer presenting a lecture. However, web conferencing technology has expanded to allow two-way communication.

How to set up a video conference

Video conferencing requires certain hardware and software:

- a desktop computer or laptop
- a webcam to record the user's image
- a microphone to record the user's voice
- a monitor to display the other participant's image
- speakers to produce the other participant's voice
- network (and internet) access to connect to the other participant
- video conferencing software to conduct and control the video conference.

Many modern devices such as laptops, smartphones and tablets already have this hardware. Smartphones and tablets are often supplied with video conferencing software installed.

Before a user can participate in a video conference, they must first register with a video conferencing service. The service will have software that the user needs to install. With the software running and the device connected to a network or the internet, the user selects another registered user and initiates a

Figure 6.08 - People can use mobile devices, such as tablets, for video conferencing calls.

conference call. The other participant can accept or reject the call.

There are a number of checks that need to be made before a video conference goes ahead:

- All participants will need to make sure they have a stable and suitable internet connection.
- Each participant will need to make sure that their microphone is inputting their voice, and that it is doing this at a suitable sound level. Most video conferencing software has a built in facility that allows a user to record their voice input and play it back to assess if it is correct.
- Each participant will need to make sure that they have correctly positioned their webcam, and that it is safely and securely placed. They will need to test that their image is being inputted into the system and that other participants can see them clearly. Most video conferencing software also has a facility to test this.

How to set up a web conference

Setting up a web conference is a similar process to a video conference. Web conference software is available, but quite often the same software that is used for video conferencing can also be used to set up a web conference.

Before initiating the web conference, the user sends an invitation to interested participants, stating the time and date of the conference. The invitation often contains an access code that allows the interested participant to log on to the conference, along with a link that specifies the network address at which the conference can be accessed. Using access codes helps keep unwanted users from participating.

At the appointed time and date, users follow the link and log on using the access code. They can now watch and participate in the conference. Participants may watch a demonstration of a product or read a document onscreen, but will not require a web camera themselves to do this. Web conferences can also be just text based, where participants will use a messaging facility to communicate.

There are a number of checks that need to be performed before a web conference goes ahead:

- Similar checks to a video conference will need to be performed for the internet connection, microphone and a web camera if used.
- In some web conferences, participants may want to share documents. Most web conferencing software will allow participants to do this. This will either be through documents being preloaded into an online meeting room, or by a link sent in a messaging facility during the web conference. A test may need to be carried out on whether the preloaded documents can be accessed, or that the text facility can be used.

Using networks in video and web conferencing

The wide-scale use of video conferencing and web conferencing would not be possible without the use of networks. The use of packet switching enables video and sound transmissions to be broken down into packets, just like any other type of data, to be transmitted. The resulting packets can be easily and swiftly transmitted across networks and the internet.

Video and web conferences held internally within organisations will make use of that organisation's LAN. The LAN may be wired or wireless. To connect externally, the conferences will also need to make use of a WAN or the internet.

Video and web conferencing requires a reasonable data transmission speed. The higher the required quality of video and sound, the higher the transmission speed that is required. As a result, for video or web conference over a WAN, one of four types of connection is usually used:

- Integrated Services Digital Network (ISDN)
- Asynchronous Digital Subscriber Lines (ADSL)
- Synchronous Digital Subscriber Lines (SDSL)
- 3G/4G mobile networks.

Integrated Services Digital Network (ISDN) is a networking technology that allows data to be transmitted digitally over analogue copper wire. This is usually with transmission speeds of up to 64 Kbps per channel. Two channels could also be used in parallel to send data at up to 128 Kbps. ISDN was popular in the 1990s and early 2000s but has largely been replaced by much faster ADSL and SDSL networks. However, ISDN is still used in areas where ADSL and SDSL technology has yet to be implemented.

Asynchronous Digital Subscriber Line (ADSL) technology, also known as broadband, is now the most common type of connection to the internet. It has typical transmission speeds of around 100 Mbs. ADSL is used in homes and businesses to deliver reliable, high-speed connections. Asynchronous means that download and upload speeds are different. This means that ADSL works by unevenly splitting the balance between download and upload speeds. Most homes and businesses will download more data from the internet than they upload to it. As a result, ADSL download speeds are usually far greater than upload speeds.

Synchronous Digital Subscriber Line (SDSL) technology uses the same data transmission technology as ADSL. However, this time the download and upload transmission rates are balanced and equal. SDSL is used by organisations that upload and download equivalent amounts of data.

Mobile devices such as smartphones make use of 3G/4G technology to allow users to use video conferencing when travelling, or when access to a LAN is not possible.

For a video conference to successfully take place, the video and audio signals must be transmitted over a network. Video signals require high volumes of data transmission. The higher the resolution of the video, the more data that needs transmission, and the greater the traffic that is placed on a network. High traffic can lead to disruption or interruption of the video conference.

To overcome this problem, video conferencing uses software called codecs. Codec is an abbreviation of the words 'coder' and 'decoder'. At the sender's end, the 'coder' element of the codec takes the video and audio signals and compresses them to reduce their file size. Reducing the file size means less data needs to be transmitted, reducing network traffic and the possibility of disruption to the conference. At the receiver's end, the 'decoder' decompresses the video and audio signals so that they can be played.

The same codec must be used at both the source and the destination of the data transmission. Different codecs compress and decompress in different ways, therefore are incompatible with each other. As a result, several codec standards exist. The H.264 codec is one of the most common and is used not only for video conferencing, but also with DVDs and YouTube videos. Other codecs for video conferencing include H.261 and H.263+.

The impact of video conferencing

KEY TERMS

Digital divide: the separation between those that have access to technologies and the internet and those that do not

Teleworking: working from home using technologies to keep in contact with an employer

Remember

Improvements in internet and communication technologies have led to affordable high-speed connections at home and at work. These high-speed connections can usually handle video transmissions. The introduction of 4G mobile networks mean that mobile devices are also capable of high-speed connections.

Additionally, many computing devices now feature inbuilt video conferencing equipment. Smartphone, laptops and tablets generally have microphones, speakers and cameras, along with the network connectivity needed for video conferencing. Free software allows cheap video conferencing.

As a result, an increasing number of users have now taken to using video conferencing as a method of communication and are enjoying the benefits it brings. Those users who live at a distance from friends and relatives have especially taken to this technology as it allows them to see, as well as hear, their loved ones. Users with hearing and speaking impairments enjoy video conferencing as it enables them to communicate using sign language.

A growing example of a video conferencing software that people use is Apple's FaceTime. Users that have an iPhone can use the inbuilt FaceTime software application to communicate with each other using video conferencing

However, the general public has yet to fully embrace this technology. Many users feel self-conscious and uncomfortable in front of a camera. Even though connection speeds have improved greatly, video

conferencing does require high-speed data transmission. High levels of network traffic can more frequently interfere with, degrade or interrupt video transmissions. This leads users to return to more reliable voice-only methods.

It could be argued that video conferencing is helping to widen the **digital divide**. Many older users are wary of technology. They are afraid of the complexity of video conferencing, opting for more traditional voice communication methods that are familiar and comfortable.

Video conferencing has not yet directly had an impact on law. However, legislation has been implemented in several countries that allows a witness to give testimony via video conferencing. This process is reserved for witnesses who may be psychologically upset by having to attend court, especially those that may have to face someone who has subjected them to physical assault or abuse.

In some countries, such as the United States, video conferencing allows defendants to make initial court appearances without having to leave jail. This saves travel expense and increases safety to the public as suspects remain in custody.

In the UK, several police forces have implemented video conferencing as a way of conducting interviews more quickly. An interviewer may be based at one police station, but can interview suspects and witnesses at other stations, without having to travel to each site.

Video conferencing has had an impact on education and the way that students learn. Rather than listening to a teacher, or reading a book or web page, video conferencing is used to engage students. Video conferencing allows students to participate in conversations and share ideas with fellow students at

Figure 6.09 - Video conferencing is used in some courts to allow witnesses to testify without being in the courtroom.

schools and universities in other parts of the world. This can lead to unexplored perspectives about subjects being shared and argued in live debates, resulting in wider, more considered points of view, especially when the students are from differing cultures.

Speaking to industry and subject experts often engages and interests students in a topic. Video conferencing allows experts to give talks and lectures without having to travel to a school. Sometimes a talk can be given to more than one school at a time, allowing many students to benefit from the experience. This is especially useful to schools in remote, isolated areas where travel would be difficult or expensive.

Universities make heavy use of video conferencing. The technology allows lecturers to teach courses at several universities, while being based at one. Sharing of such expertise is becoming more common, especially in subjects where finding a lecturer for a course has been difficult. Additionally, video conferencing allows lecturers to hold a lecture for students while away on research or at conferences.

Medicine and medical care are areas where video conferencing continues to be of growing usefulness. Consultants and physicians in different hospitals are able to discuss a patient's case and help to offer a diagnosis. External hardware components such as ultrasound imaging devices and video endoscopes can be connected and images from them shared in the video conference, helping consultants at other locations to help assess a patient's condition. This has the dual benefit of reducing travelling costs for consultants and increasing efficiency as consultants can see more cases in any given time period.

In some countries medical practices have introduced video conferencing to help doctors and nurses keep in touch with patients who have physical impairments, and for those in remote areas where travelling may be difficult or dangerous. In such situations video conferencing can bring comfort to a patient, especially the elderly, who might not otherwise have much human contact.

Sometimes the best way to do business is in a face-to-face meeting. Email and telephone provide useful media for arranging and making business deals, but when it comes to agreements of great value, people tend to prefer to do business in person. Meeting someone in person helps to promote goodwill, friendship and trust.

However, face-to-face meetings are not always possible. For example, time constraints or cost of travel may make them impossible. Video conferencing has provided a possible solution to these situations. It allows people to have face-to-face meetings without having to leave the office. This saves travel expenses and it also allows for more efficient use of an employee's time, as hours are spent working and not travelling.

Video conferencing has also helped to facilitate the growth in **teleworking**. Employee who work regularly from home can sometimes feel cut off from their employer. Teleworkers that use video conferencing tend to feel happier and less isolated from their employer and co-workers. Companies that have regional offices are finding that video conferencing brings unexpected benefits. Many companies that regularly use video conferencing to communicate with their regional offices find that employees in those offices feel more involved with the organisation, increasing employee satisfaction and productivity.

Companies are also using video conferencing for staff training. Some companies have several offices, and some, like banks, have many branches. A trainer at a company's head office can deliver a training programme via a video conference to staff at different offices or branches simultaneously.

However, video conferencing can also cause anxiety and stress among some workers. Some people are less confident in front of a camera. As a result, a video conference made by an employee with senior personnel can cause more stress than a face-to-face meeting.

One area in which video conferencing has seen a large-scale uptake is in the media sector. Video conferencing allows journalists to deliver live, on-the-spot reports in

Figure 6.10 - Dental students using video conferencing software to see and interact with a live appointment.

situations where a live broadcast might not otherwise be possible.

Another aspect to consider is press video conferencing. With businesses and organisations taking advantage of the global audience the internet permits, it is becoming increasingly common to hold international press conferences. These conferences are often held to launch new products or to make statements about political affairs. Press video conferencing allows journalists to participate without actually having to attend.

> **DISCUSSION POINT**
>
> Can you think of any other ways that video conferencing could be used in our lives?

6.07 Summary

Stand-alone computers that are connected together create what is called a network. There are different types of networks that can be categorised by their geographical and physical structure or their method for data storage.

A LAN is a network that is geographically small in area. They are usually found in homes, schools and small businesses.

A WAN is a network that is geographically large in area. The largest and most common WAN is the internet. The internet is the network infrastructure, whereas the World Wide Web is the web pages of content we can view using the internet, an ISP and a web browser. The internet is used for communication in various different ways. These include IM, VOIP, news services, video conferencing and web conferencing. Video conferencing has had an impact on many areas of society, such as personal communications, court cases, business, education, medicine and media. These impacts have been both positive and negative.

A client–server network has servers that run the network centrally. Each computer that is part of the network is called a client. A peer-to-peer network does not have servers. No single computer has control over another in this network.

A VPN is a method of allowing a remote computer to connect securely to a private network using external resources.

Review questions

1   Describe the difference between a LAN and a WAN. [4]

2   Explain what is meant by an intranet and how it could be used in an organisation. [4]

3   Explain the advantages and disadvantages of a VPN. [4]

4   Describe the difference between the internet and the World Wide Web. [2]

5   Identify four pieces of hardware that could be used when video conferencing. [4]

6   Discuss the impact of video conferencing on education. [6]

Chapter 7
Expert systems

Learning objectives

By the end of this chapter, you will be able to:

- describe the components of an expert system and how expert systems can be used
- explain how expert systems produce possible solutions, including the process of forward and backward chaining
- analyse the use of different processing systems
- explain how master and transaction files are used

7.01 What is an expert system?

KEY TERMS

Diagnosis: identifying a problem or illness by analysis of the symptoms

Artificial intelligence: computer systems that perform tasks that normally require human intelligence

Chaining: combining together instructions

Transaction: a collection of data that is exchanged

Field: an individual item of data in a database, for example forename

Remember

An expert system is a computerised system that attempts to reproduce the decision-making process of an expert human being. They are designed to try and replicate the judgement of a human that has expert knowledge in a certain field. By doing this they can be used to replace or assist a human expert.

Expert systems use a knowledge base and a set of rules to provide a **diagnosis** or a recommended course of action. They can be used to solve complex problems by reasoning, using the knowledge base they are given.

Expert systems gather data by asking the user questions about the problem. An initial set of questions can lead to further questions depending on the user's responses. The expert system reasons what questions it needs to ask, based on the knowledge it is given. It will use the responses from the user to rule out various possibilities that will allow it to eventually reach a decision or diagnosis.

The concept of an expert system was first developed in the 1970s by Edward Feigenbaum, who founded the knowledge-based system laboratory at Stanford University. Expert systems are thought to be among the first truly successful forms of **artificial intelligence**.

We rely on expert systems to help us with knowledge and understanding in a particular field. We use them in the same way as we do certain experts in our lives. For example, we will go to see a doctor if we have a health problem or we will go to see a car mechanic if our car will not start. We can use an expert system in a similar way, it will ask us questions about our health problem or car problem and provide us with a diagnosis or course of action.

Building an expert system is known as knowledge engineering and it is composed of three main components:

- the knowledge base
- the inference engine
- the user interface.

Knowledge base

Remember

The knowledge base is a database that allows the storage and retrieval of the knowledge provided by a collection of experts. It contains knowledge about the specific area for which the expert system can be used.

The developers of the expert system will interview a collection of experts to build the database of knowledge. They will look to gain two types of knowledge from the experts. The first is factual knowledge. This is knowledge that is widely shared. The second type is heuristic knowledge. This is knowledge that is more personal and is acquired through a range of experiences and reasoning.

Once the knowledge base is built, it can be used by the expert system to inform the questions it needs to ask and assist in providing the results.

Part of the knowledge base is the rules base. The rules base is a set of rules that will be used to produce an output or decision by the expert system. These rules are used by the inference engine as a base for reasoning, to obtain a solution to a problem or a decision. Each rule will contain two parts, the IF and the THEN. A rule can also have multiple IF parts that will be joined together by Boolean operators including AND and OR.

Most expert systems will have a knowledge based editor built into them. This allows the knowledge base to be checked for errors and edited ad updated when needed.

Inference engine

Remember

The inference engine is the part of the expert system that makes judgements and reasoning using the knowledge base and user responses. It is designed to produce reasoning based on a set of rules.

It will ask the user questions, and based on their answer, it will follow a line of logic. This may then lead to further questions and eventually a final result.

The inference engine is mostly a problem-solving tool. It organises and controls steps to solve the problem. To do

Advantages	Disadvantages
They provide answers to questions that are outside a user's knowledge and experience.	They do not have the addition of common sense that humans have. This means that their response can only be a logical one and cannot have a creative approach.
They can aid professionals in areas where their knowledge and experience are a little weaker.	Errors in the knowledge base or inference engine will produce errors in the results. Therefore they are only as good as the data and rules they are given.
As they use a logical process they are consistent in the answers that they give.	They are not able to automatically adapt to changing environments. This requires the knowledge base to be changed.
They will not forget to ask a question, as all the rules and knowledge is put into place to make sure that all data needed is gathered.	They are expensive to produce as they require a great deal of time and effort from experts and developers.
As they are a computer and not a human they can be accessed on a 24/7 basis.	
They can often reduce the time taken to solve a problem and the questioning and reasoning process may be much quicker than an interaction between humans.	
Using expert systems may mean that a less skilled workforce is needed, as the system will provide the knowledge and experience they need.	

Table 7.01 - The advantages and disadvantages of expert systems.

this it often uses a **chaining** method. It chains together what is known as IF–THEN rules to form a line of reasoning. The IF part of the rule is a condition, for example IF I am hungry. The THEN part of the rule is an action, for example IF I am hungry THEN I will need to eat.

There are two main methods that can be used to obtain a result. The appropriate one will depend on whether the expert system is designed to produce a final result i.e a diagnosis or course of action, or if it begins with a known conclusion i.e. a goal. If the process starts with a set of conditions and chaining moves towards a final conclusion, this is called forward chaining.

In a forward chaining system, the expert system will take the data input and match it to the knowledge and rules it contains. It will keep doing this until it can reach an end goal or outcome. A forward chaining system is data driven. Data is gathered about the problem and then the system infers what it can from the data to reach a conclusion.

If the process starts with a known conclusion, but the path to it is unknown, the chaining will work in reverse and this is called backward chaining. The system in this case has a goal or solution and the inference engine attempts to find the evidence to prove it.

User interface

Remember

The user interface is the way the user interacts with the expert system. They are often graphical in nature and have a range of selection processes or typing methods to allow the user to provide responses.

Expert systems have numerous advantages and disadvantages, see Table 7.01. The conclusion or decision the expert system reaches may not always be obvious to a user. The user may want to gain an understanding of how the conclusion or decision was determined. In order to allow this facility, some expert systems have an explanation system built into them. This will provide an explanation of the reasoning process and show how the output given by the system was reached.

7.02 How are expert systems used?

Expert systems are used by many individuals and organisations for a variety of different purposes. These include:

- medical diagnosis
- car mechanical diagnosis

- playing chess
- providing financial advice
- troubleshooting computer and printer issues
- identifying items, for example plants and birds
- using a telephone helpdesk.

EXAMPLE

The National Health Service (NHS) is the medical system in the UK. The NHS has a website that allows users to enter the symptoms of their illness or ailment and it will provide them with a possible diagnosis. This may help a person to understand which possible illnesses they may have. It can also be used by professionals within the NHS to double check a diagnosis they are giving, or to aid them with any areas of weakness they have in their medical knowledge.

7.01 - The NHS website.

EXAMPLE

The website Botanical Keys allows a user to enter a range of characteristics about a plant. The system will then identify what the plant is. Users can use this to find out what particular plants are growing in their garden or to identify a plant they have seen when out on a walk in the countryside or through a park.

Urban Forest is a non-profit website in Singapore that contains information about flora from Singapore and Southeast Asia-users can visit the site to help them with plant identification.

DISCUSSION POINT

Discuss the impact of people having the ability to self-diagnose their medical issues using an expert system.

7.03 Data processing systems

There are many types of systems that process data, and a variety of ways the processing can be carried out. A system that processes data will have a method to input the data, a method to process the data and a method to output the data.

We are going to look at three ways in which data can be processed These are batch, online and real-time processing systems.

What is a batch processing system?

Remember

A batch processing system is a system that processes batches of data at set time intervals. Data is collected from inputs and stored together in what are known as batches. These batches of data are stored until a set time when they will be processed and an output, or outputs, created.

The amount of data processed by batch processing systems is normally quite large. By storing the data together in batches, it means that the processing can be carried out at a time when the system is in less demand. This results in less disruption to a system during the times of the day when it could be in heavy demand. No user interaction is required to process the data. The system is automatically triggered at a set time.

There are issues that can occur with a batch processing system. There is a time delay for the data processing, so the output that will be provided is not always readily available. Also, if there is an error with an input, this will not be recognised until a later date when the data is processed.

EXAMPLE

A payroll system

A factory will often have a system that will register the time employees arrive at work, as well as the time they leave. This will allow the amount of hours an employee has worked to be calculated. Data about each employee's working hours can be stored in batches until the employees need to receive their pay. The data can then be processed to calculate the pay due for each employee and a payslip can be output to show this. It is not necessary to have an employee's pay calculated until they are due to be paid, so the processing to do this can be run when the factory isn't in operation, for example late at night. This will free up the processing power of the system to perform other tasks during the day.

EXAMPLE

Stock control system

A retail store will often have system a that will register the stock that is sold in a day. This system will normally be connected to the till (cash register). When an item is sold in the store, the warehouse will need to know that the item of stock will need replacing. This way the store stays fully stocked. The information about each item sold can be batched together and processed at the end of the day to be sent as a report to the warehouse. The warehouse will then know what stock to send the next day. By processing the data in this way, the system is freed up to deal with all of the sales made in the store during the day.

What is an online processing system?

An online processing system is sometimes known as an interactive processing system.

Remember

An online processing system is a type of processing system that deals with data in **transactions**. A certain amount of data is input as a transaction. This amount of data is usually small. Once the data for the transaction is collected it is processed and the next transaction can occur.

EXAMPLE

Online booking system

An online booking system, for example an aeroplane ticket booking system, will process data in transactions. All the data about the customer, flight and seat number will be collected in the transaction. This will then be processed and a ticket can be provided as an output. As each

transaction is processed in turn, this avoids a seat on the aeroplane being double-booked. Once a seat has been allocated to a transaction, until that transaction is completed that seat cannot be booked by anyone else. This is because their transaction will not be processed until the previous one is completed. The same would occur with a concert ticket booking system.

What is a real-time processing system?

TIP

A real-time processing system processes data as soon as it has been input. They are normally used when the immediacy of the data is vital.

EXAMPLE

Air traffic control

An air traffic control system is a real-time processing system. Each piece of data that is input into the system, for example the location of all the planes currently in the air, is processed immediately so that their location can be known by everybody using the system. This is imperative as this data will need to be given back to each plane that is currently in flight to make sure no collisions occur. There cannot be any delay in the processing of this data as the result could be catastrophic.

EXAMPLE

Computer games

When playing computer games the input from the user needs to be processed immediately, so that it can take effect and the game can be controlled. Each time a user asks a game character to move forward by pressing a key or button, it needs to do this immediately. In order to do this, it needs to have a real-time processing system to process the data.

DISCUSSION POINT

Why would we not make every processing system a real-time system? What would be the impact if we did?

For data to be processed it is often stored first. This can be for long periods of time or momentarily. There are two main file types that are used to store data, master files and transaction files.

Master files

A master file is normally a collection of **fields** about a main element of a data system, for example a customer or an employee.

Remember

The master file will store all of the more permanent data about the customer or the employee. Data stored in master files is normally more permanent in nature.

EXAMPLE OF A MASTER FILE

Employee number – 001

Forename – Nancy

Surname – Richards

Department – Customer services

Pay rate – $15 per hour

Pay to date – $1590

There will normally be a key field present in a master file, such as the employee number in the example above. The key field will be used to match transaction files to the correct master file.

Transaction files

The data stored in these files is normally used to update the master file. It is more temporary in nature. The key field is again present in the transaction file in order to allow it to be matched to the correct master file.

Remember

Transaction files are useful as they can act as an audit trail for a company to see what updates have been made to the master file at various times.

EXAMPLE OF A TRANSACTION FILE

Employee number – 001

Date – 01/01/2015

Hours worked – 8

In real-time and online processing systems, the transaction file is compared to the master file, by finding the matching key field, as the data is processed by the system. In a batch processing system, the transaction files are stored until a suitable time is available to update the master files. The system will then run through each transaction file and match it to the correct master file in order to update the master.

7.04 Summary

An expert system is designed to replicate the decision-making or problem-solving ability of an expert human in a certain field. Expert systems can be used to diagnose medical issues or car problems, amongst many other uses. An expert system is made up of three components: the knowledge base, the inference engine and the user interface. The knowledge base is the database of knowledge collected from the experts, the inference engine reasons what data needs to be collected and the user interface is how the user interacts with the system.

Forward chaining is when data is taken about the problem and continues to be taken until a diagnosis or course of action can be provided. Backward chaining is when an outcome is known but the chaining process is reversed to work out what is required to achieve the outcome.

There are three main types of data processing system: batch, online and real-time processing systems. Batch processing often has a time delay and processes data in batches, an online system collects data as a transaction and is processed once all data is collected and a real-time system processes data immediately.

Master files store more permanent data about a subject, for example an employee or a customer. Transaction files are used to update master files.

Review questions

1   Describe the components of an expert system. [6]

2   Explain two uses of an expert system. [4]

3   Describe two advantages and one disadvantage of an expert system. [6]

4   Describe the difference between an online and a real-time processing system. [4]

5   Define the term 'master file'. [2]

Chapter 8
Spreadsheets

Learning objectives

By the end of this chapter, you will be able to:

- create a spreadsheet
- format a spreadsheet
- create formulae and use functions within a spreadsheet
- use validation rules within a spreadsheet
- test validation rules
- test a spreadsheet model and evaluate the effectiveness of test plans
- verify and validate data entry
- search for data within a spreadsheet
- sort data in a spreadsheet
- import and export data to and from a spreadsheet
- analyse and select the most appropriate type of graph or chart
- create a graph or chart in a spreadsheet
- describe the characteristics of modelling software
- analyse the need for computer models
- evaluate the effectiveness of spreadsheet models
- describe the advantages and disadvantages of using a model to create and run simulations
- evaluate the use of simulations

8.01 Create a spreadsheet

KEY TERMS

Cell: a rectangle within a spreadsheet where data can be positioned

Formula: a mathematical calculation using +, −, × or ÷

Orientation: the direction of text, for example horizontal or vertical

Alignment: positioning text so that it is in line, for example on the left, right or centre

Function: a ready-made formula representing a complex calculation

Validation: the process of checking data matches acceptable rules

Verify: to check that data matches the original data

Import: to bring in data from another application

Export: to prepare data for use in another application

Remember
Spreadsheets are used to manipulate numbers, perform calculations, present summary data and make predictions.

A spreadsheet consists of rows, columns and **cells**. In the spreadsheet in Figure 8.01, row 4 is highlighted in green, column B is highlighted in yellow and the cell B4 is highlighted in red.

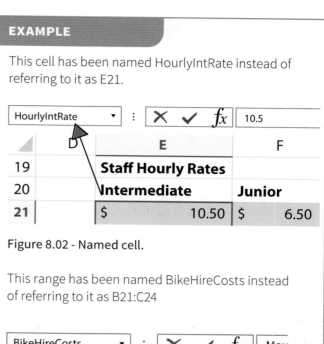

Figure 8.01 - Rows, columns and cells.

Spreadsheet elements
Cells, rows and columns

A row consists of a horizontal set of cells. A column consists of a vertical set of cells. A cell is the intersection of a row and a column. A cell is referenced by the column letter and row number. A cell that is in column B and row 4 has a cell reference of B4.

EXAMPLE

This cell has been named HourlyIntRate instead of referring to it as E21.

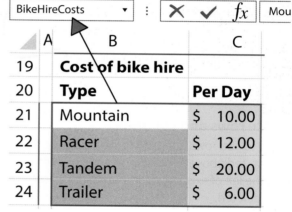

Figure 8.02 - Named cell.

This range has been named BikeHireCosts instead of referring to it as B21:C24

Figure 8.03 - Named range.

Ranges
A range is a set of one or more cells. A range can be named so that the cell or cells can be referenced by the name instead of the cell reference. Range names are easier to remember and make reference to than cell references.

Worksheets
A worksheet is a set of rows and columns. It is possible to have more than one worksheet within a workbook. Worksheets can be used to separate information such as having a worksheet for sales in each country, a worksheet for sales for each year, a worksheet for exam results for each class or separate worksheets for inputting data, storing data tables and showing the results of data processing; worksheets often take the same structure, but are storing different data.

103

EXAMPLE

This workbook contains four worksheets – one for each country. Each worksheet shows the sales made in that country. The currently active worksheet is for sales in Germany.

	A	B	C	D	E
1	City	Sales	Model	Fuel type	Cost per litre
2	Berlin	3,272	Mondeo	Diesel	$ 1.25
3	Hamburg	1,208	Saab 9-3	Petrol	$ 1.17

◄ ►	China	Pakistan	Dubai	Germany

Figure 8.04 - Worksheets.

TASK

CD 8.02 Worksheets

Explore the way worksheets have been used in CD 8.02 Worksheets.

Manipulate rows and columns

It is possible to add rows and columns by inserting them. Rows are inserted above existing rows and columns are inserted to the left of existing columns. Rows and columns can also be deleted.

EXAMPLE

In this example, you can see the option to insert a row which will be inserted above row 3.

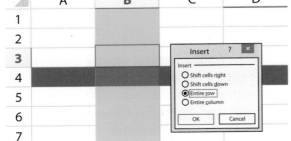

Figure 8.05 - Inserting a row.

Now you can see the effect of having added the new row.

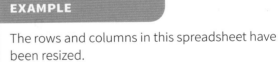

Figure 8.06 - An inserted row.

Rows and columns can be resized. Rows can be made taller or shorter and columns can be made wider or narrower. Rows are resized to enable different sizes of text to fit or to allow multiple lines of text within one cell or row. Columns are resized to allow more data to fit in the column or to save space by narrowing the column.

EXAMPLE

The rows and columns in this spreadsheet have been resized.

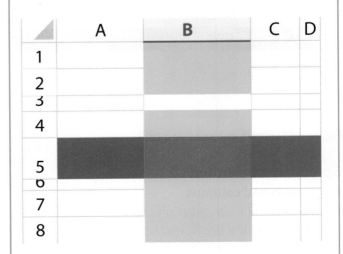

Figure 8.07 - Height and width resized.

It is possible to hide a row or column. Rows or columns are hidden because they may contain information that does not need to be seen by the user or they may contain private or confidential data that should not be seen by the user.

EXAMPLE

Here you can see the process of hiding column C.

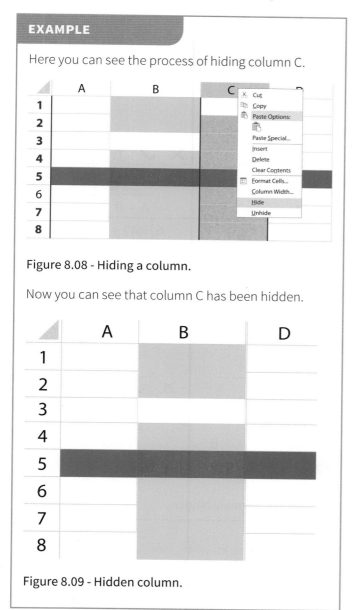

Figure 8.08 - Hiding a column.

Now you can see that column C has been hidden.

Figure 8.09 - Hidden column.

TASK

CD 8.01 Rows and columns

Open CD 8.01 Rows and columns.
1 Insert a row above row 5.
2 Delete column C.
3 Increase the height of row 1.
4 Decrease the width of column B.
5 Hide rows 2 and 3.

Spreadsheet security

Depending on the software being used, different parts of spreadsheets can be secured in a variety of ways. The simplest form of security is to protect a whole workbook from having any new worksheets added or existing worksheets removed.

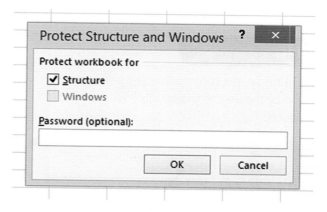

Figure 8.10 - Workbook protection.

Following on from this, it is possible to protect a worksheet from having any changes made to it.

EXAMPLE

In this example, the worksheet is protected to the extent that no changes can be made to any data and no data can be selected. No columns can be added and no rows can be added. Cells and rows cannot be formatted. This is useful if the whole worksheet contains just output data or a data table.

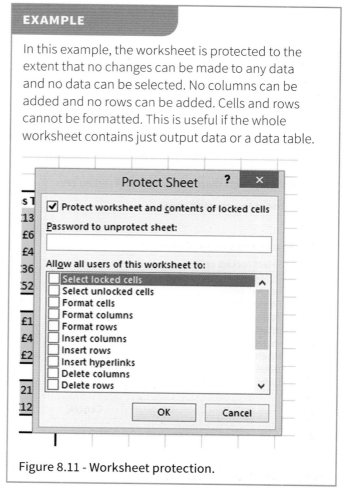

Figure 8.11 - Worksheet protection.

It is also possible to protect a worksheet but allow the user to change certain cells within that worksheet. This enables a developer to protect all the formatting, titles and structure but allow the user to enter and change input data. To do this, cells that are allowed to be edited must be unlocked prior to protecting the worksheet. It is then necessary to protect the sheet but allow unlocked cells to be selected.

EXAMPLE

In this example, the commission and prices can be changed by the user so those cells have been set to be unlocked.

Figure 8.12 - Unlocked cell.

Now that those cells have been unlocked, the sheet can be protected and only the unlocked cells can be selected.

Figure 8.13 - Worksheet protection with unlocked cells.

Cells can also be protected so that the **formula** cannot be seen by a user. This may be used to prevent users from seeing how certain confidential calculations are made but still letting them see the results of the calculation based on changing input data.

EXAMPLE

In this example, there is a formula in cell C2. It is currently visible.

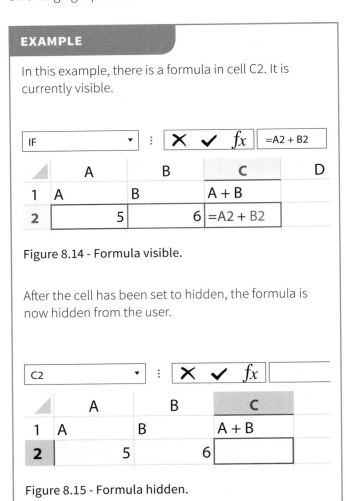

Figure 8.14 - Formula visible.

After the cell has been set to hidden, the formula is now hidden from the user.

Figure 8.15 - Formula hidden.

There will be occasions when some users will be allowed to change some data but not all data. In this case, it is possible to protect a worksheet but allow a specific range of cells to be edited by users who have knowledge of the correct password, or by selected users within the computer network.

EXAMPLE

In this example, the prices cells are left unlocked but the commission cell (B2) has been locked. In order to allow some users to edit the commission, a password has been set on that cell so that anybody with the password can edit the cell.

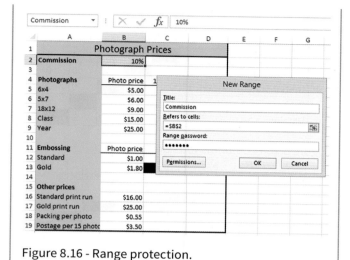

Figure 8.16 - Range protection.

Format a spreadsheet
Format data type

Cells within a spreadsheet can be formatted for an appropriate data type. Dates can be formatted to be dd/mm/yyyy where dd is the day, mm is the month and yyyy is the year. In countries like the USA, the date would be formatted mm/dd/yyyy. It is also possible to display the whole month, use leading zeros for days and months and use four digits or two digits for the year. Times can be formatted to include hours, minutes and seconds or just hours and minutes. Some times may have a.m. or p.m. whereas others will use a 24-hour clock.

Cells can be set to contain text. This is particularly useful if a set of numbers need to be entered that start with zero. Numeric cells can be set to include a specific number of decimal places including no decimal places. Currency can also be set to include a specific number of decimal places, and the currency symbol can also be chosen.

A number can be set as a percentage, in which case the number is divided by 100. For example, 58% is actually used in calculations as 0.58. Decimals can be entered into a cell and turned into fractions. For example, entering 0.25 would give a fraction of ¼.

107

TASK

CD 8.02 Worksheets

1 Open CD 8.02 Worksheets.xls
  a Try to add or delete a worksheet. The workbook has been protected to prevent this from happening.
  b Unprotect the workbook using the password 'openme'. Now try to add a new worksheet.
2 Select the Invoice worksheet.
  a Try to select any cell. This worksheet has been protected completely to prevent this from happening.
  b Unprotect the worksheet using the password 'payment'. Now try to select cells and make changes to data.
3 Protect the Breakdown worksheet so that no changes can be made at all.
4 Open the Prices worksheet.
  a Try to change one of the titles in column A. These cells are locked so that you cannot edit them.
  b Now try to change the prices of the photos. These cells have been unlocked so the prices can be changed.
  c Now try to change the commission rate in cell B2 (10%). Notice how an additional password is required to do this. This is because this cell has been set to allow users with that password to change it.
  d Enter the password 'special' and then change the rate of commission.
5 Open the Purchases worksheet.
  a Lock the cells in columns A, B and C. Unlock the cells in columns D and E. Then protect the worksheet and see what you can and cannot change.

EXAMPLE

CD 8.03 Data types

These examples from CD 8.03 Data types show different ways in which data can be formatted according to the data type. Notice how C4 contains text because, although it looks like a number, it is not really a number because it starts with zero.

	A	B	C
1	Data Type	Example 1	Example 2
2	Date	02/05/2015	02 May 2015
3	Time	3:44 PM	15:44
4	Next	abcdefg	09876
5	Numeric	25	25.33
6	Currency	$15.45	₱15.45
7	Percentage	25%	0.30%
8	Fractions	1/4	4/5

Figure 8.17 - Data types.

TASK

💿 CD 8.04 Data types task

Open CD 8.04 Data types task.

1. Change cell B2 to be a date with no leading zeros for the day and month and two digits for the year.
2. Change cell C2 to be a date with leading zeros for the day, the full name of the month and four digits for the year.
3. Change cell B3 to be a time with a.m./p.m.
4. Change cell C3 to be a time with hours, minutes and seconds.
5. Enter the value 0382 in cell B4. What happens?
6. Change cell C4 to be text and then enter the value 0382. What is different from B4?
7. Change cell B5 to have two decimal places. What happens?
8. Change cell C5 to have one decimal place. What happens?
9. Change cell B6 to be currency in euros with two decimal places. What happens?
10. Change cell C6 to be currency in Japanese yen with two decimal places. What happens?
11. Change cell B7 to be a percentage. What happens?
12. Change cell C7 to be a percentage. What happens?
13. Change cells B8 and C8 to be fractions up to one digit. Are they both correct? What do you think needs to be done to fix this?

Text orientation

Often it is difficult to fit all the necessary text into a column title without the column becoming too wide. In these circumstances, the text **orientation** can change so it is diagonal or vertical.

EXAMPLE

This spreadsheet shows the scores between international football teams. The number of goals scored by the team is shown in each row and the number of goals scored against a team is shown in each column. You will notice that in the first version the columns are too narrow to fit in the full team name and in the second version the columns are too wide.

	A	B	C	D	E	F
1		Japan	Mace	Unite	Pakis	Ukrai
2	Japan			3	2	4	1
3	Macedonia	2		3	0	0
4	United States of America	1	0		0	2
5	Pakistan	2	3	2		0
6	Ukraine	0	1	2	5	

Figure 8.18a - Columns too narrow.

	A	B	C	D	E	F
1		Japan	Macedonia	United States of America	Pakistan	Ukraine
2	Japan			3	2	4	1
3	Macedonia	2		3	0	0
4	United States of America	1	0		0	2
5	Pakistan	2	3	2		0
6		0	1	2	5	

Figure 8.18b - Columns too wide.

To overcome this problem, the text can be orientated vertically.

	A	B	C	D	E	F
1		Japan	Macedonia	United States of America	Pakistan	Ukraine
2	Japan		3	2	4	1
3	Macedonia	2		3	0	0
4	United States of America	1	0		0	2
5	Pakistan	2	3	2		0
6	Ukraine	0	1	2	5	

Figure 8.19 - Columns rotated vertically.

Alignment

By default, the **alignment** of text is to the left and numbers are aligned to the right. However, it is possible to change the way that data is aligned within columns. Data can be aligned to the left, right or centre.

EXAMPLE

One problem that often occurs is when different numbers of decimal places are used in the same column. The numbers are aligned to the right of the cell rather than by the decimal point.

	D
3	87.23
4	18.5
5	23.56
6	34.23472

Figure 8.20 - Decimal point alignment problem.

Unlike a word processor, it is not possible to change the alignment to be by the decimal point. Therefore, the number of decimal places needs to be made equal.

	D
3	87.230
4	18.500
5	23.560
6	34.235

Figure 8.21 - Decimal point alignment problem solved.

TASK

 CD 8.05 Alignment

Open CD 8.05 Alignment. This shows the election results for three areas of the UK in 2015.
1 Change the names of the parties in C2 to P2 to be vertical orientation.
2 Increase the height of row 2 if necessary.
3 Change the names of the parties to be centred.
4 Change the number of votes in C3 to I5 to be right aligned.
5 Change the number of decimal places for the percentages in K3 to P5 to be one decimal place.
6 Change the titles in B2 to B5 to be right aligned.

Cell emphasis

Cell emphasis is about changing a cell so that it stands out from the others. There are lots of ways this can be done, including changing data to be bold, italic, underlined, in a different font and in a different font size.

EXAMPLE

The cells below have been emphasised as indicated.

	A	B	C
1	colour of text		
2			
3	shading of cell		
4			
5	cell borders		
6			
7	merging 2 cells together		
8			

Figure 8.22 - Cell emphasis.

Comments

Spreadsheets can contain a lot of data and some of it may need additional information to explain what it is. However, there may not be space for that information or it may be too confusing to include the information with the data. Therefore comments can be added to cells that can be seen when selected.

109

EXAMPLE

Comments have been added to cells B5 and E2 for the Japan versus Pakistan game. Cell B5 has been selected and so the comment is showing. A comment is indicated in cell E2 by the red triangle.

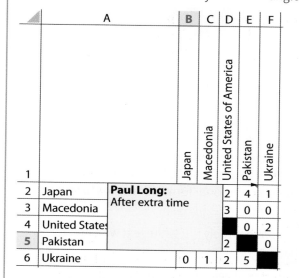

Figure 8.23 - Comments.

TASK

💿 CD 8.06 Emphasis

Open CD 8.06 Emphasis.
1 Merge cells A1 to D1.
2 Change cells A2, A4, A11 and A15 to be bold and font size 14.
3 Add borders to the bottom of cells B4, C4, B11, C11 and D11.
4 Add a thick blue border around cells A1 to D19.
5 Shade A1:D1 and A1:A19 in yellow.
6 Shade C13 and D13 in black.
7 Add a comment to cell B2 to read 'This is the commission a school will earn'.

Conditional formatting

Cells can be formatted based upon certain conditions being met. This is known as conditional formatting. Conditions can include:

- values in a cell that are equal to a set criterion (e.g. = "Good")
- values in a cell that are greater or less than a set criterion (e.g. >5)
- values in a cell that are between set criteria (e.g. between 2 and 10)
- values in a cell that are duplicated elsewhere in the worksheet
- values that are above or below average
- a scale of values from lowest to highest.

EXAMPLE

💿 CD 8.07 Conditional formatting

In CD 8.07 Conditional formatting, a questionnaire has been sent out and respondents have had to give a priority to each question from 1 to 5 or x if they disagree completely. The average response, total x responses and total blank responses has been calculated. The following conditional formatting rules have been used:

- Respondent reply = 1: white text with green shading
- Respondent reply >= 4: white text with red shading

- Respondent reply = x: white text with red shading
- Respondent reply between 2 and 3: yellow shading
- Average response < 2: white text with green shading
- Average response >= 4: white text with red shading
- Average response between 2.0 and 2.9: yellow shading
- Total x >= 4: red text with light red shading

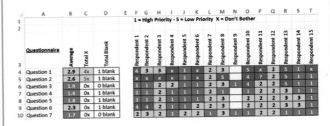

Figure 8.24 - Conditional formatting.

TASK

💿 CD 8.08 Member list

Open 8.08 Member list and conditionally format cells according to the following rules:
1 Female members: pink shading
2 Male members: white text, blue shading
3 Full, junior or patron members: green text
4 Lapsed members: red text
5 Do not email = TRUE: yellow shading with red border
6 Number of years >=10: green text
7 Number of years between 5 and 9: purple text.

Page formatting

Pages within a spreadsheet can be formatted in a variety of ways as shown in Table 8.01.

Page setup	The size of paper to print on (e.g. A4, Letter) can be set as well as the orientation (portrait or landscape). It's also possible to decide whether to print gridlines for all the cells, whether to include row and column headings and whether certain rows will be repeated at the top of each page.

Fit to page	Sometimes large spreadsheets cover several pieces of paper. In order to make it easier to follow the data and save paper, it is possible to set the spreadsheet to fit a specific number of pages. Options include, fit all columns on one sheet, fit all rows on one sheet, fit the sheet to one page or fit the sheet to a specified number of pages across and down.
Margins	The top, bottom, left and right margins can be adjusted to provide space at the edges (e.g. for hole punches) or to reduce the space at the edge and provide more space on the paper for printing.
Header and footer	Information can be included at the top and bottom of each printed spreadsheet. This could include the title and author of the document, page number, file name and date.

Table 8.01 - Formatting pages.

TASK

CD 8.09 Page formatting

Open CD 8.09 Page formatting which currently requires 20 pages to print.

1 Add a header of 'Chapter 8 figure list'.
2 Remove gridlines from printing and also on the sheet view.
3 Remove row and column headings from printing.
4 Add a footer of "Page # of n" where # is the current page number and n is the total number of pages.
5 Change the settings described above so that the document fits onto just three pages.

Create formulae and functions
Formulae

A formula uses basic arithmetic calculations. These are plus, minus, divide and multiply, for example =B5+B6. There is no limit to the number of arithmetic calculations that can be used, for example =(B5+B6)*3/100-(D1-D2).

EXAMPLE

This spreadsheet is used to calculate the cost of broadband, TV and phone packages. The formula in cell B9 adds up the monthly costs of line rental (B6), TV (B7) and broadband (B8) then multiples the result by 6. Finally it adds any setup costs from B3.

	A	B	C
1		**Broadband 1**	**Broadband 1**
2		Original	Family
3	Initial cost	$ 15.00	
4			
5	1st 6 month		
6	Line rental	$ 15.40	$ 15.40
7	TV	$ 10.75	$ 16.50
8	Broadband	$ 20.00	$ 20.00
9	Total 6 months	=6*(B8+B7+B6)+B3	

Figure 8.25 - A formula.

Relative cell references

Relative cell referencing is used when you want the content of a cell to change based on its relation to its row and column position. Often the formulae being used are performing the same calculation for a whole row or column. When this happens, it is possible to replicate the formula rather than typing it in each time.

EXAMPLE

This spreadsheet lists the number of hours it takes to produce a promotional leaflet, the cost to be charged for the leaflet and the quantity to be produced. The total to be charged is then calculated by multiplying the cost (C4) by the quantity (D4).

	A	B	C	D	E
3	Job	Hours	Cost	Quantity	Total
4	A5 Leaflet	1	$ 12.50	3	=C4*D4
5	A4 Leaflet	1.5	$ 18.75	1	
6	A3 Leaflet	2.5	$ 25.00	2	

Figure 8.26 - Replication 1.

One way of entering the formula in E5 for the total cost of A4 leaflets is to type it in again but changing row 4 to row 5 so the formula would be =C5*D5. However, it is much quicker and also more accurate to replicate the formula by copying it from E4 and pasting it into E5 and E6.

	A	B	C	D	E
3	Job	Hours	Cost	Quantity	Total
4	A5 Leaflet	1	12.50	3	=C4*D4
5	A4 Leaflet	1.5	18.75	1	=C5*D5
6	A3 Leaflet	2.5	25.00	2	=C6*D6

Figure 8.27 - Replication 2.

The cell references used in the formula in the previous example were relative cell references. This is because they point to another cell in a position relative to the current position. When referring to C4, it is pointing to a cell that is two columns to the left of column E. When referring to E4 it is pointing to a cell that is one column to the left of column E. Therefore, when the formula is replicated down to rows 5 and 6, the references continue to point to the same columns.

> **DISCUSSION POINT**
>
> The same process happens when copying formulae across a spreadsheet. The formula in B3 calculates the number of kilometres travelled. When it has been replicated to columns C and D, instead of the row numbers changing, the column letters change. B2 is referring relatively to one row above and B1 is referring relatively to two rows above.
>
> | | A | B | C | D |
> |---|---|---|---|---|
> | 1 | Start distance | 38029 | 38098 | 39273 |
> | 2 | End distance | 38087 | 39137 | 39410 |
> | 3 | Distance travelled | =B2-B1 | =C2-C1 | =D2-D1 |
>
> Figure 8.28 - Replication across.

Formulae can be used to retrieve a value from another worksheet. To do this you should include the name of the worksheet before the cell reference.

> **EXAMPLE**
>
> To use the value in cell B4 in a worksheet called 'Data source', use the following formula:
>
> ="Data source"!B4
>
> The inverted commas are only required if the name of the worksheet includes a space, but the exclamation mark must always be used.
>
> The following formula will multiply the value in B4 on the 'Data source' worksheet by C15 on the current worksheet:
>
> ="Data source"!B4 * C15

Absolute cell references

> **TASK**
>
> CD 8.10 Absolute references
>
> Open CD 8.10 Absolute references and use the worksheet Absolute 1, which is similar to the example used for relative cell references. The cost is calculated by multiplying the hourly rate in B1 by the number of hours in B4.
> 1 Replicate (copy) the formula from C4 to C5 and C6.
> 2 What has gone wrong?
> 3 Why has it gone wrong?

Absolute referencing is used when you do not want a cell reference to change when other cells are filled in, or when replicating formulae.

To stop a row from being changed, a $ symbol must be put before the row number. So C5 would become C$5. This makes the row an absolute reference but B is still relative.

> **TASK**
>
> CD 8.10 Absolute references
>
> Continuing with CD 8.10 Absolute references and the worksheet Absolute 1:
> 4 Change the formula in C4 to be =B$1*B4.
> 5 Replicate (copy) the formula from C4 to C5 and C6.
> 6 Examine the formulae in C5 and C6.
> 7 Which cell references have changed and which have not?

To stop a column from being changed, a $ symbol must be put before the column letter. So C5 would become $C5. This makes the column an absolute reference but leaves the row as a relative reference.

To stop both the row and column from being changed, a $ symbol must be put before both the column letter and row number. So C5 would become C5. This makes the whole cell reference an absolute reference.

> **TASK**
>
> CD 8.10 Absolute references
>
> Continuing with CD 8.010 Absolute references, open worksheet Absolute 2. This worksheet is used to calculate the wage bill each month.

8 Look at the formula in C4 which calculates the cost of workers in week 1 month 1.
9 Make any changes necessary to the formula in C4 before replicating it for months 2 to 4.
10 Try copying the formula from C4 to E4 for week 2 workers.
11 What has gone wrong?
12 Why has it gone wrong?
13 Change the formula in C4 so that when replicated both across and down it will still work.
14 Now replicate the formula down column C and across to columns E, G and I.
15 Complete the spreadsheet with formulae in column J.

Named cells and ranges

Ranges were introduced earlier in this chapter. A named cell is when a name is used instead of the cell reference and a named range is when a name is used instead of cell references.

Named cells can be used as absolute cell references. When referring to a named cell, whenever it is replicated it will still point to the same named cell.

Named ranges can also be used within formulae. It is easier to understand formulae with named cells and ranges than to understand formulae with cell references.

EXAMPLE

In 8.11 Tax rate, cells C4:C7 have been named as 'TaxCharged'. Instead of using a function of =SUM(C4:C8) for the total tax charged, the named range can be used instead.

	A	B	C	D
1	**Tax rate**	15%		
2				
3	**Product**	**Cost**	**Tax**	**Cost inc tax**
4	6 × 4 frame	$12.00	$ 1.80	
5	5 × 7 frame	$15.00	$ 2.25	
6	10 × 8 frame	$18.00	$ 2.70	
7	12 × 8 frame	$21.00	$ 3.15	
8	Total tax charged:		=SUM(Tax Charged)	

Figure 8.30 - Total tax charged name range.

EXAMPLE

CD 8.11 Tax rate

CD 8.11 Tax rate contains a named cell of 'Taxrate' which is cell B1. The formula in C4 is =B4*TaxRate

	A	B	C
1	**Tax rate**	0.15	
2			
3	**Product**	**Cost**	**Tax**
4	6 × 4 frame	12	=B4*TaxRate
5	5 × 7 frame	15	=B5*TaxRate
6	10 × 8 frame	18	=B6*TaxRate
7	12 × 8 frame	21	=B7*TaxRate

Figure 8.29 - Tax rate named cell.

When this formula is replicated down column C, the reference to TaxRate remains the same because it is an absolute reference.

DISCUSSION POINT

When a range of vertical cells has been named, it is possible to make reference to any individual cell in that range by using the name of the range, as long as the reference is being made in the same row.

	A	B	C	D
1	Tax rate	0.15		
2				
3	Product	Cost	Tax	Cost inc tax
4	6 x 4 frame	12	=B4*TaxRate	=Cost+TaxCharged
5	5 x 7 frame	15	=B5*TaxRate	=Cost+TaxCharged
6	10 x 8 frame	18	=B6*TaxRate	=Cost+TaxCharged
7	12 x 8 frame	21	=B7*TaxRate	=Cost+TaxCharged

Figure 8.31 - Same row named range.

In 8.11 Tax rate, cells C4 to C7 have been named 'TaxCharged' and cells B4 to B7 have been named 'Cost'. The formula in D4 calculates the cost including tax by adding the Cost to the Tax. To do this, it makes reference to the whole named range for Cost and the whole named range for TaxRate. The spreadsheet software can see that the range is in the same row so it uses the values in the same row from the Cost and TaxRate ranges. This can be replicated down and the reference is relative rather than absolute because it is relative to the same row.

TASK

 CD 8.11 Tax rate

Open CD 8.11 Tax rate.
1 Change the formula in C4 so that it uses a named range for the cost.
2 Replicate this formula to C5:C7.
3 Use a named range to calculate the total cost in B8.
4 Name the range for cost including tax.
5 Use a named range to calculate the total cost including tax in D8.

TASK

 CD 8.12 Times table

Open CD 8.12 Times table which will be used to show the times table.
1 Create a formula in B2 that will calculate the value in B1 multiplied by the value in A2. Do not use numbers, only use cell references.
2 Change the formula so that it has absolute references where needed so that you can replicate the formula across and down. You should only need one formula.

Functions

A **function** is a ready-made formula representing a complex calculation, for example =SUM(A5:B10) or =AVERAGE(cost). It is a reserved word within the spreadsheet software that processes a series of pre-defined formulae.

Summary functions

Table 8.02 shows some of the summary functions.

Function	Purpose	Example
SUM	Calculates the total of values within a range.	=SUM(B3:E3)
AVERAGE	Calculates the average of values within a range.	=AVERAGE(B3:E3)
MINIMUM	Calculates the smallest value within a range.	=MIN(B3:E3)
MAXIMUM	Calculates the largest value within a range.	=MAX(B3:E3)

Table 8.02 - Summary functions.

EXAMPLE

 CD 8.13 Student marks

CD 8.13 Student marks calculates the total, average, minimum and maximum mark that each student scores in a set of four tests. In row 2, the total has been calculated by adding up each cell individually using a formula. In row 3, this has been done using a function that requires much less effort. In row 2, the average has been calculated using a formula, but it is necessary to know how many marks there are to complete this calculation. In row 3, this has been done using a function which does not require knowledge of the number of values to be averaged and will allow extra values to be added in the future by inserting columns.

	A	B	C	D	E	F	G	H	I
1	Student	Mark 1	Mark 2	Mark 3	Mark 4	Total	Average	Minimum	Maximum
2	Name 1	98	40	36	84	=(B2+C2+D2+E2)	=F2/4		
3	Name 2	31	67	61	77	=SUM(B3:E3)	=AVERAGE(B3:E3)	=MIN(B3:E3)	=MAX(B3:E3)
4	Name 3	62	58	29	38	=SUM(B4:E4)	=AVERAGE(B4:E4)	=MIN(B4:E4)	=MAX(B4:E4)
5	Name 4	64	83	85	27	=SUM(B5:E5)	=AVERAGE(B5:E5)	=MIN(B5:E5)	=MAX(B5:E5)
6	Name 5	87	45	64	42	=SUM(B6:E6)	=AVERAGE(B6:E6)	=MIN(B6:E6)	=MAX(B6:E6)
7	Name 6	93	58	43	73	=SUM(B7:E7)	=AVERAGE(B7:E7)	=MIN(B7:E7)	=MAX(B7:E7)
8	Name 7	99	29	55	92	=SUM(B8:E8)	=AVERAGE(B8:E8)	=MIN(B8:E8)	=MAX(B8:E8)
9	Name 8	57	58	44	93	=SUM(B9:E9)	=AVERAGE(B9:E9)	=MIN(B9:E9)	=MAX(B9:E9)
10	Name 9	45	43	98	55	=SUM(B10:E10)	=AVERAGE(B10:E10)	=MIN(B10:E10)	=MAX(B10:E10)

Figure 8.32 - Summary functions.

TASK

 CD 8.13 Student marks

Open CD 8.13 Student marks. Use functions to calculate the average, minimum and maximum mark for each of the four tests.

Rounding functions

Numbers can be rounded to whole numbers or decimal places. Table 8.03 shows the functions that can be used.

Function	Purpose	Example
INTEGER	Returns the whole number value of a decimal number (the value before the decimal point).	=INT(A2)
ROUND	Rounds a number to the nearest decimal place specified. This example rounds the value in B2 to three decimal places.	=ROUND(A2,3)
ROUNDUP	Rounds a number up to the nearest decimal place specified. This example rounds up the value in B2 to two decimal places.	=ROUNDUP(A2,2)
ROUNDDOWN	Rounds a number down to the nearest decimal place specified. This example rounds down the value in B2 to four decimal places.	=ROUNDDOWN(A2,4)

Table 8.03 - Rounding functions.

EXAMPLE

CD 8.14 Rounding

In CD 8.14 Rounding you can see how the functions above have been used:

	A	B	C	D	E
1	Original number	Integer	Round	Round up	Round down
2	25817.32817	=INT(A2)	=ROUND(A2,3)	=ROUNDUP(A2,2)	=ROUNDDOWN(A2,4)
3	3852.876985	=INT(A3)	=ROUND(A3,3)	=ROUNDUP(A3,2)	=ROUNDDOWN(A3,4)
4	928.2341	=INT(A4)	=ROUND(A4,3)	=ROUNDUP(A4,2)	=ROUNDDOWN(A4,4)
5	0.03256	=INT(A5)	=ROUND(A5,3)	=ROUNDUP(A5,2)	=ROUNDDOWN(A5,4)

Figure 8.33 - Rounding functions.

You can also see the results of the calculations made by the functions:

	A	B	C	D	E
1	Original number	Integer	Round	Round up	Round down
2	25817.32817	25817	25817.328	25817.33	25817.3281
3	3852.876985	3852	3852.877	3852.88	3852.8769
4	928.2341	928	928.234	928.24	928.2341
5	0.03256	0	0.033	0.04	0.0325

Figure 8.34 - Rounding values.

TASK

Create a new spreadsheet and experiment with the four rounding functions using different values for decimal places.

DISCUSSION POINT

What happens if you change the number of decimal places to a negative number? How does this relate to rounding to significant figures? Notice how -1 rounds to tens, -2 rounds to hundreds and -3 rounds to thousands. The minus number relates to rounding to the power of 10 rather than rounding to a set number of significant figures.

Indices

If you need to calculate indices (powers), then the POWER function can be used. It uses the syntax =POWER(number,power). For example, =POWER(6,3) would raise 6 to the power of 3. It is also possible to use the ^ symbol and so =6^3 would also raise 6 to the power of 3.

EXAMPLE

 CD 8.15 Powers

CD 8.15 Powers raises the numbers in column A to the power given in row 1.

	A	B	C	D
1	Original number	Power 2	Power 3	Power 4
2	4	=POWER(A2,2)	=A2^3	=POWER(A2,4)
3	3	=POWER(A3,2)	=A3^3	=POWER(A3,4)
4	7	=POWER(A4,2)	=A4^3	=POWER(A4,4)

Figure 8.35 - Powers.

TASK

 CD 8.15 Powers

Open CD 8.15 Powers which contains random values for the number to be raised and random values for the power.

1　Create a function in B8 that raises the value in A4 to the power given in B7. Do not use any numbers, only use cell references.
2　Using absolute cell referencing where needed, copy the function from B8 across the row and down the column. You should not need to change any cell references if you have used absolute references properly.

Date and time functions

Calculations can be performed on dates and times.

Function	Purpose	Example
DAY	Calculates the day part of a date.	=DAY(B1)
MONTH	Calculates the month part of a date.	=MONTH(B1)
YEAR	Calculates the year part of a date.	=YEAR(B1)
DATE	Calculates the date from a given year, month and day.	=DATE(B4,B3,B2)
HOUR	Calculates the hours part of a time.	=HOUR(B8)
MINUTE	Calculates the minutes part of a time.	=MINUTE(B8)
SECOND	Calculates the seconds part of a time.	=SECOND(B8)
TIME	Calculates the time from given hours, minutes and seconds.	=TIME(B9,B10,B11)
NOW	Gives the current date and time (can be formatted for just date or just time).	=NOW()

Table 8.04 - Date and time functions.

TASK

 CD 8.16 Date and time

Explore CD 8.16 Date and time.

Text functions

Calculations can be performed on text to extract parts of text, join text together, calculate the length of text or change the case of text.

Function	Purpose	Example
CONCATENATE	Joins together text values.	=CONCATENATE (A1,B1,C1) =A1&B1&C1 =A1 & ”.“ & B1 & ”@” & C1 & ”.it.com”
LEFT	Extracts the furthest left characters.	=LEFT(A1,4)
RIGHT	Extracts the furthest right characters.	=RIGHT(A1,2)
LEN	Calculates the length of a string.	=LEN(A1)
UPPER	Converts text into upper case.	=UPPER(A1)
LOWER	Converts text into lower case.	=LOWER(A1)

Table 8.05 - Text functions.

TASK

Look at the spreadsheet in Figure 8.36 and the function used to calculate the username of students in a school.

	A	B	C	D
1	Forename	Surname	Year	Username
2	Harjinder	Singh	2003	=UPPER(RIGHT(C2,2)&LEFT(A2,3)&LEFT(B2,3))
3	Abigail	Drew	1999	=UPPER(RIGHT(C3,2)&LEFT(A3,3)&LEFT(B3,3))
4	Poonam	Patel	2001	=UPPER(RIGHT(C4,2)&LEFT(A4,3)&LEFT(B4,3))

Figure 8.36 - Text functions.

1　Describe what the function does and how the username is formed.
2　Calculate the usernames for each of the three students.
3　Write a function that will work out their email addresses. Their email addresses are surname.i.yy@ textfunctionschool.edu where surname is their surname, i is the first initial of their forename and yy is the last two digits of the year they joined the school. The email address should be in lower case.

Lookup functions

Lookup functions will look up a value in a table and return another value in the same row or column. VLOOKUP is used to look for a value in a column and return a value from the same row. HLOOKUP is used to look for a value in a row and return a value from the same column.

The VLOOKUP function uses the syntax:

=VLOOKUP(Search Value, Lookup Table, Column, Match)

Search Value is the value being looked up in the table. Lookup Table is the range of cells that define the location of the table. Column is the number of the column that should be returned as the result in the matching row of the value that was found. Match defines whether an exact match should be found – TRUE for approximate match or FALSE for exact match.

EXAMPLE

 CD 8.17 Months

CD 8.17 Months contains a table in the worksheet 'Months' that lists the numbers that represent months, the three-letter shortened version of each month's name, the full name of each month and the French name of each month.

	A	B	C	D
1	Number	3 Letter	Month	Francais
2	1	Jan	January	Janvier
3	2	Feb	Febuary	Février
4	3	Mar	March	Mars
5	4	Apr	April	Avril
6	5	May	May	Mai
7	6	Jun	June	Juin
8	7	Jul	July	Julliet
9	8	Aug	August	Août
10	9	Sep	September	Septembre
11	10	Oct	October	Octobre
12	11	Nov	November	Novembre
13	12	Dec	December	Décembre

Figure 8.37 - Lookup table.

The worksheet 'Number' asks the user to enter a number that represents a month and it will then look up that number in the table and return the three-letter code, full month name and French month name.

	A	B
1	Enter the number of the month:	
2	2	
3		
4	3 Letter code:	Feb
5	Month:	Febuary
6	Francais:	Février

Figure 8.38 - Number worksheet.

These are the VLOOKUP functions that were used:

	A	B
1	Enter the number of the month:	
2	2	
3		
4	3 Letter code:	=VLOOKUP(A2, Months!A2:D13,2,FALSE)
5	Month:	=VLOOKUP(A2, Months!A2:D13,3,FALSE)
6	Francais:	=VLOOKUP(A2, Months!A2:D13,4,FALSE)

Figure 8.39 - Lookup functions.

VLOOKUP functions can also be replicated in the same way as any other function. The main problem with this though is that the lookup table cell references will change as they are copied down the rows.

TASK

 CD 8.18 VLookup price categories

Open CD 8.18 VLookup price categories which calculates the prices of tickets purchased for a show.
1 Look at the lookup table on the Ticket Categories worksheet. It shows the prices for each category.
2 Look at the function in C2 on the Ticket Sales worksheet. Describe what this function is doing.
3 Replicate the function from C2 down the column.
4 What has gone wrong?
5 Why has it gone wrong?

One way of overcoming this is to change all the cell references in the lookup table (but not the lookup value) to be absolute cell references. An easier way of overcoming this is to name the lookup table as a named range.

117

118

TASK

💿 CD 8.18 VLookup price categories

Continue using CD 8.18 VLookup Price Categories.

6 Name the range containing the lookup table on the Ticket Categories worksheet (do not include the titles in the range).

7 Change the VLOOKUP function in C3 to include the named range instead of the range 'Ticket Categories'!A1:B5

8 Replicate the function from C2 down the column and it should find the correct prices for each category of ticket.

So far you have seen VLOOKUP functions that find an exact match within a table. However, there are occasions when an exact match is not required, but the closest value below or equal to the search value should be found.

EXAMPLE

💿 CD 8.19 Exam results

CD 8.19 Exam results includes a lookup table of the minimum mark required to achieve each grade. This table has been called 'GradeBoundaries' as the named range.

	A	B
12	**Mark**	**Grade**
13	0	U
14	24	E
15	30	D
16	36	C
17	42	B
18	48	A

Figure 8.40 - Non-matching VLOOKUP table.

Each student's marks are entered in cells B2 to B10 which has been named 'Mark'. The VLOOKUP

function is then used to look up the Mark in the GradeBoundaries table and return the second column, which is the grade. Not many of the marks are an exact match and so the TRUE element at the end of the function means that the closest mark below or equal to the student's mark will be found and the grade returned as the answer.

	A	B	C	D
1	**Student**	**Mark**	**Grade**	**Function**
2	1	5	U	=VLOOKUP(Mark,GradeBoundaries,2,TRUE)
3	2	30	D	=VLOOKUP(Mark,GradeBoundaries,2,TRUE)
4	3	35	D	=VLOOKUP(Mark,GradeBoundaries,2,TRUE)
5	4	22	U	=VLOOKUP(Mark,GradeBoundaries,2,TRUE)
6	5	49	A	=VLOOKUP(Mark,GradeBoundaries,2,TRUE)
7	6	47	B	=VLOOKUP(Mark,GradeBoundaries,2,TRUE)
8	7	48	A	=VLOOKUP(Mark,GradeBoundaries,2,TRUE)
9	8	39	C	=VLOOKUP(Mark,GradeBoundaries,2,TRUE)
10	9	25	E	=VLOOKUP(Mark,GradeBoundaries,2,TRUE)

Figure 8.41 - Non-matching VLOOKUP function.

It is essential that the lookup table's first column is in order from lowest to highest for this to work.

The HLOOKUP function works in a very similar way to the VLOOKUP function, but instead of searching for values down the table, it searches for values across the table.

The HLOOKUP function uses the syntax:

=HLOOKUP(Search Value, Lookup Table, Row, Match)

Search Value, Lookup Table and Match are the same as in the VLOOKUP function. Row is the number of the row that should be returned as the result in the matching column of the value that was found.

EXAMPLE

💿 CD 8.20 HLookup

CD 8.20 HLookup lists products and their prices and the discounts that are currently being applied to each of those products. The function used in D2 for the Discount Rate is:

=HLOOKUP(C2,DiscountRates,2,FALSE)

The discount rate code (C2) is looked up in the named range DiscountRates (B13:F14) and the corresponding rate in the second row of the table is returned as the discount rate.

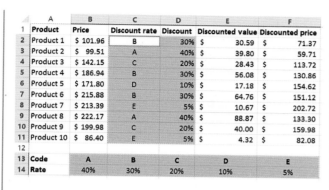

Figure 8.42 - Hlookup.

Nested formula

A nested formula is one which can include more than one function or formula. Each nested formula or function is surrounded by brackets and will be calculated before the formula or function surrounding it is completed.

EXAMPLE

 CD 8.21 Nested IFs

CD 8.21 Nested IFs calculates the average mark using separate total and average functions in columns F and G.

Figure 8.43 - Nested IF.

In column H, a nested formula has been used to calculate whether each student is above or below the average mark. It examines the average mark for the student in column G, then divides the total of all the average marks by the number of average marks to see if column G is higher. If column G is higher then "Above" is displayed otherwise "Below" is displayed.

TASK

 CD 8.22 Profit calculator

Open CD 8.22 Profit calculator.
1 Create a single nested formula for E2 that will calculate the total profit made for product 1.
2 Replicate this formula for products 2 and 3.
3 Without using the AVERAGE function, create a nested formula to calculate the average total profit in E5.

Conditional functions

The functions you have seen so far will always perform their calculation. However, a conditional function will only perform the calculation if certain criteria are met.

EXAMPLE

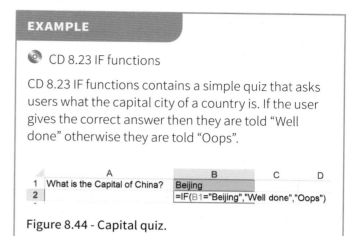 CD 8.23 IF functions

CD 8.23 IF functions contains a simple quiz that asks users what the capital city of a country is. If the user gives the correct answer then they are told "Well done" otherwise they are told "Oops".

Figure 8.44 - Capital quiz.

An IF function has three elements as shown in Table 8.06.

Element	Purpose	Example
Condition	Specifies the rules to be checked.	B1 = "Beijing"
True Value	Specifies what to display if the condition is met.	"Well Done"
False Value	Specifies what to display if the condition is not met.	"Oops"

Table 8.06 - IF function elements.

TASK

CD 8.23 IF functions

Open CD 8.23 IF functions and use the Capitals Quiz worksheet.
1 Why does the spreadsheet say "Oops" when the answer for the capital of France is correct?
2 Fix the IF function for the capital of France so it works properly.
3 Test your function by entering an incorrect answer.
4 Add another question in row 7 and write an IF function to give feedback to the user.

This is quite a slow way of creating a quiz. Try this more efficient method:
1 Put the answers to each question in column C next to where the user will put their answer in column B.
2 Change the IF function in B2 to be =IF(B1=C1,"Well done","Oops")

119

3 Now replicate this to the other two questions and write another two so you have five in total.

Notice how much quicker it is now to add the new questions because you don't have to keep editing the IF function. However, the user can see the answers.

Use security measures such as hiding columns and worksheet protection to hide the answers from the user.

Open the worksheet Mark Book.

1 Students need to get 75 marks or more to pass maths, otherwise they fail. Write a function in D4 to display Pass or Fail.
2 Replicate this function for the other maths results.
3 Students need to get 60 marks or more to pass English, otherwise they fail. Write a function in D12 to display Pass or Fail.
4 Replicate this function for the other English results.

DISCUSSION POINT

More than one criterion can be used by using AND or OR within the condition element of the IF function.

Nested IF

It is possible to have an IF function nested within another IF function. This can be useful if there are two or more alternative outputs. Sometimes the same result can be achieved with a lookup function.

EXAMPLE

 CD 8.21 Nested IFs

CD 8.21 Nested IFs contains a mark book on the Mark Book worksheet. Students who get a mark of 80 or above get a distinction. Those who get a mark below 40 get a fail. All other students get awarded a pass. Notice how a nested IF has been used to show the grades.

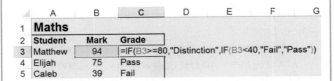

	A	B	C	D	E	F	G
1	**Maths**						
2	**Student**	**Mark**	**Grade**				
3	Matthew	94	=IF(B3>=80,"Distinction",IF(B3<40,"Fail","Pass"))				
4	Elijah	75	Pass				
5	Caleb	39	Fail				

Figure 8.45 - Nested IF example.

TASK

 CD 8.21 Nested IFs

Open CD 8.21 Nested IFs and use the worksheet Mark Book.

1 Create a lookup table for the grades.
2 Change the nested IF functions to lookup functions.

Using the same file, switch to the Ticket Sales worksheet which shows ticket sales for three different price categories.

1 Change the lookup function for the price to a nested IF function.
2 Replicate the function down the column.

Where the option for a lookup function exists, it is better to use this than a nested IF, especially if there are lots of options to choose from. However, sometimes decisions are made based on more than one item of data, in which case a nested IF function is the only possible option.

EXAMPLE

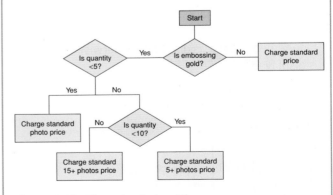 CD 8.24 Photo frames

Open CD 8.24 Photo frames which shows the charges made for a photo frame with a standard embossing or a gold embossing. The user can select Standard or Gold embossing and the quantity to purchase. The price can be determined by this algorithm:

Figure 8.46 - Flow chart algorithm.

A nested IF function is used to determine the price by following the same algorithm:

	A	B	C	D	E	F	G
1	Embossing	Photo price	5+ photos	15+ photos			
2	Standard	$ 1.00	$ 0.80	$ 0.70			
3	Gold	$ 1.80					
4							
5	Embossing:	Standard					
6	Quantity:	5					
7	Unit price:	=IF(Embossing="Gold",B3,IF(Quantity<5,B2,IF(Quantity<15,C2,D2)))					
8	Total price:	$ 4.00					

Figure 8.47 - Nested IF for unit price.

Conditional statistical functions

You have already been introduced to the SUM function and the AVERAGE function. Both of these have similar functions that will only perform that function if a certain condition is met. There is also a count function that will only count items that meet certain criteria.

Function	Purpose	Example
COUNTA	Counts all values in a range.	=COUNTA(H3:H200)
COUNTIF	Counts all values that meet a criterion within a range.	=COUNTIF(H3:H200,"Yes") Only counts cells that contain "Yes".
SUMIF	Adds up all values that meet a criterion within a range.	=SUMIF(J3:J200,"<0") Only adds up negative numbers.
AVERAGEIF	Calculates the average of all values that meet a criterion within a range.	=AVERAGEIF(J3:J200,">0") Only finds the average of positive numbers.

Table 8.07 - Conditional statistical functions.

EXAMPLE

CD 8.25 Maths results

CD 8.25 Maths results shows the marks and grades awarded to students taking a maths test. In cell

C3, a COUNTIF function is used to count only those students who achieved a Pass.

	A	B	C	D	E
1	**Maths**				
2	**Student**	**Mark**	**Grade**		
3	Matthew	91	Distinction		
4	Elijah	89	Distinction		
5	Caleb	51	Pass		
6	Joshua	38	Fail		
7	Huan	92	Distinction		
8	Junayna	42	Pass		
9	Yuki	32	Fail		
10	Menekse	54	Pass		
11					
12	Total students				
13	Passes		=COUNTIF(C3:C10,"Pass")		
14	Fails				
15	Distinctions				

Figure 8.48 - Maths results COUNTIF.

TASK

CD 8.25 Maths results

Open CD 8.25 Maths results used in the example above.
1 Use a function to count all the students in cell C12.
2 Use a function to count all the students who failed the test in C14.
3 Use a function to count all the students who achieved a distinction in cell C15.
4 Use functions to calculate the average distinction mark, pass mark and fail mark in cells C17 to C19.

CD 8.26 Member ratings

Open CD 8.26 Member ratings which shows how many meetings each member of a club has attended. Members who have attended 50 meetings or more are awarded "Gold member" status.
1 Use a function in B13 to calculate how many members have Gold member status.
2 Use a function in B14 to calculate the total number of meetings that have been attended by Gold members.

Validation rules

The principle of **validation** was introduced in Chapter 1. Spreadsheet software can apply validation rules to data that is input. If data passes the validation rule, then it will be accepted. If data fails the validation rule, then it will be rejected and an error message may be shown.

EXAMPLE

In this spreadsheet, the user is asked to enter a person's gender. They have two valid options – 'Male' or 'Female'. The user has accidentally entered 'Mal' which is not a valid option. An error message has appeared telling the user what to do to fix the problem.

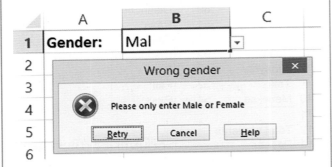

Figure 8.49 - Male/female validation fail.

This is the rule that had been set up:

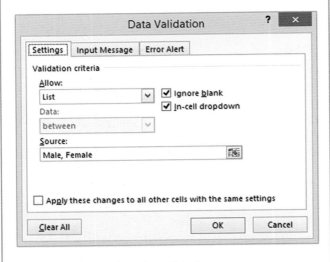

Figure 8.50 - Male/female validation setup.

The rule ensures that the only data that can be entered must exist in the list that contains 'Male' and 'Female'. It is a lookup in list method of validation.

TASK

Create a new spreadsheet.
1 Create a validation rule that will only allow the entry of 'Junior', 'Intermediate' or 'Senior'.
2 Set up an appropriate error message.

DISCUSSION POINT
Error messages must clearly tell the user what they have done wrong and what they should do to put it right. An error message that simply says 'Error' or 'Invalid Data' is not helpful to the user.

The validation rules that can be used in spreadsheet software include lookup in list, range, type (integer and real) and length. A range check can be set up with the following properties:

- between two values
- equal to a value
- not equal to a value
- greater than a value
- greater than or equal to a value
- less than a value
- less than or equal to a value.

EXAMPLE

This validation rule is a range check that checks input data is a whole number between 1 and 99.

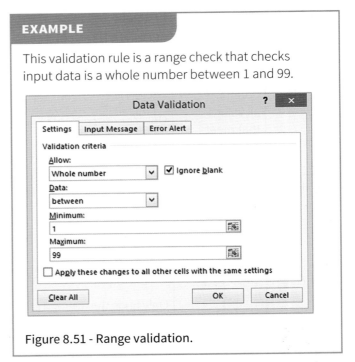

Figure 8.51 - Range validation.

TASK

 CD 8.27 Physics results

Open CD 8.27 Physics results which is ready for students' marks to be entered for tests 1, 2 and 3.
1 Create validation rules that only allow the entry of marks up to and including the maximum marks for each test.
2 The validation rule should also ensure that negative numbers cannot be entered.

Validation applied to a spreadsheet

When testing validation rules work, it is important to enter four different types of test data.

Type of test data	Purpose
Valid (normal / acceptable data)	Data that should pass the validation rule.
Invalid (erroneous / unacceptable data)	Data that should generate an error message.
Extreme valid	Data that will only just pass the validation rule because it is on the boundary of acceptable data.
Extreme invalid	Data that will only just generate an error message because it is on the boundary of unacceptable data.

Table 8.08 - Types of test data.

EXAMPLE

Here is some test data that could be used to test the validation rule whole number BETWEEN 5 and 20:

Test data input value	Type of test data	Expected result
10	Valid	Accepted
5	Extreme valid	Accepted
20	Extreme valid	Accepted
3	Invalid	Error message
-10	Invalid	Error message
abc	Invalid	Error message
10.5	Invalid	Error message
4	Extreme invalid	Error message
21	Extreme invalid	Error message

TASK

Generate test data that will test the following rules. You should use a table with three columns: test data value, type of test data and expected result. Ensure you cover all four types of test data.

- input value is a whole number <1000
- input value is a decimal >25
- input value is between 100 and 200
- input value = PASS or FAIL (there are no extreme tests for this)
- input value exists in list Junior, Intermediate, Senior (there are no extreme tests for this)

Test a spreadsheet model and evaluate the effectiveness of test plans for a spreadsheet model

Testing of validation rules is just one aspect of testing. All formulae and functions also need testing. To test a formula or function, it is necessary to identify input data that will be used for the calculation and the expected output data (result of calculation). The expected output data should be calculated using traditional methods and then compared with the result from the spreadsheet. It is also essential to identify which worksheet the input data and output data are on as they may be on different worksheets and the tester will need to find the data. Other aspects such as cell and worksheet protection and conditional formatting can also be tested. It is not possible to test every possible input value, but a good range should be used, especially extreme values which are small and large. Invalid input values should only be used if validation rules have been set up.

EXAMPLE

This test plan tests the formula in C6 of = A6 + B6

Test data input value	Type of test data	Expected result
A6 = 5, B6 = 8 on Addition worksheet	Valid	C6 = 13 on Addition worksheet
A6 = 30 000 000 B6 = 80 000 000 on Addition worksheet	Extreme valid	C6 = 110 000 000 on Addition worksheet and is fully visible
A6 = 0, B6 = 0 on Addition worksheet	Extreme valid	C6 = 0 on Addition worksheet

When a tester runs a test plan, there will be an additional column called 'Actual result' where the results of the test will be entered.

TASK.

 CD 8.28 Test results

Open CD 8.28 Test results and run the tests from the example above.
1 Record the results in CD 8.28 Test results.
2 If a test fails, record what happened.

TASK

📀 CD 8.29 Invoices and CD 8.30 Test plan

Open CD 8.29 Invoices and CD 8.30 Test plan and complete the test plan with at least six other tests. Calculate the expected result using traditional methods and then enter the input data and compare with the actual result.

Test data input value	Type of test data	Expected result	Actual result
Quantity for Product 3 on Invoice worksheet = 36 Cost for Product 3 on Invoice worksheet = $1,345.00 VAT rate on Data worksheet = 20%	Valid	VAT for Product 3 on Invoice worksheet = $9,684.00	

Test plans are often written during the design stage of a system life cycle. At this point, cell references are unlikely to be known. Therefore, cell references can be replaced with a description of the input. It must be clear to the tester where to input the test data.

Verify data entry

In Chapter 1 you learned that data that has been validated is not necessarily correct. It is therefore necessary to **verify** data. When inputting data into a spreadsheet, you should verify that the data has been input correctly by comparing what has been entered with the original source.

Filter data

When there is a lot of data listed in a spreadsheet, users may want to view just some of that data. This can be achieved by filtering the data that is required. The term filter is used to relate to the user's mental model. When coffee is filtered, the granules are left in the filter while the flavoured drink flows through the filter.

Figure 8.52 - Coffee filter paper in use.

EXAMPLE

In this example, people with a title of 'Dr' have been filtered.

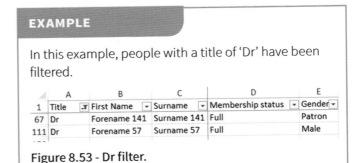

	A	B	C	D	E
1	Title	First Name	Surname	Membership status	Gender
67	Dr	Forename 141	Surname 141	Full	Patron
111	Dr	Forename 57	Surname 57	Full	Male

Figure 8.53 - Dr filter.

TASK

📀 CD 8.08 Member list

Open CD 8.08 Member list and apply the following filters:

1 People with a membership status of Full.
2 People who do not want to be emailed.
3 People who have been a member for one year.
4 People who are either Full or Patron members.

In the task above, the last filter that you applied was to find members who were either Full or Patron members. This uses a Boolean operator known as OR. It means that either condition can be true. Other Boolean operators include AND and NOT.

EXAMPLE

This filter shows members who have NOT lapsed their membership:

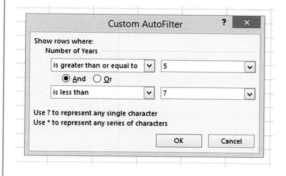

Figure 8.54 - NOT.

This filter will show members who have five or more years of membership AND less than seven years of membership:

Figure 8.55 - AND.

This is the result of the filter:

Figure 8.56 - AND result.

Special text filters can be applied as shown in Table 8.09.

Filter	Purpose	Example
Contains	Selects data in a column that includes the text specified.	Contains 'CH' will select all data in a column where CH exists anywhere within each data item. Chicken, Reach, Church and Ache would all be included, but not Card.
Starts with	Selects data in a column that starts with the text specified.	Starts with 'CH' will select all data in a column where the data starts with CH. Chicken and Church would all be included, but not Reach, Ache or Card.
Ends with	Selects data in a column that ends with the text specified.	Ends with 'CH' will select all data in a column where the data ends with CH. Church and Reach would be included but not Chicken, Ache or Card.

Table 8.09 - Text filters.

Filters that find a range of data can be used with numbers, dates and times as shown in Table 8.10.

Filter	Purpose	Example
Greater than	Selects data in a column that is greater than the value specified.	>10 Lists 11 but not 9 or 10.
Less than	Selects data in a column that is less than the value specified.	<10 Lists 9, but not 10 or 11.
Greater than or equal to	Selects data in a column that is greater than or equal to the value specified.	>=10
Less than or equal to	Selects data in a column that is less than or equal to the value specified.	<=10

Table 8.10 - Filtering for a range.

125

TASK

 CD 8.31 USA addresses

Open CD 8.31 USA addresses and apply the following filters:
1   State is Arizona 'Az' OR California 'CA'.
2   City starts with 'San'.
3   Company ends with 'Inc'.
4   Company includes '&'.
5   Position is <=10.
6   Position is >10 AND <=50.
7   State is NOT = 'FL' AND NOT = 'OH.

Sort data

It is possible to sort data into ascending or descending order. If only a selection of columns are sorted, then only the data within those columns will be sorted. To keep all data in each row together, do not highlight the data. To sort on more than one column, it is necessary to specify the sort order for each column and which column should be sorted first. If you wanted to sort by surname and then sort any matching surnames by forename, then you would sort by surname first.

TASK

 CD 8.31 USA addresses

Open CD 8.31 USA addresses and sort data into the following order:
- Position from 1 to 500.
- Position from 500 to 1.
- State in alphabetical order from A to Z.
- City in reverse alphabetical order.
- Surname in alphabetical order from A to Z with Forename as the secondary sort.

It's not just text and numbers that can be sorted into order. Dates and times can also be sorted.

Import and export data

Data can be **imported** from other formats such as a comma separated values (CSV) file, text (TXT) file or from a database. When importing, you should already have the spreadsheet software open and open the file to be imported from within the spreadsheet software. You will often have to ensure that when opening you have selected the option to show all files.

TASK

 CD 8.32 Instructors

Within your spreadsheet software, open CD 8.32 Instructors and select options which will cover the following:
1   This is a delimited file that is separated by commas.
2   The file has data headers in the first row.
3   The Date of Birth should be in date format with no time.
4   The charge should be in currency.
5   Use the find and replace option in the Weekends column only to replace 1 with 'Yes' and 0 with 'No'.

 CD 8.33 Driving school.accdb

Within your spreadsheet software, open CD 8.33 Driving school.accdb and import the Learner table.

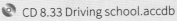

DISCUSSION POINT

 CD 8.34 Lessons

Try to open CD 8.34 Lessons from your spreadsheet software. It is unlikely that your spreadsheet software will recognise how to import this data. It is essential to ensure that the data being imported is structured in a way in which the spreadsheet software can understand it by using rows of data and separating columns with a special symbol such as a comma.

Data can also be **exported** so that it can be used in other software. If it is exported in a common format such as CSV or TXT, then other software will be able to recognise the rows and columns. Formats such as portable document format (PDF) will enable the data to be viewed by a wide variety of users but not manipulated, so PDF is good for showing output data.

TASK

 CD 8.31 USA addresses

Open CD 8.31 USA addresses and export it to the following formats:
- CSV
- TXT
- PDF
- Open Document Spreadsheet (ODS) – works with Open Office
- Web page (HTML).

View the files that you have exported the data to and note how the data has been stored.

QUESTIONS

1 Describe the purpose of a named range of cells.

2 Describe the difference between a formula and a function.

3 Explain how a user could verify data on a spreadsheet.

4 Compare absolute cell referencing with relative cell referencing.

5 Using an example, describe how absolute cell referencing could be used in a spreadsheet.

8.02 Graphs and charts

Analyse and select a chart

Graphs or charts are used to show information in a way that makes it easy to compare values. This could be as simple as showing the monthly sales in a column or bar chart or it could be more complex and show how hospital waiting times vary during a month compared with their targets. Charts that show more than one set of data are known as comparative charts because data for one set can be compared against data for another set.

EXAMPLE

CD 8.35 Graphs and charts

CD 8.35 Graphs and charts includes some examples of graphs and charts. The worksheet Monthly Sales contains a bar chart showing the Monthly sales over a period of 12 months. Notice how a chart title and x-axis title have been included:

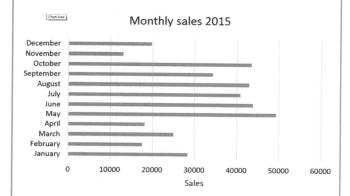

Figure 8.57 - Monthly sales bar chart.

The comparative bar chart on the worksheet Worldwide Sales compares the sales of different continents for each of the months in 2015. Notice how a legend is used to show which continent is represented by which colour:

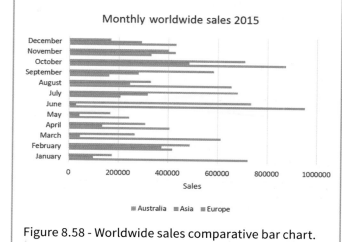

Figure 8.58 - Worldwide sales comparative bar chart.

Line graphs are similar to bar charts in that they show the size of data, but they are mainly used to show how data changes over a period of time.

EXAMPLE

CD 8.35 Graphs and charts

The first line graph on the worksheet Waiting List in CD 8.35 Graphs and charts shows how waiting times at the Kerslake Hospital have fallen over a four-year period. Notice how the minimum value on for the x-axis scale is 2.0 hours and the maximum value for the y-axis scale is 3.6 hours. The y-axis scale has intervals of 0.2 hours. Both y and x-axes have been given axis titles.

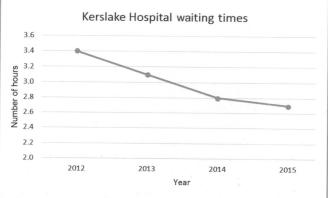

Figure 8.59 - Kerslake Hospital line graph.

The comparative line graph on the worksheet Waiting List compares the waiting times of three hospitals over a four-year period with the target waiting time of 2.5 hours. Notice how the y-axis scale has intervals of 0.5 hours, the maximum value for the y-axis scale is 5.0 and the minimum value for the y-axis scale is 1.5.

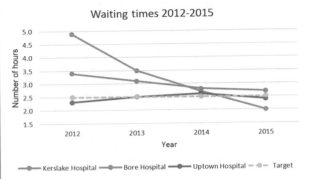

Figure 8.60 - Hospital waiting times comparative line graph.

Pie charts are used to show proportional data. This differs from bar charts or line graphs because instead of showing the actual values, the proportion or percentage of each data item is shown.

128

EXAMPLE

 CD 8.35 Graphs and charts

The worksheet Head Prefect in CD 8.35 Graphs and charts contains a pie chart showing the proportion of votes received for each student standing in an election for head prefect of a school. Notice how a legend is not necessary because each legend has been labelled with the name of the data item. Each segment has also been labelled with the percentage of the total vote that each data item represents:

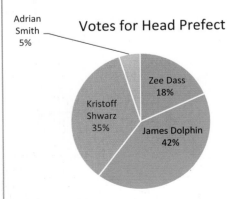

Figure 8.61 - Head prefect pie chart.

When selecting which type of graph or chart to produce, you should consider the general rules shown in Table 8.11.

Type of graph / chart	Purpose
Bar / column chart	Used to show a single series of data in columns or rows.
Comparative bar / column chart	Used to compare more than one series of data in columns or rows.
Line graph	Used to show how a single series of data changes over a period of time.
Comparative line graph	Used to compare how more than one series of data changes over a period of time.
Pie chart	Used to show the proportion that is used by each item of data.

Table 8.11 - Rules for selecting type of graph or chart.

Create a graph or chart

When creating a graph or chart, you should ensure that it is labelled appropriately.

Label	Purpose
Title	A brief overview of what the graph or chart is showing.
Legend	A key to show what the colours used represent.
Value axis	Each of the axes (usually x and y) should include the values including any units.
Category axis	Each of the axes should include a title to state what the data represents.
Percentages	When using a pie chart, the percentages may need to be displayed for each segment.
Segment label	Instead of a legend, each segment in a pie chart could be labelled with its description.
Segment value	As well as, or instead of the percentage, each segment in a pie chart could be labelled with its quantity.
Scale	The interval between each value on an axis.
Axis scale maximum	The maximum value to be used on an axis.
Axis scale minimum	The minimum value to be used on an axis.

Table 8.12 - Labelling graphs and charts.

TASK

💿 CD 8.25 Maths results

Open CD 8.25 Maths results.
1 Create a bar chart to show the marks for each student.
2 Include a title and axis titles.

💿 CD 8.27 Physics results

Open CD 8.27 Physics results.
1 Enter some marks for each student for each test.
2 Create a comparative bar chart to show the marks for each student in each of the tests 1, 2 and 3.
3 Include a title and axis titles.
4 Include a legend for the tests.
5 Change the y-axis maximum scale value to be 50.
6 Change the y-axis scale to have intervals of 5.

💿 CD 8.36 School attendance

Open CD 8.36 School attendance.
1 Create a comparative line graph to show the attendance of each of year 1 and year 2 over the period of the year compared with the target.
2 Label the chart appropriately.
3 Adjust the y-axis scale and maximum scale values appropriately.
4 Include a legend.
5 Change the line type of the target series to be dashed.

💿 CD 8.08 Member list

Open CD 8.08 Member list.
1 Open the worksheet Pie Chart. Change 'Count of Membership Status' to 'Count of membership status', 'Membership Status' to 'Membership status' and 'Grand Total' to 'Grand total'.
2 Create a pie chart to show the proportion of members for each status.
3 Give the chart a sensible title.
4 Add the percentages and membership statuses to the pie chart segments.

💿 CD 8.20 HLookup

Open CD 8.20 HLookup.
1 Create an appropriate chart to show the products, original price and discounted price.
2 Label the chart appropriately.

A chart can be created in a spreadsheet and then used within other software by copying the graph and pasting it into the other software, such as word processing for a report, or presentation software for a presentation. It is also possible to link the exported chart to the original spreadsheet data so that if the data changes within the spreadsheet then the chart will update in the software to which it has been exported.

TASK

💿 CD 8.35 Graphs and charts

Open CD 8.35 Graphs and charts.
1 Copy the graph Monthly sales 2015.
2 Open a word processor or presentation software.
3 Select the option to paste as a link (you may find this under paste special).
4 Ensure that the link option is selected and the object type (graph) is identified.
5 Save this new document and close it.
6 Change some of the data in the Monthly sales worksheet.
7 Save the spreadsheet.
8 Reopen the new document you created and check that the graph has changed to reflect the updated data in the spreadsheet.

QUESTIONS

6 Identify and give reasons for the most appropriate type of chart or graph to show the number of missed refuse collections shown in the table below:

Year	Vesey	New Hall	Trinity
2010	2502	4571	3271
2011	2786	5728	3102
2012	1987	5645	2905
2013	2057	4972	2647

7 Identify and give reasons for the most appropriate type of chart or graph to show the data shown in the table below:

Student	Mark 1	Mark 2	Mark 3	Mark 4	Average
Name 1	98	40	36	84	65
Name 2	31	67	61	77	59
Name 3	62	58	29	38	47
Name 4	64	83	85	27	65
Name 5	87	45	64	42	60
Name 6	93	58	43	73	67
Name 7	99	29	55	92	69
Name 8	57	58	44	93	63
Name 9	45	43	98	55	60

12

8.03 Modelling

Characteristics of modelling software

KEY TERM

Model: a representation of a process

Remember

A **model** is a computer representation of a real-world process. A model is created through mathematical analysis of the real-world process. Modelling software is used to create a model. Spreadsheets can be used to create computerised models, but there are also custom-written solutions that are used to model specific processes.

EXAMPLE

A network simulator such as Cloonix can be used to model a computer network. The software will be able to produce a diagrammatic view of the devices connected to the computer network. It will be possible to identify the Internet Protocol (IP) addresses used on the network and how they are assigned through a Dynamic Host Configuration Protocol (DHCP) server. Wireless networks can be added and security can be configured to see what the effects will be. Devices can be connected to specific switches and the throughput of data traffic can be analysed.

Computer Aided Design (CAD) enables designers to produce a model of a physical object. This could include a kitchen, a building, a motor vehicle or an aeroplane. CAD software can include features such as viewing an object in two dimensions (2D) or three dimensions (3D), manipulating objects within the model, adding or removing objects, viewing the model from different angles, applying different effects such as colour and lighting, and focusing on specific features such as the electrical cabling or heating system within a building.

Modelling software will include some essential features:

- the ability to change variables within the software
- asking what-if questions to see what the result of changing variables might be
- formulae and functions to carry out the mathematical calculations that form the basis of the model
- automatic recalculation of formulae and functions

- rules that define how the model behaves
- layers of abstraction so that different parts of the model can be viewed and analysed separately.

EXAMPLE

A model of a roller coaster can be built. Variables can include the height of each drop, the radius of loops, the starting speed of the carriage, length of each section and the weight of each carriage. Calculations will be used to define rules such as the amount of friction and how that will slow carriages down, the effect of gravity on carriages as they move up and down and the g-force that will be experienced by passengers. What-if questions could be asked such as 'What would happen if we increased the starting speed by 2 km/h?' or 'What would happen if we increased the initial drop by 5 km?' The effect of these changes in variables can then be modelled.

TASK

Experiment with the digital single-lens reflex (DSLR) camera simulator at http://camerasim.com/apps/camera-simulator/ by changing the variables and seeing what the end results are.

The need for computer models

There are a variety of reasons why models might be used, including training, forecasting and construction. Whatever the reason, a model must be able to answer what-if questions.

Models can be used for the purpose of training people to use equipment. This could range from learning to drive a forklift truck to flying an aeroplane or operating a nuclear power plant. Models are used for training because there is less risk of injury to the trainees and instructors than learning in a real environment. When learning to drive a forklift truck, the trainee may make a mistake by lifting a load too high and toppling the truck. In real life this could cause serious injury as well as costing money in terms of repairs, but using a model removes both of these risks. Costs are saved because real equipment does not suffer wear and tear, fuel is not required to operate machinery and instructors do not need to be present all of the time. It is also possible to test the trainee in unpredictable situations such as turbulence for an aeroplane or driving a heavy goods vehicle on ice. Unpredictable situations that would happen in real life can also be removed for trainees when they first start learning so they can focus on basic controls.

Models can also be used for forecasting. One of the most common models for this purpose is weather forecasting. Patterns that have happened in the past can be analysed along with current data to predict what the weather might be in the future. Businesses and governments use financial modelling to predict what might happen to profits or the economy. It is too risky for a business to make sudden changes in the marketplace without testing them out with a model first. A variety of what-if questions can be asked using a model to determine how to make the most profit. Variables that could be changed include selling prices, adjusting the quantity of products to supply at any given time, times of year to sell products and the effect of weather on seasonal sales.

Constructing buildings, kitchens, gardens, motor vehicles and other objects can be a very costly process. It is important to get it right first time as any adjustments that have to be made in the real world will incur financial costs. Models help to experiment with different designs to see which look is most aesthetically pleasing and which ones react best to environmental conditions. When designing a kitchen using modelling software, variables such as lighting, worktops, cupboard doors, position of units, flooring and tiling can be changed to see which configuration looks the best. Cupboards, drawers, dishwashers and cookers can be opened to see if they use the space efficiently. The angle of view can be changed in a 3D environment to see what the kitchen might look like from a variety of angles.

Evaluating the effectiveness of spreadsheet models

TIP

Spreadsheet models are mainly used for financial forecasting, but there are a lot of other models that can be used.

There are a variety of tools within a spreadsheet that can be used to help with modelling:

- variables which can be changed to ask what-if questions
- formulae and functions which define the rules of the model
- graphs and charts which can show a graphical representation of the forecast

- instant, automatic recalculation of formulae, functions and graphs/charts to answer what-if questions immediately
- conditional formatting to highlight the effects
- goal-seek to find out what variables need to be changed to achieve a given outcome.

EXAMPLE

Some examples of what-if questions in a financial spreadsheet model might include:

- What happens to the total income for the month if we increase the selling price by 20%?

- What happens to our costs if we use a different supplier for one of our parts?

- What happens to our total expenditure for the next five years if we move to new premises?

Some examples of goal-seek questions might include:

- What price do we need to sell at in order to sell 5000 items per month?

- How many items do we need to sell to break even (zero profit and zero loss)?

Other advantages of spreadsheet models include the ability to share the spreadsheet with colleagues easily so that many people can experiment with the model, and the fact that most organisations already own spreadsheet software which reduces the need for training and purchase costs.

Spreadsheets do have their limitations though. They are only as accurate as the formulae and functions that are the rules that represent the real world. Unless extremely complex rules are used, then a spreadsheet model will never be an accurate representation. These complex rules require mathematical and computer expertise in order to set them up and it can take a very long time to create models that are truly representative of the real world. Spreadsheets can only be used to simulate numbers, but cannot simulate the effect on objects.

QUESTIONS

8 Identify three characteristics of modelling software.

9 Describe, using examples, how a spreadsheet could be used to model the costs or savings to an organisation of moving premises.

8.04 Simulations

Advantages and disadvantages of using a model to create and run simulations

 KEY TERM

Simulation: using a model to predict real-life behaviour

A **simulation** is the use of a computerised model to predict how a real-life system might behave. As with modelling, simulations can be used for training, forecasting and construction.

Advantages include:

- it is not necessary to create expensive prototypes or the real thing in order to experiment with different variations and answer what-if questions
- changes to the model can be made very quickly and the effect can be seen just as quickly
- alternative models and designs can be used to see how they react differently
- unusual events (e.g. earthquakes) can be tested without the need to wait for them to happen in real life
- equipment does not suffer from wear and tear or damage when being tested or experimented with
- dangerous situations such as aeroplane equipment failure can be simulated without putting people in danger
- simulations can be 'sped up' so that effects can be analysed over a long period of time without having to wait for that period of time to elapse.

Disadvantages include:

- the way a simulation reacts is only as good as the model it is based upon
- simulation software and equipment can be very expensive to purchase
- people need to be trained to use simulation equipment and software
- complex models take many years to develop, especially if they are designed to react like the real process
- it is impossible for a simulation to be a perfect representation of the real-world process.

The use of simulation
Natural disaster planning

When planning for natural disasters, it is necessary to know what the effects of a natural disaster might be.

It is impossible to do this in real life without the actual disaster happening and, as they are natural disasters, it is impossible to force them to happen. If the planners wait for the natural disaster to happen, then it is too late to plan.

Simulations based on models of natural disasters such as earthquakes, volcanic eruptions, hurricanes, bush fires and tsunamis can be used to see what the effects might be. Planners can experiment with different variables such as wind speed and direction to see how quickly a fire might spread, which will help them to plan evacuations and firefighting.

As with all simulations, these rely upon the accuracy of the model. There will be many things that the model can't predict completely such as sudden changes in wind direction or wind speed and emotional reactions to being evacuated. However, planners can experiment with lots of what-if questions in order to plan for a large variety of circumstances, which means that when a natural disaster does occur they can be better equipped to deal with it.

Pilot training

Part of the thrill of flying an aircraft is being in the air. However, when it comes to large aircraft, it can cost thousands of pounds just to take off, fly and land. This cannot be repeated too often as it will become too costly to train pilots. Flight simulators can help by removing the fuel costs associated with flying. They can also remove the danger that a trainee pilot might pose if they make a mistake while in the air.

Flight simulators not only include software, but very specialised equipment which can cost hundreds of thousands of pounds. The equipment will be designed to react in a similar way to a real aircraft, so that the pilot can feel the physical effects of any movements that they make (including take off, landing, turbulence or even a crash landing) in a way that is as close to real life as possible. The software will include the rules of the model that define how the aircraft should react in a variety of circumstances.

Pilots can also practice landing and taking off at airports they have not visited before, including some of the most dangerous airports in the world such as Toncontin Airport in Honduras. Simulations give pilots the opportunity to respond to malfunctions such as an engine failure, cabin pressure failure or landing gear failure. These would be far too dangerous to attempt in real life.

Figure 8.62 - Toncontin Airport.

Car driving

Simulators can be used to learn to drive a car. In most countries, learner drivers start immediately on the road having never used any of a car's controls before. They immediately have to deal with hazards such as other cars, pedestrians, cyclists, potholes and dangerous junctions. In addition to this, other drivers on the road are held up because of the learner driver being slow and hesitant.

Simulations can enable a learner driver to become familiar with the controls of a car and dealing with hazards before taking a car onto the road for the first time. This is a safe environment and could reduce insurance premiums for driving instructors. The simulator could also be used when the learner driver needs to attempt manoeuvres such as turning in the road or reversing around a corner for the first time, rather than having to do this straight away on a real road. Even after a learner driver has passed their test, they could use simulators to learn how to drive on a motorway, drive in icy conditions and how to handle a car if it gets out of control such as in a skid.

Simulations can also be used for racing drivers to experiment with different car setups to find the optimum configuration for a racing circuit, rather than risking crashing. Racing drivers would be able to take the car to the limit knowing that the virtual crash will not result in an injury. However, a simulation will never behave exactly the same as the real car as the rules of the model will never be perfect. Therefore it is still necessary to practice using a real racing car.

Nuclear science research

Nuclear science is very dangerous. Even a small accident could expose a person to radiation that could cause serious disfigurement or death. It is therefore not possible

to experiment with nuclear reactions in the real world in the hope that something might work. Simulations can be used to try out different nuclear reactions by adjusting the coolant temperature, changing the way the control rods are used and the rate of reaction. What-if questions can be asked such as 'What happens if I increase the temperature?' and the outcomes can be seen. It's also possible to speed up the simulation so that rather than waiting hours, days or even years to see what the effects might be, results can be seen much more quickly.

Nuclear science requires a lot of computing power in order to simulate nuclear reactions. For example, reactors convert uranium and plutonium through nuclear fission which involves millions of collisions every microsecond. Even with supercomputers, nuclear scientists cannot represent all of these collisions in a simulation.

> **EXAMPLE**
>
> There is an online nuclear power plant simulator at www.nuclearpowersimulator.com/.

> **TASK**
>
> Try the nuclear reactor simulator at www.dalton.manchester.ac.uk/engage/nrs/.

> **QUESTIONS**
>
> 10 Describe two advantages of using a simulator for pilot training.
> 11 Describe one disadvantage of using a simulator for learning to drive.

8.05 Summary

A spreadsheet consists of worksheets. Each worksheet consists of rows and columns. Cells are referenced by the column letter and row number. A range is one or more cells that are named.

Cells within worksheets can be protected so they can't be altered and worksheets can be hidden. Data within a cell can be assigned data types including date, time, number, text, currency, percentage and fractions. Text within a cell can be aligned left, centre or right and can be rotated.

Comments can be added to cells. Conditional formatting can be used to format cells based on their content.

A worksheet can be set up to print on a specific size of paper, with a header/footer and set margins. It can also be specified to fit on a set number of pages.

Formulae are basic arithmetic calculations and functions are ready-made formulae representing complex calculations. Functions can include summary functions, rounding functions, date/time functions, lookup functions and conditional functions. Absolute cell references do not change when replicated and relative cell references change when replicated.

Validation rules can be used to ensure that data is sensible and allowed. Valid, invalid and extreme data

should be used to test validation rules. Verification is the process of checking data has been transferred correctly.

Data can be selected using filters. Data can be sorted into ascending or descending order. Data can be imported into a spreadsheet from another data source or exported so it can be used in other software. Graphs and charts can be used to analyse data.

Models represent real world processes for training, forecasting and construction. Spreadsheets can be used for financial forecasting and other models that rely on mathematical analysis. Simulations use computerised models to predict how real-life systems might behave.

Review questions

The spreadsheet below shows cars that are owned by a driving school. It calculates the fuel type of each car, the cost per litre of each fuel type and the cost per gallon.

	A	B	C	D	E	F
1	Registration	Make	Model	Fuel type	Cost per litre	Cost per litre
2	BX56JWL	Ford	Mondeo	Diesel	$ 1.25	$ 5.69
3	BX56JWM	Saab	Saab 9-3	Petrol	$ 1.17	$ 5.32
4	BX56JWN	Land Rover	Discovery	Diesel	$ 1.25	$ 5.69
5	BX56JWP	Smart	Smart Car	LPG	$ 0.85	$ 3.87
6	BX56JWR	Ford	Mondeo	Petrol	$ 1.17	$ 5.32
7	BX56JWS	Saab	Saab 9-3	Diesel	$ 1.25	$ 5.69
8						
9				Fuel type	Cost per litre	
10				Diesel	$ 5.69	
11				Petrol	$ 1.17	
12				LPG	$ 5.69	

Fig 8.63 - Rental company spreadsheet.

Rows and columns are used in the spreadsheet.

1 a Use an example from this spreadsheet to describe a row. [2]

Formulae and functions have been used in the spreadsheet. There are 4.55 litres in a gallon.

1 b i Describe a formula. [1]

1 b ii Write the formula used in F2. [1]

1 b iii Describe a function. [1]

1 b iv Identify the type of formula used in E2. [1]

The driving school would like to see all their petrol cars but not the other cars.

2 a Explain how the driving school could see all their petrol cars but not the other cars without losing any data. [2]

2   b   Explain how the fuel types could be identified quickly using a different colour for each without changing them all one by one. [2]

Absolute and relative cell referencing have been used within the spreadsheet.

3   Using examples, explain how absolute and relative cell referencing have been used. [4]

The spreadsheet model is going to be used to calculate the costs of using each car.

4   a   Describe three advantages of using a spreadsheet to model the costs of using each car. [3]

4   b   Describe one disadvantage of using a spreadsheet to model the costs of using each car. [1]

The driving school is considering purchasing a simulator to help students to learn to drive.

5   Give reasons for the use of a simulator for this purpose. [4]

Chapter 9
Database and file concepts

Learning objectives

By the end of this chapter, you will be able to:

- create a database with tables, queries, forms, reports and relationships
- assign appropriate data types to fields and set primary, compound and foreign keys
- understand relationships, entity relationship diagrams and referential integrity
- evaluate the difference between a flat file, and relational and hierarchical databases
- use validation and verification to check for accuracy
- search a database using multiple criteria, static parameters, dynamic parameters and nested queries
- summarise data within a table or query
- import and export data to and from a database
- understand normalisation and be able to normalise a database to third normal form
- describe the components of a data dictionary
- understand the different types of files that can be used
- explain the use of different methods of file access
- understand how a management information system can be used

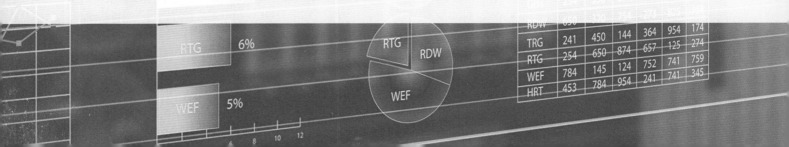

9.01 Create a database

KEY TERMS

Database: a structured method of storing data

Table: a set of similar data (about people, places, objects or events)

Record: a common word for entity

Entity: a set of data about one thing (person, place, object or event)

Attribute: a category of information within an entity

Field: a common word for attribute

Primary key: a field that contains the unique identifier for a record

Database management system: software used to manage a database

Relationship: the way in which two entities in two different tables are connected

Foreign key: a field in a table that refers to the primary key in another table

Normal form: the extent to which a database has been normalised

Index: a list of keys or keywords which identify a unique record and can be used to search and sort records more quickly

Entity relationship diagram: a diagram that represents the relationships between entities

Flat file: a database stored in a single table

Compound key: two or more fields that form the primary key

Referential integrity: data in the **foreign key** of the table on the many sides of a relationship must exist in the primary key of the table on the one side of a relationship

Query: a question used to retrieve data from a database

Parameter: data used within the criteria for a **query**

Introduction to databases

Remember

A **database** is a structured method for storing data in sets of tables. Each **table** contains similar data about people, places, objects or events.

EXAMPLE

Figure 9.01 from CD 9.01 Sales processing.mdb contains data about customers (people):

Customer ID	Contact Forename	Contact Surname	Street Address
1	Reina	Wolchesky	305 W Washington St
2	Marc	Wenger	33 Harrison Ave
3	Damion	Matkin	5830 Downing St #-d
4	Lucius	Winchester	670 S Barrington Rd
5	Petra	Mcnichol	670 S Barrington Rd
6	Katina	Ramano	580 Fountain Ave

Figure 9.01 - Customer table.

Within a **table** are rows known as **records**. Each record is an **entity** which is a set of data about one single thing (person, place, object or event). In the example above, the data about Marc Wenger is a single record/entity.

Each entity has categories of information. These categories are known as **attributes** or **fields**. In the example above Customer ID, Contact Forename, Contact Surname and Street Address are all field/attribute names.

One of the fields will be known as the **primary key**. The primary key contains a unique value for each record. This means that each value can only exist once in that table so it is possible to identify each record using the primary key. In the example above, Customer ID is the primary key.

Remember

The software that is used to manage the database is called a **database management system** (DBMS). Sometimes, this is referred to as a relational database management system (RDBMS) as it is managing a database that includes **relationships**.

TASK

CD 9.01 Sales processing.mdb

Open CD 9.01 Sales processing.mdb and then open the table Product.
1 Identify four field names in the Product table.
2 Identify the primary key in the Product table.
3 How many records are in the Product table?
4 Identify two other tables within the database.

Data types and field sizes

DISCUSSION POINT
You should read the section about data types in Section 9.03 below.

Each field in a table will have a data type assigned to it. Data types include:

- text
- alphanumeric
- numeric (integer/decimal)
- date/time
- Boolean.

137

EXAMPLE

 CD 9.02 Sales processing 2.mdb

The Product table in CD 9.02 Sales processing 2. mdb has the following data types:

Field Name	Data Type
Product ID	AutoNumber
Product Name	Short Text
Supplier ID	Number
Category ID	Number
Quantity Per Unit	Short Text
Unit Price	Currency
Units In Stock	Number
Reorder Amount	Number
Units On Order	Number
Reorder Level	Number
Discontinued	Yes/No

Figure 9.02 - Product data types.

- Product Name and Quantity Per Unit are alphanumeric (Short Text is the term used by Microsoft Access) which means they can include letters, numbers and symbols.

- Units in Stock is a Number (numeric) which has been set as an integer because it only contains whole numbers.

- Unit Price is Currency (numeric) which has been set as a decimal (real) because it can contain decimal values.

- Discontinued is Yes/No (Boolean) because it can only contain Yes or No values.

The Order table has the following data types:

Field Name	Data Type
Order Number	AutoNumber
Customer ID	Number
Order Date	Date/Time
Notes	Long Text

Figure 9.03 - Order data types.

- Order Number is numeric but it is also set as an AutoNumber which means a numeric value will be automatically assigned to it.

- Customer ID is numeric which has been set as an integer. It also matches the data type of the Customer ID in the Customer table which you can find within the database.

- Order Date is Date/Time and has been set as a date.

- Notes is alphanumeric but has been further defined as Long Text which means that any amount of text can be assigned to it.

DISCUSSION POINT

Different database management systems use different names for data types. If you are using Microsoft Access, you will notice that text is used for alphanumeric data and number is used for numeric data. Sometimes the software will also use formatted data as a data type such as currency. Currency is actually numeric (usually decimal) and is just formatted by displaying a currency symbol with the number.

Fields within a table will have field sizes applied to them. This is because most fields are a fixed length. This means that only a specified amount of data can be stored in each field.

Text and alphanumeric fields will have a length to specify the maximum number of characters that can be stored. For example, the Product Name in the Product table is limited to 40 characters. This avoids having lots of wasted storage space where field space is not used if the length is too long.

Numbers can also have a field size. This could be defined as the number of digits or it could be defined as the maximum numeric value.

Dates will always be the same field size as they will always store the date is the same way, but they can be formatted to be displayed differently.

Some text fields can be formatted to be a variable length which means they can store as little or as much data as possible. These are sometimes referred to as memo or long text data types. These are useful for fields that will contain notes or comments.

DISCUSSION POINT

It's important to ensure that the field length is not too long because this will waste storage space, but it is also important to ensure that the field length is long enough to store the longest required data item.

TASK

CD 9.01 Sales processing.mdb

Open CD 9.01 Sales processing.mdb and explore the data types and field sizes used within the tables.

The three relationships

Relationships within a database can be used to connect entities together. A **foreign key** is an attribute (field) in one entity that connects to a primary key in another entity. This allows related data to be looked up and found.

EXAMPLE

(a)

Order Number	Customer ID	Order Date
1	2	28/05/2015
2	1	22/05/2015
3	5	06/05/2015
4	3	05/04/2015
5	7	06/05/2015

(b)

Customer ID	Contact Forename	Contact Surname
1	Reina	Wolchesky
2	Marc	Wenger
3	Damion	Matkin
4	Lucius	Winchester
5	Petra	Mcnichol
6	Katina	Ramano

Figure 9.04 - Foreign key. a) Order table; b) Customer table.

In the Order table, the foreign key is Customer ID which connects to the primary key Customer ID in the customer table. For Order Number 4, the Customer ID 3 is looked up in the Customer table to find Damion Matkin.

One-to-one

A one-to-one relationship is when each record in one table only connects to one record in another table. Each foreign key value will link to one primary key value and each primary key value will only be linked to by one foreign key value. The foreign key can exist on either side of the relationship.

EXAMPLE

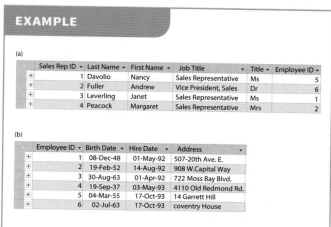

(a)

Sales Rep ID	Last Name	First Name	Job Title	Title	Employee ID
1	Davolio	Nancy	Sales Representative	Ms	5
2	Fuller	Andrew	Vice President, Sales	Dr	6
3	Leverling	Janet	Sales Representative	Ms	1
4	Peacock	Margaret	Sales Representative	Mrs	2

(b)

Employee ID	Birth Date	Hire Date	Address
1	08-Dec-48	01-May-92	507-20th Ave. E.
2	19-Feb-52	14-Aug-92	908 W.Capital Way
3	30-Aug-63	01-Apr-92	722 Moss Bay Blvd.
4	19-Sep-37	03-May-93	4110 Old Redmond Rd.
5	04-Mar-55	17-Oct-93	14 Garrett Hill
6	02-Jul-63	17-Oct-93	coventry House

Figure 9.05 - One-to-one relationship. a) Sales Rep table; b) Employee table.

The Sales Rep table stores details of the sales representatives within a business. This only contains basic information about their name but their full employee details are stored in a separate table called Employee. Each sales representative only has one employee record and each employee record can only refer to one sales rep record.

One-to-many

A one-to-many relationship is when each record in one table can connect to many (zero or more) records in another table. A foreign key will exist within the table on the many side of the relationship and will connect to a primary key in the one side of the relationship. This is the most common type of relationship within relational databases.

EXAMPLE

The Category table stores data about the different categories of products being sold. Its primary key is Category ID. The Product table stores data about the products. The Product table has a foreign key of Category ID. Each product can only have one category. Each category can have many products. There is **one** Category to **many** Products.

139

(a)

Product ID	Product Name	Category ID
1	Chai	1
2	Chang	1
3	Aniseed Syrup	2
4	Chef Anton's Cajun Seasoning	2
5	Chef Anton's Gumbo Mix	2
6	Grandma's Boysenberry Spread	2
7	Uncle Josef's Organic Dried Pears	7
8	Northwoods Cranberry sauce	2
9	Mishi Kobe Niku	6
10	Ikura	8
11	Queso Cabrales	4
12	Queso Manchego La Pastora	4

(b)

Category ID	Category Name	Description
1	Beverages	Soft drinks, coffee, teas, beers and ales
2	Condiments	Sweet and savory sauces, relishes, spreads and seasoning
3	Confections	Desserts, candies and sweet breads
4	Dairy Products	Cheeses
5	Grains/Cereals	Breads, crackers, pasta and cereal
6	Meat/Poultry	Prepared meats
7	Produce	Dried fruit and bean curd
8	Seafood	Seaweed and fish

Figure 9.06 - One-to-many. a) Product table;
b) Category table.

Many-to-many

Many-to-many relationships are only conceptual. They are not used in relational databases because they are converted into two sets of one-to-many relationships. In a many-to-many relationship, each record in one table can connect to many records in another table but each record in the other table can also connect to many records in the original table.

EXAMPLE

(a)

Order Number	Customer ID	Order Date	Product IDs
1	2	28/05/2015	1, 8, 4, 3
2	1	22/05/2015	1, 7
3	5	06/05/2015	2, 5, 6
4	3	05/04/2015	4
5	7	06/05/2015	3, 8

(b)

Product ID	Product Name	Category ID
1	Chai	1
2	Chang	1
3	Aniseed Syrup	2
4	Chef Anton's Cajun Seasoning	2
5	Chef Anton's Gumbo Mix	2
6	Grandma's Boysenberry Spread	2
7	Uncle Bob's Organic Dried Pears	7
8	Northwoods Cranberry sauce	2
9	Mishi Kobe Niku	6
10	Ikura	8
11	Queso Cabrales	4
12	Queso Manchego La Pastora	4

Figure 9.07 - Many-to-many. a) Order table; b) Product table.

The Order table stores data about the orders that are placed including which products are being sold. It has a field called Product IDs which lists the products being sold on each order. Each order can have many products. Each product can exist on many orders. There are **many** Orders to **many** Products.

DISCUSSION POINT

The problem with the many-to-many relationship is that it is not possible to store single data items within the foreign key. In the Order and Product example, the Product ID field contains more than one Product ID per Order and this causes a problem of non-atomic data, breaking the rules of first **normal form** which you will learn about later in this chapter.

TASK

 CD 9.01. Sales processing.mdb

Open CD 9.01 Sales processing.mdb and examine the relationships. Identify the relationships that currently exist. For example, the relationship between Sales Rep and Employee is One Sales Rep to One Employee.

Create and use relationships

One-to-many

When creating a one-to-many relationship, there are some rules to follow:

- the table on the one side must have a primary key
- the table on the many side will have a foreign key
- the data type and field size of the foreign key must match the primary key on the one side
- only data items that exist in the primary key on the one side can be used in the foreign key.

TASK

CD 9.01 Sales processing.mdb

Open CD 9.01 Sales processing.mdb and open the relationships.
1 Create a one-to-many relationship between Supplier and Product.
2 Create a one-to-many relationship between Order and the Sales Rep that dealt with the order. You will need a new foreign key in the Order table.

One-to-one

When creating a one-to-one relationship, there are also some rules to follow:

- at least one of the tables (table A) must have a primary key
- the other table (table B) must either have
  - a primary key that is also a foreign key and will link to the primary key in table A
  - or a foreign key field with a unique **index** that will link to the primary key in table A
- the data type and field size of the foreign key in table B and primary key in table A must match
- only data items that exist in the primary key in table A can be used in the foreign key in table B.

TASK

💿 CD 9.01 Sales processing.mdb

Open CD 9.01 Sales processing.mdb and open the relationships.

1 Create a one-to-one relationship between Sales Rep and Employee. Employee ID should be used as the foreign key in the Sales Rep table and it will need a unique index.

❗ **DISCUSSION POINT**

If you don't have a unique index or a primary key as the foreign key, then the database software is likely to assume you want to create a one-to-many relationship instead of a one-to-one relationship.

Create and interpret an entity relationship diagram

An **entity relationship diagram** (ERD) shows the relationships (connections) between each entity. Each entity is represented by a rectangle. Each relationship is represented by a line.

EXAMPLE

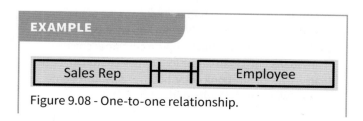

Figure 9.08 - One-to-one relationship.

Figure 9.08 shows a one-to-one relationship between a Sales Rep and an Employee. Each sales rep is related to one employee and each employee can only be one sales rep.

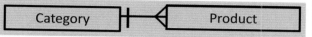

Figure 9.09 - One-to-many relationship.

Figure 9.09 shows a one-to-many relationship between Category and Product. Each category can have many products, but each product has only one category.

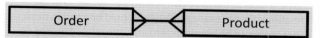

Figure 9.10 - Many-to-many relationship.

Figure 9.10 shows a many-to-many relationship between Order and Product. Each order can be for many products and each product can exist on many orders. This is a conceptual diagram only.

TASK

Describe each of the relationships in Figure 9.11.

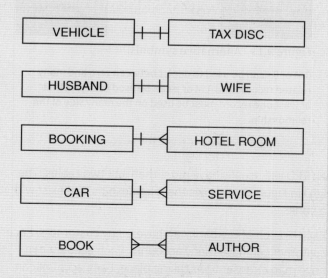

Figure 9.11 - Relationships.

DISCUSSION POINT

Different RDBMSs use different symbols. For example, Microsoft Access uses the infinity symbol for the many side of a relationship.

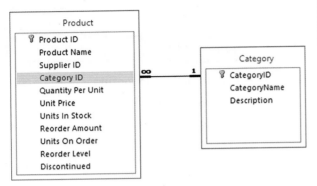

Figure 9.12 - Infinity symbol.

Other RDBMSs may use two symbols at each end of the relationship. For example, 0:1 or 0| could be used to depict that there can be between zero and one related record on that side of the relationship, whereas 1:1 or || could be used to depict that there must be exactly one related record on that side of the relationship.

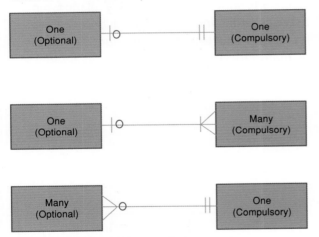

Figure 9.13 - Alternative symbols.

0:M or 0< can be used to depict between zero and many related records and 1:M or |<can be used to depict that at least one record must be used on the many side of the relationship.

An ERD will usually have more than just two tables. The ERD in Figure 9.14 shows the relationships that exist within a bank.

Each branch of the bank can have many customers. Each customer can have many accounts. Each account can have many transactions taking place. Each account can be of only one type but each type of account can exist as many accounts.

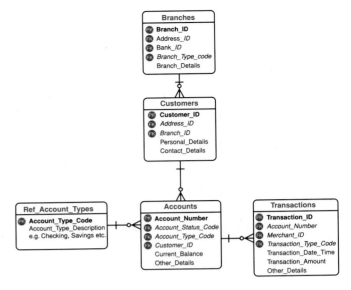

Figure 9.14 - Bank relationships.

EXAMPLE

💿 CD 9.02 Sales processing 2.mdb

The Product table in CD 9.02 Sales processing 2.mdb has the following relationships that have been implemented:

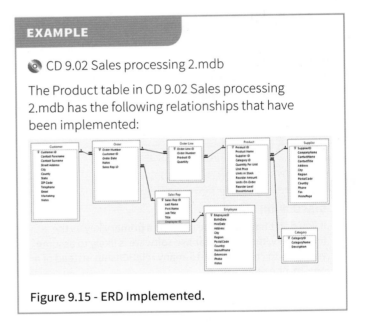

Figure 9.15 - ERD Implemented.

TASK

Draw ERDs to represent the following relationships:

1 One Airline Seat to one Customer.
2 One House to many Occupants.
3 Many Coaches to many Drivers.

Draw an ERD to represent a library model. Within the library, there are several **books**. There may be many copies of the same **book** which are known as **book copies**. **customers** can **loan** a **book copy**. **a customer** can have many **loans** but a **loan** will be for just one **customer**. Each **loan** will be for one **book copy**. but over a period of time each **book copy**. can be **loaned** out many times.

When a many-to-many relationship exists, it is necessary to break it down into two one-to-many relationships. The general rule for this is to put a LINK table between the two entities as shown in Figure 9.16.

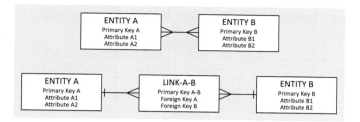

Figure 9.16 - Many-to-many.

A new primary key (Primary Key A-B) is created in the LINK table. The primary keys for each of the original entities are then used as foreign keys in the LINK table.

EXAMPLE

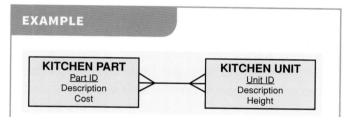

Figure 9.17 - Kitchen.

In this example, each **kitchen unit** can include many **kitchen parts**. As each **kitchen part** can be used for many **kitchen units**, a LINK table is required.

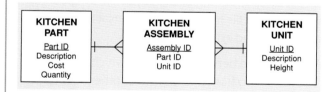

Figure 9.18 - Kitchen resolved.

The LINK table **kitchen assembly** is for each combination of unit and part. It has its own primary key, but the primary keys from **kitchen unit** and **kitchen part** are also used as foreign keys. The quantity of each part needed for each unit is also stored. This is what some of the data might look like:

KITCHEN UNIT

Unit ID	Description	Height
DR3-700	3 drawer unit	700
BU-700	Base unit	700
LR-2000	Larder unit	2000

KITCHEN PART

Part ID	Description	Cost
HNG	Hinge	0.30
HND	Handle	1.45
SHL	Shelf	4.50

KITCHEN ASSEMBLY

Assembly ID	Unit ID	Part ID	Quantity
1	DR3-700	HND	3
2	BU-700	HND	1
2	BU-700	HNG	2
2	BU-700	SHL	2
3	LR-2000	HND	1
3	LR-2000	HNG	4

TASK

Resolve the following many-to-many relationships and suggest attribute names for all three tables:

- many Orders to many Products
- many Hire Car to many Drivers
- many Authors to many Books
- many Students to many Classes
- many Employees to many Skills
- many Doctors to many Patients.

The difference between a flat file and a relational database

A **flat file** is a database that consists of a single table with no relationships. It is like looking at all the data in a single worksheet in a spreadsheet. It is called 'flat' because it only has two dimensions – fields and records.

EXAMPLE

This is an example of a simple flat file to store data about cars:

ID	Registration	Make	Model	Reg Year	Transmission
1	BX03HMW	Ford	Focus	2013	M
2	BR54URS	Vauxhall	Astra	2011	M
3	BA55WEP	Volkswagen	Beetle	2012	M
4	BC53PRS	Mini	Cooper	2013	M
5	BD05ABC	Nissan	Almera	2012	A
6	BE04RTJ	Renault	Megane	2011	M

EXAMPLE

The flat file below stores data about driving lessons, the cars used and the learners taking the lessons.

LESSON

Lesson ID	Lesson Date	Time Slot Start	Registration	Make	Model	Reg Year	Transmission	Forename	Surname	Telephone
1	27/08/2013	08:00	BR54URS	Vauxhall	Astra	2011	M	Aimee	Fenson	0555 555 556
2	28/08/2013	08:00	BD05ABC	Nissan	Almera	2012	A	Roger	Drake	0555 555 557
3	31/08/2013	11:00	BD05ABC	Nissan	Almera	2012	A	Roger	Drake	0555 555 557
4	31/05/2014	16:00	BC53PRS	Mini	Cooper	2013	M	Aimee	Fenson	0555 555 556
5	01/06/2014	16:00	BR54URS	Vauxhall	Astra	2011	M	Aimee	Fenson	0555 555 556
6	29/08/2013	19:00	BC53PRS	Mini	Cooper	2013	M	Sally	Mastock	0555 555 555

The data about the car is repeated and the data about the learner driver taking lessons is also repeated. This example only contains a small amount of redundant data, but imagine if data about the distance each car had travelled was stored, or the full address of the learner and their date of birth.

In the flat file example box, the data about cars was very similar to a table you would find in a relational database. However, with larger flat files there is a problem when all the data is in one table because there will be redundant data. Redundant data is data that is unnecessarily repeated.

Redundant data uses up additional memory. It can also cause problems with inconsistency and maintaining the flat file. If Aimee Fenson changes her telephone number, then it will need to be changed for every lesson that Aimee has taken. If some are missed, then there will be inconsistent data, meaning that a search will not produce accurate results because Aimee has more than one phone number. When a new lesson is entered, all the details of the car and the learner have to be entered rather than just their primary keys. This can lead to further inconsistent data and errors.

Flat files do have their uses though. They are often simple to set up as sometimes data can be entered into the file without needing to set up data types, field sizes or relationships. They can be shared easily through email and across the internet because the data is not dependent upon specific file types or software. It is also easy to add additional information to a flat file because it's a simple case of adding new columns. As all the data is in one single table, it is also very quick for the computer to process the data.

Relational databases are more useful when data needs to be managed properly. They resolve the problems of inaccurate data, inconsistencies and redundant data by using related tables.

Relational databases are used to reduce redundancy. Where data is likely to be repeated if stored in a single flat file then it is preferable to store this data in a set of related tables. For example, a relational database about a library would include separate tables for books, borrowers and loans. Flat files are used when processing speed is essential. Data is likely to have been stored in a relational database originally but exported to a flat file for processing. Flat files would be used in transactional processing systems such as when processing monthly salary payments by updating the master payment file from employee transactions such as hours worked and expenses claimed.

Links are created between the tables which means data can be looked up from one table to another. This takes time and expertise to plan in order to ensure that it is all set up correctly. It also means that processing time can be a bit slower, especially when there are large data sets. It is possible to share a relational database across a network or even the internet and apply security permissions to each table so that different types of users can access different tables. This is not possible with a flat file as it is all in one table. Queries can be created that enable data to be searched and sorted efficiently using a relational database and they can also join data together from related tables. It's also possible to produce detailed and customised reports of the data stored within a relational database. Relational databases are also flexible because additional fields and tables can be added without disturbing the rest of the data.

EXAMPLE

The flat file in the previous example could be stored in a relational database as a set of three tables:

LESSON

Lesson ID	Lesson Date	Time Slot Start	Registration	Learner ID
1	27/08/2013	08:00	BR54URS	
2	28/08/2013	08:00	BD05ABC	
3	31/08/2013	11:00	BD05ABC	

CAR

ID	Registration	Make	Model	Reg Year	Transmission
2	BR54URS	Vauxhall	Astra	2011	M
4	BC53PRS	Mini	Cooper	2013	M
5	BD05ABC	Nissan	Almera	2012	A

LEARNER

Learner ID	Forename	Surname	Address 1	Address 2	Post Code	Gender	Telephone	Mobile	Licence Number
9	Sally	Mastock	15 Cloud Road	Kingston-Upon-Hull	KI8 6GU	F	0555 555 555	0777 777 777	MAST9999999SA9XX
10	Aimee	Fenson	23 Yandle Lane	Shrewsbury	KN3 7YY	F	0555 555 556	0777 777 778	FENS9999999AI9XX
11	Roger	Drake	19 Spion Kop	Liverpool	L15 9PL	M	0555 555 557	0777 777 779	DRAK9999999RA9XX

Table 9.01 further examines the types of searches and queries that can be applied to flat files and those that can be applied to relational databases.

Flat file database	Relational database
A search or query has to load the entire database in order to find the data needed. For example, to find information about the car with registration BC53PRS, the database would need to search for every occurrence in the whole lesson flat file.	A search or query only has to load the tables required. For example to find the same information, only the CAR table would need to be loaded.
A search or query will find all the data required in one file. For example, to find all lessons taken by Aimee Fenson, a filter could be applied to the Forename and Surname columns.	A search or query would have to assimilate data from more than one table. For example, to find all the lessons taken by Aimee Fenson, her Learner ID would need to be looked up in the LEARNER table and then the Learner ID would need to be found in the LESSON table.
Running a query to find the number of vehicles with manual transmission would mean searching the whole file and then identifying unique occurrences of each car and then counting only those that are manual transmission.	To run the same query would simply require filtering the CAR table to show only manual transmission and then a summary count of the number of records.

Table 9.01 - Types of searches and queries that can be applied to flat file databases and relational databases.

Import data

Data can be imported from text files so that data that has been created in another system or for another purpose can be used within the database. The text files must be structured in such a way that fields can be recognised and records can be separated. Comma separated values (CSV) is a common format used for this purpose. Fields are separated by commas, records are separated by line breaks and speech marks are used to identify text. The use of a separation character means that the field lengths are delimited, which means each field can be any length.

> **EXAMPLE**
>
> This is a CSV file for books. The first row contains the field names.
>
> "ID","Book title","Genre","Reading age","ISBN","Author"
>
> 1,"A Soldier's Tale","Thriller",12,"0-321-93561-1","B Rushmore"
>
> 2,"Hidden Gold","Mystery",10,"0-342-92763-X","J T King"
>
> 3,"Fearless","Action",14,"0-250-34751-9","K Lawrence"

CSV is only one common format. Text files (TXT) can also be used. Text files can be formatted in exactly the same way as a CSV file or they can use different characters to separate fields. They can also be structured to have fixed length fields, which means spaces are used to fill the gaps.

> **EXAMPLE**
>
> This is a fixed length field text file for students.
>
> ```
> 1    Smith        Larry      9F
> 2    Nyakatawa    Paul       9B
> 3    Kalsi        Waheed     10R
> 4    Woolfenden   Howard     11M
> 5    Patel        Poonam     9N
> ```

Some DBMSs allow data to be imported from rich text format (RTF) files. The data must be in a table within the RTF file.

> **EXAMPLE**
>
> Figure 9.19 is a RTF file with field headings as the top row of the table.
>
> | ID | Loan date | Return date | Student ID | Copy ID |
> |---|---|---|---|---|
> | 1 | 12/11/2010 | 29/11/2010 | 9 | 21 |
> | 2 | 12/11/2010 | 24/11/2010 | 3 | 22 |
> | 3 | 05/01/2011 | 01/02/2011 | 4 | 23 |
> | 4 | 01/02/2011 | | 9 | 17 |
>
> Figure 9.19 - RTF file.

> **TASK**
>
> CD 9.03 Book
>
> CD 9.04 Student
>
> Create a new database and import the following files:
> - CD 9.03 Book (file includes row headings)
> - CD 9.04 Student.

Create a relational database

The first step in creating a database is to create the file that will be used. Other steps can then include creating:

- tables
- relationships
- forms
- reports.

> **TASK**
>
> CD 9.03 Book
>
> CD 9.06 Student
>
> CD 9.07 Copy
>
> CD 9.08 Loan
>
> Create a new database called CD 9.15 My library that will be used to store information about books in a school library.
> 1. Create a new database file.
> 2. Import the files:
>   a. CD 9.03 Book
>   b. CD 9.05 Student
>   c. CD 9.06 Copy
>   d. CD 9.07 Loan.
> 3. Check the data types for each field in each table and change if necessary.
> 4. Check the field lengths for each field in each table and change if necessary (do not leave them as 256 characters in length).

Keys

Primary key

A primary key is a unique identifier for each record in a table. Therefore, the field used for the primary key must contain unique values and not have any repeating values. Examples of primary keys could include:

- registration plate for a car
- student number for a student
- product code for a product.

It is important that data within primary keys never changes as it can be used within a relationship. Therefore, some fields that may appear on the surface to be suitable as a primary key may not be suitable in the long run. For example, a registration plate for a car can be changed in some countries. For this reason, it is always best to use separate ID fields as primary keys.

Order Number	Product ID	Quantity
1	1	1
1	2	2
2	3	1
2	3	1
3	4	1
4	5	1
4	6	1
5	5	1
5	6	2

EXAMPLE

Table name	Primary key
Car	CarID
Student	StudentID
Product	ProductID

These ID fields should be used purely for the structure of the database. It is still possible to set another field to be unique, but the primary key should be used for relationships. If possible, the primary key should be set to increment automatically (e.g. AutoNumber).

Compound key

A **compound key** is two or more fields combined to form a unique identity. These should not be used in relational database design as they can be complex to use, especially within relationships. Instead, you should use a separate field as a primary key.

EXAMPLE

The Order Line table below shows the products and quantities ordered for each order. As long as each order only includes each Product on one Order Line, then the combination of Order Number and Product ID is unique.

! DISCUSSION POINT

The table below shows appointments for a doctor. If Doctor ID and Patient ID were selected as the compound key, then this would mean each patient could only see each doctor once and so this combination would not be suitable. If Doctor ID, Patient ID and Date were selected as the compound key then this would mean each patient could only see each doctor once each day. It may be acceptable to the doctor to see a patient only once per day, but if the doctor needs to see the same patient more than once on the same day, then a combination of all four fields including Time would be needed as the compound key.

Doctor ID	Patient ID	Date	Time
1	1	5/11/17	12:00
1	2	2/9/17	13:00
2	3	18/9/17	13:00
1	1	12/11/17	12:00
2	3	18/9/17	17:30

Foreign key

A foreign key is a field in a table that refers to the primary key in another table. It is used to create the relationship between the two tables. The foreign key must always have the same data type and field size as the primary key to which it is linking. The foreign key must always be on the many side of the relationship. The foreign key will always link to a single primary key field.

EXAMPLE

Customer ID in the Order table is a foreign key which links to the Customer ID in the Customer table.

Order

Order Number	Customer ID	Order Date
1	2	28/05/2015
2	1	22/05/2015
3	5	06/05/2015
4	3	05/04/2015
5	7	06/05/2015

Customer

Customer ID	Contact Forename	Contact Surname
1	Reina	Wolchesky
2	Marc	Wanger
3	Damion	Matkin
4	Lucius	Winchester
5	Petra	Mcnichol
6	Katina	Ramano
7	Leslie	Cackowski
8	Cristopher	Wiget

Figure 9.20 - Foreign key.

TASK

CD 9.15 My library

Open CD 9.15 My library that you created earlier.
1 Assign primary keys to existing fields in each table.

Each book has several copies. Each copy of the book can be loaned out several times. Each loan is for only one student and only one copy of a book. Each student can take out several loans.
2 Create relationships between the tables.

CD 9.08 Driving school.mdb

Open CD 9.08 Driving school.mdb
3 Set the primary key for the Instructor table.
4 Create a new primary key for the Car table (do not use Registration).
5 Create a new primary key for the Learner table.
6 Create a compound primary key for the Lesson table. You will need at least three fields for this.

Each car can be used in several lessons. Each student can have several lessons. Each instructor can give several lessons. Each lesson will be for one student with one instructor in one car.
7 Create relationships between the tables.

Referential integrity

Referential integrity exists when data in the foreign key of the table on the many side of a relationship exists in the primary key of the table on the one side of a relationship.

EXAMPLE

In the Order table below, Customer ID 5 does not exist in the Customer table. This means that the Order table does not contain referential integrity because the related customer does not exist.

Order

Order Number	Customer ID	Order Date
1	2	28/05/2015
2	1	22/05/2015
3	5	06/05/2015

Customer

Customer ID	Contact Forename	Contact Surname
1	Reina	Wolchesky
2	Marc	Wanger

Figure 9.21 - No referential integrity.

Without referential integrity a relationship cannot be properly set within a database. It is a type of lookup validation where the database will check to see if the related record exists before allowing it to be entered. If the related record does not exist, then the database will prevent the foreign key data from being entered.

This is important for maintaining the accuracy of the data within the database. If details of which classes you attend were entered into a database, but those classes did not exist, then the database would not be able to give you any information about the classes.

TASK

CD 9.09 Sales processing 3.mdb

Open CD 9.09 Sales processing 3.mdb

1 Open the order table and add Sales Rep IDs 4, 5, 8, 11 and 15 to the records.
   a Which ones worked?
   b Which ones did not work?
   c Why didn't they work?
2 Try to create a relationship between Product and Category and enforce referential integrity.
   a What happens?
   b Why has this happened?
   c Correct any data that is causing this problem and try to create the relationship again.

Validate and verify data
Validation rules

The principal of validation was introduced in Chapter 1. Database management systems can apply validation rules to data that is input. If data passes the validation rules, then they will be accepted. If data fail the validation rules, then they will be rejected and an error message may be shown.

EXAMPLE

In this database, the user is attempting to enter the title that a Sales Rep will be addressed by. They have four valid options – "Mr", "Mrs", "Miss" or "Dr". The user has accidentally entered "Msr" which is not a valid option. An error message has appeared telling the user what to do to fix the problem.

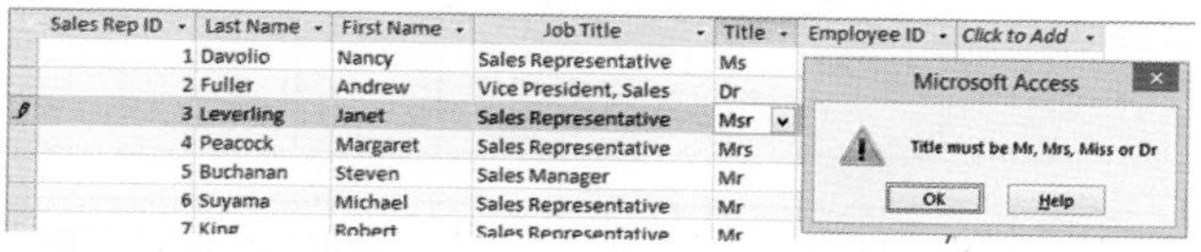

Figure 9.22 - Error message.

This is the rule that had been set up:

| Validation rule | In('Mr', 'Mrs', 'Miss', 'Dr') |
| Validation text | Title must be Mr, Mrs, Miss or Dr |

Figure 9.23 - Validation rule.

The rule ensures that the only data that can be entered must exist in the list that contains "Mr", "Mrs", "Miss" and "Dr". It is a lookup in list method of validation.

TASK

CD 9.10 Sales processing validation.mdb

Open CD 9.10 Sales processing validation.mdb and open the table Employee.
1 Create a validation rule that will only allow the entry of "UK" or "USA" for the Country.
2 Create an appropriate error message.

There are a variety of validation rules that can be used within a database including:

- lookup in list (by looking up in a list entered within the rule)
- lookup in list (by using referential integrity)
- lookup in list (by using a lookup table)
- range
- data type
- format
- length
- presence.

EXAMPLE

Type	Field	Rule
Lookup in list	Gender	"M" or "F"
Lookup in list	Title	IN ("Mr", "Mrs", "Miss", "Dr")
Range	Date of Birth	>DATE() (must be after today's date)
Range	Date Joined	>28/02/1995
Range	Reorder Amount	Between 1 and 2000
Range	Reorder Level	>0
Data Type	State	Like "[A-Z][A-Z]" (must be two text characters)
Format	Email Address	Like "*@*.*" (* means any character)
Length	Colour	Like "??" (must be two characters)
Presence	Forename	IS NOT NULL

150

TASK

💿 CD 9.10 Sales processing validation.mdb

Open CD 9.10 Sales processing validation.mdb and open the table Customer.

1 Create a validation rule to ensure the surname is present.
2 Create a validation rule to ensure that an email address includes the @ symbol and a full stop.
3 Create a validation rule to ensure the telephone number is 12 characters long.

Open the table Product.

4 Create a validation rule to ensure the Units in Stock is a positive number.
5 Create a validation rule to ensure the Reorder Amount is less than 1000.
6 Create a validation rule to ensure the Reorder Level is at least 0 and no more than 100.

Open the Employee table.

7 Create a validation rule to ensure the Hire Date is at least today.
8 Create a validation rule to ensure the region is two characters long and only contains letters.
9 Create a validation rule to ensure the extension is either three or four characters long and only contains numbers.
10 Create a validation rule to ensure the Hire Date is after the Birth Date.

Validation applied to a database

You should follow the same process that you learned in Chapter 8 by using valid, invalid, extreme valid and extreme invalid data.

TASK

💿 CD 9.10 Sales processing validation.mdb

Open CD 9.10 Sales processing validation.mdb and open the table Customer

1 The State field has a validation rule applied to it.
  a Try changing the state for Reina Wolchesky to NN. What happens? Why does this happen?
  b Try changing the state for Reina Wolchesky to NM instead of MN. Why was this error allowed to happen?
  c Identify five items of test data that could be used to test this validation rule.
2 The ZIP Code field has validation applied to it.
  a Try different combinations of data to see if you can work out what the validation rule is.

b Identify eight items of test data that could be used to test this validation rule. You should use valid, invalid, valid extreme and invalid extreme data.

Verify data entry

In Chapter 1 you learned that data that has been validated is not necessarily correct. It is therefore necessary to verify data. When inputting data into a database, you should verify that the data input has been entered correctly by comparing what has been entered with the original source.

TASK

💿 CD 9.10 Sales processing validation.mdb

Open CD 9.10 Sales processing validation.mdb and open the table Customer.

1 Visually check that the data for Damion Matkin matches the original data below:

Contact Forename	Contact Surname	Street Address	City	County	State
Damion	Matkin	5830 Downing St	Denver	Denver	CO

ZIP Code	Telephone	Email	Marketing	Notes
80216	303-295-4797	damion@matkin.com	Yes	

2 Add the following data to the customer table and then visually check the data matches the source:

Contact Forename	Contact Surname	Street Address	City	County	State
Joel	Nardo	5150 Town Cir	Boca Raton	Palm Beach	FL

ZIP Code	Telephone	Email	Marketing	Notes
33486	561-395-2277	joel@nardo.com	Yes	

Searches

So far you have looked at whole tables. It is also possible to view only records which meet certain conditions known as criteria. This can be achieved by creating a **query** which asks questions about the data in order to retrieve the required records.

Simple queries

A simple query has only one criterion (singular for criteria). A criterion is the rule that will be applied to the data.

When creating a simple query, it is also possible to specify which fields will be listed.

EXAMPLE

The following table shows examples of when you would use a simple query for a particular outcome.

Field	Criterion	Outcome
State	="CA"	Lists all customers who live in CA (California)
Marketing	True	Lists all customers who have agreed to receive marketing
Mark	100	Lists all students who achieved 100 marks
Mark	<50	Lists all students who achieved less than 50 marks
Price	>3.99	Lists all products with a price more than 3.99 (i.e. 4.00 or above)
Distance covered by car	>=50000	Lists all cars with a distance travelled of at least 50 000 kilometres
Width	<=50	Lists all products with a width up to and including 50 mm
Date of Joining	<01/01/2010	Lists all employees who joined the company before 1 January 2010
Appointment Time	>= 12:00pm	Lists all appointments in the afternoon
Surname	Like "A*"	Lists all customers with a surname starting with A
Product Code	Like "??B??"	Lists all product codes where the third character is B
Allergy	NOT "Nut"	Lists all students who do not have a nut allergy

EXAMPLE

CD 9.02 Sales processing 2.mdb

In CD 9.02 Sales processing 2.mdb a simple query has been created to show all Sales Reps who have a Job Title of Sales Representative:

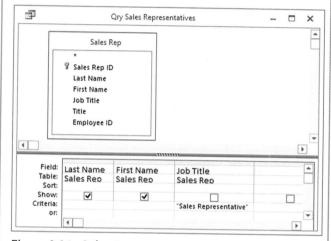

Figure 9.24 - Sales Rep query.

The criterion of Job Title = "Sales Representative" means that only sales reps with that job title will be listed. The only fields that will be listed are Last Name and First Name. Job Title will not be listed because the option to show it has been deselected. This is what the result of the simple query looks like:

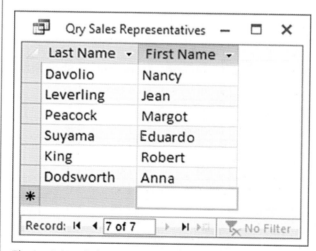

Figure 9.25 - Sales Rep query result.

It is also possible to include data from a related table.

EXAMPLE

⊙ CD 9.02 Sales processing 2.mdb

In CD 9.02 Sales processing 2.mdb a query has been created to show all Products over $75 including their categories:

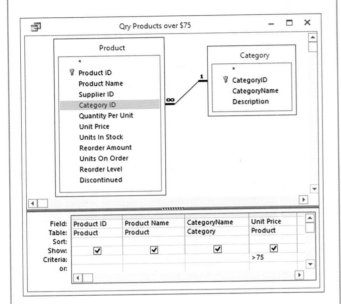

Figure 9.26 - Product Category.

The CategoryName has been included from the Category Table which is related to the Product Table through the Category ID.

TASK

⊙ CD 9.02 Sales processing 2.mdb

Open CD 9.02 Sales processing 2.mdb, identify which query is most suitable and then create queries for the following:

1. All UK employees.
2. All employees from Seattle.
3. All employees who were born on or after 1/1/1960.
4. All products that include the word "bottles" in the quantity per unit.
5. All products with no units in stock.
6. The product name and supplier company name of all products that have been discontinued.
7. The names and categories of all products with at least 100 units in stock.
8. The names and price of products that are in the category "Condiments".
9. A list of all orders that were not placed on 6/5/15.
10. A list of all Sales Reps who do not have a job title of "Sales Representative".
11. A list of all products where the Units in Stock is less than or equal to the Reorder Level.

Complex queries

Complex queries are queries that have more than one criterion. They use either the AND or OR Boolean operators. If all specified criteria need to be satisfied, then the AND operator is used. If any one of the specified criteria needs to be satisfied, then the OR operator is used.

Complex queries are not restricted to just two criteria. They can have as many criteria as necessary for the query.

EXAMPLE

The table below lists characteristics about some people.

Surname	Forename	Height	Shoe Size	Eyes	Nationality	Occupation	Sex
Greer	Wendy	1.85	7	Blue	British	Firefighter	F
Percy	Hugo	1.75	8	Blue	French	Welder	M
Pearce	Madison	1.85	8	Blue	American	Musician	F
Gardiner	Felicia	1.85	9	Blue	South African	Waitress	F
Ivanova	Sofia	1.65	8	Brown	Russian	Road sweeper	F
Joo	Haeun	1.35	9	Brown	South Korean	Firefighter	F
Goswami	Lamar	1.75	9	Brown	Indian	Shop Assistant	M
Kaya	Yusuf	1.95	10	Blue	Turkish	Teacher	M
Danshov	Aleksander	1.8	6	Hazel	Russian	Politician	M
Mallapati	Smriti	1.6	11	Hazel		Singer	F
Martinez	Maria	1.85	5	Green	Argentinian	Bus Driver	F

152

The complex query Eyes = Blue **AND** Shoe Size = 8 would return the following:

Surname	Forename	Height	Shoe Size	Eyes	Nationality	Occupation	Sex
Percy	Hugo	1.75	8	Blue	French	Welder	M
Pearce	Madison	1.85	8	Blue	American	Musician	F

As both parts of the query have to be satisfied, only people with both blue eyes and a shoe size of 8 will be listed.

The complex query Eyes = Hazel **OR** Eyes = Green would return the following:

Surname	Forename	Height	Shoe Size	Eyes	Nationality	Occupation	Sex
Danshov	Aleksander	1.8	6	Hazel	Russian	Politician	M
Mallapati	Smriti	1.6	11	Hazel		Singer	F
Martinez	Maria	1.85	5	Green	Argentinian	Bus Driver	F

As any one part of the query can be satisfied, all people with either hazel or green eyes are listed.

The complex query Eyes = Brown **OR** Nationality = Russia would return the following:

Surname	Forename	Height	Shoe Size	Eyes	Nationality	Occupation	Sex
Ivanova	Sofia	1.65	8	Brown	Russian	Road sweeper	F
Joo	Haeun	1.35	9	Brown	South Korean	Firefighter	F
Goswami	Lamar	1.75	9	Brown	Indian	Shop Assistant	M
Danshov	Aleksander	1.8	6	Hazel	Russian	Politician	M

Aleksander Danshov does not have brown eyes, but he is Russian and so is included in the list. Similarly, Haeun Joo and Lamar Goswami are not Russian but because they have brown eyes they are included in the list.

EXAMPLE

The following nested query uses a combination of AND and OR and includes more than two criteria:

Sex = F AND (Eyes = Blue OR Eyes = Brown) AND Height > 1.5

These are the results of the nested query:

Surname	Forename	Height	Shoe Size	Eyes	Nationality	Occupation	Sex
Greer	**Wendy**	**1.85**	**7**	**Blue**	**British**	**Firefighter**	**F**
Pearce	Madison	1.85	8	Blue	American	Musician	F
Gardiner	Felicia	1.85	9	Blue	South African	Waitress	F
Ivanova	Sofia	1.65	8	Brown	Russian	Road sweeper	F

TASK

CD 9.02 Sales processing 2.mdb

Open CD 9.02 Sales processing 2.mdb, identify which query is most suitable and then create queries for the following:
1   All customers from Texas (TX) or Illinois (IL).
2   All customers who would like to receive marketing and live in Ohio (OH).
3   All products priced at least $50 with no units in stock, showing the Product Name and Supplier's Company Name.
4   All products over $30 supplied by companies in Germany.
5   All products under $30 supplied by companies in Denmark or Sweden.
6   A list of all products where the Units in Stock is less than or equal to the Reorder Level and the Units on Order is zero.

Nested queries

So far, each query that you have seen has been based upon existing tables within a database. It is also possible to create a query on an existing query. This means that the results of the original query will be narrowed down further by the new query. This is called a nested query.

EXAMPLE

CD 9.02 Sales processing 2.mdb

In CD 9.02 Sales processing 2.mdb a query has been created to show all customers who live in California (CA). A nested query is then created on top of the California Query to find customers in the California Query who placed an order on 6/5/15:

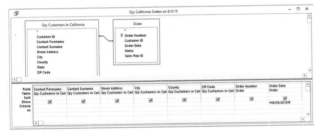

Figure 9.27 - Nested query.

The new query is based upon the California query and the Order table.

DISCUSSION POINT

A nested query is effectively a query that has multiple criteria and is equivalent to using AND. However, they can be used to make very complex queries easier to follow and set up by breaking down the individual steps required to create the query. There are also occasions when a nested query is necessary to achieve the desired results, such as creating a cross-tab query based on two or more tables.

TASK

CD 9.02 Sales processing 2.mdb

Open CD 9.02 Sales processing 2.mdb, identify which query is most suitable and then create a query based on the existing query "Qry Products over $75" that will show those products in the Meat/Poultry category.

Summary queries

A cross-tab query is a type of summary query used to summarise data. It can be used to show the total number of records, the sum of values within a field, averages or other statistical data.

EXAMPLE

CD 9.12 People.mdb

CD 9.12 People.mdb contains a cross-tab query that shows the total number of people of each nationality. It also breaks this down into how many males and females there are in each nationality.

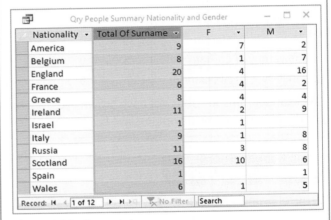

Figure 9.28 - Cross-tab query.

In order to set this up, it is necessary to identify which fields will be used as row headings, which fields will be used as column headings and which field the summary of data will be used:

Nationality	Sex1	Sex2	Sex3
Nationality 1	Count (Surname)		
Nationality 2			
Nationality 3			
Nationality 4			

Figure 9.29 - Cross-tab wizard.

This can also be seen in the configuration settings where the data is grouped by nationality and sex as row and column headings and the surname is counted:

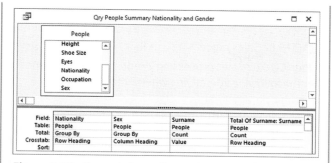

Figure 9.30 - Cross-tab configuration.

You will notice that a new calculated field of "Total of Surname" has been added that counts the total number of people. This is not essential unless the overall totals are required.

DISCUSSION POINT

To create a cross-tab query based on data from more than one table, you should use a nested query by first creating a query that joins the tables together and then creating the cross-tab query based on the original query.

A pivot table is another type of summary query that allows data to be summarised by selecting the row headings and column headings to be used to give summary data. For example, within a database that keeps records of orders placed by customers, a pivot table could be used to show how many customers from each area of the country purchased each product.

TASK

CD 9.11 People.mdb

Open CD 9.11 People.mdb and create cross-tab queries to show:
1 The number of people of each gender with eyes of each colour.
2 The number of people of each occupation (no need to have a column grouping).
3 The number of people of each gender with each shoe size.

CD 9.02 Sales processing 2.mdb

Open CD 9.02 Sales processing 2.mdb and create cross-tab queries to show:

1 The number of suppliers in each country.
2 The number of customers in each state.

3 The number of products in each category (the category names must be showing so you will need to join the Product and Category tables first).
4 The total price of each product in each category.

Using simple, complex, nested and summary queries

Simple queries should be used when only one criterion is required, such as Gender = Male.

Complex queries should be used when more than one criteria are required, such as Gender = Male AND Country = Israel, or Gender = Male OR Country = Israel.

A nested query can be used in the following situations:

- When an OR needs to be combined with an AND as this will avoid the problem of having to repeat the AND part of the query for each OR. It will also avoid the problem of not getting the criteria in the correct order.
- When there are lots of criteria and nesting the queries will make the criteria easier to understand.
- When a query can be reused and so creating a nested query saves the developer having to recreate some of the criteria.

A summary query can be used in the following situations:

- When multiple tables are required within a cross-tab query.
- When a cross-tab query is summarising data from another cross-tab query.

Static parameters

So far all the queries you have used include static **parameters**. The parameters are the values used within the criteria. Each time the query is run, the values of the parameters will not change.

EXAMPLE

The query for all customers from Texas (TX) or Illinois (IL) had static parameters of TX and IL. These values do not change

Dynamic parameters

Dynamic parameters allow the values within the criteria to be chosen at the time of running the query. This can

155

be useful when the user needs to decide what those parameters might be.

156

EXAMPLE

💿 CD 9.02 Sales processing 2.mdb

In CD 9.02 Sales processing 2.mdb, a query has been created to show all customers in the state that will be chosen by the user:

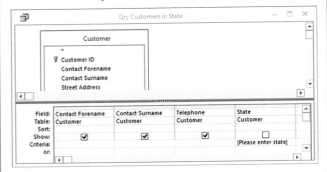

Figure 9.31 - Dynamic query.

The criterion of [Please enter state] will be a prompt to the user to enter the state. This is what the prompt looks like when the query is run:

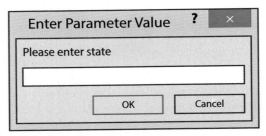

Figure 9.32 - Parameter.

If the user enters AZ then all the customers in Arizona will be listed:

Contact Forename	Contact Surname	Telephone
Prince	Kauk	623-581-7435
Danny	Dales	602-225-9543
Lucas	Santellana	602-225-3469
Sabrina	Deppert	602-954-4343
*		

Figure 9.33 - Arizona.

Dynamic parameters can be used with ranges (<, >, <=, >=) and Boolean operators (NOT, AND, OR). They can also be used alongside static parameters within a complex query.

TASK

💿 CD 9.02 Sales processing 2.mdb

Open CD 9.02 Sales processing 2.mdb and create queries for the following (identifying whether to use static or dynamic parameters):

1 All sales reps with a Title of the user's choosing.
2 All products with a price below the user's choosing.
3 All products with a reorder amount above the user's choosing.
4 All products with more than 100 units in stock that have a unit price below the user's choosing.
5 All products with a category of the user's choosing that are also above a price of the user's choosing.

Analysing and evaluating when static and dynamic parameters should be used in queries

Static parameter values should be used when those parameter values will not change, no matter how many times the query is used. For example, if you wanted to search a table on a regular basis for all customers based in China, then you would use a static parameter query with the criterion of Country = "China". Dynamic parameters should be used when the user is likely to want to change the value each time the query is run. For example, if you wanted a query that would enable you to search for a specific product code, but that product code could be different each time, then you would use a dynamic query with the criterion of Product Code = [Please enter product code].

Perform calculations within a database

Within a database, calculations can be performed on fields. This can be done within forms, reports and queries. Within a form, a text box can be added to the form which includes the calculation. As with spreadsheets, the calculation must start with the equals (=) sign.

EXAMPLE

💿 CD 9.02 Sales processing 2.mdb

In the Order Form from CD 9.02 Sales processing 2.mdb, the Total Price for each order line has been calculated by multiplying the Quantity by the Unit Price. The Order Total has been calculated by adding up all the Quantities multiplied by their corresponding Unit Prices.

The calculation for Total Price is = [Quantity] * [Unit Price]

The calculation for Order Total is = SUM ([Quantity] * [Unit Price])

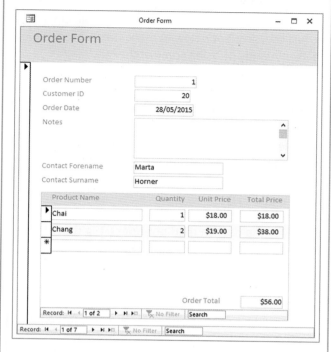

Figure 9.34 - Order Form.

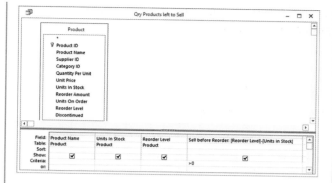

Figure 9.35 - Query calculation.

The calculation subtracts the Units in Stock from the Reorder Level. In order to remove any products that are already below their Reorder Level, a criterion has been added that the total must be greater than zero. Here is an extract of the result of the query:

Product Name	Units In Stock	Reorder Level	Sell before Reorder
Chang	17	25	8
Aniseed Syrup	13	25	12
Queso Cabrales	22	30	8
Sir Rodney's Scones	3	5	2

157

DISCUSSION POINT

In some database management systems, such as Microsoft Access, calculated fields such as Total Price cannot be used in a SUM function. Therefore, the SUM has to use the full calculation rather than simply referring to =SUM([Total Price]).

TASK

CD 9.02 Sales processing 2.mdb

Open CD 9.02 Sales processing 2.mdb and create a query to calculate the new Units In Stock when the Units On Order are added to the current Units In Stock.

Calculations within reports are carried out in the same way as within forms. Within a query, the calculation needs to be defined by giving it a name and then identifying what the calculation will be.

Sort data

Ascending/descending

Data can be sorted in ascending or descending order. This can be done within a table, within a query or within a report. The order can be based on numbers, alphabetical characters, dates or times.

Grouped

More than one field can be used to create the sort. This is commonly used when sorting names into order. The surname would be set as the first sort order and then if there are any people with the same surname, the forename would be set as the second sort order.

EXAMPLE

CD 9.02 Sales processing 2.mdb

In CD 9.02 Sales processing 2.mdb, a query has been created to calculate how many products are left to sell before more need to be reordered:

EXAMPLE

The data below is sorted in order of colour of eyes and then within each colour, it is sorted by height:

Surname	Forename	Eyes	Height
Percy	Hugo	Blue	1.75
Hughes	Carl	Blue	1.8
Gardiner	Felicia	Blue	1.85
Greer	Wendy	Blue	1.85
Young	Rose	Blue	1.9
Cox	Arnold	Blue	1.9
Inan	Menekse	Blue	1.9
Hansen	Mathias	Blue	1.95
Xu	Huan	Brown	1.35
Li	Fen	Brown	1.64
Petrova	Alisa	Brown	1.7
Truong	Dinh	Brown	1.85
Saltings	Damien	Brown	1.85
Fontana	Giuseppe	Brown	1.95
Himura	Yuki	Green	1.75
Martinez	Maria	Green	1.85
Brown	Joseph	Green	1.9
Danshov	Aleksander	Hazel	1.8
Banton	Cedric	Hazel	1.85
Hammer	Daniel	Hazel	1.9

Data entry forms

As its name suggests, a data entry form is used for the entry of data. It can also be used to view existing data.

When designing a data entry form, you should consider who will be using it and how to make the form effective and user friendly by using some of the following techniques.

Appropriate font styles and sizes

Fonts should be plain and easy to read. A consistent font style should be used throughout so the user does not have to adjust to viewing different font styles. The colour of fonts should either be dark on a light background or light on a dark background so that the user can read the fonts clearly. The size should be big enough for the user to read but not so big that all the data does not fit on the screen. Titles and subtitles should be in larger fonts.

Spacing between fields

There should be enough space for the user to be able to distinguish between the data within each field. If you look at Figure 9.36, you will see that the fields on the left are separated by providing space between them and each field has a box around it to separate it from other fields. On the right you will see that there is

EXAMPLE

CD 9.12 Outlet monitoring.mdb

The form from CD 9.12 Outlet monitoring.mdb is used for monitoring inspections carried out at retail outlets within a shopping centre.

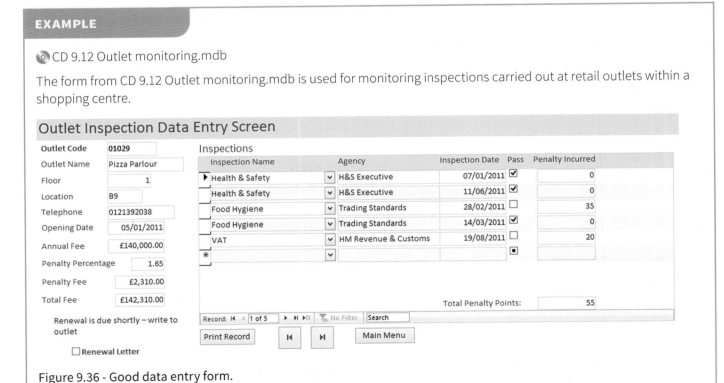

Figure 9.36 - Good data entry form.

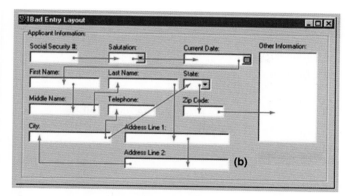

Figure 9.37 - A badly designed input.

sufficient horizontal space between each field to know which field belongs to which title.

Character spacing of individual fields

There should be enough space between each character within the data for each field to enable the data to be viewed. If there is too much spacing then the user will struggle to read the data because it is spread out too much. If there is too little spacing then characters will overlap. If single words have been used for field names (e.g. Outlet Code), then when using field names on the form, the labels for the fields should include appropriate spacing (e.g. Outlet Code).

Use of white space

White space can be used to separate data and also to make sure a screen does not look too cluttered. In the example, you will see that there is white space used between the left and right hand sides, between field names and the data and between buttons. Having white space between controls such as buttons means that the user is less likely to select the wrong button by having the pointer slightly in the wrong position.

Navigation buttons

Navigation buttons allow the user to browse through records by choosing the next record, previous record, first record in a file or last record in a file.

Radio buttons

Radio (option) buttons allow a user to select one mutually exclusive option.

Check boxes

Check (tick) boxes can be used to select an item. It can be true (ticked) or false (not ticked). Check boxes are used for Boolean data types. In Figure 9.36, a tick box has been used for whether or not a renewal was sent to the outlet

EXAMPLE

When printing a document, print options may be available regarding how much of the document to print, such as all of the document, a range of pages or selected records (or pages).

Figure 9.38 - Radio buttons.

Only one of the radio (option) buttons can be chosen at a time.

and tick boxes have been used to identify whether each inspection was passed or not.

Drop-down menus

Drop-down menus allow the user to select from a set of options. They are used instead of radio buttons when space is limited. In Figure 9.36 you can see that each inspection can be selected from a drop-down menu. This means that the user is only able to select from the list so will not make any spelling mistakes or enter an inspection that does not exist. This also helps to maintain referential integrity.

Highlighting key fields

If the key field is useful to the user, then it may be appropriate to highlight it. Figure 9.36 shows the Outlet Code in bold. However, if the key field is only used for the

TASK

CD 9.13 Library.mdb

Evaluate the data entry form from CD 9.14 Library.mdb.

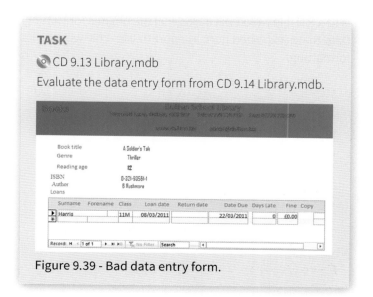

Figure 9.39 - Bad data entry form.

159

database structure, then it may not even be displayed. In Figure 9.36, there are no key fields displayed for the inspections or agencies.

Switchboards/menus

A menu can be used to help users navigate between elements of a database including forms, reports and action queries. A menu should include a title, clear instructions and buttons for each element.

Export data

In the same way that data can be imported from common formats, it can also be exported to common formats. This allows data to be used by other users who either do not have DBMS software or do not know how to use it. It can also be used to transfer data to other systems.

Table

Data in tables can be exported as a delimited file in CSV format, as fixed length fields in text format or as a table within a RTF file. It is sensible to save the field names when saving to CSV or text files.

Query

Data from queries can be exported in the same way as tables, but only the data that meets the criteria of the query will be exported.

Report

Reports include formatting, so the best method of export is to a RTF file which will include all the original formatting. Data that is exported from a report to a text file will lose its formatting.

160

TASK

CD 9.01 Sales processing.mdb

Open CD 9.01 Sales processing.mdb and export the following:
1 The Customer table in CSV format.
2 The UK Sales Reps query in fixed length fields text format.
3 The Categories of Products report in RTF format.

QUESTIONS

1 Define the term primary key.
2 Describe the difference between a simple query and a complex query.
3 Give an example of when a dynamic parameter query might be used.
4 Identify the decisions involved in exporting data from a table.
5 Explain the importance of referential integrity.

9.02 Normalisation to third normal form

 KEY TERM

Normalisation: process of structuring data in a database

Normalisation is the process of structuring data within a database. The process starts with a flat file and finishes with a set of related tables. It is a formal method of ensuring that each table is structured correctly and does not contain redundant data. There are stages throughout the process known as normal forms. Each normal form measures the extent to which the data has been normalised.

When describing tables, the following conventions will be used:

TABLENAME
<u>Primary Key</u>
Attribute 1
Attribute 2
TABLENAME (<u>Primary Key</u>, Attribute 1, Attribute 2)

Table names will be in capitals, primary keys will be underlined and all attributes will be listed below the table name or within brackets.

Unnormalised form

Data in unnormalised form (UNF) is a flat file. It will contain non-atomic data, repeating groups of data and possibly redundant data. Non-atomic data is where a field contains more than one item of data.

EXAMPLE

This table contains non-atomic data:

Product ID	Description	Price
327BLF	Brown, Leather, Female	₹ 3510
327BPM	Brown, Plastic, Male	₹ 2540
327CLF	Cream, Leather, Female	₹ 3510

The colour, material and gender are three separate items of data within the description. This causes a problem when trying to sort data by a specific characteristic, such as colour, or when trying to search by a specific characteristic. (Note: ₹ is the symbol for rupees.)

Repeating groups of data is when fields are repeated for each record or a record appears to have more than one set of data for a group of fields.

Redundant data exists when data is repeated unnecessarily. This can be spotted when data can be identified by knowing it is dependent upon another field.

First normal form

Data in first normal form (1NF) must satisfy the following criteria:

- all fields must contain atomic data
- there must be no repeating groups of data
- there must be a unique key.

EXAMPLE

This table contains fields that are repeated for each record:

Surname	Forename	Subject 1	Subject 2	Subject 3	Subject 4
Jones	Ifor	Welsh	English	History	
Rushton	Ken	Politics	Literature	Philosophy	Physics
Smallwood	Steven	Maths	Physics	German	

The Subject field has been repeated. This can be a problem when trying to search for all students studying the same subject or when a student only studies one subject (leaving several blank) or when a student needs to study a fifth subject.

This table contains more than one set of data for a group of fields:

Surname	Forename	Book	Date Out	Date Due
Jones	Ifor	Everything in Colour	12/5/16	12/6/16
		Guardian	12/5/16	12/6/16
Rushton	Ken	Saving Grace	14/5/16	14/6/16
Smallwood	Steven	Delirious	26/11/16	3/1/17
		Stretch Out	5/1/17	5/2/17
		Always Faithful	5/1/17	5/2/17

Each student is borrowing more than one book and so the fields Book, Date Out and Date Due contain more than one set of data per record. This could also be classed as non-atomic data as there is more than one data item per field.

EXAMPLE

The table below contains redundant data:

Order ID	Order Date	Product	Quantity	Price
3857	12/9/16	Marzipan	1	$1.50
		Flour	2	$0.75
2320	15/10/16	Marzipan	3	$1.50
		Sugar	1	$0.83
		Eggs	6	$0.15

The price is dependent upon the product and therefore it is being repeated unnecessarily. If we know the product, we know the price.

TASK

Describe the characteristics of data in 0NF using examples from the table of driving lessons:

Learner	Lesson Date	Instructor ID	Instructor	Price
Rob Pocock	30/5/16	4	Marcus Brown	$35
	6/6/16	4		$35
			Marcus Brown	
Graham Alkins	31/5/16	3	Mike Joyce	$30
	1/6/16	4	Marcus Brown	$35

EXAMPLE

The ORDER table below contains details of products ordered by customers:

ORDER
Order Date
Customer ID
Customer Name
Customer Address
    Product Code
    Description
    Quantity
    Price

Indented fields are a repeating group for each order.

To be in 1NF, this table needs:

- a unique key (Order Number)
- atomic data (Customer Name and Customer Address need breaking down)
- no repeating groups of data (products being ordered).

The ORDER table becomes:

ORDER (Order Number, Order Date, Customer ID, Customer Forename, Customer Surname, Customer Address 1, Customer Address 2, Customer Address 3, Customer ZIP Code)

A new table for the order of products needs to be added, but it needs to retain information about which order each order of products belongs to:

ORDERLINE (Order Number, Product Code, Description, Quantity, Price)

Order Number is retained in the ORDERLINE table as a foreign key. However, it is not unique and so cannot be used as the primary key. However, a combination of Order Number and Product Code are unique and so these becomes a compound key.

TASK

Normalise the table of driving lessons below to 1NF:

LESSON (Learner, Lesson Date, Instructor ID, Instructor, Price)

Learner	Lesson Date	Instructor ID	Instructor	Price
Rob Pocock	30/5/16	4	Marcus Brown	$35
	6/6/16	4	Marcus Brown	$35
Graham Alkins	31/5/16	3	Mike Joyce	$30
	1/6/16	4	Marcus Brown	$35

Second normal form

Data in second normal form (2NF) must have no partial key dependencies. This means that no non-key fields can be dependent upon part of a primary key. This therefore only applies to tables with compound keys because they are the only tables that can have partial keys. Dependencies exist when the data is known because of its direct relationship to another field.

When identifying partial key dependencies, there will be fields that are dependent on just one part of the compound key. These fields and that part of the compound key will form a new table.

EXAMPLE

The orders database from the previous example now contains two tables:

ORDER (<u>Order Number</u>, Order Date, Customer ID, Customer Forename, Customer Surname, Customer Address 1, Customer Address 2, Customer Address 3, Customer ZIP Code)

ORDERLINE (<u>Order Number</u>, <u>Product Code</u>, Description, Quantity, Price)

Only the ORDERLINE table contains partial keys. Description and Price are dependent on Product Code which is part of the compound primary key. Therefore, a new table needs to be created for products:

PRODUCT (<u>Product Code</u>, Description, Price)

The information stored in the ORDERLINE table that is not part of the PRODUCT table needs to be retained:

ORDERLINE (<u>Order Number</u>, <u>Product Code</u>, Quantity)

The Product Code field is retained in the ORDERLINE table as a foreign key because it is still necessary to know which products were ordered.

TASK

Normalise the table of ingredients below to 2NF:

RECIPE-INGREDIENT (<u>Recipe ID</u>, <u>Ingredient ID</u>, Ingredient Name, Measure, Quantity)

Recipe ID	Ingredient ID	Ingredient Name	Measure	Quantity
1	B	Flour	Grams	200
1	D	Eggs	Eggs	2
1	K	Water	Tablespoons	2
2	C	Milk	Millilitres	250
2	B	Flour	Grams	100

Third normal form

Data in third normal form 3NF must have no non-key dependencies. This means that there should be no fields that are dependent upon another field that is not a primary key. Therefore primary keys and compound primary keys can be ignored. All other fields should be examined to see if they are dependent on any other non-key field.

EXAMPLE

The orders database from the previous example now contains three tables:

ORDER (<u>Order Number</u>, Order Date, Customer ID, Customer Forename, Customer Surname, Customer Address 1, Customer Address 2, Customer Address 3, Customer ZIP Code)

PRODUCT (<u>Product Code</u>, Description, Price)

ORDERLINE (<u>Order Number</u>, <u>Product Code</u>, Quantity)

In the ORDER table, all the customer data is dependent on the Customer ID which is a non-key field. A new table needs to be created called CUSTOMER:

CUSTOMER (Customer ID, Forename, Surname, Address 1, Address 2, Address 3, ZIP Code)

The ORDER table now becomes:

ORDER (<u>Order Number</u>, Order Date, Customer ID)

Customer ID is retained in the ORDER table as a foreign key so it is still known which customer placed the order.

TASK

Normalise the table of students below to 3NF:

STUDENT (<u>Student ID</u>, Forename, Surname, Class, Teacher Title, Teacher Surname)

Student ID	Forename	Surname	Class	Teacher Title	Teacher Surname
1	Hayley	Barrow	3	Mrs	Stokes
2	Harriet	Chew	1	Miss	Spicer
3	Jessica	Lang	3	Mrs	Stokes

161

Normalise a database to 3NF

TASK

The PROJECT table below contains details of the employees working on projects for clients. It is currently in 0NF. Normalise the data to 3NF.

PROJECT

Description

Start Date

End Date

Client ID

Company

Contact Name

    Employee ID

    Employee Name

    Employee Hours

Here is an example of the data:

Description	Start Date	End Date	Client ID	Company	Contact Name	Employee ID	Employee Name	Employee Hours
Barton Towers	28/2/15	31/12/16	512	Barton Estates	Jerry Dean	PK32	Fred Havers	1052
						JH45	Janice Spring	575
Haywood Manor	31/3/15	15/6/15	987	Haywood Estates	Peter Gates	JH45	Janice Spring	153
						YR27	Mike Rawson	372

> **DISCUSSION POINT**
>
> There are also fourth (4NF) and fifth normal forms (5NF) as well as another one called Boyce-Codd Normal Form (BCNF). However, these have little relevance to a designer of a database and are used mainly in higher academic studies.

Advantages and disadvantages of normalisation

Normalisation removes duplicate data from a database. Not only does this reduce the size of the database, it also removes the potential for errors and inconsistencies. Data that is duplicated may be edited for one record but not another, meaning that it becomes inconsistent. This causes problems when searching for matching data.

The database will perform better if it is normalised because searches can be carried out on indexed fields and data can be looked up from related tables. However, each lookup does take time to perform and will use up processor time, which means that some queries that require access to more than one table may be slow.

As tables no longer contain redundant data, maintenance tasks such as rebuilding indexes can be completed more quickly. However, it can be difficult to understand the data stored in each table because foreign keys consisting of numbers or codes are used and they mean very little to the user. This means that the user will need to build queries to look up data from related tables. These queries can be quite complex and require expertise from the user.

The database becomes more flexible in that it is easy to add new fields to tables without affecting other columns and it is easy to add new tables without affecting existing tables. Having smaller tables also means that data can fit onto one screen or one page more easily because there are fewer fields and security permissions can be applied to individual tables. However, it is also necessary to design the database properly and to understand the process of normalisation. This is a high level skill that requires a database designer to understand the real world data structures and represent them in a relational database. An average user would not be able to do this.

QUESTIONS

6   Identify two characteristics of data in 1NF.
7   Describe one characteristic of data in 3NF.
8   Explain two advantages of normalisation.

9.03 Data dictionary

 KEY TERM

Data dictionary: metadata (information) about the database

A **data dictionary** is a document or file that describes the structure of the data held within the database. It is known as metadata which means 'data about data'. It is a tool that is used by database developers and administrators. It will include the following items:

- data about fields:
  - field names to identify each field
  - data types, such as text, integer, date/time
  - field size, such as the length of a text field or the maximum value of a numeric field
  - format of fields
  - default values which are values a field is set to be initially when a new record is created
  - primary keys, compound keys and foreign keys
  - indexed fields which improve search times
  - validation rules that restrict data entry for that field
- data about tables:
  - the primary key of the table

- what sort order to use when displaying data
- relationships to other tables
- total number of records
- validation rules that apply based on multiple fields within the table
- permissions and security as to which users can access the table.

EXAMPLE

This is part of a data dictionary for fields in a product table:

Attribute	Data Type	Field Size	Format
Product Code	Alphanumeric	6	XX99XX
Description	Alphanumeric	20	
Category Code	Integer	4	9999
Price	Decimal	3.2	$999.99

Attribute	Validation Type	Rule	Error Message
Product Code	Format	Must be in the format of two letters, two numbers, two letters	Please enter a code that is two letters, two numbers, two letters
Description	Presence	Must be present	Please enter a description
Category Code	Look up in List	Must exist in Category Code in Category table	Please enter a category code that exists in the category list
Price	Range	Between 0.01 and 999.99	Please enter a price between 0.01 and 999.99

.66

TASK

Complete the data dictionary below for employees:

Attribute	Data Type	Field Size	Format
Employee ID			
Surname			
Forename			
Date of Birth			
Telephone			
Email			
Year Joined Company			
Pension Scheme?			

Data types

It is necessary to know the type of data in order to store it correctly and process it efficiently.

Product	
Field Name	**Data Type**
Product ID	Number
Description	Short Text
Retail Price	Currency
Date Started	Date/Time

Figure 9.40 - Product data types.

Text

Text data types come in different formats. They can also sometimes be known as string or alphanumeric. A text data type can contain any letter, number or symbol.

EXAMPLE

Jane Atkins

M

Female

W6749PR

O'Connor

info@alphabeta.rtq

00 44 208 555 5555

Numeric

Numbers can be stored in two main formats which are integer and real.

Integers are whole numbers. These can be negative or positive but must not contain decimals.

Real numbers can contain decimals. They can be positive or negative.

Numbers can also be formatted as percentages or as currency. Currency values are presented with a currency symbol. The currency symbol isn't actually stored with the data, but is presented when the data is displayed.

Percentage values are stored slightly differently to other number values. The number that is displayed is stored as a one hundredth (1/100) of the value. When using 25%, for example, the computer would store it as 0.25 (25/100). However, it would display 25%. So when the computer displays a percentage data type, it multiplies what is stored (e.g. 0.63) by 100 and adds the percentage symbol (e.g. 63%)

EXAMPLE

Integer	Real	Currency	Percentage
9	9.05	$9.05	0.09 (9%)
-6	-6.2	-$6.20	-0.06 (6%)
232 382 109	232 383 109.00	$232 383 109.00	2 323 821
-238	-238.00	-$238	2.38 (238%)

TASK

Use a spreadsheet to enter the following numbers:

5

60

0.32

0.2

Now format the cells as percentages. What has happened to the data and why?

DISCUSSION POINT

Some people get confused with telephone numbers because the word 'number' is used. However, a telephone number is actually a set of digits. The number data types cannot include the spaces or hyphens or brackets which are often used within telephone numbers. The number data types also cannot start with a zero because numbers cannot start with a zero. Arithmetic calculations can be performed on numbers but not on telephone numbers. Therefore telephone numbers are stored as text.

Try typing this telephone number into a spreadsheet (without using spaces) and see what happens: 00442085555555

If this was a number it would actually be 442 085 555 555 which is 442 billion, 85 million, 555 thousand, 5 hundred and fifty-five.

Date/time

This data type is used to store dates and times. The number data type cannot be used because it works in 10s, 100s, 1000s, but a date/time data type will be able to work with days, months, years, hours, minutes and seconds. It will also enable dates and times to be sorted into a logical order.

EXAMPLE

Dates can be formatted in a variety of ways such as:

18/7/1965
18-07-65
18th July 1965
July 18, 1965

However, they are always stored in the same way: day 18, month 7, year 1965. The symbols (such as th, / and -) are not stored. They are just displayed.

EXAMPLE

Times can also be formatted in a variety of ways:

12:55 p.m.
14:02.45 (hours, minutes, seconds)
0305 hrs (five past three in the morning)

Dates and times can also be combined to give a specific time on a specific date, for example:

12:55 18-07-65

DISCUSSION POINT

Internationally, days, months and years can be stored in a different order. It is important to specify this order when setting up a data type. For example, in America, they use month, day, year (e.g. 7/18/1965), whereas in the UK they use day, month, year (e.g. 18/7/1965). This can become a problem when the day part is 12 or less. What date is 5/10/2019? Is it 5 October or 10 May?

Boolean/logical

Boolean or logical data types can have only one of two values. These two values are TRUE and FALSE, but are sometimes represented as YES and NO. If you use

Microsoft Access you will notice that this data type is referred to as the Yes/No data type.

DISCUSSION POINT

Data is only a Boolean data type if the two possible answers are TRUE/FALSE or YES/NO. Boolean/logical data types do not include data like 'M' or 'F' for Male or Female. These are actually text data types. Just because there are two possible answers for the data does not mean that it is a Boolean.

Select appropriate data types

You will need to know how to choose an appropriate data type for a given situation. You will also need to be able to select appropriate data types when creating spreadsheets and databases. The following guidelines should help you:

Rule	Data type
The data contains whole numbers only	Integer
The data contains a decimal number	Real
The data starts with a zero (e.g. telephone number)	Text
The data includes letters, symbols or spaces	Text
The data is a date, a time or both	Date/Time
The only values for the data are TRUE/FALSE or YES/NO	Boolean/Logical

Table 9.02 - Data type rules.

TASK

Data is to be stored in a database about party bookings. Select the most appropriate data type for each of the following fields:
- Date of Party
- Time of Party
- Room being Booked
- Number of Guests
- Deposit
- Price Charged
- Paid?

68

QUESTIONS

9 Identify and describe three components of a data dictionary.

10 Select the most appropriate data type for the following information stored about flights:

Flight number (e.g. BA372)
Departure date
Departure time
Airport code (e.g. ACF)
Max number of passengers
Type (e.g. scheduled or charter)
Arrived?

11 Give reasons for the use of the text data type for storing a mobile phone number.

9.04 File and data management

File types

When data is saved it is stored in a file. Different software applications use data in different ways and so the way the data is stored differs between application types. For example, a database stores data in tables, whereas graphics software stores data about pixels.

Each file will typically include a header, which will be metadata (data about the file), then the main content will be stored followed by an end-of-file marker.

To a user, file types are usually identified by their extension. For example, Students.txt has an extension of txt which identifies it as a text file.

EXAMPLE

Examples of file types include:

Extension	File type	Purpose
.txt	Text	Stores plain text without any formatting. It is useful for transferring data between applications, but any formatting is lost.
.csv	Comma separated values	Stores structured data as plain text in rows with each column separated by commas. It is useful for transferring data between databases and spreadsheets or other applications which require data in a structured format.
.rtf	Rich text format	Stores text-based documents and includes the formatting (rich text). It is used to transfer data between different word processing or other text-based applications.
.docx	Microsoft Word XML document	Stores Microsoft's word processing documents in open XML format by saving all objects separately within a compressed file.
.pdf	Portable Document Format	Used to share read-only documents in a common format that can be accessed by any PDF reader software. It is commonly used for storing documents on the web as its contents can be indexed by search engines.
.odt	OpenDocument Text	An open-source file type for word processor documents that is used by open-source word processors and is not tied to one manufacturer.
.ods	OpenDocument Spreadsheet	An open-source file type for spreadsheets that is used by open-source spreadsheet software and is not tied to one manufacturer.
.odp	OpenDocument Presentation	An open-source file type for presentations that is used by open-source presentation software and is not tied to one manufacturer.
.html	Hypertext Markup Language	Stores web pages that can be opened by any web browser.
.xml	Extensible Markup Language	A data file that uses markup language to define objects and their attributes. They are used to transfer data between applications and can be read by a simple text editor.
.avi	Audio Video Interleave (video file)	Microsoft's method of storing video files with very little compression. File sizes are very big but no data is lost.

Extension	File type	Purpose
.mp4	Moving Pictures Experts Group (MPEG) Layer-4 (video file)	Audio and video are compressed and videos can be shared across the internet.
.wav	Waveform Audio File Format	Stores audio files as waveform data and enables different sampling rates and bit rates. This is the standard format for audio CDs but does not include compression so files are large.
.mp3	MPEG Layer-3 audio compression	Stores audio files in a compressed format approximately 10% the size of .wav files. Enables audio files to be shared across the internet.
.bmp	Bitmap image	Stores images as uncompressed raster images, storing each pixel individually. They are large files but can be accessed by any software.
.jpg	Joint Photographic Experts Group (compressed image)	Stores images as compressed raster images. It is used by most digital cameras and is a common format for web graphics but its use of lossy compression can mean some quality is lost.
.png	Portable Network Graphic	Stores images as compressed raster images and can include background transparency making it useful when images are required on different colour backgrounds.
.svg	Scalable Vector Graphics	Stores images as two-dimensional (2D) vector graphics. It is a standard format for using vector graphics on the web.
.exe	Executable program file	Stores program object code which enables the program to be executed by the computer.

Proprietary and open-source file formats
Proprietary file formats

Proprietary file formats are file types that have been developed by software manufacturers solely for use within their software. Using their own formats means that software manufacturers are free to develop software features that will store data in a way that is most suitable for the software and without waiting for a standard format to adapt to the software's needs. This enables software to improve and provide new features that otherwise would not be available.

Open-source file formats

Open-source file formats are file types that have been developed for the purpose of being used by any proprietary software or open-source software. They are free from copyright, patents and trademarks, and their structure is known publicly. They are usually maintained by an international standards organisation or a public interest group. Their main advantage is that the files can be shared between users of different software. However, they can hold back development of open-source software because new features will require the file format standard to be updated.

EXAMPLE

Some examples of proprietary file formats include:

Extension	Software / file type	Manufacturer
.docx	Word processor	Microsoft Word
.wpd	Word processor	Corel Word Perfect
.msg	Email message	Microsoft Outlook
.ra	Audio / video streaming	Real Networks
.MOV	Movie	Apple
.psd	Graphics	Adobe Photoshop
.ai	Graphics	Adobe Illustrator
.accdb	Database	Microsoft Access

EXAMPLE

Some examples of open-source file formats include:

File type	Type of data	Standards organisation
JPG	Compressed raster graphics	Developed by the Joint Photographic Experts Group (JPEG) and standardised by the International Organization for Standardization (ISO)

File type	Type of data	Standards organisation
PNG	Compressed raster graphics with transparency support	ISO
ePub	E-book	International Digital Publishing Forum
XML	Extensible Markup Language	World Wide Web Consortium (W3C)
MPEG	Compressed video	Developed by the Moving Picture Experts Group (MPEG) and standardised by the ISO

Generic file formats

Generic file formats enable data to be transferred between software. Data can be exported from software to a generic file format and generic file formats can be imported into software. They store the essential data but will not include any formatting.

The two main file formats used within databases are CSV and TXT. These were described earlier in this chapter in the section about importing data.

Indexed sequential access

Many years ago, data was often stored on tape, which required records to be written one after another onto the tape. This was known as storing the data serially. To access the data, all the records would need to be read from the first onwards until the required record was found or until the end of the file was reached. It could take a very long time to read through a whole table of data and so indexed sequential files were developed.

Indexed sequential files still store records one after each other but they are sorted into an order based upon a field. For example, data about customers might be sorted into surname order or customer ID order. Sequential files are particularly useful when data is being batch processed such as when gas bills are being generated and the master customer file will be processed in order of customer ID and any transaction files will also be processed in order of customer ID.

EXAMPLE

Here is an example of part of a master customer file showing the customers, the date the current meter reading was taken, the previous meter reading (amount of gas used) and the current meter reading:

Customer ID	Surname	Date of reading	Previous reading	Current reading
10	Black	12/1/16	32721	34872
11	Brown	15/12/15	02717	03281
12	White	8/1/16	47270	48572
13	Green	8/1/16	21827	23593

Here is an example of part of a transaction file that will be processed to update the master customer file with new gas meter readings:

Customer ID	Date of reading	Meter reading
11	12/3/16	03692
13	12/3/16	23997

This is what the master customer file will look like once the transaction file has been processed:

Customer ID	Surname	Date of reading	Previous reading	Current reading
10	Black	12/1/16	32721	34872
11	Brown	**12/3/16**	**03281**	**03692**
12	White	8/1/16	47270	48572
13	Green	**12/3/16**	**23593**	**23997**

When reading the data in sequential files, it was necessary to read the whole file serially from the beginning because there was no way of knowing where each record was stored. Indexed sequential files are stored in exactly the same way as sequential files but the file also has an index based on the field used to sort the file. A field with an index is known as a secondary key. The index file stores each secondary key value and the address in storage (e.g. tape or disk) where the first record containing that value is stored.

The index is small enough to store in main memory and so all that needs to be done to find a record is to search the index, find the location in storage and then read the records from that point until the record is found.

EXAMPLE

If Employee ID is the secondary key, then an index will exist with Employee ID as one column and the storage address as the other column. Rather than storing every single Employee ID, the index may store every tenth Employee ID for example.

Employee ID	Storage address
0001	A8FB2DC3
0011	9AEB08E3
0021	8C4DDDF5

Direct file access

The use of indexed sequential file access still requires some serial access of data and there are problems with trying to maintain a file in a sequential order as new records are added and old records deleted.

With direct file access, records are stored in a random order. There is no sequence. When storing a file, a hashing algorithm (calculation) is performed on the key field to determine the storage address where the record should be stored. Then, when the record is searched for, the same hashing algorithm will be performed on the key field to determine where the record can be found. The computer system can then

directly access that record without having to read through other records.

Hierarchical database management systems

The hierarchical database model was created in the 1960s and is not commonly used today. The model relies upon a tree structure where each parent branch is the one side of a relationship and each child branch is the many side of a relationship. The tree structure can only deal with one-to-many relationships and can only work in one direction. Hierarchical databases are only suitable for models which have a strict hierarchy.

One such hierarchy is the file system used within computer systems. The file system may look something like this:

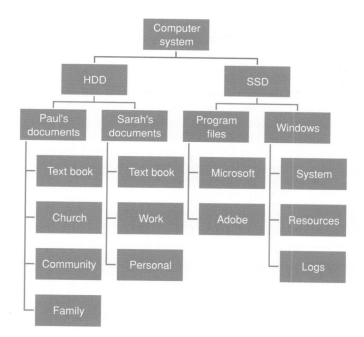

Figure 9.41 - Folder structure.

Each disk contains folders and there may be further subfolders within each folder. Each subfolder has only one folder at the level above it. To find the data, the user browses through the system, selects the disk the data is stored on, then selects the folder, then selects the next subfolder until eventually the file is found.

This same process is used when searching for data within a hierarchical database. This means that data at the top of the tree is very quick to access.

EXAMPLE

A bank could store data about customers and the accounts they hold:

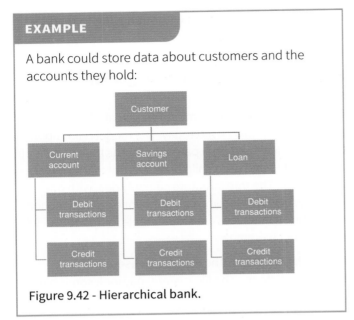

Figure 9.42 - Hierarchical bank.

Management information systems

Remember

A **management information system** (MIS) provides summary information to managers to enable them to make decisions. The MIS will collate data from a database and present it in the form of reports and charts. These reports and charts can be produced within the database system itself or they may be part of an additional piece of software that is used to analyse the data.

The additional software is likely to collate data from more than one database and interconnect the data from those databases to produce reports that analyse all the data together. When additional software is used to collate data from more than one database, it is often referred to as an executive information system (EIS).

A MIS has the following essential features:

- data is collated from databases and other sources
- data is interconnected from different sources
- data is analysed to provide the data that is required by management
- summary reports and charts are produced for managers that will help with decision making.

The reports and charts are created by people, but once they are created they can be reused as the data changes within the data sources. It's important that the reports and charts provide information that managers need.

Using MISs

TIP

Information from a MIS is used by managers to make decisions. Managers can examine the summary information and then decide upon actions to take. Reports are provided at regular times and it's also possible for managers to request ad hoc reports if they need additional information.

EXAMPLE

Managers within a large second-hand car dealership need to be able to monitor sales. They need to be able to identify trends in sales for different makes and models of cars at different times of the year. This will enable them to identify which cars are selling the most and which are making the most profit. They can then decide which second-hand cars they want to acquire to sell.

Marketing managers can analyse how effective a marketing campaign was by comparing sales figures during an advertising campaign with sales figures outside the advertising campaign. This will help them to decide whether to run similar campaigns in the future.

QUESTIONS

12 Explain why generic file types are needed.

13 Describe the steps involved to find a file using indexed sequential access.

14 Explain why direct access is used for databases in preference to indexed sequential access.

15 Describe two features of management information systems (MISs).

9.05 Summary

A database contains structured data in tables which consist of records and fields. Data in fields has a type assigned to it, such as text, alphanumeric, integer/decimal, date/time or Boolean.

A flat file is a single table and has no relationships. Relationships connect entities (tables) together and can be one-to-one or one-to-many. Hierarchical databases are based on a tree structure to deal with one-to-many relationships. Relationships are depicted in an entity relationship diagram (ERD). A primary key is a unique identifier for a record, a compound key is a primary key consisting of more than one field and a foreign key relates to a primary key in another table.

Referential integrity ensures that data exists in a related table. Validation rules can be used to ensure that data is sensible and allowed. Verification is the process of checking that data has been transferred correctly.

Simple queries use one criterion to search for data and complex queries use two or more criteria. Summary queries can be used to find statistical information from a database. Static parameters are used in queries when the value of the parameter does not change and dynamic parameters are used when the user is likely to want to change the value each time the query is run.

Indexed sequential access involves the use of an index to determine where to start searching a file for a record.

Direct file access involves using a hashing algorithm to find the location of a record in a file.

Normalisation is the process of structuring data within a database and is measured using normal forms. A data dictionary, known as metadata, describes the structure of the data held within the database.

Data entry forms are used for inputting data into a database. Data can be imported into a database from another data source or exported so it can be used in other software. Different software applications require different data types in order to store data.

Proprietary file formats are developed by manufacturers for their own software and open-source formats are developed for use by any software.

A management information system (MIS) provides summary information to managers to enable them to make decisions.

Review questions

A website accepts donations for charities. Each donor may make several donations to one or more charities. This information is stored in a relational database.

1a Identify three tables that should be used within the database. [3]

1b Describe two relationships that would be used within the database. [2]

1c Explain how referential integrity is important to this database. [2]

An apartment complex stores data about its customers, their bookings and the rooms they are staying in. The entity relationship diagram (ERD) is shown below:

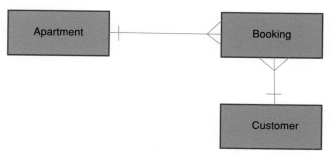

Figure 9.43 - Entity relationship diagram.

2a Identify two foreign key fields that should be used within the database. [2]

2b Select the most appropriate data type for each of the fields below in the apartment table: [3]

    (i) Telephone Number

    (ii) Swimming Pool

    (iii) Bedrooms

2c Describe how a dynamic parameter query could be used to produce a list of customers that have stayed in an apartment during a specified time period. [4]

2d Explain why this query would be a complex query. [2]

2e Identify and describe three items of a data dictionary that could be used in this database. [6]

Students in a college belong to tutor groups. Each tutor group has one tutor. The students are able to borrow books from the college library.

3 Normalise the unnormalised data below to 3NF. Show each table, its attributes and its primary keys. [4]

STUDENT
Name
Address
Telephone
Tutor Group
Tutor Name
    Book ID
    Title
    Due Date

4 Describe the difference between proprietary and open-source file formats. [2]

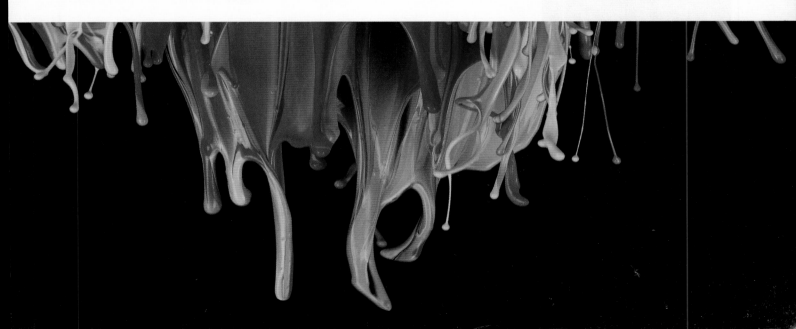

Chapter 10
Sound and video editing

175

Learning objectives

By the end of this chapter, you will understand how to:

- edit a video clip in various ways to meet the requirements of its audience and purpose
- edit a sound clip in various ways to meet the requirements of its audience and purpose
- describe how video and sound editing features are used in practice
- compress video and sound files for different media

176

KEY TERMS

Pixel: a very small square area of one colour that is illuminated on a display screen. These are combined to create a bitmap image

Frame: a single still image in a video file

Rendering: combining the effects created in a video file to create an output video file

Transition: The movement from one clip to the next

Filters: an effect, often colour related, that can be applied to a clip

Track: a single audio section in a sound or video file

Pitch: the highness or lowness of a tone

10.01 Video editing software

Most video editing software will have similar features. The level and complexity to which these features can be used may differ between the software available. Some will allow simple effects and editing to take place. Some will allow much more complex effects to be added and editing to take place. Most software has a similar set-up in that they have a preview pane to view the video creation progress and an area where the editing takes place, often referred to as the timeline.

To be able to edit video in the software package, any clips or images to be included must first be imported into the software. Each clip or image can then be dragged or placed onto the timeline to be edited.

Setting an aspect ratio

Video today can have several different aspect ratios.

Remember

An aspect ratio is the ratio of the width to the height of a screen. There are many different formats of media that require different ratios, such as television, computer monitors, cinema screens and mobile devices.

Setting an aspect ratio is determined by the media for which you are creating the video. 16:9 is the current high-definition standard for television and monitors, and photography often uses 4:3 or 3:2 aspect ratios.

A resolution can also be set for a video. The resolution is the number of **pixels** horizontally compared to the number of pixels vertically. The current resolution for high definition is 1920 p × 1080 p. This means that each **frame** in a video has 2 073 600 pixels.

Setting an aspect ratio and resolution can be done when initially setting up the video project. It can also be set or changed when **rendering** a video file at the end of a project.

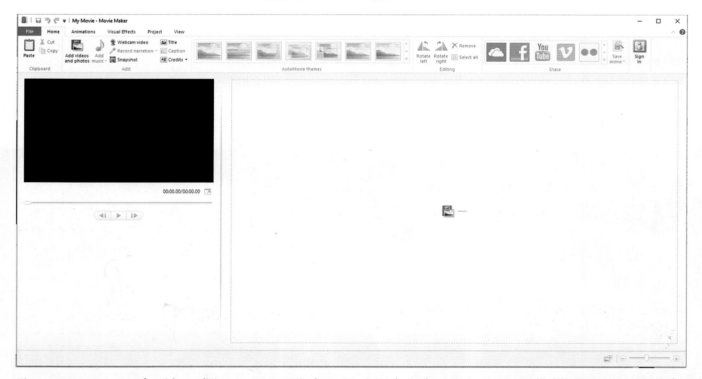

Figure 10.01 - Layout of a video editing program, Windows Movie Maker. The preview pane is the black space on the left and the timeline the large white space to the right.

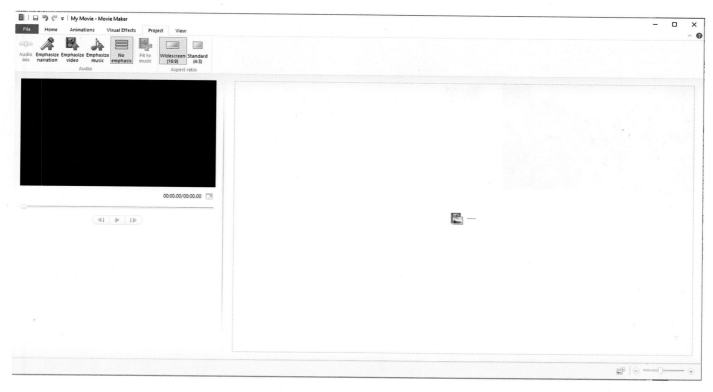

Figure 10.02 - Setting the aspect ratio in a video editing program.

TASK

Change the aspect ratio to each of the settings available in your software package. What effect does this have on the preview pane?

Trimming a video clip and joining clips together

When we trim video clips we cut out parts of the video. This is mostly from the start or the end of the video. Trimming video clips is an essential skill to have when editing videos. For a video to be well edited, video trimming needs to be a key focus for the project.

TIP

Trimming videos is done to create more concise videos that do not continue for too long, and become boring as a result.

To trim a video, there is normally a 'trim/cut' tool. This is often used by simply finding the point in the clip you need

trim and then highlighting the video to this point, either from the start of the clip, or the end, depending on what you need to remove. When the trim/cut tool is clicked, it will remove the highlighted part of the video. The tool can also work by dragging the clip from the start or the end, to the point you want to trim to. Some software will allow you to set a start point and an end point for a clip and will remove any video that is not within this.

Once you have trimmed the video clips you may want to join several clips together. Joining together video clips can be done by dragging video clips in the timeline next to each other. Clips can also have **transition** effects applied to make the change between clips more visually interesting. Joining together clips is done to create effects such as jump cuts for action scenes, to start new scenes or to sometimes imply that time has passed by in the video.

TASK

Import two video clips into your video editing software. Trim the start and finish of your video clips to a suitable point, then join them together. Apply a suitable transition effect between one video clip to the other.

Figure 10.03 - Example of trimming a video.

Figure 10.04 - Example of adding a text-based slide to the start of a video.

Creating text-based slides and credits

Text-based slides in videos are often used for a title slide at the start of a video, or credits at the end of a video to show who was involved. They were also used throughout old movies, before sound was part of films, to show what had been said by a character. Text-based slides can also be used at the beginning of videos in order to establish any background information that may be important for the video.

Text-based slides are often created by having a still image or block of colour as the background. Text is then layered on top of this to give the information needed.

> **TASK**
>
> Add a text-based slide to the start of your video. Introduce the theme or topic of your video on the slide. Experiment with any effects available to display the text on the slide.

Adding captions and subtitles

Adding captions and subtitles is often done to provide a message, emphasise a point or to help the hard of hearing. These are created by using text, and sometimes visual effects, that is displayed over a number of frames in the video. These effects have to be very carefully timed with what is being said so as not to distract the viewer from the experience.

> **TASK**
>
> Add a caption over part of your video to explain what is currently on the screen.

Adding animation and effects

Animation and effects can be added as a transition between video clips and text-based slides. They can be added to the text on text-based slides and for captions and subtitles. They can also be added to the video clips themselves to change the overall look of the clip. The animations and effects available can differ greatly between different software, but most have a standard set including effects such as fading and adding **filters**.

Adding fade effects to video clips allows for calm, smooth transitions. It can be used to overlay two video clips, which is often used to convey something happening simultaneously. However, mostly it is used simply to either gently establish a scene or close one. A slow fade in an action scene could be unsuitable and ruin the action effect. However, if it is a scene that has

179

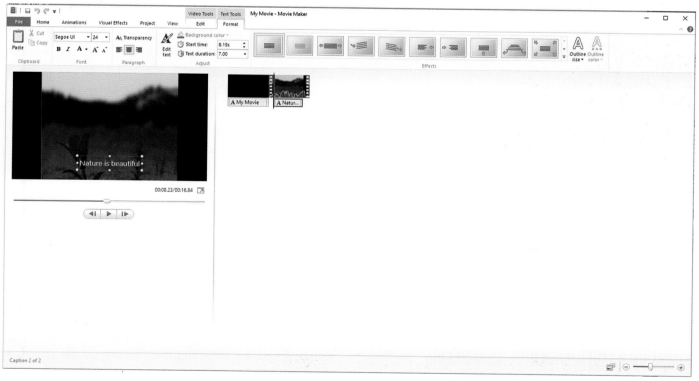

Figure 10.05 - Example of a caption added over a video clip.

Figure 10.06 - An example set of filters available in a video editing program. A sepia tone effect has been applied to the video. This can make it look older.

a solemn note, a fade can be used to enhance that feeling. Animation effects can be used to create different feelings and provoke different emotions about a video.

> **TASK**
>
> Add a filter to your first video to change the overall look.
>
> Create a credits slide at the end of your movie. Add a fade effect from your final video clip to your credits.

Extracting a still image from a video clip

Video footage can often contain some frames that would make excellent still images. Therefore, we may want to take one individual frame and extract it as a still image. It would then be more like a digital photograph. Editing software will often allow you to navigate through the video to a certain frame and extract that frame to save as an individual image. This can be called taking a snapshot in some software, extracting an image or taking a picture in others.

Inserting a still image into a video clip

Inserting a still image into a video is usually done by importing the image into the software, then dragging or placing the image onto the video's timeline. A limit can then be set for the length of time the image needs to be displayed.

The still image may take up the frame or just be part of the overall view. Having a still image as part of a frame is what is often done in news programmes. The news anchor reads the news and has a still image off to the side giving some context to the story.

Inserting still images is done in videos for many reasons, such as adding visual cues in news programmes, to show a close-up still of a product in advertising campaigns or referencing something in a review video on media such as YouTube.

Adding and removing sound from a video clip

Adding sound to a video clip is often done by importing the sound clip and dragging or placing it onto the timeline of the project. The sound timeline can be separated from the video timeline in most editing software. Sound clips are often added to videos to provide a sound track, a voice-over or to add sound effects to the video.

Removing sound from a video clip in most software is a simple process. It often requires clicking on the sound clip, and either pressing the delete key, dragging it off the timeline entirely or right clicking and selecting

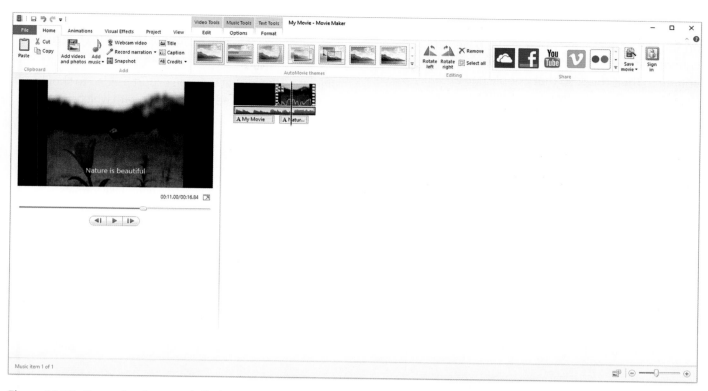

Figure 10.07 - Example of a sound clip in a video. The sound clip can be seen in green under the video timeline.

'remove/delete'. This is done to remove any unwanted sound from a video clip, to either create a silent situation or to add a different sound clip to the video. Often videos will be recorded with sound, but when the editor begins to edit the video, they may find the sound is not clear enough or does not work effectively. This means they may want to remove it and replace it with something better.

TIP

Slowing down a clip is an effect used in, for example, action movies and sporting events. The video clip is slowed down to show events that happen very quickly in real life in a much slower time. This allows the audience to appreciate the action or to have a prolonged emotional reaction to the clip.

TASK

Add a sound track to your video. Make the sound track start after your title slide and end when your movie does. You could try adding a second sound clip and have a different sound track on your video for your credits.

TASK

Highlight part of your video and experiment with changing the speed of the video for that part. What effect does this have on your video clip? Does it change what the clip shows? Does it make is funnier? Does is make it more sad?

Altering the speed of a video clip

Altering the speed of a video clip is another effect that can be applied. It can be used for various reason such as creating time-lapse videos, where an event happens over a prolonged amount of time. Normally this type of video is created by having a camera record one frame of video every few seconds/minutes. This video, which can often be quite long, can then be sped up to demonstrate the process.

Exporting video clips in different file formats

When we export a video clip we join together all the editing elements that we have carried out and create a single file again. This file can then be used on different media. Many people do not realise that different file formats store video in many different ways. They think they are the exact same format or don't even consider format at all. It is just a video. This is not the case! Depending on the media for which you are creating your video, the format can be very important. For example on YouTube, a social networking video website, you cannot just upload any format you want to. It needs to adhere to their rules, so that people can actually watch the video on YouTube from many different devices.

Remember

Some formats allow for higher quality but create larger file sizes and some formats compress video files greatly, losing much of their quality in the process. MP4 is a common file format that will compress a large video file but retain quite a lot of its quality.

Some file formats will be more suitable for different media. For example, video files on most websites will be .mp4, .avi or .mov files. Many videos on websites used to be flash files. However, with the invention of the iPad, this changed. The iPad did not support flash files, so many people could not

view videos on websites using them. With the popularity of the iPad growing so much, websites began to change their video file formats so that iPad users were able to view them.

Ultimately the format that you export a video to should match what is allowed by the media with which you want to work.

TASK

Try exporting a video clip into different file formats. Compare the exported files to see what differences can be seen between the clips.

10.02 Sound editing software

As in video editing software, most sound editing software will have similar features. The level and complexity to which the different features can be used may again differ

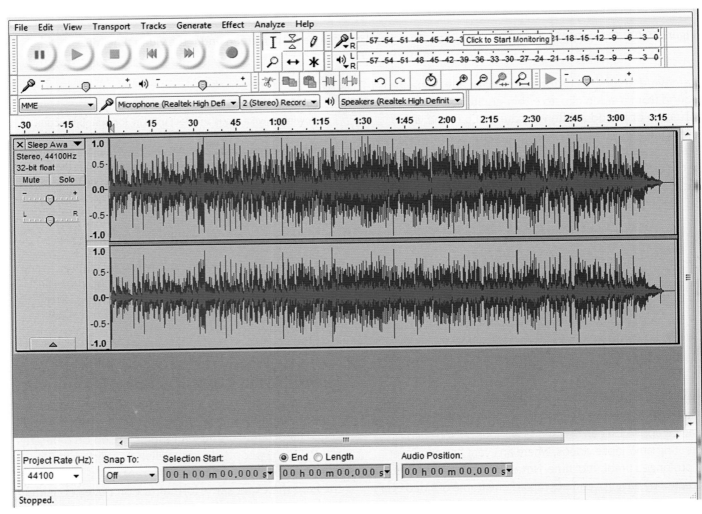

Figure 10.08 - Example of sound editing software called Audacity. The sound clip imported has two different tracks.

between the different software available. Most software has a similar set-up in that it has a way to view different **tracks** in the sound clip. Each track is often represented as a sound wave.

To be able to edit sound in the software package, any clips to be included must first be imported into the software.

Trimming audio clips and joining clips together

Trimming audio clips is used in order to remove unwanted parts of the clip. This can sometimes be done to synchronise the sound clip with a video clip. If you've already trimmed part of the video, you'd also need to trim the equivalent audio section in order for the video and the sound to end together.

To trim an audio clip you simply find what you want to trim and then use a 'cut/trim' tool to remove the unwanted parts. This is often done in sound editing software by

highlighting the section of the clip that needs to be removed and selecting 'delete'.

In the same way that video clips can be joined together, sound clips can be too. Multiple sound clips can be imported, edited and placed straight after the previous clip. The software will continue from one clip onto the next. Effects, such as fading, can also be applied between the clips when joining them together.

> **TASK**
>
> Import two sound clips into suitable sound editing software. Trim each a section off each clip and join them together.

Fading in and fading out an audio clip

Like video clips, sound clips can be faded in and out. This often involves the end of one clip becoming quieter and the

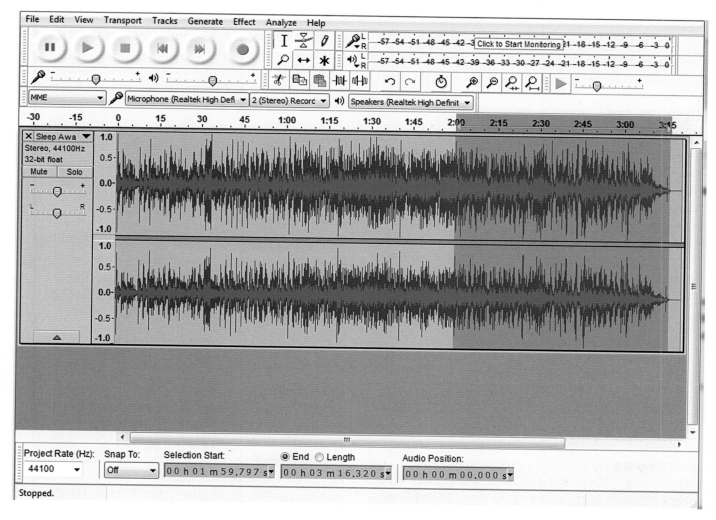

Figure 10.09 - Example of the end of a sound clip highlighted ready to be removed.

start of the next beginning quietly and getting louder. If a clip is faded in it will start quietly and get louder. If a clip is faded out it will start at a louder volume and get quieter. This is done in order to create a gradual transition and gentler start to a clip that is more pleasant to listen to, rather than just starting a clip at full volume. Imagine a host on a radio show about to play a loud song. Without a fade-in effect, the song would just burst into sound and could shock listeners. Instead, it is much more enjoyable to get a gradual transition over a couple of seconds to allow listeners to readjust in their own time.

Fading in or out is normally an effect that can be applied to an audio track. Normally the part of the track that needs to be faded is selected and a fade effect can be applied. You can often choose what volume the clip will be at the start of the fade and what it will be at the end of the fade. You can also often choose how long you want a fade effect to last in terms of time. For example, apply a fade-out effect to the last 10 seconds of a sound clip.

> **TASK**
>
> Fade in the start of the sound clip you have created for 5 seconds, then fade it out at the end for 10 seconds.

Altering the speed of a sound clip and changing the pitch

Altering the speed of a sound clip is similar to altering the speed of a video clip. The section of the clip to be altered is highlighted and an effect is applied to the clip to speed it up or slow it down. The speed can often be set very accurately with an input method allowing a value to be entered. Changing the speed of a sound clip has a similar effect to changing the speed of a video clip. It also alters the mood and emotion felt when listening to the clip.

Remember

Issues can arise when speeding up or slowing down sound clips. When playing back a sped up clip the sound can appear very high pitched and squeaky. When playing back a slowed down clip the clip can sound deep and have too much bass to it.

To counter this, some software is able to allow you to adjust the **pitch** of the recording while altering the speed. This will change the level of the sound track to be higher or lower in pitch, changing the notes to be higher or lower as a result. You may want to lower the pitch on a sound clip that has been speeded up to counter the

squeaky effects that could be created in speeding the track up.

> **TASK**
>
> Experiment with changing the speed and the pitch of the sound clip you have created. What effect does this create for your sound clip?

Adding or adjusting reverberation

Reverberation, often shortened to reverb, is the effect that is created on sound when it repeatedly bounces back off a surface. In an auditorium, the sound from a musical performance will bounce off all the walls. When this effect is layered on top of each other, by bouncing off multiple surfaces, reverberation is created. Reverberation is noticed most when the performers stop playing but the sound can still be heard. It lingers on for a time. Adding reverberation onto a sound track can create a similar effect. It adds a type of echo onto the section of the track selected in order to create a reverberation effect. This effect can be enhanced and made very obvious, or can be decreased and made more subtle if you feel it is too much.

Most sound editing software will have a reverberation effect that can be applied to the sound track. The effect of this can normally be altered, by imitating things such as making it sound like the clip is recorded in a large auditorium.

Overdubbing a sound clip with a voice-over

Overdubbing a sound clip is often done to provide a voice-over without removing the noise from the clip that is already there, such as background noise. This is done to allow many of the originally recorded sounds to remain, otherwise it becomes a less interesting clip without some background noise to accompany it.

Overdubbing is when presenting news clips, using a translator, reviewing entertainment or just giving extra information, such as in nature documentaries. To overdub, you must record an entirely new sound track of just the voice-over work. Once that is recorded it is imported into the software as a separate track. This track can then be edited separately to the other sound track and the two can be exported together at the end to create a single sound file.

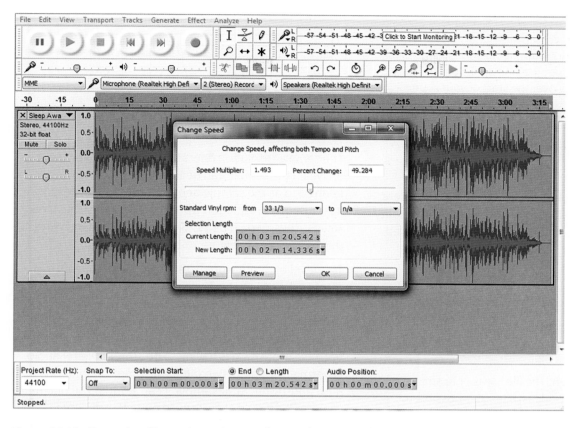

Figure 10.10 - Example of inputting values to change the speed of a sound clip.

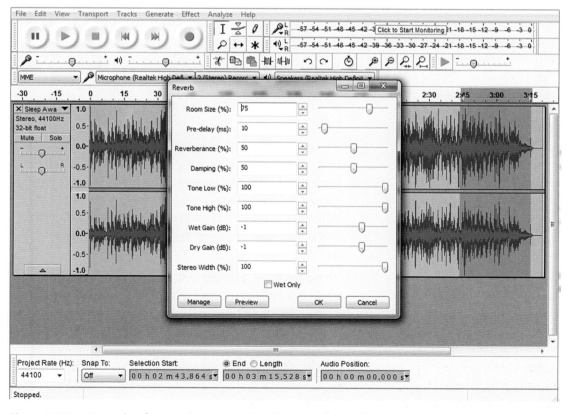

Figure 10.11 - Example of a reverberation effect that can be applied to a sound track.

186

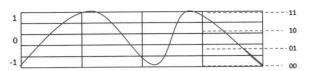

Figure 10.12 - A 2-bit sample resolution.

TASK

Record a voice-over to introduce your sound clip. Import this into your sound file and apply it to start at the beginning and lay over the start of your sound clip.

Exporting sound clips in different file formats

Like video clips, sound clips can be exported in different file formats. This will again depend on the desired quality of the final track and the media for which it will be used.

Remember

MP3 is a common sound file format. It is a format that allows most of the quality of the sound file to be retained, but compresses the file to make it smaller.

Reducing the file size means the file is easier to stream or download from music or podcast sites. It is possible to export a sound file without compressing it. This can be done with file formats such as .wav.

TASK

Research further file formats such as .flac, .wma and .alac. How are they different? What kind of compression do they use? What can they be used for?

Sampling rate and resolution

The sampling rate is the number of samples of the recorded sound taken in a second. The sample rate is normally measured in hertz (Hz) or kHz (1000 Hz). A sample rate of 40 Hz would mean that 40 000 samples of the sound are taken in a second.

The more samples taken in a second, the higher the quality of the sound file. Therefore, the lower the amount of samples taken, the lower the quality of the track. When the sample rate goes beyond 50 kHz it is thought that the human ear will not be able to recognise any further quality in the track. The standard sampling rate used by most digital recording equipment is 48 kHz.

The sample resolution refers to the number of bit values on which the sample can be taken. This can also be referred to as the sample depth. In a very simple example, a 2-bit sample resolution would have four possible binary values. These would be 11, 10, 01 and 00. A sound wave for this can be seen in Figure 10.12.

This level of depth would create a very low quality recording and is not sufficient for most recordings. The higher the sample resolution, the higher the quality of the file and the more accurate the file will be. It will, however, also increase the size of the audio file because more data is having to be stored. Digital audio is normally found in two different sample resolutions: 8-bit and 16-bit. 8-bit sampling can sample 256 different values. This would still produce quite low quality audio. 16-bit sampling can sample over 65 000 different values. This is a higher quality than any human ear can recognise.

10.03 Summary

Most available video and sound editing software have very similar features. The level and complexity to which these features can be used may differ in different software.

There are many different features that can be used to edit a video. In most cases, you will need to set the aspect ratio and the resolution of the video, then export the video in a suitable format at the end. The editing that happens between this will depend on the effect you wish to create and the software you are using.

There are many different features that can be used to edit sound. In most cases, you will need to import the sound clip(s) into the software to be edited, then export them in a suitable format at the end. The editing that happens between this will depend on the effect you wish to create and the software you are using.

Review questions

1 Describe how changing the speed of a video clip can be used to affect the mood or emotion of the clip. [4]
2 What is a frame in a video file? [2]
3 What is a track in a sound file? [2]
4 Describe how overdubbing is used in sound tracks. [4]
5 Explain what is meant by sample rate. [4]

Chapter 11
Emerging technologies

Learning objectives

By the end of this chapter, you will be able to:

- describe a wide range of emerging technologies, including how they work and what they are used for
- evaluate the impact of emerging technologies on individuals, organisations, the environment and medicine
- discuss the advantages and disadvantages of storing data in the cloud

KEY TERMS

Heuristic: discovering knowledge through experience

Biometrics: the measurement of a person's physical characteristics

Cloud computing: using remote servers hosted on the internet to store data

Encrypt: converting data into a scrambled code

Key: a sequence or algorithm used to encrypt or decrypt data

11.01 Technology and our lifestyle

With the introduction and development of smartphones and other mobile devices, people are able to perform many of the tasks for which they previously needed a PC or a laptop, and they are able to perform them on the go. This means that people can often better utilise their time. For example, when travelling on public transport they are able to use their mobile device to perform many tasks, from online banking and shopping, completing work tasks, to keeping up with their favourite news sites and social networking. As people no longer need to sit down at a PC or laptop to perform many work tasks, such as creating or editing a word processed document, they have much more freedom about when and where they are able to complete tasks. This has also had a negative impact, most especially on people's working lives. Companies now expect their employees to be much more available, often outside working hours, and they often provide the technology to enable this. They know their employees have the technology to send emails and read and edit reports and documents on the go, so this has become far more common. This means that people may be working much longer hours than previously and longer than the company actually recognises. This could mean an increased level of stress and fatigue for employees.

As a result of this, we tend to want the most up-to-date technology to make sure we can perform tasks with the greatest level of efficiency. This has meant that technology has become very throwaway to us and this has had a profound effect on our environment as this can hugely increase the amount of landfill created by all the discarded technology. There are many organisations trying to counter this effect by encouraging people to recycle their old technologies rather than throw them away. Some even offer a monetary award for doing this.

Technology is extensively used in many areas of our lives. One area in which it has become highly vital is in medicine. We are able to provide many cures for disease and many

aids, such as replacement limbs, due to the presence of technology in medicine. Technology can be used for many of the more complex elements in medicine such as tissue engineering. This is when stem cell technologies are combined with tissue to grow new body parts and organs. The ability to use technology in this way is hugely beneficial. One of the main issues with implanting organs from one person's body to another is that a body will often reject the organ and attack it. As tissue engineering allows organs to be grown from a person's own cells, their body accepts it and does not see it as being a foreign part.

DISCUSSION POINT

Research the first organ to be grown and transplanted using tissue engineering. What do you think about scientists using technology in a laboratory to grow body parts to order in this way?

Technology is constantly evolving. There are better, more efficient technologies, and new technologies are emerging all the time. We are going to have a look at a variety of emerging technologies and the impact they are having on individuals, organisations and the environment.

11.02 Three-dimensional printing

Remember

Three-dimensional (3D) printing is where an object is created based upon a blueprint made with modelling software. It works by taking thousands upon thousands of cross-section layers of the model, from the bottom to the top, to create the object. It uses heated plastic to print a single layer at a time. 3D printing takes a very long time to produce an object.

Up until now, 3D printing has only been used by larger organisations and not individuals. Developers are currently trying to make it more readily available with the creation of smaller, personal printers that would be more accessible for the use in the home.

There have been many uses for 3D printing to date:

- In medicine, 3D printing has been used to create casts for broken bones. These casts are far more flexible than previous casts and don't completely cover up the broken body part.
- In medicine, prosthetics have been created, as well as replacement organs.
- In medicine, it is possible to print artificial blood vessels that can be used to replace damaged ones.

- In China, it has recently been used to create houses using large-scale printers.
- It has been used by the National Aeronautics and Space Administration (NASA) to print different tools and automobile parts, and spare parts for vehicles in space.

These examples show that 3D printing has a great potential:

- Using a 3D printer to build houses could mean that in the event of a natural disaster, which left many civilians homeless, the affected people could quickly be rehoused.
- In medicine a big issue is often the long waiting lists for organs. In the future this may not be an issue as organs may be printed on demand. Individuals may not have to worry about their short life expectancy or if an organ will be a blood match.
- In space, a team may not need to abort its mission if part of the spacecraft becomes broken. It could print out a spare part using a 3D printer and replace the broken part.

However, not all effects of 3D printing are positive:

- A 3D printer can be used to create a gun. This is a huge safety concern both for countries with and without guns, as anyone who previously could not get access to one, could potentially print one.
- 3D printers use plastic to create the objects that are printed, and plastic can be a large environmental concern as it is not biodegradable. However, some 3D printers now use 'bio-plastics' that are plastics made from renewable sources. This means they can be made by repurposing waste products from farming or recycling previous plastic items. This can help lower the negative impact on the environment.

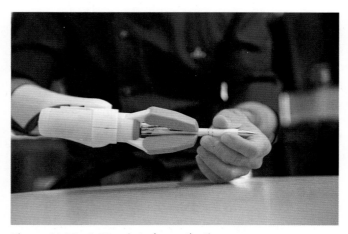

Figure 11.01 - A 3D printed prosthetic arm.

11.03 Fourth generation and fifth generation cellular communications

Cellular communication is progressing through different generations. Initially we had first generation (1G), then second generation (2G). This developed into third generation (3G) and now that has advanced into fourth generation (4G) and fifth generation (5G). All of the names refer to the generation of wireless communications that the technology has gone through. 3G developed in the late 1990s and early 2000s. This has more recently developed into 4G and we are now starting to see 5G.

Remember

The aim of each different generation development is to improve the speed and capability of the wireless connection. It is only data that is carried by the later generations though, as voice is still mostly carried using 2G technology.

3G is the third generation of mobile communication standards. The development of 3G opened up more services that mobile providers could offer, including mobile broadband. It allows devices that are enabled with 3G technology to deliver broadband speeds for the internet. This made it much easier for people to check their emails and browse websites whilst travelling around. 2G did offer access to the internet, but it was often very slow and could be expensive. As 3G uses airwaves more efficiently than 2G the speed of internet access was increased and mobile internet access became cheaper.

The development of 3G was necessary to deal with the growing number of mobile users. 2G technology was not robust enough or fast enough to deal with the rapidly increasing number of mobile phone users. The signal used did not allow enough data to be carried at a time to create efficient use of mobile devices.

3G services work by using cellular based technology. The 3G signal is passed from each cellular mast or phone tower. The mast that is nearest to a phone is the one that will be used when using the mobile device. If a person is moving, the mast used may change if another becomes closer. This is why the signal strength that a mobile device has can change, depending on a person's proximity to a mobile mast. 3G technology is capable of allowing internet speeds that can reach 7 Mbps, but this speed is normally unrealistic and it is often approximately 2 to 3 Mbps.

People felt that the speeds reached by 3G technology were better, but that speed and access could still be improved regarding the internet and mobile devices. This encouraged the development of 4G technology, the 4th generation of mobile communication standard.

The development of 4G technology provided two main benefits, increased upload and download speeds and reduced latency. 4G technology is approximately five times (and sometimes more) faster than 3G technology. This meant that the speed at which files could be downloaded was significantly increased. This increase in speed meant that files could be downloaded in a much faster time. Typically with 3G technology, a 2GB file could take approximately 30 minutes to download. However with 4G technology that download time could be potentially cut to approximately 3–4 minutes. This significantly improved the experience of mobile devices and internet usage for the user.

The deduction in latency with the development of 4G technology also improved the experience of using mobile devices. The reduction in latency means that 4G enabled devices get a quicker response time to the requests made by their mobile device. The quicker response time improves the experience of streaming online video and playing online games using mobile devices.

Access to 4G technology is still limited in many areas. Many countries are trying to build the infrastructure to provide as wide a coverage as possible to enable a 4G signal to be accessed.

DISCUSSION POINT
Find out what developments are being made in your country to make 4G technology accessible.

The race to develop the next mobile communication standard, 5G technology, is well underway. 5G technology is set to dramatically affect the use of mobile internet. In order to provide 5G access there is a major restructure occurring on parts of the radio network that is used to transmit data. This restructure is reported to allow data to be transmitted approximately 100 times faster. In a test of 5G by Samsung in 2013, a high definition movie could be downloaded in less than 30 seconds. It is thought that 5G technology has the potential to eventually provide much faster speeds than this, speeds of approximately 800 Gbps, meaning that 30 high definition movies could be downloaded in a single second!

The development from 3G to 4G technology and further developments into 5G technology will enable a number of advancements. These may include:

- greater speed in internet access
- faster loading speeds of applications, such as maps
- the ability to have multiple people in video conferencing calls
- more effective location services to allow for real-time updates, such as traffic and weather
- the ability to stream high-definition (HD).

The development of 4G (and in the future 5G) technology can affect the use of mobile devices in many ways. With the increased speeds and reduced latency of the technology, organisations can make use of mobile technologies in their business. This means that workers could be travelling around meeting clients and having meetings and still keep in touch with each other and the organisation through the use of applications such as video conferencing facilities on mobile devices. They could also use their mobile device as a navigation device to aid their travel.

The development of 5G technology could influence key areas of society, such as medicine. It will be critical in enabling specialist doctors around the world to watch and advise in an operation on a patient located in a completely different place. This would mean that the best medical attention could be accessible to a person, no matter where they are in the world, as long as the technology needed is available. The doctor would not need to travel to perform the surgery and may be better prepared and more rested as a result.

11.04 Artificial intelligence

One of the earliest pioneers of artificial intelligence was Alan Turing. During World War II he cracked the Enigma code, the code generated from the Enigma machine used by the German army to communicate, and decrypted German messages. He became intrigued by the possible intelligence of machines. This came from the notion of providing machines with **heuristic** knowledge to enable them to make decisions in a way more like humans.

Remember
Artificial intelligence is when a computer is able to make decisions based upon stimuli, much as a human would. Artificial intelligence is very hard to create. Some say that it is not at all possible to have a computer think like a human being. Artificial intelligence systems are made by programming rules to be obeyed.

True artificial intelligence can also be learnt from actions taken and modifying behaviour based on them. This can give the illusion that a computer can think, but in fact it is still responding to programmed elements.

A simple example of artificial intelligence is an opponent in a game of Tic-Tac-Toe/Noughts and Crosses. If you were to place an 'X' in two corners, a computer would know to place its 'O' in-between your 'X's, in order to prevent you from winning. This is a very low-level example of artificial intelligence. A well-known example of artificial intelligence is the computer system Deep Blue. Deep Blue is a computer that plays chess. The more chess Deep Blue played, the better it became at chess. This is because it was able to learn from the errors it made in previous chess games and become a better chess player as a result. It became so intelligent that it was the first computer ever to beat a world chess champion at the game.

More recently, artificial intelligence has emerged in the market of self-driving cars. Car manufacturer Tesla recently released their line of autopilot cars. These are cars that are able to automatically change lanes, maintain speed and slow down if they sense they are approaching another car. The chief executive officer (CEO) of Tesla has stated that this is not a fully self-driving car but that in perhaps five years' time such a car will have been developed.

Artificial intelligence is even in most of our phones today. Applications such as Siri and Google Now are examples of artificial intelligence. They can help with tasks such as searching the web and setting up calendar events, all from simple voice commands.

Artificial intelligence has already had a wide impact on our lives:

- Those with disabilities can use voice-activated systems, such as Siri or Google Now, to search the web, message family and friends and more.
- The development of self-driving cars may mean that those with disabilities will also be able to travel independently in a car. It may also make the task of driving a car safer, by removing the element of human error.
- The level of entertainment provided by games is much greater. This is because an enemy or opponent in a game can be made more challenging to beat.
- It can be used to create expert systems that allow easy diagnosis or problem solving of issues that require expert knowledge.

However, artificial intelligence is not without its issues:

- In the case of self-driving cars, there is a debate about who should pay in the event of an accident on the road, where the self-driving car is at fault. Should the user have to pay? Should the company who made the car have to pay? This issue is as yet unresolved.
- Voice activated systems are improving, but they still suffer from lots of input errors. If artificial intelligence is dependent on a voice-activated system, it will be limited by the ability of this system.
- Artificial intelligence is only as good as its programming. If there are errors in the programs that allow the intelligence to be created, then it will not operate correctly.

Figure 11.02 - Inside a Tesla Autopilot car.

DISCUSSION POINT
Many people find the concept of allowing a computer to be responsible for major tasks, such as driving a car, an extremely scary prospect. What do you think about placing your life in the hands of a computer?

11.05 Augmented reality

Remember
Augmented reality is where technology overlays computer-generated images onto the real world. It works by taking signals from the real world using a camera. It then checks to see if there is a point in the camera image that is telling it to draw an image on screen.

Imagine using your phone's camera to take a picture of a sign in a foreign language that you cannot read. The camera uses image processing to understand what is written on the sign. It then uses a translation tool to translate the sign into a language you do understand. It then draws that translation on your camera view replacing the original image.

Augmented reality is a very interesting technology and one that is gaining a lot of attention at the moment:

- An example of using augmented reality is Google Glass. Users can wear a pair of glasses that overlay information about the world around them, such as the name of the street they are on. They allow you to take images and share them on social media, and can also provide news updates.
- Augmented reality has also been used as part of computer games. The Nintendo 3DS has 'AR Cards' at which you can point your 3DS camera lens. It then builds, for example, a 3D model of a Nintendo character in that spot.

Augmented reality does have some potential issues:

- Using a product such as Google Glass can mean your vision is impeded. You might easily bump into someone or, if driving, it could distract a driver and cause an accident.
- The technology still has issues with object recognition due to lighting or the angle of the camera.
- A product such as Google Glass can suffer security issues when streaming data. The streaming is often done from a mobile device to the Google Glass using a Bluetooth connection. There is the potential for someone to possibly exploit a security flaw and look at your private data or disrupt your Google Glass.

Figure 11.03 - Google Glass.

DISCUSSION POINT

Find out about Microsoft's augmented reality product the HoloLens. What impact could this product have on a person's life?

11.06 Biometrics

Remember

Biometrics is the use of technology that tracks user values. This could be as simple as their heart rate with fitness devices, or it could be voice recognition software, fingerprint and iris recognition or even recognition of DNA patterns.

Biometrics works by taking several examples of whatever is being measured, so for a voice command a user may have to say 'Hello' five times for the computer to get an average measurement. This data is then saved and attached to a user account, just like a username and password. The user simply gives the same command of 'Hello' and this is compared with the values stored to determine if there is a match. If the vocal pattern matches closely enough to the original values taken, the user will be able to access their account.

Some uses have been developed for biometrics:

- Some mobile devices and laptops currently have a fingerprint recognition device attached. When the device is locked, the user places their finger on the scanner to unlock it.
- Anyone who has watched enough spy movies has probably seen biometric devices being used, such as iris scanners or hand scanners that measure the size, shape and fingerprints of the user's hand.
- Some airports now have the capability of reading biometric passports. This means that a person's biometric data, often their facial and iris image, is attached to their passport. They can go through a special gate at passport control that will scan their passport and their facial features and if there is a match they will be allowed to pass through.

Biometric technology is incredibly personalised because of the data it takes in and stores. This can cause issues:

- Very personal details are stored about users. These could be used against them if someone were able to hack into the database where the data is stored. In fact, the database could be abused and have data values replaced, locking original users out and giving access only to those who hacked into it.
- There isn't anything stopping a user from presenting fake biometric material, such as a fake fingerprint or a recording of a voice command. These would need to be very high quality to be undetected, but it is possible.

193

- Some people feel that their human rights are being violated through the collection and use of their biological data for security reasons. They feel that it is a huge invasion of their privacy to have this kind of data stored and used in this way.

Figure 11.04 - A biometric passport control system.

11.07 Cloud computing

Remember
Cloud computing is where a collection of servers are used to store or process data instead of doing this on your own computer. Your computer simply needs an internet connection in order to communicate with the bank of servers.

A number of uses have been developed for cloud computing:

- There are many online services that provide cloud computing services, most of them emerging in the late 2000s. Providers include Dropbox, Google Drive and Microsoft's OneDrive, along with many others. These services allow you to upload your own files and manage them. This means that you can be away from your computer and still be able to access those files through the online service.
- Data can be uploaded onto a cloud from numerous mobile devices. This means the data can then be accessed by each device that has access to the cloud. This is a great way of sharing files between your own personal devices and with others.
- Cloud computing can also be used to process data. The game Crackdown 3 uses cloud computing to outsource the calculations needed to be able to render the destruction of very large buildings. Therefore a high-quality effect can be achieved, while not affecting the performance of the console too much. This means

that a reasonable computer, or console, can be used alongside cloud computing to perform tasks far beyond the capabilities of the computer on its own.

There are issues with cloud computing:

- A big issue is security. If someone hacked into one of the services for file management and started reading people's files, this could reveal personal details that could be used for acts such as credit card or even identity theft.
- Another concern is the need for a constant internet connection. This is not an issue for some. However, not everyone has a connection all day or even just one that does not get interrupted periodically. This is an even bigger issue when you consider that the provider you choose might have a power outage, which means that even if you did have a perfect internet connection, you still would not be able to access your files. Therefore it is important to regularly synchronise the files from the cloud with the files on the computer or device, to make sure that the data is always accessible.

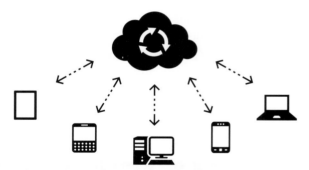

Figure 11.05 - Data from many different computers and devices can be uploaded into the cloud.

11.08 Computer-assisted translation

Remember
Computer-assisted translation tools work by giving the software either a document or a string of text. The software then removes anything that is not text, such as pictures or tables, and simply takes what is left over and translates it into the language of choice.

There are some well-known computer-assisted translation tools, such as Google Translate.

Access to computer-assisted translation can have its benefits:

- When in a foreign country, as long as an internet connection is available, a person can quite quickly and easily translate words and phrases by entering them into a site such as Google Translate. This can improve their ability to communicate with people in that country.

- It can be used to translate whole documents and websites into a language of choice, quickly making it possible to read them.

There can be issues with computer-assisted translation:

- Sites such as Google Translate are designed to give direct translations, rather than the meaning behind the sentence. This means that if you enter a French sentence, the structure is kept the same when it is translated into English, which can break the grammar. As an example 'the blue car', when in French, might be directly translated as 'the car blue' in English. There are, however, more sophisticated computer-assisted translation tools than many of the web-based services, which are designed to overcome this issue, such as OmegaT or memoQ.
- One of the biggest issues is being able to restructure grammar across translations, picking the correct meaning of a word that has multiple uses, and also handling issues where there is no actual translation for the word in question.

11.09 Holographic and fourth generation optical data storage

Remember

The traditional methods of data storage, magnetic and optical, rely on each bit of data being stored as magnetic or optical changes on the surface of the medium. Holographic data storage works by recording data throughout the volume of the medium.

Holographic data storage is a developing medium of high capacity data storage.

Magnetic and optical storage methods store data in a linear way: each bit is placed side by side. Holographic data storage can store bits in parallel, meaning many bits are stored layer upon layer.

Holographic data storage can be beneficial as it can provide companies with the ability to archive vast amounts of data for a long period of time. This is because this medium will degrade a lot less than others. Many argue, though, that this benefit may not be completely worthwhile. Technology develops and moves on so rapidly that in years to come the technology to read the holographic storage may no longer be available.

One of the largest issues with holographic data storage is the cost. The drive to read the data costs thousands of dollars and each medium used to store the data will cost hundreds.

Fourth generation optical media refers to the next generation of the traditional optical media we know about, at present. The third generation of optical media allowed the storage of HD video, with the ability to store data files of around 400 GB. The fourth generation will bring about the potential to hold up to 1 TB of data on optical media. This will be done by using smaller pits and lands (the indents made on the disk to record data), and using more layers.

11.10 Holographic imaging

Holographic imaging, sometimes known as holography, is the ability to make holograms. A hologram is a 3D image that is created with photographic projections. A hologram is a free-standing 3D image that you can see around. It does not need to mimic depth like a 3D image or virtual reality. In time, it may become possible to transmit a hologram electronically to special devices in our home or workplace. Think of the possibilities this could create!

DISCUSSION POINT

How could the introduction of holograms that can be transmitted into our home change the way we live?

11.11 Quantum cryptography

Quantum cryptography is thought to be one of the safest ways to **encrypt** data. Most encryption methods use mathematics and algorithms to encrypt data. Quantum cryptography uses physics.

Remember

The process of encryption is carried out in a similar way to mathematical algorithms, in that it uses a **key**. This key is generated using photons, which are tiny packets of light. The key scrambles the data.

The data will then be transmitted using fibre optic cable. The reason the encryption is much safer is because it is much more difficult to crack the key. In a normal key, a mathematic algorithm would be used, but a human could actually manage to recreate this algorithm and decrypt the message. The key in quantum cryptography is made up of a stream of light particles that individually vibrate in all different directions. Creating these different vibrations is called polarising. Once transmitted, the light particles will then be passed through a filter that will reverse the polarisation and unscramble the data.

When the light photons are polarised, it is not possible to accurately measure their activity, it is only possible by using a device to reverse the polarisation. This is what makes quantum cryptography a very safe method for data transmission.

At present, quantum cryptography has been successful over short distances of around 60 km, but it is yet to prove it can be used without error over longer distances.

11.12 Robotics

Remember
Robotics is the creation of computers that perform tasks that humans cannot or are less efficient at performing.

The word robot itself has a Slavic origin, *robota*, which means slave or work. A robot works by having a processor that controls its movement. This can be a set task, for example moving an arm forwards and backwards, repeatedly, or its action can depend upon the environment it is in. This requires sensors to be attached to the robot and they feed data back to the processor so it can decide what to do next.

Remember
Robots are heavily used in manufacturing, for example moving items down a conveyor belt or moving heavy items such as car doors or chassis.

When the term robot is used, some people automatically think of human-like computers from science fiction. This interpretation of a robot does exist and they are able to do many impressive things. One of the most famous examples of a humanoid robot is ASIMO. It is currently one of the most remarkable pieces of technology. It is able to visually recognise people, understand a lot of people talking at once, run and lift both feet of the ground as it does so, climb up and down stairs, hop and a great deal more.

Robots can be beneficial:

- They can be used to complete mundane and repetitive tasks, removing the need for humans to do them.
- They can be used for tasks that may possibly be dangerous to humans or require presence in a dangerous atmosphere, such as in a chemical factory.
- They can provide great entertainment value and can be used for many everyday tasks.

Robots can cause issues:

- Many people get angry when humans are replaced by robots to do certain tasks. This takes away jobs from people, and often their livelihood.
- Many people get scared by the ability of robots, especially when they are equipped with artificial intelligence. They fear that robots could begin to overpower human beings.
- Robots cannot respond with any kind of emotion and can only carry out the task(s) that they are programmed to do. They can become a little more sophisticated if they are programmed with a level of true artificial intelligence. With this, they may be able to respond to learned situations and experiences and provide a more human-like response.

Figure 11.06 - A robot arm at work in a factory.

11.13 QR codes

Remember
Quick response (QR) codes are a type of barcode that is made up of black and white squares. They are printed on many products in order to give extra information about the object.

The QR code is scanned by a camera acting as a QR code reader, which can then carry out an action, such as linking to a page of information related to the object.

Figure 11.07 - QR code.

QR codes can be used to provide information in a variety of ways:

- Some gyms have QR codes on the equipment to show you how to use them, as well as providing information about what muscle groups are being used.
- They can be used on foods to share more about the company who makes the product, or about the product itself and its nutritional information.
- They are used for marketing purposes. They are printed in magazines or other advertising outlets to attract a user into scanning them and viewing the marketing material.
- They are an easy way of giving the user the choice to learn more about the product, instead of overloading the product packaging itself with information.
- They can be used as a trigger to open different applications. They can also register data within the application.

However, QR codes have several issues:

- As they are based on image processing, the QR code can only be scanned if there is enough light for the code to be fully recognised by the camera.
- Companies have to be very careful about QR codes being distorted when they are resized, as the image may not be exactly the same as before and therefore will not scan and link to the information.
- They may require less text placed on a product. However, they need ample space so as not to interfere with the recognition of the code. Any text or image that is too close to the code can make the code very hard to read.
- As QR codes often act as a link, if you do not have a stable internet connection, then you may not be able to access the linked information.

11.14 Wearable computing

Remember
Wearable technology can take many forms. However, there are two major forms with which most people are currently familiar. These are fitness devices and smartwatches.

Wearable computing, or wearable technology, is either clothing or accessories that somehow involve a computer-based component. Some serve an actual purpose. Others are just fashion statements.

Fitness devices are often worn on the wrist, similar to a watch, but they measure your activity, such as steps taken, sleeping patterns, calories you have burnt, and they can even wake you up by vibrating. There are many fitness devices available from several major brands.

Smartwatches are not as popular. This is mainly due to their price, but they perform similar functions to fitness devices, as well as allowing you to pair them with your smartphone. Currently a range of companies make smartwatches, including Microsoft, Apple, Sony, Motorola and Pebble. Products such as Google Glass also count as wearable technology. These headsets can send the wearer news updates, incoming messages and information about where they are and directions for where they're going.

There are also some wearable technology T-shirts, often displaying either a message or a .gif type image that moves, such as an equaliser for music. These serve no function other than to look stylish and fashionable.

There can be issues with wearable technologies:

- They are easily subject to moisture, especially fitness devices, and this could affect the operation of the technology. This could break devices if they are not protected or built for dealing with it. They need to be carefully designed and be able to deal with this potential issue, which may increase the cost.
- Another problem is with connectivity. Using Bluetooth and wireless networks to send data back and forth does mean that people may try to hack the connection and gain access to private information and documents.

Figure 11.08 - A range of smartwatches that are available.

11.15 Ultra-high definition television

Remember
Ultra-high-definition is now firmly established in screen and monitor definition. This refers to the measure of the horizontal number of pixels for the screen, so ultra-wide screens (2560 x 1080) and standard desktop monitors (1920 x 1080) both count as 2K, which is classed as HD.

4K has nearly twice as many pixels horizontally, while maintaining aspect ratios. It is also possible to get an 8K screen and this is the up and coming technology in ultra-high-definition.

4K and 8K definition is still expensive as they have not been adopted widely enough for consumers to benefit from a cheaper manufacturing process. There are several companies creating both 4K and 8K televisions and computer monitors. Cinema screens are sometimes 4K depending on the size, so you may have already had an experience with 4K resolution without realising it.

The main issue with 4K and 8K is simply content. While films are able to be high resolution and many have been filmed in 4K for quite a while now, everyday television programmes and many video games are often not made at such a high resolution. Users therefore do not buy 4K and 8K devices because there is not enough content and creators of television programmes do not create 4K and 8K programmes as it would prove very expensive and not many consumers can currently view them. It is also very difficult to stream content that is ultra-high-definition because of the amount of bandwidth required. Many people stream their movies and television programmes from online providers and this is a further barrier to the regular use of ultra-high-definition.

11.16 Vision enhancement

Vision enhancement is a field of technology which is able to restore, vision, one of our five senses, to those who have lost it. The ultimate goal of vision enhancement is to be able to provide blind people with images of their surroundings so that they can work and enjoy themselves just as others do.

However, the field is not solely focused on those who are blind. A recent development in the field has allowed those who are colour-blind to see the world in the same way that everyone else sees it. This means that they are better able to distinguish between colours and in some cases see new colours that were muted before.

Remember
Vision enhancement is normally provided in the form of a type of glasses or lenses. These alter the stimulus that enters through the eyes and filters it in a way that can enhance a person's vision. The glasses or lenses can be tailored to the person and their current level of vision for greatest effectiveness.

11.17 Virtual reality

Remember
Virtual reality is where a 3D space is made by a computer. The user is then effectively put into that 3D space by wearing some sort of technology, usually a headset, which displays that space and their position within it.

The headset uses two camera feeds, one for the left eye and one for the right, in an attempt to mimic the human field of vision. The user can then walk around the room and possibly interact with it. This can require handsets or gloves to monitor the user's hand position.

Currently there are many game-related virtual reality projects, such as the Oculus Rift, HTC Vive and PlayStation VR. As many games already take place in a 3D environment, it is often a case of splitting the camera view to match the user's field of vision. While the headsets do place the user into the game, there is no way of interacting with the game other than by controllers, such as keyboard and mouse or console controller. Google Cardboard is a very inexpensive and simple virtual reality experience that is already available. This requires users to wrap their mobile phone in a cardboard structure, and, by using certain apps, they can create a simple virtual reality experience.

Virtual reality also has many applications outside games. For example, several medical procedures make use of virtual reality by allowing doctors to practice surgery. This can allow them to gain confidence and experience, and become more comfortable with procedures.

Virtual reality has been used in several training programmes, including flight simulators to give pilots experience in dealing with certain scenarios and in demonstrating military situations.

Virtual reality does pose some issues:

- Achieving calibration between the camera and user has not yet been perfected. Many users have mentioned issues with motion sickness because of the difference between what they feel and what they can actually see.
- Virtual reality can also cause users to injure themselves if they are not in a large, empty space, as they could easily walk into objects and hurt themselves.
- In some cases, users have experienced seizures because of virtual reality, so epileptic users must be very cautious.

There is a constant race to create the next better, more efficient, more glamorous, more functional technology. This means that more and more technologies are emerging all the time. As a result many technologies, such as mobile devices, have become far more throwaway than they were. The desire to have the newest technology encourages people to discard the items they have in favour of the functionality and services provided by that new technology. This creates a problem with how to deal with the technology that is being discarded.

Figure 11.09 - The Samsung Gear virtual reality experience.

Discarding technology into landfill is bad for the environment. If people choose to do this the amount of landfill created will be great. Some countries have incentives in place to recycle old technology and this can discourage people from discarding the old technologies into landfill and having a negative impact on the environment.

11.18 Summary

Technology is constantly developing and affecting our life in a variety of ways.

From faster internet speeds, more accurate and safer systems, to enhanced enjoyment through improved entertainment, technology is having an impact on areas of our lives such as sport, manufacturing and medicine.

It is also having both a positive and a negative effect on our environment. With technology advancing at such a rate, there is a fear it will become more and more throwaway, causing our landfill sites to increase.

Review questions

1   Discuss the impact 3D printing has on medicine. [8]

2   Evaluate the impact of artificial intelligence being used to create self-driving cars. [8]

3   Discuss the impact of emerging technologies on our personal entertainment. [8]

Chapter 12
The role and impact of IT in society

Learning objectives

By the end of this chapter, you will be able to:

- explain how technology is used in e-business and evaluate the impact of technology on e-business, society and learning
- evaluate the impact of digital currency
- discuss how organisations mine data
- evaluate how social networking has changed social patterns
- describe video conferencing and the hardware and software used
- describe web conferencing and the hardware and software used
- discuss the advantages and disadvantages of video conferencing on employers and employees
- discuss the advantages and disadvantages of web conferencing on employers and employees
- describe teleworking
- discuss the effects of teleworking on employers and employees

KEY TERMS

Transaction: the action of buying or selling an item or service
Public key: used in encryption to encrypt data
Private key: used in encryption to decrypt data

12.01 What is an e-business?

An e-business is one that performs either all or the majority of its business online. Large online companies such as Amazon are e-businesses, even though they supply physical products, most of their **transactions** occur online. Another example is gaming businesses such as the Xbox and PlayStation online stores. These are businesses that are purely online and deal with digital products.

Remember
Commerce has changed hugely through the introduction of technology. Online business is now commonplace and is often seen as an easier way of buying goods and services than in a physical store. Goods and services are often cheaper online because of cost savings from not needing shop space and reduced utility bills.

12.02 Online shopping

Remember
Information technology has caused the rise of online shopping by providing a more convenient platform on which to sell items to a customer or purchase items as a customer.

One of the main advantages of this is how quickly the customer is able to receive products. Online shopping has become even more popular with the rise of smart devices, because of applications that allow you to order anything online by using your phone, regardless of where you are. This is even more convenient for the customer as they could be out shopping, not able to find their product in store, but able to order it from the online store straight away from their phone.

Online shopping can be better for the environment, as less vehicles may be used as people are not driving to shops. This will depend on whether the amount of people travelling to the shops is reduced by people shopping online. Some people argue that the amount of vehicles on the road that are delivering the online shopping does not make it much better for the environment. It is also very difficult for people to see the quality of products online or check the size of them. This can mean that many

products end up being returned. This may also increase the amount of vehicles used.

12.03 Online banking

Online banking is a computerised version of the majority of services that a normal bank would offer. It is a way for customers to manage their bank account and use other

Remember
As well as buying and selling goods, the ability to bank online is ever increasing. The speed and capacity of computers allows for very complex online models to be set up to better help serve customers.

banking services electronically via the internet. Online banking is also known as internet banking or e-banking.

A customer's bank provides access to online banking using a website. A customer requests an online banking account from their bank. The bank will set up electronic access to the customer's account and send the customer login details to access the account. The customer will enter these login details into the website each time they want to log onto their online bank account. Many banks now also provide access to an online bank account using a mobile app. Customers download the app onto their mobile device, set up access to their account by entering their personal details and use their login details (or set up new ones) to access their online account using the app.

Online banking services now allow people to check their bank account quickly using technology. They can carry out most banking services online, such as:

- checking their bank balance
- viewing bank statements
- setting up direct debits
- applying for loans and overdrafts
- paying bills
- transferring money between accounts.

To be able to use services such as these, people would previously have needed to go into a bank branch. Often they would only have one or two local bank branches, so their choice may have been limited if they wanted their branch to be close to home. Also, those people that live in remote locations may have had to travel a great distance in order to get to a bank. The introduction and developments in online banking have allowed people to have more choice over which bank to choose and saves people a lot of time in using banking services. There are many benefits brought about by online banking, these include:

- Needing to visit a branch less as many services can be used online.
- Avoiding queues in bank branches.
- The ability to use banking services 24 hours a day, 7 days a week.
- Using banking services without leaving home.
- Viewing transaction online without needing to wait for paper statements to be delivered.

Some banks have chosen to encourage online banking by offering better deals on interest rates and loans online. They have done this as online banking can help cut their costs, from printing statements to the number of branches they need to have.

12.04 Electronic funds transfer

Information technology can be used in many areas of business. Many business transactions are carried out through electronic funds transfer. This is when money is transferred from one account to another electronically. This transaction could be from a person paying for their purchase with a credit card. No actual money will change hands when doing this. The money will be moved electronically from their bank account to the business's bank account. Another method of electronic funds transfer is direct debit. This is when a person sets up an agreement with a business that allows the business to take a set amount of money from their bank account. This could be just once or could be on a regular basis, for example each month. Many people choose to pay their bills in this way. This type of transfer can be beneficial as it means that the person does not need to remember to pay the business each month, as the money will automatically be transferred.

All of these services are, however, not without their issues. Online transactions are a cause for concern for many people because of the safety of their financial details being stored on a company's or several companies' servers.

Financial details in the hands of hackers is a great concern. This is identity theft in its very simple and most common form. This is a very serious issue. If you use a credit card, you may not notice fraudulent activity until you start getting asked for large payments that you cannot identify. If someone obtains simple personal details such as full name, current address, credit card number and date of birth, they can do great financial damage. If they get access to full financial details, then they could have enough information to do many things, such as take out a loan, access other accounts and even take out a lease or make very large purchases. It is therefore imperative to

check the security of any online website that you use to carry out any financial transactions.

> **TIP**
> The simplest way to check that the website has a secure protocol is by looking for https:// at the start of a website address, or the security padlock symbol.

Figure 12.01 - The security padlock symbol that can be checked for on e-business websites.

12.05 Automatic stock control

In business, information technology can be used in ways other than as a method of purchasing goods and making payments. It can be used to control other elements such as stock levels. A business that sells or manufactures products will most likely need to keep track of the number and type of products it has in stock. Stock will most likely be stored in a warehouse or stock room and it may not be easy to see how much stock a business has at any moment in time. Therefore a business needs a way to automatically measure the amount of stock it has. It is important they are able to measure their stock levels for several reasons including:

- holding too much stock means more storage space for the stock is needed and this can be very costly
- having too little stock in storage may mean that stock might run out before more can be ordered and sales could be affected as a result.

Products that are purchased can have a barcode that will contain data about the product. This data, when scanned, can be used to automatically control stock levels. It can look to see what the product is that is being sold and deduct one of those products from the stock level available in the warehouse. This means it is easy to see how much stock for a product a business currently has in its stock room or warehouse. This system can then also be programmed to reorder stock when it gets below a certain level. This means that a business does not need to manually count and reorder stock when it is running out. As new stock comes into the warehouse, the barcode on the product can be scanned and the total stored for that product will be updated. This means that the business can measure how much new stock has arrived in the warehouse and add it to the previous total.

By automatically monitoring stock, a company can perform checks to see whether the stock the system shows they should have actually matches the physical stock they have manually counted. If the two stock levels do not match, for example the physical stock level is lower than the one shown on the system, this could highlight possible theft from the store. The business could then monitor this to establish how and why it is occurring.

Automatic stock control can be carried out in two ways. The stock control system could be real-time or batch. If it is a real-time system it will process each addition or deduction to stock as it is sold or enters the warehouse. This type of stock control system is used by businesses such as large supermarkets. This is because they sell large volumes of stock and need to restock regularly. A stock control system can also be batch. In this kind of system each item of stock sold, when scanned, is recorded in a database in a file called a transaction file. At a suitable time, normally during an off peak period for the business, for example when it is closed, the transaction files will be processed and a master file in the database will be updated.

12.06 Digital currency

Digital currencies are an internet-based form of money. They have a value that can fluctuate much like normal currency. However, they can be used instantly and without the need for exchange rates. This can be seen as beneficial when trading internationally.

Remember
The simplest way to check that the website has a secure protocol is by looking for https:// at the start of a website address, or the security padlock symbol. The digital currency most people are familiar with is Bitcoin. This allows people to trade anonymously as it requires no link to your identity. Bitcoin does not keep data on their customers, it only tracks the value attached to an address that is made up of two **keys**, a **public** one and **private** one.

While digital currency can quickly overcome the issue of exchange rates, it has a level of anonymity that appeals to criminals. It is used in a lot of transactions involving criminal activity, especially on the dark web (a collection of websites that will not appear when using search engines and hide the IP address of the server that runs them). This is because it is far less likely for the criminal to be traced as the transaction is anonymous.

Digital currencies can also fluctuate a great deal more than most standard currencies. This could result in a great amount of money being made for those people who invested by using the currency at the right time, but also a great deal of money being lost by those people who invested at the wrong time.

Figure 12.02 - The currency symbol that is used for the digital currency Bitcoin.

TASK
Research two further digital currencies.

12.07 Data mining

Data mining is the act of sorting through large sets of data to identify patterns and establish relationships. The goal of mining data is to extract information from sets of data that can be used to inform and instruct future decisions, by identifying past and present trends.

Remember
Data mining involves finding trends and then applying a theory to new data sets in order to try and validate the changes that are occurring. The overall goal is to be able to predict changes before they actually occur. This means that a business can be in the right place at the right time.

Data mining normally involves analysing data in different ways. These include:

- Anomaly detection – identifying unusual data that may require further investigation.
- Association rule – finding relationships between variables. This is how recommendation services work for shopping sites.
- Cluster detection – identifying groups and subgroups in data.
- Classification – classifying data into existing groups or categories. This is how a spam filter works for an email.
- Regression – creating predictive models based on a range of variables.

Data mining is a huge step forward for businesses. If they are able to predict what will be wanted beforehand, they are able to make the most profit by changing what they offer early, to easily meet the new demand.

12.08 Social networking

Social networking has developed a great deal in a very short period of time. Originally this was limited to very simplistic forms of communication such as email, forums and chat rooms. Instant messaging and email were early forms of social networking and both still exist today. Many more forms of social networking have now developed, such as websites like Facebook, Twitter and Tumblr. These later methods make use of earlier features, such as instant messaging, which is a form of social networking that enables real-time text communication over the internet – either between two people or, more recently, between groups of people. They also include newer features such as blogs and microblogs. Forums have also become a popular social networking method and are used to post questions

Figure 12.03 - Taking and posting a 'selfie' is a popular way of using social networking sites.

on many different topics so that other people can post replies. Many people use this to get advice on a variety of subjects and areas of interest. The forms of communication in each of these services is slightly different and allows for different forms of expression. Most have developed to try and cater for people who want different things from social networking websites. Access to social media sites can be an issue because content disseminated can be inaccessible, for example, frequent hashtags, abbreviations or acronyms are not easily decipherable for people with certain disabilities.

There is also a great concern for young children growing up, who see these sites, and the communication that takes place on them, as normal. There is a fear that this will leave them unable to recognise social cues and body language, harming their ability to socialise properly. It is also easier for them to access, or be targeted by, inappropriate content or communication.

Remember

Social networking websites are used for many purposes, both good and bad. They have allowed many people to stay in touch over great distances and with greater ease. However, they leave people open to abuse from issues such as online bullying, identify theft and other criminal acts.

Another issue with social networking websites is that they enable companies to track and assess your online data to target advertising. For example, if a company wants to advertise a sports product, they can find out how many people on Facebook are interested in that product, and information about them. Some see this as a benefit as they are only presented with what they would like to buy. However, this involves tracking and sometimes selling your personal data and online actions and some people feel this is extremely intrusive. It is also limited in the sense that not all of a company's target audience will necessarily be on a particular social networking site.

TASK

Research how websites track your online activity and use it to target you with advertising on social network sites.

Blogs are also a form of social networking. They are a more one-way communication channel as the person blogs about their life, interests or other topics. The word blog comes from web log. Blogging is probably older than you think. It developed towards the end of the 1990s with services such

204

as Open Diary, LiveJournal and Blogger all launching during 1998 to 1999. Blogging started as the work of one person on a single topic. These were often quite personal, such as an individual opinion on changes in their industry, or something more personal, such as events in their life.

Blogging then became even more popular and the amount of authors and subjects increased. Blogging, in fact, has become so universal as a form of social networking that it has expanded into several formats. Microblogging is a new format of blogging and is carried out on sites such as Twitter, Facebook and Tumblr. Microblogging is when people use short and frequent posts to inform their followers about what they are doing. Video blogs or 'vlogs' have become a popular video format on sites such as YouTube. The content is the same as a normal blog but, with the added visual and audio cues, points can be presented more coherently. This can feel more personal as the person is vocally describing their passion for a subject. Blogging has become such a huge part of social interaction that some people are able to make money through it or turn it into an actual business.

The effects of these forms of social networking have their benefits and drawbacks. The ability to find others who think as you do can be a comfort to people because humans like to feel part of a group. Followers of certain social media figures describe themselves as fans, and can feel as if they are friends. However, those figures have sometimes abused this by launching online hate campaigns against those with whom they have disagreements, rallying support from other fans. This has also happened in reverse, with some people attacking others even without the public figure wanting them to do so, because of a public disagreement between the two. Social networking has brought the world together in many different ways. At the same time, it has also created some very large divides. The anonymity that people are able to have online, if they choose to, can cause them to do or say things that they would never do in a face-to-face situation. It is also nearly impossible to delete data from the internet once it is published, so once someone has posted text, photos or videos to a social networking site, it is extremely difficult for them to take it back.

12.09 Video conferencing

Video conferencing is when computers are used to provide a video link between two or more people. Previously people made conference calls by logging into a telephone based system and several people could speak on a telephone call at any one time. Video conferencing aims to provide this same service, but with the added addition of video, so people can see each other as they speak.

To carry out a video conference, a range of equipment is needed. This includes:

- a computer system
- a web cam
- a microphone
- speakers
- a good broadband connection
- video conferencing software.

Specialist video conferencing systems can be purchased that incorporate all the equipment needed to make a video conferencing call.

Video conferencing has a range of advantages and disadvantages as shown in Table 12.01.

Advantages	Disadvantages
Employers do not need to pay expenses for employees to travel to meeting venues.	A video conferencing system that is suitable for business use can be very costly to buy initially.
Meetings can be carried out, without the need to travel, between employees from many different offices.	Employees may be in different time zones and this could mean that some employees will need to be present for the conference outside working hours.
People can be seen as well as heard, so additional conversation aspects can be seen, such as body language.	It may not be possible to see all people involved in the meeting at the same time, using the camera. This would not happen in a face to face meeting.
Documents can be shown, shared and emailed. This can encourage the generation of ideas from employees.	If any person's equipment breaks down they are not able to be part of the meeting and may miss vital contribution.
	A very reliable and fast internet connection is required to effectively carry out a video conference. This can be an extra cost.

Table 12.01 - Advantages and disadvantages of video conferencing.

Ultimately, a business will need to look at the benefits of using video conferencing against the drawbacks of not meeting face to face. Video conferencing may mean global meetings between employees are much easier to organise and cost less because of the lack of travel. However, the equipment to set up the facilities for a video conference is costly and if it breaks then meetings are heavily disrupted.

12.10 Web conferencing

A web conference is another form of carrying out a meeting or event. It is a real-time communication where a number of people are viewing the same content on their computer screen at the same time. A business may set up a web conference to hold a meeting, make a presentation or provide online education, amongst other services.

To carry out a web conference, a range of equipment is needed. This includes:

- a computer system
- a web cam (this is optional and only needed if video is required for the conference)
- a microphone (this is mostly necessary for the host, but optional for other attendees, unless voice communication is required)
- speakers
- a good broadband connection
- web conferencing software.

The web conference host or presenter will lead the web conference. They will mostly control what is shown on the screen. To see the same screen, each attendee will be sent (normally by email) a link to enter the web conference meeting. This will normally require the person to download the necessary software to do this, if they have not attended a web conference using that software before.

The link will take the attendee to what is often referred to as a virtual room. To get into the room they may need to enter login details, if they are provided with them. Once in the room they will be able to see the content the host chooses to display. The host can upload documents to the web conferencing room. These documents may be displayed on the screen for attendees to view, they can also be made available for download if the host chooses to do this.

The host will mostly control the content on screen, they may speak to attendees as they do so. The host can hand over control of some content on screen to another person attending. They may choose to do this if they want the attendees to read through a document at their own pace. This way each attendee can scroll through the document at a different rate.

Web conferencing has a range of advantages and disadvantages as listed in Table 12.02.

Advantages	Disadvantages
The host controls the content on screen and can make sure everyone keeps on task, despite not being in the same location .	It is difficult to tell if a person is closely following the web conference as they mostly cannot be seen.
Web conferencing saves time that would be spent travelling to see, for example the presentation.	It can be time consuming for the host to set up all the content and the 'room' for the web conference to take place.
Web conferencing saves travel costs for each of the attendees.	Web conferencing software can be very costly.
Pre-recorded content can be used in the web conference. This saves the host repeating part of the content each time the presentation is given.	The host will likely need a lot of training to use the web conferencing software. Some attendees may also need training in how to navigate around the 'room'.
Documentation can be made available for attendees to download as a quick and easy way to share resources.	If an attendee has a poor internet connection, they may not have a very good experience in the web conference. They may miss vital elements.

Table 12.02 - Advantages and disadvantages of web conferencing.

12.11 Teleworking

Teleworking is essentially using IT to work away from an office. Employees of a business use IT to work from their home or another location. This could include using their PC, laptop, tablet, mobile and internet connection, amongst other devices, to carry out their work.

Teleworking has a number of advantages and disadvantages for an employee. It allows an employee more freedom over the hours they want to work. It can give them freedom as to what time they want to start and finish their work. They can also take a break and have their lunch whenever they want to. This means they have more freedom to organise other elements of their days, such as family commitments around their work, or vice-versa. Employees may still be restricted to company working hours though if their employers requires this. Employees may also find that there are too many distractions in their home and their productivity may suffer as a result.

If an employee can work from home, this can save on costs as they will not need to travel to their place of work every day. Reducing this travel can also have a positive effect on the environment as not as much fuel is being used by transport, so, in this way, the carbon footprint is lowered. However, the employee will need to use extra electricity being at home all day, so the effect may be countered by this, thus harming the environment.

Teleworking has a number of advantages and disadvantages for an employer. If an employer does not have as many employees in an office at any one time, they may be able to have a smaller building, less facilities and use less energy. This will reduce costs for them, quite considerably in some cases. However an employer may feel that they have less control over their employees as they cannot see them to monitor how much they are working. They may also have to worry about the confidentiality of any sensitive documents. They will need to rely on an employee to store and them safely if they have them in their home or another location.

12.12 Technology in society

Technology has changed so many aspects of society, and these effects are mostly global. Many of us own one if not several technology devices. Technology also features in a great variety of industries. Manufacturing, sport, teaching, medicine, banking and commerce have all been heavily affected by developments in technology.

12.13 Technology in sport

In sport, technology has been introduced to aid referees in making important decisions that could change the outcomes of games. In rugby union, the referee will regularly use technology to see if the ball was put over the goal line for a try to be scored. This was very difficult to judge without the use of technology, as the referee was often having to see around a pile of players trying to aid or stop the try occurring. Technology has been both welcomed and criticised in sport for this use. People support its use as it means the outcome of games are often more accurate, as decisions made can be carefully considered based on recorded footage that can be accessed. Other feel that the introduction of this kind of technology stops the flow of games and makes them less enjoyable to watch. Technology is also used in sports such as tennis, to allow players to challenge the decisions

of the officials judging the match. Some feel this is a welcome addition to the game as it can help the decision making process become more accurate. Some feel that the system used is not very accurate and will often provide incorrect outcomes as a result.

> **TASK**
> Research the use of Hawk-Eye in tennis.

12.14 Technology in medicine

In medicine, technology has given us the ability to monitor patients and make sure they are healthy. We're able to measure their heart rate, analyse DNA samples to see if an infection is present, and even use technology to train doctors and nurses in how to perform certain procedures through simulations.

Technology has enabled many advancements to occur in medicine. It is now possible to provide people with artificial limbs that can be controlled through the use of technology. This means that people who previously had debilitating disabilities can be provided with a new life through the use of these artificial limbs. They could be given the ability to walk again or regain the use of their arms and hands, allowing them to live a fuller life. This type of treatment has been very beneficial to soldiers who have been wounded, by providing them with the ability to use their wounded limbs again, or have them replaced altogether.

The use of nanotechnology in medicine has provided great advancements, especially in the use of drugs to treat disease. Nanotechnology is when technology is used to manipulate individual atoms and molecules. In medicine, it can be used to target the delivery of drugs in a very precise way. Particles can be engineered to locate particular cells in the body to which to deliver the drug, cancer cells for example. This can help to reduce any damage or unnecessary treatment being delivered to healthy cells.

The use of technology in medicine is constantly developing because of the vast benefits it can bring. One development in progress is the use of smart devices that are designed to be implanted into different parts of the body, such as the brain or heart. By monitoring the body, these devices can detect health issues a long time before they fully develop, for example Parkinson's disease. This can enable treatment to start much sooner and this may prove more effective, or avoid the disease developing altogether.

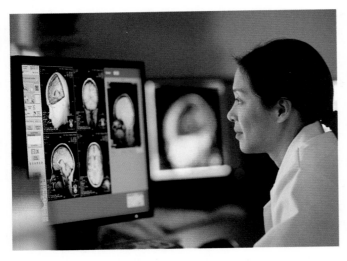

Figure 12.04 - Technology is used in a great variety of areas in medicine.

12.15 Technology in manufacturing

Manufacturing uses robotics to create assembly lines of products such as cars, where heavy elements like the chassis are moved to an area where humans can then fit items to them to build a car. This has meant that humans can be removed from working on the more dangerous elements of manufacturing. By using robotics in manufacturing, it is possible to create a more consistent and accurate product. This is because the robot can be programmed to produce a product and will do this to the same standard repeatedly. A human may differ in their standard of production depending on the mood they are in or how tired they feel that day. Also, if a manufacturing system is completely robotic, it can run for much longer periods of time and will not require the same level of rest as a human. With the correct level of maintenance, robotic manufacturing could be set to run for 24 hours a day.

Some feel that the introduction of robotics into manufacturing has resulted in a loss of jobs for people. This has often created animosity toward the use of robotics in manufacturing, despite their benefits. Also, if a company cannot afford the robotic equipment, this can sometimes put them at a competitive disadvantage against those companies in their industry that can.

12.16 Technology-enhanced learning

Teaching has not only been improved by technology, but now also involves subjects such as information technology and computer science. Computers are a feature in most classrooms now and teaching can also be provided at a distance using online courses. Students can be provided with resources and guidance online, and with services that allow them to upload work to a portal where it will be marked. Interactive whiteboards can be used to enhance the teaching and the demonstrations that are being carried out. This means that students may benefit from a greater understanding of the subject because of an increase in the quality of the demonstrations that can be carried out and the level at which resources can be shared.

A large part of technology's growing influence on society is the introduction of online learning and online courses. There are many tutorials available on websites such as YouTube, and more educationally oriented sites like Lynda.com. There is no shortage of people willing to teach and learn online through small courses on websites such as Codecademy for learning computer coding, or offering accredited courses on websites such as Coursera and Udacity. This means that people can now gain access to teaching often without a fee, other than the cost of their internet connection. This also means they are able to learn at their own pace and in their own time. With sites such as YouTube, they also have a greater level of visual aids available when learning. The quality of the resources available through these sites can often differ greatly. There is also no governing body looking at the level of teaching that is taking place, as there often is with schools. This means it may be difficult and time-consuming for a person to pick through all the tutorials they can find to get one that is of a high quality. It could also mean that a person could use a tutorial that teaches them incorrectly.

One of the biggest online learning methods is through the use of massive open online courses (MOOC). These are courses that are not limited in the number of people that can access them and have open access using the web. MOOCs are mostly free and will be used by a large number of learners of a topic at any one time. They will often include filmed lectures and other resources, and have forums that can be used to interact with other learners and the educators. MOOCs allow people in similar industries to learn more about their industry from other people within that industry. They allow this to happen at the convenience of the learner.

Online courses can vary a lot in terms of quality, cost and the subjects offered. Whether it is for self-interest or accreditation, it is often much easier to learn at your own pace and in your own time. It can sometimes be difficult to find the exact course you want as there are so many available. Another issue with online learning is finding effective teachers that are able to break down problems and help students in the process. This is partly because of the difficulty in finding someone who is capable, but also it can be because of the way how the customers want to learn. Do they prefer to be lectured or do they want a small bit of information and then be set off on a piece of work and learn as they go?

Remember

One of the greatest benefits of people being able to learn through the use of technology is that it is easier for people to improve themselves or help their own career.

12.17 Summary

An e-business is one that performs either all or the majority of their business online. They use a variety of technologies to carry out their business transactions online. E-business is constantly growing as it has many benefits to both the business and the customer.

Information technology has helped with the rise of online shopping by providing a more convenient platform on which to sell items to a customer or purchase items as a customer. Online shopping has also become even more popular with the rise of smart devices. This is because there are applications available that allow you to order anything online, using your phone, regardless of where you are.

Online banking is growing, with many banking services now being available online.

Digital currencies are an internet-based form of money. The currency with which most people are familiar is Bitcoin.

Data mining involves finding trends and then applying a theory to new data sets in order to try and validate the changes that are occurring. The overall goal is to be able to predict changes before they actually occur.

The use of social networking is ever growing. It has had both a positive and a negative effect on our social patterns, bringing us closer together, yet creating issues in our lives at the same time.

Technology can be used to enhance learning in a great way. Education is now more accessible than ever with a variety of free and paid-for courses available online.

Review questions

1 Explain what is meant by a digital currency. [3]

2 Discuss the impact of online shopping for the customer. [6]

3 Evaluate the effect that social networking has had on our social patterns. [6]

4 Explain what is meant by data mining. [4]

5 Describe two benefits of software-based training. [4]

Chapter 13
Networks

Learning objectives

By the end of this chapter, you will be able to:

- describe components within a network
- understand bandwidth, bit rate, bit streaming and the importance of bandwidth
- understand different methods of data transmission
- describe protocols
- understand security issues and the need for security measures and evaluate their effectiveness
- understand the need for data protection
- understand how satellite communications work and are used

13.01 Network components

Network: a set of computers and devices connected together so they can communicate and share resources

Switch: connects devices on a network

Packet: a set of bits which represent data to be transmitted

Hub: similar to a switch but does not examine each data packet that is received; instead simply transmits each data packet to all connected ports

Wireless access point: connects Wi-Fi enabled devices to a network

Wi-Fi: wireless Ethernet which allows devices on a LAN to connect wirelessly

NIC: network interface card which connects the motherboard of a device to a network cable

WNIC: wireless network interface card which enables a device to use Wi-Fi

Router: a switch which can forward data to the correct location in the most efficient manner

LAN: local area network which connects devices in a single building or area

WAN: wide area network which connects devices that are geographically remote

Repeater: amplifies the signal on a network cable. It is also another name for an active hub

Gateway: connects two different types of networks

Bridge: connects two LANs

Firewall: prevents external devices from gaining unauthorised access to a computer system

Server: a computer on a network which provides resources that can be used by client devices

Virus: software that replicates itself in order to corrupt data

Bandwidth: the range of frequencies available for a communication method which determines the transmission rate

Bit rate: the number of bits that can be transferred per second

Streaming: a method of displaying sound or video without waiting for the whole file to be downloaded

Circuit switching: a single communication path which is opened for the duration of data transmission

Packet switching: data that is broken down into packets that are sent through different routes and reassembled by the recipient

Message switching: a method of transmitting data through intelligent node

Infrared: a communication method used by most remote control devices

Fibre optic: a fine strand of glass that transmits data as light beams

Laser: an intense beam of light used for transmitting data

Bluetooth: a short range wireless communication standard

Biometric: unique physical characteristics of a person that can be used by a computers for identification purposes

RFID: radio-frequency identification

NFC: near field communication

Protocol: a set of rules that ensure data is transferred between devices correctly

> **TIP**
>
> In order for devices in a **network** to communicate with each other and share resources, certain components are required.

Data packet

An Internet Protocol (IP) data **packet** will include header information and the data that is being sent. Within the header information will be the source address, destination address, IP version being used (e.g. IP v4), the length of the data packet and an identification number to enable packets to be sequenced if they have been fragmented during transmission. The source address and destination address will both be 32 bit IP addresses (if using IP v4), for example, 212.35.0.89. The source is the original device that sent the data packet and the recipient is the final device that will receive the data packet. The IP addresses do not change during transmission.

An IP packet resides within an Ethernet packet that also includes a TCP packet. The Ethernet packet also includes a receiver MAC (machine address code) address and sender MAC address. The sender MAC address will change during transmission to the address of the most recent device each time the data packet passes through a device such as a **router**. The receiver MAC address will change to the address of the next device (known as hop) on its route to the final destination.

Switch

Figure 13.01 - Switch.

A **switch** connects devices on a network. It is a necessary component in any wired Ethernet network. A switch will have several ports into which network cables are plugged. Each network cable will connect to another device (e.g. printer, computer, another switch). A switch examines each

211

data packet that it receives and sends the data packet to the desired port where it will be transferred to the next device.

Hub

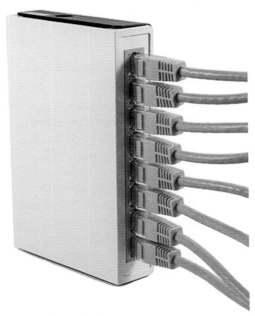

Figure 13.02 - Hub.

A **hub** is similar to a switch but it does not examine each data packet that is received. Instead, it simply transmits each data packet to all connected ports. A hub can also be classed as a multi-port **repeater**.

Wireless access point

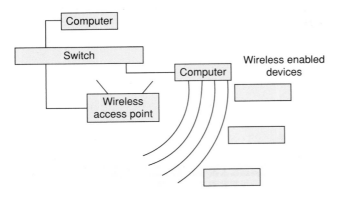

Figure 13.03 - Wireless access point.

A **wireless access point** connects **Wi-Fi** (wireless) enabled devices to a network. It uses radio waves at frequencies of 2.4 GHz or 5 GHz to transmit data. A wireless access point is usually connected to a switch by a cable, although it is possible in the home to have a combined wireless access point/switch/router. A wireless enabled

device can transmit data to the wireless access point, which will then either send the data on to the switch or directly to another wireless enabled device that is using the same wireless access point. Similarly, data that is transmitted from elsewhere in the network can be sent to a wireless access point to be transmitted wirelessly to a wireless enabled device.

Network interface card

In order to connect a network cable to a computer or other device, a network interface card (**NIC**) is required. This is a set of electronics on a circuit board that connects to the motherboard of the computer, although many motherboards now include the NIC circuitry as standard. Each NIC has a unique address called a media access control (MAC) address.

Wireless network interface card

Figure 13.04 - Wireless network interface card.

A wireless NIC (**WNIC**) makes a device 'wireless enabled' meaning that it can connect to a network wirelessly through a wireless access point. It is most often part of the motherboard circuitry of a laptop, printer, tablet or mobile phone. However, it is also possible to add a wireless NIC to a non-wireless enabled device by using a wireless dongle to a Universal Serial Bus (USB) port or an expansion card to the motherboard. Each wireless NIC has a unique MAC address.

Router

Figure 13.05 - Domestic router.

A **router** is often used as the gateway to a network and in most cases connects the local area network (**LAN**) to the internet via an internet service provider (ISP). An ISP is wide area network (**WAN**) that provides a connection to the internet. A router's role is to determine the most efficient route to use to transfer data to its destination, and in order to do this it needs to store the addresses of all devices connected to it. In domestic use, a router is often combined with a switch and wireless access point.

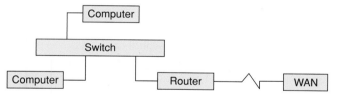

Figure 13.06 - Router.

Repeater

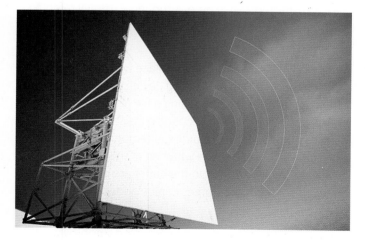

Figure 13.07 - Repeater.

A **repeater** is another name for an active hub. It boosts the signal along a network cable. A booster requires a power source and receives data packets from an incoming network cable. It will then retransmit those data packets along its outgoing network cable. This is necessary when long cable lengths are required (typically over 100 m) and the signal would not be strong enough to reach the destination on its own. A similar degradation of signal happens with wireless access points and so wireless repeaters carry out the same function with wireless signals.

Gateway

A **gateway** connects two networks of a different type. It is typically used as a router to connect a LAN to a WAN. When data leaves one network to move onto another network, it must pass through the gateway.

Bridge

A **bridge** connects two physically separate LANs of the same type together so that devices on one LAN can communicate with devices on the other LAN.

Firewall

A **firewall** prevents external users gaining unauthorised access to a computer system. It is usually positioned at the gateway to a network and will examine all incoming data to determine if it should be allowed. Data that is not allowed will be prevented from gaining access to the network. A firewall can also prevent certain types of data from exiting a network. As well as preventing unauthorised users from gaining access, a firewall can prevent malicious data packets from causing disruption to a computer system such as a denial of service (DOS) attack.

A firewall is often configured as part of a router but it can also be software that is installed on a proxy server or individual computers. A proxy server would sit between the gateway and the LAN so that data cannot pass through to the network without being examined by its firewall software. Firewall software can also be installed on individual computers in order to prevent any unauthorised access or malicious attack from within a network.

Servers

A **server** is a computer on a network which provides resources that can be used by client devices. Individual servers or groups of servers can perform a variety of functions depending on how they are configured.

A **file** server's role is to make files available for users on the network. These files might be for individuals who have access to their own user area for file storage or they may be files that are shared between groups of users. Depending on the permissions given to each user or group of users, files can be created, read, modified and deleted.

TASK

Explore the files available on your school's file server. Find out what documents are available to you and what permissions you have. Ask your teacher or technician what other documents are available to other user groups and the permissions that they have.

A **print** server deals with all the print jobs on a network. Each time a client computer sends a request for printing, it will be added to the queue on the print server. The print server will then deliver each print job in turn to the printer. There may be several printers that are managed by the print server. Some client computers or users may be given priority and so may be able to jump the queue. It's also possible for the print server to charge users for each print job, which is usually done by reducing the number of print credits available to the user.

A **mail** server receives and sends all emails for an organisation. The mail server can be part of a LAN or a WAN. Incoming emails are checked for **viruses**, phishing or spam and then sent to the user's mailbox. When a user sends an email the mail server will either direct it to another user within the organisation or send it on to the internet for delivery to another mail server.

An **application** server delivers software to client computers. This can be done by the clients accessing the software direct from the server or by the server managing the installation of the software onto each client computer.

A **proxy** server deals with all requests to the internet. It sits between the LAN and the gateway. It will check that each request is allowed and filter out any undesirable requests such as pornographic websites. It will also store web pages in a cache which will speed up the time it takes for a user to receive a web page. A proxy server often also includes firewall software.

Bandwidth and bit rate

Bandwidth measures the range of frequencies available on a communications channel. This defines its capacity. Bandwidth is measured as a frequency range in kilohertz (kHz) or as a transmission rate in bits per second (bps). Although the bandwidth is often thought of as a speed,

it's actually the number of bits per second that the line is capable of transmitting, rather than the actual speed of transmission. It is therefore the maximum possible speed of data transfer. The transmission speed is often referred to as the **bit rate**.

EXAMPLE

A 1 Gbps line in a network is capable of transmitting a maximum of 1 billion bps. A 38 Mbps fibre optic internet connection from an ISP is capable of transmitting a maximum of 38 million bits per second. If a computer within the network is downloading data from the internet, then the maximum transmission speed is 38 Mbps and not 1 Gbps as the connection to the ISP is a bottleneck.

DISCUSSION POINT

Note that bits are different to bytes. There are eight bits in a byte. Therefore, a bandwidth of 32 Mbps is actually four megabytes per second.

TASK

Find out what bandwidth your school has for its connection to the internet and compare that with the bandwidth you have at home.

Bit streaming

A bit stream is a series of bits which represent a stream of data transmitted at one time. Although it usually refers to communications, it can also apply to data in memory or storage.

In networking, **streaming** takes place when video or audio files are sent to a receiving device for viewing or listening to without downloading a file to save in storage. With a video, the first few seconds consisting of several frames will be sent to fill a buffer (a temporary area of storage) which can then be watched at the receiving device. As the frames within the buffer are viewed, they are removed so that more frames can be added to the buffer to keep it full.

A buffer is used to keep the video running smoothly. Without a buffer, any data congestion would be noticed by the video pausing, missing out frames or pixelating until the full transmission rate was available again, even if it was only for a split second. It's still possible that a buffer could be fully used during data congestion but it is much less likely than if a buffer was not present.

Data congestion can be caused by devices on the same network using up so much bandwidth that there isn't enough left for the full video transmission or a similar situation at the sending end of the transmission.

The same situation regarding buffering applies to audio streaming as it does to video streaming. This is not just used for video and audio streamed on demand but also when streamed live, for example when watching a sporting event or live news. This means that live events that are streamed are actually delayed by the size of the buffer. This is why you could be watching a rugby match on television and see a try being scored before you see it on a live stream.

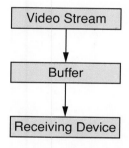

Figure 13.08 - Buffer.

> **DISCUSSION POINT**
> A byte stream is a bit stream that consists of bytes. It is also known as an octet.

Circuit switching, packet switching and message switching

These three switching methods are all methods of communication used to transmit data from the sender to the receiver.

Circuit switching

This method of data communication sets up a physical network path from the sender to the receiver before any communication starts. All the data is then transmitted using this single path. While the circuit is open, no other devices can transmit data using that path. When transmission is complete, the path is released for other data transmissions.

> **EXAMPLE**
> Traditional voice telephone calls using the Public Switched Telephone Network (PSTN) are transmitted using **circuit switching**.

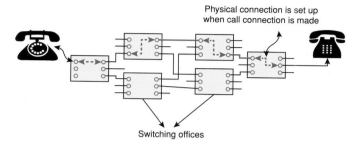

Figure 13.09 - Circuit switched telephone network.

Packet switching

This method of data communication splits the data to be transmitted into packets, which are groups of bits. Packets will include header data which identifies the source and destination, some of the data and error control bits. Each packet can take its own route from source to destination. As each packet is received by a network node, such as a switch or router, it will be routed to the next node.

> **EXAMPLE**

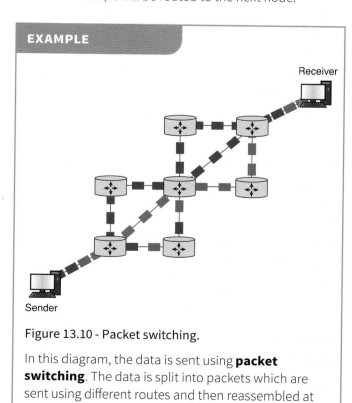

Figure 13.10 - Packet switching.

In this diagram, the data is sent using **packet switching**. The data is split into packets which are sent using different routes and then reassembled at the receiving device.

Message switching

Message switching transmits the whole set of data together from source to destination. It does not have a predefined route. The data is sent to one network node (e.g. switch or router) at a time and is temporarily stored there before being passed to the next node. This is known as 'store and forward'. Each message includes a header which contains the source and destination.

This method is quite slow because it depends on processing taking place at each node and it also requires network nodes with adequate storage capacity. This makes it unsuitable for streaming real-time games or real-time communication.

Optical communication methods

Optical communications make use of light to transmit data. The big advantage of this is that the speed of light is far faster than any other method. Light travels at 300 million m/s. That means it can travel around the whole earth 7.5 times every second or that it only takes 0.065 seconds to travel halfway around the world. This means that there is negligible latency (delay) between sending and receiving data, which makes it suitable for real-time applications.

Infrared

Infrared is the communication method used by most remote control devices. It is cheap to produce and a well-recognised standard method of transmitting simple commands. It works by transmitting electromagnetic radiation that is just past the red end of the visible light spectrum, so it cannot be seen by the human eye. It does not have a very high bandwidth and so is only suitable for transmitting small amounts of data. It can also be affected by sunlight, meaning that the transmission of data is not always successful. Infrared requires line of sight between the sending and receiving devices so it cannot bend around corners but it can reflect off light surfaces. Infrared will only work for short distances.

Infrared can also be used by mobile phone devices to act as a remote control and is used within active sensors, which were introduced in Chapter 3.

Fibre optic

Fibre optics are fine strands of glass that transmit data as light. As the strands are very fine, a large number can be fitted into a small space, meaning that it is possible to transmit a lot of data at once. The fine strands are also flexible, which means that the cables can be used in buildings and around corners. The light is retained within each strand of glass and so, unlike copper cables, fibre optics are not susceptible to electrical interference. All these factors combined mean that fibre optics have very large bandwidths. A single fibre optic strand used in an internal network can easily carry 1 Gbps of data. Security is another advantage of fibre optics because they cannot be 'tapped' in the same way that copper cable can be. The main disadvantages of fibre optics are that if they are broken they can be complicated to repair, especially if there are several hundred strands to fix, and they are more costly to produce than copper cables.

Figure 13.11 - Fibre optic strands.

Because they suffer hardly any degradation of signal, they can be used over large distances, including in LANs where copper cable limits are typically 100 m. They are also used in aircraft where weight is an important factor, because they are lighter than copper cables. The lack of degradation of signal means that they are suitable for passing data across the globe as well as throughout towns and cities. ISPs often use a method called fibre to the cabinet (FTTC) to provide internet connectivity to homes. With FTTC, fibre optics are used to connect a communications exchange to a cabinet in the street and the last portion of the connection to the house is by copper cable. In the UK in 2015, Virgin Media were able to offer bandwidths of 200 Mbps using this method.

Laser

Laser is an intense beam of light that can be used to transmit data. Like infrared, line of sight is necessary, but, unlike infrared, laser beams can cover large distances. Laser still travels at the speed of light, but it does not require a physical connection like fibre optics.

Lasers can be used to connect LANs between buildings. They are suitable for this because very few data packets are lost as there is little interference in normal atmospheric conditions, although adverse conditions can cause some interference. Laser communications are quick to set up and can be portable, making them suitable for live events such as sports and music concerts.

The military use lasers to transmit live video from aircraft because the video feed will arrive in real time because it is travelling at the speed of light. Laser beams tend to be secure because they are narrow and aimed directly from sender to receiver, meaning that to intercept the transmission would mean interrupting it, which would alert the sender and receiver.

Wireless communication/transmission methods

Bluetooth

Bluetooth is a wireless communication method used for the transfer of data between devices. It uses wireless frequencies between 2402 and 2480 MHz. Bluetooth splits transmission data into packets which can be transmitted on 1 of 79 channels, each with a bandwidth of 1 MHz. It is typically used within mobile phone devices to connect to a range of equipment including:

- a car's audio system for hands-free communication
- a headset for hands-free communication
- communicating with a Bluetooth enabled smartwatch so that some of the phone's features can be used on the watch
- sending and receiving data to and from devices that measure **biometric** data, such as heart rate
- streaming videos to a larger display screen
- streaming music to Bluetooth speakers
- transferring files from one phone to another phone or other Bluetooth connected device.

Bluetooth can also be used to network devices together in a small area as long as a high bandwidth is not required.

Bluetooth doesn't require a radio frequency licence and is a common standard that is used on many different devices. Bluetooth requires very little power to operate. It doesn't require line of sight and it is possible to set up security so that only authorised devices can connect. However, it has a limited data transfer rate, its range is only approximately 10 metres and a master device is limited to connecting to a maximum of seven devices.

Wi-Fi

Wi-Fi is a wireless communication method. It operates in the 2.4 GHz and 5 GHz frequencies. There have been many Wi-Fi standards that have evolved over the years and they are all referred to by the number 802.11 followed by a letter. These letters have included a, b, g, n and, in 2015, ac was introduced. Devices supporting a version are backwardly compatible with devices that support previous versions, but the communication will be limited to the highest common version the two devices support.

The 802.11ac standard supports speeds of up to 1.3 Gbps, compared to just 450 Mbps (0.45 Gbps) on the previous 802.11n standard. These are theoretical maximums and don't reflect the actual maximum speeds that are experienced in practice, which were around 150 Mbps and 300 Mbps respectively. Another big advantage of 802.11ac over 802.11n is that it uses the 5 GHz wireless spectrum rather than the 2.4 GHz spectrum used by 802.11n. The 2.4 GHz spectrum was very crowded because in urban areas there can be several wireless access points overlapping, as well as other wireless devices such as baby monitors, smart home equipment and even microwaves, which cause interference and therefore reduce the connection speed.

DISCUSSION POINT

Wi-Fi does not provide direct access to the internet. Wi-Fi enables a wireless enabled device to connect to a network. That network may then have a connection to the internet which is shared with the devices connecting to it.

Wi-Fi is used for a range of applications including:

- connection of portable devices such as laptops, tablets and mobile phones to a network, which could be a corporate LAN, a home LAN or a wireless hotspot

- 'smart' televisions which use services from the internet and so require a connection to a LAN that is connected to the internet
- printers that can be located anywhere in a room, without having to run additional cables
- 'casting' of a devices screen to another device wirelessly. Typically this could be casting a laptop's display to a projector or casting a mobile phone's display to a television
- smart home devices.

The main advantage of Wi-Fi is that devices can connect to a LAN without the need for cables which can be costly to install, unsightly and a potential hazard. This means devices can use any location where Wi-Fi access is available. Line of sight is not required and the international Wi-Fi standards mean that any compatible device can connect. Mobile phones which usually rely on fourth generation (4G) for data can connect to Wi-Fi networks for internet access, which will save the user money and allow for larger amounts of data to be downloaded. Connection speeds are not massively smaller than wired connections, meaning that data can be transferred quickly.

However, the range offered by Wi-Fi is restricted by distance and objects. The connection speed is dependent on the bandwidth available and the number of devices that are using the Wi-Fi connection at the same time. Security is a potential issue because a hacker does not need to make a physical connection to a network in order to gain access and so it is necessary to ensure that sufficient encryption is in place with a secure key.

> **TASK**
>
> Investigate screen casting methods including Miracast, Chromecast, AirPlay and AllShare.

Radio

Bluetooth and Wi-Fi both use radio waves. Another transmission method that uses radio waves is radio-frequency identification (**RFID**). RFID uses electromagnetic fields to identify and track small RFID chips. One use of RFID is to monitor the location of parcels from a distribution warehouse to the delivery point. Each parcel can have a RFID tag that is unique to the parcel. As it moves through the warehouse and onto a delivery van, the tag is read

by a RFID reader and the parcel's location is updated in a database. The RFID reader will be continuously sending interrogation signals through its antenna to identify the location of any RFID tags. These types of tags are also used by shops as security tags prior to a product being purchased.

Figure 13.12 - RFID.

Another use of RFID is for wireless key cards that are used to unlock doors. These can be part of an identification badge for employees or could be a card issued to guests in a hotel. The card can be used to unlock a door without it actually touching the lock. This is the same type of system used in ski resorts where skiers can keep their lift pass in their pocket and then just move their pocket towards the RFID reader. These close proximity RFID chips are known as near field communication (**NFC**). NFC is also used by mobile phones to emulate a NFC tag on a credit or debit card and make contactless payments. The mobile phone can also read NFC tags, which can be used to activate an application, change phone settings or open a web page.

Figure 13.13 - Contactless payment.

NFC is also a secure method of RFID which means it is suitable for payment transactions. Its disadvantage is that the card has to be next to the reader, but this can also be an advantage as it prevents accidental transactions from taking place. RFID does not require a line of sight and does not require somebody to manually scan the tag, which is what would have to happen with a barcode.

TASK

Complete the table below summarising the advantages and disadvantages of each wireless communication method:

Method	Advantages	Disadvantages
Bluetooth		
Infrared		
Wi-Fi		
Radio		
RFID		

The importance of bandwidth and bit rate when transmitting data

Bandwidth governs the maximum speed that data can be transferred; the bit rate is the actual transmission speed. They are therefore important to consider when large amounts of data need to be transferred in a short amount of time. There are two main scenarios when bandwidth is important:

- accessing content within a time limit
- accessing content in real time.

If a user wants to download a large file, then the higher the bandwidth the quicker it will be to download if the bit rate is higher and the bandwidth is sufficient for the bit rate. However, bandwidth and bit rate are only important if it is important to download that file within a specific time limit. For example, if a user needs to download a 50 Mb high quality photograph but doesn't need to view it until several minutes later, then bandwidth may not be a major issue. However, if that user needs to examine the photograph within a couple of minutes, then it is important the user has a higher bit rate and sufficient bandwidth.

When a user needs to access streamed or live content in real time (or with a short buffer delay), it is essential that there is sufficient bandwidth to stream the content without the buffer emptying at any point. If the buffer empties due to the content not being streamed quickly enough, then the user will experience pauses, pixelation or missing video or sound.

EXAMPLE

A person who is travelling decides to download some television programmes onto their mobile phone, tablet or laptop while at home before they make the journey. One of the reasons for this is to save having to 'eat' into a limited 4G data allowance. Another reason is that the 4G connection may not always be available and Wi-Fi connectivity at a hotel may be slow due to congestion, meaning that live streaming is not effective.

Different types of communication/ transmission media govern bandwidth
Cables

Copper cables are the main method used for connecting devices in a LAN. The most common form of copper cable is unshielded twisted pair (UTP), which is also known as an Ethernet cable. The cables consist of four twisted pairs of cables and are protected by plastic tubes, but there is no earth wire, which can result in lost data packets at high frequencies.

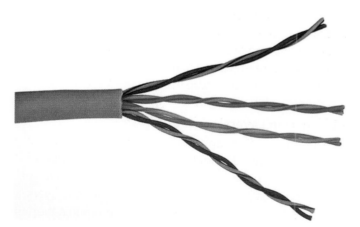

Figure 13.14 - Unshielded twisted pair cable.

Copper cables are suitable over distances up to 100 metres but beyond this the signal weakens. The bandwidth available is governed by the frequencies that the copper cable can accommodate, and electrical interference which can result in lost data packets that will affect the transmission rate.

When higher bandwidths are required, shielded twisted pair (STP) cables can be used. They include a metal shield around each twisted pair and an earth wire.

Wireless

Less frequencies are available to wireless communication methods than to copper cable, which means there is less bandwidth available. Wireless transmission is also susceptible to interference from other wireless devices, including conflicting wireless access points, baby monitors and even microwave ovens. This interference causes lost data packets which reduces the transmission rate. Obstacles such as walls and ceilings can reduce the strength of a wireless signal, which means there is even less bandwidth available the further away a device is from a wireless access point.

Optical

As fibre optics are not susceptible to electrical interference, it is far less likely that data packets will be lost, meaning that the total bandwidth available is considerably higher than with copper cables.

What a protocol is and different types of protocols

A communication **protocol** is a set of rules that ensure data is transferred between devices correctly. These rules are required so that a variety of devices and applications can communicate together successfully. A protocol defines the method of addressing to use, the type of error checking to be used, how sending devices will indicate the start and end of a message, how a receiving device will confirm it has received a message and any data compression methods to be used.

Abstraction Layers

The International Organization for Standardization (ISO) published a layered model in 1983 known as the Open Systems Interconnection (OSI) model. This defined a framework that put protocols into seven different layers with each layer being an abstraction of communication. The physical layer of communication deals with electrical and mechanical operations. The data link layer deals with data packets. The network layer deals with how data is switched, routed and addressed. The transport layer ensures data flows correctly without errors. The session layer defines protocols between applications during a communication session. The presentation layer ensures that data is in a format that can be recognised such as types of image, types of video file and the text encoding method to use. The application layer deals with specific types of communication application such as file transfer or email.

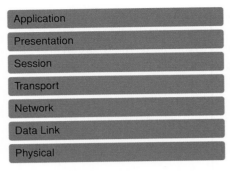

Figure 13.15 - ISO OSI 7 layer model.

POP

Post office protocol (POP) defines the rules for email client software to retrieve emails. The main method that is applied is to connect to an email server, download all messages and store them on the client computer and then delete the messages from the server. POP also supports encrypted transmission of emails. POP is part of the application layer of the OSI model.

IMAP

Internet message access protocol (IMAP) is an alternative method for email client software to retrieve emails. Instead of downloading the email and then deleting it from the server, its default mode is to leave the email on the server and download a copy to the client. This means the emails can still be accessed from a remote location. IMAP also supports multiple folders on a server whereas POP only supports a single folder on the server. IMAP is part of the application layer of the OSI model.

TCP/IP

Transmission Control Protocol / Internet Protocol (TCP/IP) is the basic communication protocol used on the Internet and in most LANs and WANs. TCP/IP consists of two layers. TCP deals with breaking a message down into small data packets that are transmitted and then reassembled at the receiving end. IP deals with the address to ensure that each packet reaches the correct destination. The address will be checked each time a packet reaches a gateway and routed towards the destination. The IP protocol uses IP addresses which consist of four numbers between 0 and 255 separated by dots. Some of these are addresses used for private networks which start with 10, 172 or 192 (eg 192.168.0.0) but most are for external networks (eg 212.58.246.90). There are approximately 4 billion of these addresses but they started to run out in 2011. Therefore, IP v6 was introduced which has the potential for over 3.4×10^{38} addresses.

FTP

File transfer protocol (FTP) is part of the TCP/IP suite and is used to define how computer files should be transferred from one location to another. FTP allows for users to be authenticated by username and password but also has an option for anonymous connectivity. This protocol sets the rule for how a server should respond using ASCII codes, the data format to use (eg ASCII, binary, EBCDIC) and the mode of data transfer (stream, block or compressed). FTP is part of the application layer of the OSI model.

HTTP

Hypertext transfer protocol (HTTP) is also part of the TCP/IP suite and is used by web browsers to send requests to a web server to view a web page. When the request is received by the web server it sends the web page information back to the web browser. HTTP is insecure and so HTTPS is a secure version that encrypts the transmissions. HTTP is part of the transport layer of the OSI model.

> **TASK**
>
> Research some of these protocols:
> - SMTP
> - PPP
> - Telnet
> - UDP

BitTorrent protocol

The BitTorrent protocol specifies how multiple downloads can take place from the same file source concurrently. Several clients (peers) download portions of the file. The peers then connect to each other directly to send and receive those portions of the file between themselves. This reduces the bandwidth required by the original host of the file and can increase download speeds for clients downloading large files.

The protocol only works effectively if there are lots of peers downloading the same file, as without lots of peers there are less opportunities to receive portions of the file. To download a file using BitTorrent, clients need client software such as μTorrent. To provide a file for download, a server must run a tracker which coordinates all the peers.

A torrent is a metadata file which identifies the locations (Uniform Resource Locators (URLs)) or trackers which

coordinate communication between the peers in the swarm. The swarm is the set of peers that are downloading parts of the file and uploading parts for each other to download on a peer-to-peer basis. When a peer wants to start downloading a file, it announces that it wants to join the swarm. Peers will periodically report information to the tracker regarding their download status and receive in exchange information about other peers to which they can connect. Peers will eventually become seeders, which are clients that have a full download of the torrent and are still making it available to upload to other peers. If there are a large number of seeders, then there is a good chance of achieving a high transfer rate for the download. The total seeders for a file is known as the availability, which refers to the number of fully distributed copies.

> **QUESTIONS**
>
> 1 Describe the role of a repeater in a network.
> 2 Identify two different types of a server in a network.
> 3 Describe the difference between bandwidth and bit rate.
> 4 Explain why a buffer is needed when streaming.
> 5 Identify three types of switching used for the delivery of data through a network.
> 6 Describe two advantages of fibre optics for the transmission of data.
> 7 Identify two different ways in which Bluetooth could be used.
> 8 Describe three disadvantages of Wi-Fi.
> 9 Explain why bandwidth is important during a video conference.
> 10 Compare and contrast the POP and IMAP protocols.

13.02 Network security

Security issues

> **KEY TERMS**
>
> **Malware:** malicious software
> **Spyware:** malicious software that records what a user is doing on a computer system

228

TIP

When computers are connected together through networks, there are increased security risks due to access being available from other computers.

Unauthorised access

Commonly known as hacking, unauthorised access takes place when a person or device gains access to a computer network without permission. Hackers can guess usernames and passwords to gain access to a network, particularly when users set up weak passwords. Once a hacker has access, they can read data on the system. This data may be confidential to people or to the organisation. The hacker may also make changes to the data, such as changing payment details, or the hacker might destroy data deliberately to cause harm to the organisation or individual.

Malware

Malware is a word used to describe any software that is designed to cause damage. In relation to networks, the main problems are viruses and **spyware**. Viruses copy themselves automatically to other devices and so the connectivity of a network makes the spread of viruses more likely. Viruses are designed to cause damage to data or cause problems to the operation of a computer system. Parasitic viruses attach themselves to files on a computer system and are triggered by certain events such as a date and time. Macro viruses attach themselves to macros that are part of macro-enabled documents. Email viruses arrive as attachments to emails and are triggered by the user opening the attachment. Unique to networks are worms which spread automatically through networks. Worms don't require files to attach to as they create their own executable file. Trojan horses are malicious programs that disguise themselves as normal software, but if they are run they will actually cause damage. Trojans are often found on websites when a user tries to download some illegal music or films and they end up downloading a Trojan instead.

TASK

Find out how the Blaster worm infected networked computers in 2003.

Spyware is software that secretly collects information without the user being aware. Spyware can log user activity including identifying credit card information or usernames and passwords. Once a username and password is ascertained by the spyware, the perpetrators can log onto the network as that user. Another problem for networked computers is that spyware can collect data and then transmit it to another server so that the perpetrator can access that information. If a key logger is used, then every keystroke made by a user is recorded and this could include confidential data.

Denial of service attack

A denial of service (DoS) attack is designed to send more requests to a server than it can deal with. These are easy to launch and difficult to track. They are carried out to cause disruption to an organisation's network or website and often result in users not being able to use the network and customers not being able to access the website. Website attacks are measured in requests per second (RPS) and it can only take around 50 RPS to cripple a website. Network attacks are measured in gigabits per second (Gbps) and it can only take around 20 Gbps of data to make a network unusable. DoS attacks are not designed to gain access to data, but purely to cause disruption. A DoS attack can last for hours, days or weeks.

DoS attacks involve the perpetrator using a single internet connection to overload the target, but distributed denial of service (DDoS) attacks use multiple connections distributed across the internet. These are much more difficult to defend because they are coming from so many different locations.

The motivations of perpetrators of DoS attacks can be pure vandalism (cyber vandalism) or it could be as part of an activist campaign (hacktivism) to express criticism of, or displeasure with, an organisation.

TASK

Find out how the hacktivist group Anonymous used DoS attacks against ISIS websites and social media in February 2015.

Security methods
Access rights

When a user logs onto a network, they are given rights to access different parts of that network. These access rights are usually related to data but can also be related to services that are available, such as accessing the World Wide Web, accessing email accounts and running software.

The most common access rights that are given are:

- create (C): users can create new items of data
- read (R): users can read existing data
- update (U): users can make changes to data
- delete (D): users can delete data.

EXAMPLE

A school or college may give the following access rights to users:

- visitors: access to internet services only
- individual users: CRUD access to all data in their own user area
- students: R access to a shared area for educational resources and executable access to software that has been allocated to them
- teachers: CRUD access to the shared area for educational resources for their department and CRUD access to a staff shared area for their department
- staff: R access to a whole school staff shared area of information about the school
- head teacher's secretary: CRUD access to the whole school staff shared area
- network administrators: CRUD access to the whole network.

Websites may be restricted based upon each student's age. Software can be restricted so that some software is only available to authorised users, such as the school's management information system which is only available to staff. Some email accounts may be shared between users such as the main incoming inbox being shared between administrative staff.

In order to gain these access rights it is necessary for a user to identify themselves. This is usually done by entering a user ID, but other methods can be used such as an email address, swipe card, NFC using a phone or card or biometric methods. A user ID on its own is weak because this would often be known by other people. It is for this reason that a user is also expected to authenticate themselves using a password or personal identification number (PIN) to prove they are who they claim to be. It's also possible that a physical login device such as a swipe card or phone could be stolen and so these should also be used in partnership with an authentication method.

It's possible for hackers to try and guess usernames and passwords and so a password should be strong enough to prevent a hacker from guessing it. Hacking software can be used to try different passwords in order to gain access and so security measures should be put into place to lock a user account if a password has been entered incorrectly a certain number of times. It is essential that a user selects a password that is secure and is less likely to be guessed. Users also need to be careful that potential hackers (including co-workers) aren't looking over their shoulder to try and see what is being typed in. One of the biggest problems with passwords is that a user must be able to remember it. If the user writes the password down then it can easily be stolen. If a user uses the same password for several accounts then, once it is known for one account, it can be used by hackers for another account. This leads to another problem: when a user has several passwords for several accounts it is difficult to remember which ones have been used, especially if the user is required to change their password on a regular basis.

TASK

Research what makes a good password. Define a set of rules for a password that is not too restrictive on users but also ensures that the password is secure.

It's also possible to disable accounts at certain times of day so that users who work from 9 a.m. to 5 p.m. can only access their accounts during that time and this prevents somebody from trying to use their account outside those hours. Security measures can also be put into place to ensure that certain user accounts can only be accessed from specific computers. This can be limiting if a user genuinely needs to use a non-authorised device for their user account, but it also prevents hackers from trying to gain access from anywhere within the network or even anywhere on the internet. This can be especially useful if users are given access from home, where they can be limited to using approved devices.

Where security is critical, two-factor authentication (2FA) can be used which requires two security components to gain access. This can be as simple as using a swipe card and a PIN but it can also include more complex methods. The user could also be issued with a token which could be a small device that generates one-time passcodes or a USB key that includes a secret token stored on it. One of the downsides of requiring a swipe card or token is that the user must always have it available, which means carrying it around. It can also be lost or stolen.

TASK

Find out about how Vasco's DIGIPASS tokens work. You could work as a group so that each person finds out about each different DIGIPASS token and then reports back to the rest of the group.

Mobile phone 2FA involves the system sending a one-time passcode by text message to the user's mobile phone, which the user has to enter to confirm it is them trying to access the system. This is often used by banks to confirm the user's identity before setting up a transfer of money to another account. The main advantages of mobile phone 2FA are that each code that is issued is for a single use and the user is likely to always have the mobile phone available. However, not all users may have a mobile phone and the phone must have enough battery charge and be in range of a mobile network in order to receive the text message. Text messages also cost money for an organisation to send and there may be a delay in the user receiving the text message.

Biometric methods

Biometrics are biological characteristics that can be measured. Biometric security uses these biological characteristics to authenticate a user's identity. The biological characteristic has to be unique to each user in order to be able to authenticate the user. Characteristics used for biometric security include retina recognition, facial recognition, fingerprints and voice recognition.

Figure 13.16 - Fingerprint security image.

Fingerprints and retina scans are tried and tested methods and are known to be very secure. Each person has a unique fingerprint and retina pattern that can confirm their identity. There are concerns about whether fingerprints are the right method to use as they can also be used for identifying criminals. However, if people aren't carrying out criminal acts, then they shouldn't have any concerns. The difficulty arises when corrupt governments use these methods to track individuals who might be opposed to their regime. If a person had to provide their fingerprint every time they used public transport or entered a building, then it would be very difficult to avoid being monitored.

Facial recognition is a developing field of study and is being used within some applications. Microsoft's Windows 10 includes a feature that will detect a user and log them on automatically when they sit in front of their computer. Voice recognition has never been an ideal security method as there are so many parameters that can change, such as a person having a cold that affects their speech, background noise or the potential for a voice to be recorded and played back.

Biometric security can be used as a 2FA method by requiring both biometric security and a password. However, as biometrics used for security should be unique to each human being, it isn't actually necessary to require a password. Users can both identify themselves and confirm their identity using biometric security. This method is also user proof in that fingers or eyes can't be forgotten as an ID card or password can be.

Firewalls

Networks that have access to a WAN or the internet have two-way traffic into and out of the network. A firewall controls what data can flow into and out of the network. A firewall may be part of a router or it may be software installed on a server that sits between the network and the gateway. It is effectively a barrier between the network and external data traffic.

Firewalls include an access control list (ACL) that uses a technique called packet filtering. An ACL controls which data packets are allowed through the firewall. The ACL will include a set of rules that determine which protocols, port numbers, source addresses and destination addresses are allowed or not allowed. If data packets are not allowed, then they will be dropped. For example, if the ACL includes a rule to block FTP, then all data packets for port 21 (the FTP listening port) will be dropped. The ACL can also include rules that direct certain traffic to specific destinations. For example, requests for website data into the network would be directed to the web server on listening port 80. Another rule in the ACL could be that requests for access on certain ports are only allowed from predefined IP addresses on the internet. This could be used to control devices that have virtual private network (VPN) access or devices that could be used to initiate Telnet sessions to administer the network.

A firewall often includes a proxy server. The proxy server makes requests to the internet on behalf of client computers within the network. If a client wants to request a website, then the request will be sent to the proxy server and the proxy server will then fetch the website and return it to the client. Any requests for data from the internet or from outside the network must be made through the proxy server.

Some data packets may be disguised and so proxy firewalls include an application layer which can block specific content such as malware or block content that is misusing a protocol. The application layer firewall will perform a deep inspection of data packets to check for any malicious commands, executable programs or other inconsistencies.

Firewalls offer a certain level of protection from hackers and malware, but it all depends on how the firewall has been configured. If the ACL is configured to block all data packets except those which are deemed safe, then the network will be very secure, but it can also cause inconvenience when users legitimately try to transmit or receive data that has not been configured as safe. On the other hand, if the ACL is configured to allow all data packets except those which are deemed unsafe, then there are more opportunities for hackers and malware to sneak into the network. A healthy balance needs to be found between security and usability.

Backup

A backup is a copy of the original data. A backup is required if something goes wrong and the original data is either damaged or lost. In the event of a problem with the data then the backup copy can be restored. A backup does not stop a hacker from gaining access to data, nor does it stop viruses from causing damage to data, but it is essential when recovering from an attack. A backup can also be used to restore data when non-malicious destruction of data has occurred, such as a file becoming corrupt or physical storage media being destroyed by fire or water.

In a network, backup processes should be set to run automatically and regularly. The more regularly a backup process is run, the more storage that will be required for the backup data. However, if a backup process is run less regularly, then there will be more new data that has not been secured in case of a problem. In a network environment, backups are usually stored on tapes or remotely at another location. That location might be a server at another organisation or it might be servers in the 'cloud', which are effectively internet-based storage.

Storing data remotely has advantages which include not having to change tapes each day and the data being away from the original in case of fire or flood. However, it also means that the data is 'connected' and part of a network which could also suffer a security breach. Storing data on tapes means that the tapes have to be changed each day and then relocated to a secure location away from the main servers.

Encryption

Encryption is the process of changing the data so that if it is accessed without authorisation, then it will be unreadable. This is done by using an algorithm to change the cipher. Although encryption can stop a hacker from reading data, it does not stop a hacker from destroying data and it does not stop malware. However, it is important when data is being transmitted, particularly if that data is sensitive and if the data is being passed through an open network such as a Wi-Fi hotspot or the internet.

When data has been encrypted, only the intended recipients will be able to decipher (decrypt) it using a decipher algorithm. Random encryption keys are used to encrypt the data so that the same algorithm is not used each time. Therefore, anybody trying to intercept the data not only needs to be able to view the data, but must also have access to the decryption key.

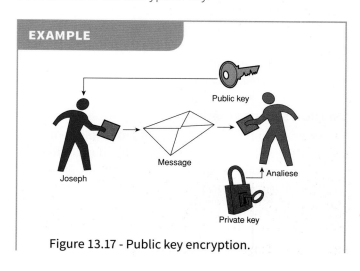

Figure 13.17 - Public key encryption.

Public key encryption is a method used whereby the recipient doesn't know the decryption key to use. In this example, if Joseph wants to send secure data to Analiese, his computer will use Analiese's public key to encrypt the data. Analiese will then use her private key to decrypt the data. This means that the decryption key does not need to be sent to the recipient. Even if somebody knows the public key, they cannot work out what the private key is.

Websites that use encryption for passing data will use the HTTPS protocol rather than the HTTP protocol. Email protocols can also use encrypted protocols, as can many other protocols.

Malware security (anti-virus and anti-spyware)

Anti-virus software now tends to be referred to as anti-malware software as it deals with other threats, such as adware and spyware, as well as viruses. Together, these threats are known as malware. Anti-malware software has two main functions. The first is an anti-virus monitor that is continually monitoring the system for malware. If the anti-virus monitor detects any unusual behaviour or tell-tale signs of malware, then it will prevent that malware from being executed so that it cannot cause damage to files or programs. The second function is to check for malware that may already be on a system. This is usually known as scanning the system. If any malware is found, then the user will usually be given the option to disinfect the malware, put it into quarantine or ignore it. Ignoring it is very dangerous because it means the malware will be executed and may have unexpected results. Disinfecting the malware is the safest option as it completely removes the malware from the system, but it does mean that any data or program that included the malware will be deleted. The compromise is to put the malware into quarantine. This is a safe area where the malware cannot be executed, but the data or program remains isolated until it can be checked more thoroughly.

Physical security methods

Physical security methods are about protecting computer equipment. This can include standard methods that are used to secure other equipment and buildings or specialist physical devices that are designed to protect computer equipment.

Security guards can be used to verify every person who enters a building or specific rooms to ensure that they are authorised to gain entry. Physical locks can be used on server room doors to prevent unauthorised access to those rooms. These can be key locks, swipe card locks or numerical code locks. This type of security should also be applied to backup tapes, which should be stored in a safe that is kept off site.

Main servers should be protected against electrical surges. This can be done using extension leads that offer surge protection, but most servers will be protected by uninterruptible power supply (UPS) units which are basically battery packs that will provide power in the event of a power cut, but will also ensure that the power supply is uniform.

Server rooms should be located in areas that are protected from fires and floods. This should include providing additional fire protection, such as a server room with fireproof doors, carbon dioxide fire extinguishers and putting backup tapes in fireproof safes. Server rooms should not be located on the ground floor, which can be susceptible to floods, and they should be away from any water pipes that could potentially burst.

Data protection act principles

A data protection act can be used to protect people about whom data is stored. They are known as data subjects. It is not in place to protect general information.

In the United Kingdom, the Data Protection Act of 1998 includes the following principles which state that information about data subjects must be:

- used fairly and lawfully
- used for limited, specifically stated purposes
- used in a way that is adequate, relevant and not excessive
- accurate
- kept for no longer than is absolutely necessary
- handled according to people's data protection rights
- kept safe and secure
- not transferred outside the European Economic Area without adequate protection.

TASK

Find out what the principles of data protection law are in your country or another country.

The need for a data protection act

Data protection law is required in order to protect data subjects and the information that is held about them. People have a right to know what information is being stored and that it is stored accurately.

To process data fairly, data subjects must be informed if information is collected about them and they must give their permission for this to be done. It is also expected that data subjects should be made aware of the purpose for which information stored about them is used. Organisations that use this data (data users) must ensure that they only use the data for that purpose and that they inform the relevant governing body of why that data is being stored.

Data subjects expect that enough information will be stored about them by data users in order to carry out necessary data processing. For example, if salary payments are being made to employees, then the employees would expect their employer to keep records of any tax that has been deducted and any tax allowances that should be applied. Data subjects also expect that only necessary and relevant data will be stored about them, as they have a right to privacy. For example, person applying for a travel pass for public transport would not expect the transport authority to be storing information about their mental health.

Data subjects have the right to expect that their data will be accurate and up to date. It is the data user's responsibility to ensure that data is entered accurately in the first place, but the data subject must also have a right to request that any inaccurate data is corrected. The data subject must also take responsibility for informing data users of any changes to personal information, such as change of address, of which data users should be made aware. Data users can make use of validation and verification techniques to reduce errors during data entry.

EXAMPLE

Naomi applies for a credit card. She is declined the credit card because her credit history shows that she has not made payments on a loan for the past six months. Naomi had paid off the loan in full six months ago, but the bank had not updated their records to show that payments no longer needed to be made. Naomi has suffered embarrassment due to the bank's error and has been unable to access a new credit facility.

Data users should only store data for as long as is necessary. This means that they should remove data when it is not needed any more. Data subjects have a right to expect that their data will be kept secure. It is therefore the responsibility of data users to put security measures in place, as described earlier in the chapter. If data is lost, damaged or accessed unlawfully, then the data user could be prosecuted for not providing adequate security.

DISCUSSION POINT

European countries have to follow a European directive (Directive 95/46/EC) which imposes data protection requirements upon member countries. As part of this, the European Union requires that any data transferred outside the European Economic Area is only transferred to countries which have adequate data protection so that data subjects remain protected. This has caused all sorts of problems for multinational companies such as Facebook and Google who store data on servers in the cloud, which can often be servers in the United States of America where data protection laws do not meet European Union requirements. Facebook currently store European users' data in Ireland, which is a member of the European Union. It can be very complicated for multinational companies to comply with such regulations that vary from country to country in a world that is globally connected.

TASK

Find out what organisations might be exempt from certain parts of data protection law, particularly in relation to national security.

QUESTIONS

11 List three security issues that could arise from networking computers.

12 Explain how two-factor authentication could be used to protect against unauthorised access to online banking.

13 Explain why backup security methods do not protect against unauthorised access.

14 List four principles of a data protection act.

15 Explain why employees would want their employers to store accurate and up-to-date information.

13.03 Satellite communication systems

KEY TERMS

Satellite: an object in space that follows an orbital path

GPS: global positioning system which uses satellites to determine the current location

Satellites are objects in space that follow an orbital path. A satellite is different to a satellite dish. In satellite communications, a satellite in space will send microwave signals to a satellite receiving dish on earth. There are three different levels or orbit used by satellites:

- low earth orbit (LEO) at 500–1500 km from earth requiring 40–80 satellites for global coverage
- medium earth orbit (MEO) at 5000–12 500 km from earth requiring 8–20 satellites for global coverage
- geostationary earth orbit (GEO) at fixed points 35 800 km from earth requiring just three satellites for global coverage.

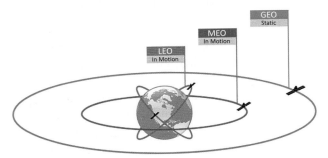

Figure 13.18 - The three different orbits used by satellites.

TASK

Search for videos online that show how LEOs, MEOs and GEOs orbit the earth.

Data transfer systems

Satellite broadband is an option for people who live in areas that are not covered by wireless or wired broadband connections. These could be rural areas, deserts, at sea or in deprived communities. Satellite broadband uses GEOs. As GEOs are such a long way from earth, there is a delay (known as latency) between the sending and receiving of data. This means that satellite broadband is not suitable for real-time applications such as internet gaming.

There are two methods of using satellites for broadband. One-way satellite broadband sends data for download from the internet to the client and uses a public switched telephone network (PSTN) connection for the client to upload data. This means that uploading data can be very slow because of the limitations of the telephone network. The other method is to use two-way satellite broadband, which allows the client to upload data directly to the satellite as well as to receive data from the satellite. However, this requires more expensive equipment that is able to transmit microwaves to space as well as to receive them.

The bandwidth available for the end users of satellite broadband is not as high as other broadband connections, such as fibre optic, but it is improving. Satellite broadband also tends to be far more expensive than fibre optic and asymmetric digital subscriber line (ADSL) broadband and users usually have to pay higher premiums if they are using a lot of data.

TASK

Investigate the satellite broadband options available in your country and compare the prices, bandwidth and download limits with cabled alternatives.

Television and radio broadcasting

Television and radio can be broadcast to end users by radio waves, cables or satellite. As radio waves are dependent on the frequencies available, they are limited to the number of channels that can be offered. Cable broadcasts are limited to areas where cables are installed. Satellite broadcast systems are able to offer far more channels because of being able to broadcast over a larger range of frequencies using microwaves.

All a user requires to watch satellite television is a set-top box (STB) and a satellite dish. Television companies send their television signals from earth to satellites in space. The broadcast channels will be compressed and if necessary encrypted. The end-user's satellite dish receives the broadcast from the satellite in geostationary orbit and passes it on by a cable to the STB. The STB will then decrypt any encrypted signals and send them onto a television.

Encrypted signals are used for television channels to which viewers have to subscribe. This is so that they cannot be watched by viewers that have not paid a subscription fee and enables television companies to charge for additional channels. Free-to-air channels are not encrypted as these are available to all viewers.

Although many people living in urban areas will subscribe to satellite television for the additional channels, one of the big benefits of satellite television is that broadcasting is available in remote areas. This can be very useful for people who like to go camping or caravanning and for those using boats. It also means that viewers can watch their own country's television in neighbouring countries where there is overspill of the broadcast signal.

Although the equipment can be a little expensive to purchase initially, this cost is often spread over 12 months by providers of satellite television. As a satellite receiving dish is required, there does need to be somewhere to position it and this can be quite unsightly in urban areas where several properties all have satellite dishes. There can be some problems where the microwave signals are lost in severe weather conditions, but this does tend to be rare.

Global positioning systems

Global positioning system (**GPS**) receivers use satellites to calculate their current location on the earth. They use a process called trilateration (see Figure 13.19) using at least three satellites to determine the distance between the GPS receiver and each satellite, which enables the exact location to be calculated. There are 24 LEO satellites that orbit the earth twice every day and at least four of these are always in the line of site from any flat point of the earth.

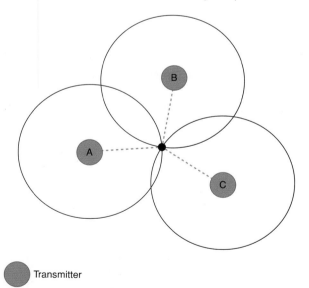

● Transmitter

----------- Time between satellite and receiver

● Receiver

Figure 13.19 - Trilateration. The figure shows three GPS satellites each sending a transmission in order to determine a target's location. The calculation of time from each of the satellites to the receiver works out the distance and then than pinpoints the location. The location is at the intersection of each transmission.

TASK

Complete the trilateration exercise at http://www.gps.gov/multimedia/tutorials/trilateration/

GPS is almost becoming an everyday part of life for many people. Applications that use GPS include:

* locating emergency vehicles so they can be dispatched to emergencies
* finding a nearby private hire taxi and calculating the taxi fares
* tracking people, objects and vehicles
* geotagging photographs
* satellite navigation (sat nav) systems
* treasure hunt games such as Geocaching
* tracking cycling and running routes.

When used with sat nav systems, GPS can provide real-time locations on a live map and so drivers can focus on their driving with occasional glances at their progress on the sat nav. If the driver misses a turn, then a new route can be quickly calculated based on the current location of the driver. If using a sat nav application within a mobile phone, then the maps will be regularly updated, but if the sat nav is a stand-alone device, then the owner will need to update the maps manually by connecting it to a computer. There are concerns about the use of sat navs in cars, though, when drivers attempt to input a destination while driving at the same time, which can be potentially very dangerous.

GPS isn't a perfect system. Line of sight is required and so finding an exact position can be difficult or impossible when the line of sight to the satellites is blocked by a bridge, tunnel, tall buildings or mountains. As with other satellite systems, the signal is dependent upon good atmospheric conditions and so problems can occur in heavy snow or thick cloud, for example.

229

QUESTIONS

16 Describe two disadvantages of satellite broadband.

17 Explain why satellite television networks might encrypt their broadcasts.

18 Explain two advantages of GPS.

13.04 Summary

A variety of components are required to connect devices together in a network, both physically and wirelessly. Servers provide resources that can be used by client devices. Switching methods are used to transmit data packets from the sender to the receiver.

Streaming takes place when video or audio files are sent to a receiving device for viewing or listening without downloading a file to save in storage. Bandwidth measures the range of frequencies on a communications channel in kHz and defines the transmission rate in bps. Bandwidth is important when content needs to be accessed in real time or within a time limit. The bandwidth will be affected by the type of transmission media used, such as cables, wireless and optical.

Optical communications, including infrared, fibre optic and laser, use light to transmit data. Bluetooth, Wi-Fi and radio are all methods of transmitting data wirelessly.

Communication protocols are required so that a variety of devices and applications can communicate together successfully. The BitTorrent protocol specifies how multiple downloads can take place from the same file source concurrently.

When computers are connected together, there is an increased security risk from unauthorised access, malware and denial of service attacks. Security measures need to be put in place and include access rights, biometric methods, firewalls, backups, encryption and physical security methods.

A data protection act is used to protect people about whom data is stored. They are known as data subjects.

Review questions

Levi wants to set up a home network in his one-bedroom apartment. He will be using a desktop PC, a laptop, a mobile phone and a printer.

1a   Identify the physical component that will connect Levi's network to the internet. [1]

1b   Describe three other physical network components that Levi will need within the network. [3]

Levi will be using his laptop and mobile phone to stream music and videos. He also participates in live video conferences for some of his university lectures.

2   Explain the importance of bandwidth to Levi. [4]

Levi rents his apartment.

3   Explain why Wi-Fi might be more suitable for his desktop computer than a wired connection. [4]

Levi will use HTTP when browsing websites.

4a   Describe the term protocol. [1]

4b   Describe the purpose of HTTP. [2]

4c   Identify a protocol that Levi might use for receiving emails. [1]

Levi wants to download an item of freeware from the World Wide Web.

5a   Explain how Levi can take precautions against malware when downloading freeware. [4]

5b   Describe two other ways in which malware could infect Levi's computer. [2]

Levi is able to access his university network from home using a fingerprint recognition device.

6a Suggest with reasons two different access rights that Levi might have to the university network. [2]

6b Explain why the fingerprint device is all that is required for him to access the network. [2]

Levi has decided to subscribe to satellite television.

7a Explain two advantages of Levi subscribing to satellite television instead of using television broadcast by radio waves. [4]

7b Explain one limitation to Levi of satellite television. [2]

Chapter 14
Project management

Learning objectives

By the end of this chapter, you will be able to:

■ describe the stages of project management
■ discuss different types of project management software and describe their features
■ describe, interpret and create critical path analysis and Gantt charts
■ describe disaster recovery management
■ understand different methods of prototyping
■ understand computer-aided design and computer-aided manufacturing

KEY TERMS

Conception: start of a project

Gantt chart: a chart used for planning a project

Execution: the development stage of a project

Closure: completion of a project

14.01 Stages in project management

Remember

Every project needs to be managed properly in order to ensure deadlines are met, resources are available and everybody knows what they are doing.

Traditional project phases

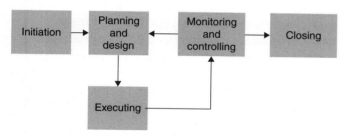

Figure 14.01 - Project stages.

Conception and initiation

During the **conception** and initiation stage, the initial ideas for a project are identified and goals set. Key stakeholders are identified and decisions are made as to whether it is appropriate to undertake a project or not by conducting a feasibility study. The feasibility study will determine whether or not the project is of benefit to an organisation based on resources, time and finance. Requirements for the project will be identified so that all stakeholders are aware of the expectations of the project. Objectives of the project, its scope, risks, approximate budget and approximate timescales will be defined and agreed with all stakeholders.

Planning

There is a common phrase, 'failing to prepare is preparing to fail'. This is very true in all parts of life, but particularly with project planning. It is essential that the project is planned well so that all stakeholders know their responsibilities during all stages. A comprehensive budget will be formulated along with details of timescales for the progress of the project. Milestones will be set, by which time certain aspects of the project must be complete. Tasks that have to be completed between each milestone will be

identified and prioritised. A **Gantt chart** will be produced to show which tasks need to be completed in which order. Resources including personnel will be allocated to tasks in a coordinated manner so that they are available at the right times. A very important part of planning is to ensure that appropriate amounts of time are allocated to each task and resource so that tasks can be completed on time, resources (especially personnel) are not over used and that personnel have work to do rather than not being used.

Execution

Once all plans are in place and the start date arrives, the project can commence. It is critical that the plan is followed so that resources are used at the appropriate times. Any delays to a task can have a knock-on effect to successor tasks. The project manager will be expected to communicate roles and responsibilities to team members and set interim targets for each member to achieve within the timescales of the overall plan.

Monitoring and control

Throughout the **execution** of the project, the project manager must monitor the progress and control what is happening. They will be responsible for ensuring tasks are completed on time and rescheduling any tasks if there are delays. The project manager will need to monitor the performance of team members to ensure they are carrying out their agreed roles effectively. The project manager will need to monitor expenditure and compare it against the budget to ensure that overspends don't occur and keep a close eye on the scope of the project to make sure it doesn't extend beyond its agreed boundaries. There should be regular project review meetings where key stakeholders can discuss the progress of the project. At times, the project plan will need to be adjusted, so there is regular iteration between the execution, monitoring and control, and planning phases as shown in Figure 14.01.

Closure

When the project is ready to complete, a handover will take place from the project team to the client. Contracts will be terminated, which means some people may need to be deployed elsewhere or may need to look for alternative employment. Resources that have been assigned to the project will be released. A review of the project will take place between the client and the project management team, where requirements will be evaluated and successes will be celebrated. The client will be expected to sign off the project as completed, so that it is clear there is no further work to carry out and **closure** will have been achieved.

234

EXAMPLE

Before writing a textbook, authors are given a project brief that outlines the scope of what they are required to write about, the types of pedagogical items to include, the timescales for the delivery of manuscripts and payment information. This is all part of planning.

Prior to this, a publisher will have decided that they want to publish that particular textbook, and will seek approval from an exam board, which makes the publisher and the exam board the key stakeholders. During planning, the publisher will have identified a project manager, an editor, a reviewer and authors, all of whom are required resources.

The execution stage includes the authors writing chapters for the textbook. This is monitored and controlled by the editor who stays in regular communication with the authors to check on their progress and to collect completed chapters. If timescales slip, then the project plan is revised as other execution stages such as reviewing, typesetting and proofreading are all dependent upon the manuscript being delivered.

The project comes to a close when the textbook is ready to be sent to the printers, the authors have signed off their copyright and the publisher and exam board have approved the final proof.

QUESTION

1   Explain why it is necessary to iterate between the planning, execution, and monitoring and control stages of project management.

14.02 Types of project management software

KEY TERM

Collaboration: working together

Desktop

Desktop project management software requires installation to a specified computer or set of computers. Licences are required for each installation and this will

incur a cost. Where there is only one project manager who will be closely monitoring the whole project, this can be useful as desktop software can be sophisticated and cover a large variety of tasks. Some desktop solutions allow multi-user access, but this will require the software to be installed on several desktops and a central network location being used to store the project files.

The software will be responsive as it is installed locally and the interface can be highly graphical. However, where **collaboration** is required on documents or plans are regularly changing and need to be communicated, this type of software can have its limitations.

Web-based

Web-based software can be accessed through a browser. The main software could be installed on an intranet that is also made available as an extranet or it could be installed in the cloud. As the software is not installed locally, there can be delays in waiting for data to be processed or delivered to the end user and the data isn't available offline, meaning that if the network connection is broken, then data is not available to the user. The graphical capability will also be limited due to bandwidth limitations.

However, web-based software has many advantages over desktop software including:

- access from any computer without the need to install software
- access from a smartphone or tablet
- multiple users can access the data at once
- collaboration on documents is possible as they are stored centrally
- only one version of the software will be installed and maintained.

Single-user

Single-user project management systems are usually desktop systems and it is often the case that desktop systems are usually single-user systems, too. For small projects where there is just one project manager and maybe only a couple of people assigned to tasks, then this software is appropriate, but it prevents any type of collaboration and communication from within the software itself, meaning that alternative tools will need to be used.

Personal

Personal project management software is typically used by home users for small projects such as managing a building extension or planning a holiday. It will be single-user software and include a simpler interface that a non-experienced project manager is able to use. It will include basic features such as a timeline/calendar, task management and resource planning, but it won't include any collaboration features or complex features required by larger organisations.

Collaborative

Collaborative project management systems are used by several users at once. There may be several sub-project managers who are responsible for updating different parts of the plan both during the planning stage and when monitoring and controlling. This type of software is often web-based or delivered on a client–server model, with project and task information being stored on a central server. Some client–server tools include a desktop application for detailed project management and a web interface for other project team members to access when required.

TASK

Copy the table below on a separate sheet and complete it with the advantages and disadvantages of each type of project management software.

Type of software	Advantages	Disadvantages
Desktop		
Web-based		
Single-user		
Personal		
Collaborative		

DISCUSSION POINT

In groups, research the different types of project management software available in each category. One person should choose one piece of software from each category. Report back to your group on costs, features and any overlaps with other categories.

QUESTION

2   Contrast two advantages of web-based project management software with two disadvantages of single-user desktop project management software.

14.03 Project management software

KEY TERM

Critical path: the tasks which must be completed on time for a project to complete on time

Planning

Most of the planning involved using project management software is concerned with scheduling tasks and allocating resources to those tasks. However, key milestones can be identified in advance. These are when crucial points in the project should be reached, so tasks should be scheduled to meet these milestones. Documents that are likely to be required can be allocated to milestones, such as success criteria and specifications. Templates can be used for setting up an initial project plan. These templates can be provided by the software or they could be templates that are created based upon an organisation's previously successful projects. Through the use of project templates, company standards can be set up for the way projects should be planned, so employees have a common, collaborative and recognisable structure.

Scheduling of tasks

Tasks are jobs that need to be completed as part of the project. Project management software will enable a project manager to create a Gantt chart to show an overview of the tasks that need completing on a timeline. Tasks will be assigned an estimated number of hours or days that they will take to complete, together with a deadline for completion. The project manager will be able to identify which tasks are dependent upon other tasks and so cannot start until those other tasks have been completed. Tasks can be delegated to other members of the team and prioritised to identify which should be completed first. Team members will be able to record how many hours have been spent on each task and identify when the task is complete. Milestones can be identified for crucial points of the project and these can be highlighted. The project manager will be able to see an overall calendar of all tasks that need to be completed, together with calendars for each team member that is responsible for those tasks.

Allocation of resources

Resources can be equipment, property or people that are required to complete a task. These resources will need to be defined within the project management software and their availability can be identified so the project manager knows when they can be utilised. Costs can be assigned to any resource, so the project manager can see how their use will affect the budget. Resources can then be assigned to tasks and a number of hours or days be assigned to the use of that resource. The software will help the project manager to avoid resource conflicts and also identify clearly situations where team members could experience overload. This is when they have too many tasks to complete during a period of time.

Costings

All resources will have costs allocated to them, so the project manager will be able to calculate the total cost of each task based on how many hours each resource is used for each task. The software can be used to keep a record of any expenses incurred by team members and account for these in the overall costs. Daily, weekly, monthly or custom analysis of expenditure and its comparison to the budget can be provided. The software can report on the total costs for each individual resource or set of resources. The costings information will be able to be exported to common formats such as spreadsheets for further manipulation and analysis.

Communications

Project management software can offer a large variety of communication tools which help team members to collaborate throughout the whole project:

- Calendars: each team member will have a calendar showing what they are doing at any time. These can be synchronised with third-party calendars, such as Google, iCal or Outlook, so that each member's availability is always up to date. This enables meetings to be scheduled with each team member. Documents can be attached to these meetings so that they are readily available to each participant.
- Instant messaging / video chat / video conferencing : these tools will enable team members who are working remotely from each other to communicate in real time so that they can share ideas and discuss progress.
- Shared documents: all documents should be stored in a central repository so that they are available to the team members who require access to them. Documents can be assigned to tasks, resources or milestones so that they are available at the right time to the right people. Changes to the documents can be tracked so that each

team member knows what modifications have been made and which is the latest version of the document. The software can email team members to inform them when changes to documents have been made or display an alert on their project dashboard, their home page for the project management software. This is a much more controlled manner of dealing with documents than the nightmare of email attachments and mixed revisions.

- Discussions/forums: these can be set up for tasks, documents or milestones so that discussions between team members can be held. This is particularly useful when all team members are not available at the same time. Team members will be able to see comments and suggestions that have been made by others and respond to them. Email notifications of new contributions to discussions can be sent or alerts can be displayed on project dashboards.
- Progress: the software can inform team members and the project manager of progress that is being made. Team members can update tasks to show how near to completion they are and this progress can be fed into the whole project plan. If changes are made to the project timeline, automated email notifications can be sent out to all affected team members.

Decision making

All communications within the project management software can be logged and tracked so that if decisions have been made, then it is possible to clearly identify who made each decision and for what reasons. If problems or issues have been experienced, then these will be highlighted by the software and decisions can be made as to what adjustments need to be made, such as changing the timeline or allocating additional resources. These issues can also be monitored to check on progress of the resolution.

Graphs, charts and reports can be used to analyse the budget, scheduling and task progress. Comparisons can be made between the plan and what is actually happening during the execution of the project, and then decisions can be made to make changes if necessary. The software can show how much time was spent on each task compared to how much time was planned for that task, so that lessons can be learned for future tasks that are similar in nature.

The software will identify a **critical path**, which will show all tasks that must complete on time if the project is to meet its deadline. This can then be monitored closely and delays can be anticipated in advance and resources diverted to critical tasks if necessary. The software will show an overview of the availability of resources and the time allocated to each and their respective costs, so that the project manager is able to reallocate them as necessary.

QUESTION

3   Explain how project management software can be used for allocating resources to tasks.

14.04 Critical path analysis

KEY TERM

Predecessor: a task in a project that must be completed before another task can start

A critical path analysis (CPA) finds a project's critical path. The critical path identifies which tasks must complete on time in order for the whole project to complete on time, and defines the minimum time in which the project can be completed.

EXAMPLE

Figure 14.02 shows a CPA for making a cup of tea.

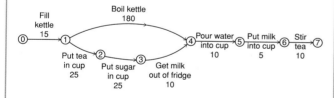

Figure 14.02 - CPA for cup of tea.

The circles represent milestones in the project and are numbered for identification purposes. The tasks are represented by arrows. The numbers next to each task represent the number of seconds the task will take. For example, pouring water into the cup will take 10 seconds.

Some tasks can be completed in parallel to other tasks. For example, boiling the kettle can take place at the same time as putting tea in the cup, putting sugar in the cup and getting milk out of the fridge. Where there are parallel tasks, the longest timeline forms the critical path. In this case, 180

seconds to boil the kettle is longer than the 60 seconds it takes to do the three parallel tasks.

Sequential tasks cannot be carried out at the same time because they are dependent upon other tasks completing first. For example, boiling the kettle is dependent upon the kettle being filled with water and so cannot start until the kettle is filled with water. In this case, the kettle being filled with water is a **predecessor** to boiling the kettle.

The total length of the critical path is calculated by adding up all the sequential tasks plus the longest of each of the parallel sets of tasks. In this case that is 15 + 180 + 10 + 5 + 10 = 220 seconds, which is the shortest time it will take to complete the project. If any of the tasks on the critical path takes longer than planned, then the whole project will be delayed.

Some tasks aren't critical and have what is known as float time. The float time is the time an activity can be delayed without affecting the rest of the project.

In the example CPA for making a cup of tea, getting the milk out of the fridge has a float time of 120 seconds as it can be delayed this long before it would catch up with milestone 4.

TASK

Interpret the CPA in Figure 14.03 for building an extension to a house.

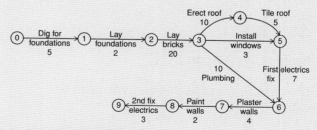

Figure 14.03 - CPA for extension.

1   Identify the longest task.
2   How many milestones are there?
3   Which tasks are dependent upon the bricks being laid?
4   Which tasks can run parallel to installing the windows?
5   How many days is the critical path?
6   Which tasks form the critical path?

To create a CPA it is necessary to know the following information:

- the list of tasks
- how long each task will take
- which tasks are dependent upon predecessors.

This information can be shown in an activity dependence table

EXAMPLE

Task	Days	Dependencies
A	**3**	
B	2	A
C	6	A
D	1	B
E	3	C
F	5	D
G	4	E, F
H	3	G
I	2	G
J	3	G

First, add any tasks to the diagram that have no predecessors.

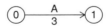

Figure 14.04 - CPA part 1.

Then add on any tasks that are dependent on task A.

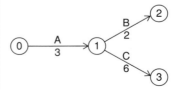

Figure 14.05 - CPA part 2.

Continue task by task until there is a completed diagram.

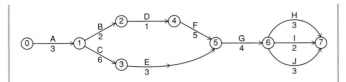

Figure 14.06 - CPA part 3.

TASK

Complete a CPA for the following scenario:

Task	Days	Dependencies
A	3	
B	5	
C	4	
D	18	A
E	16	B
F	12	C
G	7	E, F
H	11	D, G
I	2	H

14.05 Gantt charts

A Gantt chart is used to show the start and finish dates of each task, the predecessors for each task, the progress of each task and the current position within the project. Tasks are listed with their start and finish dates. A bar will represent each task. Each bar can be shaded in to show the percentage of the task that has been completed. Arrows are used to show which tasks are dependent upon other tasks. A line or other indicator can be used to show the current position (time) within the project. It's also possible to identify the resources required, usually by listing the person responsible for each task.

Creating a Gantt chart follows a similar process to creating a CPA. In addition to knowing the list of tasks, how long each task will take and which tasks are dependent upon predecessors, you will also need to know the start date of the first task and the resources that are allocated to each task.

EXAMPLE

Figure 14.07 shows a Gantt chart for developing a book.

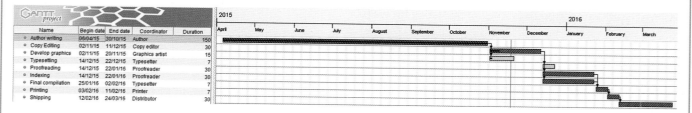

Figure 14.07 - Gantt chart.

On the left-hand side you can see the task list together with beginning dates and times, coordinators and the duration. The yellow bars represent the time that each task takes. This makes it much easier to see the float time that is available. Dependencies are shown by the arrows from the end of a predecessor to the start of another task. The black lines represent how much of each task has currently been completed and the red line represents the current time. Therefore, assuming that the progress is correct, the project is running slightly behind schedule. The diagonal lines on the yellow bars represent the critical path.

DISCUSSION POINT

Figure 14.08 is the PERT chart that has been generated from the Gantt chart using the GanttProject software.

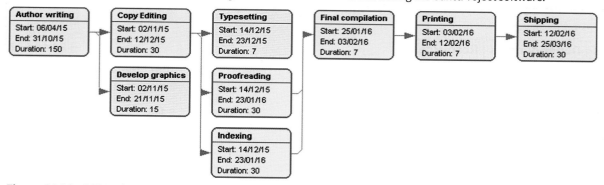

Figure 14.08 - PERT chart.

Look at the similarities and differences to a CPA and a Gantt chart.

TASK

CD 14.01 House extension.gan

Interpret the Gantt chart in Figure 14.09 for building a house extension. The Gantt chart is saved as CD 14.01 House extension. gan and was created using GanttProject, which can be used to open the files.

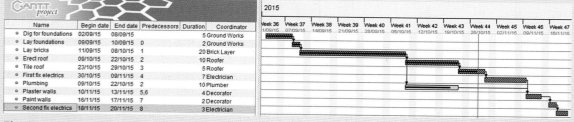

Figure 14.09 - Gantt chart for house extension.

239

1 Which task has float time?
2 Which tasks are currently in progress (started but not finished)?
3 The plumbing appears to be behind schedule. Will this affect the whole project finish date? Why?
4 Which tasks are the predecessors for plastering the walls?

DISCUSSION POINT

Figure 14.10 is the resources chart for the house extension project. You can see when each resource will be being used, with gaps for weekends.

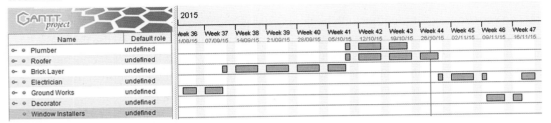

Figure 14.10 - Resource chart for house extension.

EXAMPLE

Task A starts on 1 January 2016.

Task	Days	Dependencies	Resources
A	3		R1
B	2	A	R1
C	6	A	R2
D	1	B	R1
E	3	C	R2
F	5	D	R3
G	4	E, F	R3
H	3	G	R5
I	2	G	R2
J	3	G	R6

First, create a list of tasks, the duration and the resources required and identify the start and finish dates of the first task.

```
                          JAN
                       1 2 3 4 5 6 7
Task   Duration   Start      End       Resources
  A       3      1-1-16    3-1-16        R1        ▭
  B       2                              R1
  C       6                              R2
  D       1                              R1
  E       3                              R2
  F       5                              R3
  G       4                              R3
  H       3                              R5
  I       2                              R2
  J       3                              R6
```

Figure 14.11 - Gantt chart part 1.

Then add on any tasks that are dependent on task A, to start the day after task A finishes.

```
                                    JAN
                              1 2 3 4 5 6 7 8 9
Task   Duration   Start      End     Resources
  A       3      1-1-16    3-1-16      R1
  B       2      4-1-16    5-1-16      R1
  C       6      4-1-16    9-1-16      R2
  D       1                            R1
  E       3                            R2
  F       5                            R3
  G       4                            R3
  H       3                            R5
  I       2                            R2
  J       3                            R6
```

Figure 14.12 - Gantt chart part 2.

Continue task by task until there is a completed Gantt chart.

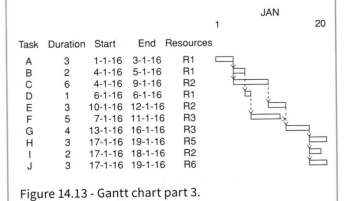

```
                                 JAN
                          1                    20
Task  Duration  Start      End    Resources
  A      3     1-1-16    3-1-16     R1
  B      2     4-1-16    5-1-16     R1
  C      6     4-1-16    9-1-16     R2
  D      1     6-1-16    6-1-16     R1
  E      3    10-1-16   12-1-16     R2
  F      5     7-1-16   11-1-16     R3
  G      4    13-1-16   16-1-16     R3
  H      3    17-1-16   19-1-16     R5
  I      2    17-1-16   18-1-16     R2
  J      3    17-1-16   19-1-16     R6
```

Figure 14.13 - Gantt chart part 3.

241

TASK

Complete a Gantt chart for the following scenario commencing on 1 April 2017.

Task	Days	Dependencies
A	3	
B	5	
C	4	
D	18	A
E	16	B
F	12	C
G	7	E, F
H	11	D, G
I	2	H

14.06 Disaster recovery management

Sometimes disasters occur, such as a power cut, flood, fire, theft of data, malware, corruption of data, loss of network admin password or loss of the network manager. When this happens it is necessary to recover from the disaster. A disaster recovery plan (DRP) is needed for such events so that recovery can be completed as quickly and effectively as possible, minimising disruption to the organisation.

Risk assessment

Risk assessment involves identifying the potential risks to an organisation, analysing the potential impact to the organisation and the likelihood of each risk occurring. This is often carried out alongside a systematic process known as business impact analysis (BIA), which quantifies the impact of a disaster in terms of financial and non-financial costs.

A risk assessment will identify a number of potential hazards including:

- power cut
- fire
- flood
- denial of access to premises
- malware
- unauthorised access to data

- theft of data
- corruption of data
- loss of key personnel.

Some of these risks involve people who could deliberately cause problems. These people are known as perpetrators. Each risk will then be quantified in terms of its likelihood on a scale from 0.0 to 1.0, where 0.0 represents it never happening to 1.0 which represents it as being almost inevitable.

Within an organisation, there will be a number of business activities that are carried out. Each business activity will need to be identified. The impact of that business activity not being able to take place then needs to be analysed. The impact for each activity not being able to take place will be measured on a scale from 0.0 to 1.0 where 0.0 means that there is no impact to 1.0 meaning that the impact is absolutely critical to the aims of the organisation.

Impacts could include:

- loss of revenue
- damage to organisation's image
- penalty fees
- cost of recovery
- effect on other business activities.

From this analysis, activities can be categorised, for example:

- activities which must continue
- activities which could be scaled down
- activities which could be suspended.

Analysis of the impacts should also cover how the impact changes over different time periods, for example in the first hour, 24 hours, 48 hours, week etc.

The overall risk to an organisation of each potential disaster/risk can now be quantified by multiplying the likelihood by the impact:

$$Risk = Likelihood \times Impact$$

This will now show which risks are the most important to guard against and ensure that recovery plans are robust. This can be done for each risk, for each business activity or for a combination of each.

TASK

Search the web for risk analysis templates and investigate the sorts of risks to which organisations are susceptible.

242

DISCUSSION POINT

Different methodologies exist for analysing risks. Another way of quantifying the risk is to use a matrix like the one in Figure 14.14 which shows how important each risk should be considered based on the combination of impact and likelihood.

Very high 5					
High 4					
Medium 3					
Low 2					
Very low 1					
Impact Likelihood	1 Rare	2 Unlikely	3 Possible	4 Likely	5 Almost certain

Figure 14.14 - Risk mitigation overview.

Securing the risk

Once the risks have been identified and prioritised, measures need to be put into place to protect against those risks. Most of these measures have been discussed in Chapter 13 (Networks), including access rights and passwords, biometric methods, firewalls, backups, encryption, malware security and physical security methods.

One of the risks that hasn't been discussed previously is the potential to lose key personnel. If a person leaves, is suddenly ill, dies or has to be dismissed, then the organisation loses all of that person's knowledge which has not been documented. It is therefore important to guard against personnel loss by requiring key personnel to document procedures that they follow. It's also wise to have at least two people who know the main system administration password or to have a copy of it written down in a sealed envelope in a safe that has limited access.

Recovery management

Procedures need to be put into place to plan for recovery after a disaster has occurred. This can include planning for:

- restoration of backups
- replacement of hardware
- reinstallation of software
- emergency replacement of key personnel
- emergency office accommodation.

When planning for these situations, any resources in terms of personnel, technology, data, supplies and premises that are required to recover from the disaster must be identified and planned for. The recovery point objective (RPO) must also be identified. The RPO is the point in time prior to the disruption to which data must be recovered.

It is important to plan how long each recovery process will take. There will be some parts of recovery where the time is fixed, but other parts where if more resources are allocated then the recovery can be quicker. When planning for the recovery time, two key measurements should be considered:

- maximum tolerable downtime (MTD): this is the maximum time that each business activity could tolerate not having access to their essential system functionality
- recovery time objective (RTO): this is the estimated maximum amount of time that the organisation or business activity has in which to recover its systems and resume operations.

Priorities will be identified based on the MTD for each business activity, therefore ensuring that activities with the lowest MTD are functioning again the soonest.

Recovery testing

Plans are important, and a plan is better than no plan, but plans don't always work. It is therefore important to test disaster recovery plans. This is particularly applicable to restoring data and systems. Backed up data should be tested daily to ensure that the backup process has succeeded and that the backup data is accessible. Full system restorations should be tested periodically by attempting to restore whole server backups onto a clean server and testing their success.

TASK

Back up your personal data from your school network. Now recover it to your home computer and test whether you are able to open the files.

QUESTIONS

4 Identify three risks that should be considered during disaster recovery planning.

5 Explain why it is important to test recovery procedures.

14.07 Prototyping

🔑 **KEY TERMS**

Prototype: a 'mock-up' of a software or manufactured solution

RAD: rapid application development

A **prototype** is a 'mock-up' of a software solution in a primitive form. It is used during the design stage to demonstrate how a system will look and work. It is usually focused on the user interface, rather than any data structures. It is used so that the client can get a feel for the new system before it is developed and can provide feedback that can then be acted upon. The client is also able to compare the prototype against the requirements specification. The client also has an opportunity to explain their requirements more clearly having seen the designer's interpretation.

Types of prototyping
Evolutionary/incremental prototyping

This type of prototyping takes an iterative approach in that requirements are specified, an initial prototype is developed, the prototype is reviewed and then requirements are clarified and the prototype is improved based on feedback.

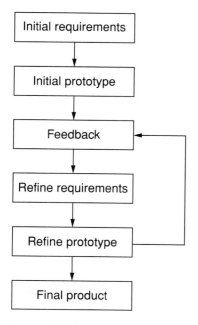

Figure 14.15 - Iterative prototyping.

Each prototype will be build upon the previous one and include more functionality until a final product is built. At each stage, only clearly understood requirements are developed. Each prototype can be functional and if required can be used by the client until the next evolution of the prototype is ready. This means that the end users may request enhanced or new features that they discover they require as the prototypes are being developed, features they wouldn't have envisaged at the initial requirements specification stage.

Throwaway/rapid prototyping

With throwaway prototyping, also known as rapid prototyping, the prototype will never become part of the final delivered software, but will be discarded. A loosely working model is created following a short investigation, with the aim being to get something tangible to the client as soon as possible for feedback as to how well the requirements are being met.

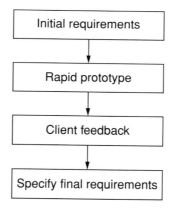

Figure 14.16 - Throwaway prototyping.

This enables the requirements to be fine-tuned early in the process, which is more cost-effective than trying to make changes later when considerable work has been carried out. The main aspect to the prototype will be the user interface which the client will be able to test and experience. The interface will appear to work by being simulated.

The advantages and disadvantages of prototyping

The advantages and disadvantages of prototyping are shown in Table 14.01.

243

Advantages	Disadvantages
Problems can be identified early during the process and modifications made before it becomes very costly to make changes.	Requirements analysis can be rushed, meaning that prototypes don't reflect much of what the end users were expecting.
Requirements can be clarified and refined following feedback on the prototypes.	With rapid prototyping, the prototype can become rushed and, when trying to develop it into a working system, it may have significant design flaws or structural errors that carry through to the end solution.
The end users will be involved more in the process, giving them more ownership of the solution and providing valuable feedback.	When users see the prototype, they can often get lots of new ideas about features they would like to be included, which can lead to disappointment if these features can't be funded. This is known as 'feature creep'.
If the prototype is evolutionary, then users can get used to using parts of the system before having to use the whole system, which will reduce the need for bulk training. It's much cheaper to make changes earlier in the process than after real development has taken place.	When users see what looks like a working interface with a throwaway prototype, they don't realise how much more effort is required to make it into a working solution and may have false expectations as to the timescale. The iterative process of feedback can sometimes last too long if the user is regularly wanting changes to be made to the latest prototype.
By listening to feedback from end users, the developers will have a much better understanding of what the users are expecting and so a better quality solution will be provided.	The initial costs of developing a prototype are high compared with traditional designs.

Table 14.01 - Advantages and disadvantages of prototyping.

Methods of software development
Rapid application development

Rapid application development (**RAD**) uses prototyping to develop a system in a very short time frame, usually less than six months. Instead of following a traditional requirements gathering approach, requirements are gathered through focus groups. Users are key players in the prototyping stage and provide feedback for refinements. This type of user involvement is known as joint application development (JAD) because the user is jointly involved with the developer in the development of the system. Less time is spent on planning and design and more emphasis is put on the development phase.

Strict deadlines are allocated throughout the development of the system to ensure that the product is developed and finished on time by allocating time boxes to the development of each requirement. This requires understanding from the user that, if requirements are too complex, then they must be simplified or removed from the project. The RAD approach will also try to reuse any modules of software that already exist and are available, rather than always developing from scratch. Software application frameworks can be used to develop the solution whereby a complex graphical user interface can be created using drag and drop functionality. This enables users to be involved in the actual design of the interface as part of the JAD approach and they can see the interface taking shape in real time.

Waterfall method

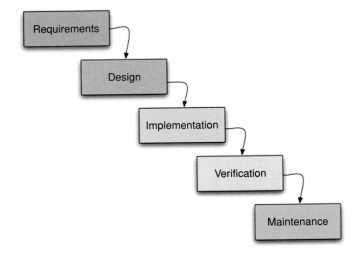

Figure 14.17 - Waterfall method.

The waterfall method involves gathering all the user requirements at the beginning of the project. There will be considerable communication with the user at this stage in order to elicit the requirements of the potential solution. When the requirements are defined, the process runs 'downhill' like a waterfall.

During the design stage, the interface and the structure of the system will be designed. During implementation, often referred to as development, the system will be developed, which often involves programming. The purpose of the verification phase is to ensure that the project meets the customer's requirements. The system will then be used and during its use there may be problems that are discovered that need to be corrected or other changes that need to be made. This is known as maintenance.

The waterfall method relies upon the requirements being clearly defined, which is an unrealistic expectation, so it is fundamentally flawed. It was originally used in manufacturing and then adopted into computing, but with adaptions that included the need to revisit the requirements.

The system life cycle, discussed in Chapter 15, is based on the waterfall model and there are many variations in existence.

The advantages and disadvantages of RAD

The advantages and disadvantages of RAD are shown in Table 14.02.

Advantages	Disadvantages
The high level of user involvement means that the end solution is more likely to be suitable for the end users, who will also have ownership of the solution.	Requirements are not clearly specified from the outset and so the final solution may not meet the entire needs of the organisation.
Users are often not sure of what the requirements of a system should be from the outset and so the evolutionary approach of RAD enables the requirements to evolve.	Users are required throughout the whole process and they also have their normal day jobs to do. This can lead to work overload or the need for temporary staff.

Advantages	Disadvantages
As users are involved throughout the whole project, it is quickly recognised when a requirement is over-ambitious and therefore the requirement can be simplified or removed at an early stage.	The structure of the system may be compromised, leading to instability, as the focus is on the user interface and getting a system developed rapidly.
The strict deadlines ensure that the project will be completed on time and prevents 'feature creep'.	The strict deadlines mean that some parts of the project could be rushed and not completed to a high enough quality.
Prototyping of the interface with user involvement means less time is spent on design and more on development, leading to a shorter overall project.	Existing software modules will not have been designed for the exact requirements of the system and so may not provide sufficient functionality.
Software application frameworks mean that a user interface can be developed quickly and users can even be involved in configuring the layouts of screens and reports.	Software application frameworks don't produce particularly efficient code and so the end solution will not run as quickly as if it had been developed from scratch.
	Users who are not involved in the JAD approach may be disappointed that they didn't have a say in the process and the system may not meet their specific needs.

Table 14.02 - Advantages and disadvantages of RAD.

QUESTIONS

6   Compare and contrast evolutionary and throwaway prototyping.

7   Describe joint application development.

14.08 Computer-aided design and computer-aided manufacturing

KEY TERMS

CAD: computer-aided design

CAM: computer-aided manufacture

Computer-aided design (**CAD**) involves the use of computers to design physical products. Computer-aided manufacturing (**CAM**) involves the use of computers to manufacture physical products. CAD/CAM applications involve the use of computers to design the physical products and then the application uses the design to manufacture the physical product to match the exact design.

Figure 14.18 - Motor vehicle design.

CAD uses vector graphics to create objects in two dimensions (2D) or three dimensions (3D). Due to the manufacturing nature of CAD, it is common to use 3D tools. A plan view is often used in 2D and the CAD software will render a 3D view, which can be viewed from any angle and zoomed in or out. Objects can be stretched, resized and moved and properties such as material and colour can be changed.

Object libraries will be available within CAD software so that the user can select standard objects. For example, if designing a house, an object library could include steel beams, walls, paving slabs, windows and doors. Other applications for CAD/CAM include:

- landscaping
- vehicle manufacturing

- textiles production
- carpentry
- manufacturing of components
- printed circuit boards.

EXAMPLE

IKEA provides CAD tools to its customers for designing living spaces such as kitchens, bedrooms and bathrooms. This enables a customer to position furniture in a virtual room and to try out different layouts. The customer can view the layout from different angles in a 3D view. Different options for colours of walls, style of cupboards and worktops can be selected and modified until a preferred solution is found. The customer is also given a full breakdown of the parts needed and the cost for each part.

The benefits and drawbacks of CAD and CAM

The benefits and drawbacks of CAD and CAM are shown in Table 14.03.

Benefits	Drawbacks
Expensive prototypes are not always necessary as users can experience 3D models, and stress testing can be carried out on these 3D models.	Both CAD and CAM have led to the loss of jobs and the need for reskilling of employees.
CAD drawings can be modified and enhanced without manufacturing cost until a final version is completed.	Testing using a model will never provide the same results as testing using the manufactured product and so at least one manufactured prototype is required before mass production.
A list of required materials can be produced from the CAD drawings automatically.	Although a user can experience a 3D model, it is not the same as walking through a real building or holding a real product.
CAD models can be viewed from many angles by rotating the model and elements can be magnified by zooming in.	CAD software is very complex and so highly trained staff are required to use it.

Benefits	Drawbacks
Components that have been designed once can be reused.	Initial costs of purchasing CAD software can be high.
CAD requires fewer designers than traditional drafters and so is cheaper for business.	Designs developed with CAD will include errors made by the designer as the software is not intelligent enough to know when the wrong materials have been used.
CAM enables products to be mass-produced consistently.	Designers are limited to using vector objects based on geometrical modelling.
CAM is more precise than manufacturing by hand and can deal with tiny measurements.	
Manufacturer's drawings can be created seamlessly.	
CAM removes the need for manual labour and so reduces costs for business.	

Table 14.03 - Benefits and drawbacks of CAD and CAM.

TASK

Find out how CAD/CAM is used in dentistry and prosthetics.

8 Describe how CAD could be used to design an extension to a house.

9 Give one disadvantage of CAM.

14.09 Summary

The five stages of project management include conception and initiation, planning, execution, monitoring and control, and closure.

Different types of project management software include desktop, web-based, single-user and collaborative. Project management software can be used for planning the project, scheduling tasks, allocating resources, budgeting, communicating and making decisions.

Critical path analysis identifies which tasks must complete on time in order for the whole project to complete on time.

Gantt charts show start and finish dates of tasks, allocated resources, predecessors, progress and the current position within the project.

Disaster recovery management involves writing a disaster recovery plan in case there is a disaster. Disaster recovery plans should include an assessment of risks, methods of securing the risks, methods of recovery and plans for testing the recovery methods work.

Prototyping is a 'mock-up' of a software solution in a primitive form and can be evolutionary/incremental or throwaway/rapid. Rapid application development uses prototyping to develop a system in a very short time frame. The waterfall method of development identifies user requirements at the start of the project, similar to the system life cycle. Computer-aided design is the use of computers to design physical products and computer-aided manufacturing turns those designs into physical products.

247

Review questions

A landscape gardening company has commissioned a software development company to develop a new piece of software that can be used by customers to view a model of what their new garden might look like. A project manager has been appointed to oversee the project.

1 Identify four stages of project management that will be coordinated by the project manager. [4]

The project will involve a large team.

2a Give reasons for the use of web-based collaborative project management software. [4]

2b Identify one other type of project management software that would not be suitable. [1]

3 Describe how the project management software can help the project manager to allocate resources to the project. [2]

The project manager has the option of using critical path analysis (CPA) and a Gantt chart for planning the timescales of the project.

4a Compare CPA with a Gantt chart. [2]

4b Identify two features available in a Gantt chart that are not shown on CPA. [2]

An evolutionary prototype approach will be used during the design and development of the software.

5a Define the term 'prototype'. [1]

5b Evaluate the reasons for the project manager choosing an evolutionary approach. [4]

The software will include CAD tools.

6 Suggest three objects that could be included in the object library for the CAD software. [3]

Chapter 15
System life cycle

Learning objectives

By the end of this chapter, you will be able to:

- evaluate different methods of analysis
- describe the contents of specifications
- design a solution
- evaluate suitable hardware and software
- explain and analyse different types of testing
- create a test plan
- describe and analyse different implementation methods
- design, develop and explain the need for documentation
- evaluate a new system
- explain different types of maintenance

KEY TERMS

Maintenance: changes made to a system after its implementation

Requirements specification: what a user needs a new system to do

System specification: the hardware and software needed to run the system

Design specification: illustration of how the system will look, what the data structures will be and how the system will work

Some terms are used differently by different models. Of particular note is the term 'implementation'. In the traditional system life cycle, implementation is the stage where the design is implemented, which means the system is programmed or developed. Throughout this chapter, this stage will be called development, which is the term used by Cambridge International Examinations. Other versions use implementation to refer to the point at which the new system is implemented, which means the system is installed. Cambridge uses the term 'implementation' to mean the 'installation' phase. Some models include a documentation stage. However, the traditional model assumes that documentation is happening throughout the whole life cycle.

Feasibility and **maintenance** are not usually carried out by the main development team of a new system. Therefore, the analysis, design, development, testing and installation phases are a subsection of the system life cycle known as the system development cycle.

15.01 Analysis

Analysis involves finding out how the current system works and what the requirements of the client are for the new system.

A variety of methods can be used to research current systems and the requirements of a new system.

Questionnaires

Questionnaires are used when information is required from a large number of users when it would be impractical to interview them all. A large number of users also means there is a large sample size for the results of the questionnaire to be quantified and compared. They are not suitable when there are only a small number of users involved as there is not a large enough sample size to gauge opinion and it would

be quicker to conduct interviews than spend time preparing questionnaires. An exception to this would be if it is impossible to arrange an appointment time with a user or users, in which case questionnaires could be used as an alternative to interviews. The disadvantage of this is that it doesn't allow the analyst the opportunity to ask the user to elaborate on answers without contacting the user again.

Questions need to be asked in a way in which the required information can be elicited from users, but also so that the responses can be analysed collectively. This often means providing multiple choice responses so that each response can be counted. It's also important to ensure that the questionnaire does not take too long for users to complete as otherwise not many responses may be returned.

EXAMPLE

During the analysis for a new school reports system, the analyst wants to find out from pupils, teachers and parents what information should be included on the report. One question that could be asked would be:

Please rate from 1 to 5 the importance of the following information on the school report (1 is not important, 5 is very important):

- Attendance total half days
- Attendance percentage
- Number of negative behavioural events
- Number of positive praise events
- Academic grade for each subject
- Position/rank in class for each subject
- Percentage score for each end of year exam
- Average score for all exams
- Comment from subject teacher
- Targets from subject teacher
- Comment from house tutor
- Target grade.

This will allow the analyst to consider the importance attributed to each piece of information by the three different groups of people, which will contribute to deciding what is included on the reports and how prominent a position each piece of information will take.

An alternative way of asking this question would be:

Please list any information you would like to be included on the school report.

This would make it very difficult to quantify the responses and analyse the findings as each respondent would give very different answers. By providing the list, the analyst is able to give the respondents a starting point.

A mixture of multiple choice questions, opinion ratings and open questions should be used. This will provide a balance of quantitative analysis of closed questions and a qualitative analysis of open questions where users are able to suggest alternative ideas to those presented by the questionnaire. Questions should also be written in a way which does not threaten users and the way they currently do their work. Users should be given the opportunity to return their questionnaires anonymously because that means more honest answers are likely to be given.

DISCUSSION POINT

Questionnaires should ideally be completed online. This means that the results are immediately stored and readily available for detailed analysis in the form of graphs and tables. Filters can be applied to the results and responses can be compared based on the answers given to another question. For example, a filter could be applied to compare the responses of all males who work part-time compared with males who work full-time.

Interviews

Interviews involve a direct conversation between the analyst and the client. Where there is a single end user or small group of end users then interviews are the perfect solution, because questions can be asked of the users and a conversation can take place which can expand upon answers that are given with follow-up questions searching for further detail. Even in large organisations, interviews can still be used with key stakeholders or representatives of user groups.

Questions to be asked during interviews should be planned and designed to elicit the required information from the client. The questions will vary depending on who is being interviewed. If management are being interviewed, then the questions will focus on the requirements of the organisation as a whole and the information that is required for decision making. If end users are being interviewed, then the questions need to be aimed at finding out what the users need to make their jobs more efficient. Interviews don't have to be with individual users. They can take place with groups of users or focus groups that represent user groups or customers.

The logistics of each interview also needs to be planned. It can sometimes be difficult to find a time when both the analyst and the client are available, especially if the client has a busy schedule. Honesty is important during interviews so that the analyst can get an accurate picture of how tasks are completed. This can sometimes be difficult to achieve as end users may not want to admit to taking shortcuts in their tasks or not carrying out tasks to the best of their ability. In these situations, anonymous questionnaires can get more honest responses. With interviews, the analyst has to be involved with every interview and this can result in a lot of time being used up early in the project.

Observation

Observation involves the analyst watching the processes that take place within an organisation to find out how everyday tasks are completed. This can involve sitting with users to understand the tasks they have to complete, with an opportunity to ask questions of the users to elicit further information that could be needed for a **requirements specification**. This can give a very good understanding of the current input data, processing methods and output information. Other options can include wandering around an office throughout the day to see how information is shared amongst users.

One disadvantage of this method is that when users are being observed, they may do things differently from normal or they may be more efficient and so this does not give the analyst a true picture of what is happening. The analyst needs to be able to identify how long tasks genuinely take and any inefficiencies that could be improved upon. By observing users directly, the analyst can get first-hand experience of the inefficiencies and can plan to overcome these. Of course, some users may not like being watched and this may cause them some stress, which means they don't perform as they would do normally. Although this method can take up a lot of time, it is the most insightful method of finding out how an organisation works.

Document analysis

Existing documents within an organisation can tell an analyst a lot about the information that is currently being used.

TASK

Examine the receipt in Figure 15.01.

Figure 15.01 - Receipt.

1 Identify the output information that is included on the receipt.
2 Identify any calculations that are likely to have taken place on the receipt.
3 Identify which information is likely to be the same for all receipts and which information is likely to be different for each receipt.

The analyst will need to see examples of any documents that show output information or give an indication of what data is being collected for input to a system. The analyst can sometimes also identify processes that take place by looking at documents. It's also possible to estimate the amount of data that is likely to be required if the volume of documents is known.

This method is not to be used on its own but must be used in conjunction with other analysis methods, as it is difficult to identify the processes just by looking at documents. Examination of the documents also only shows data that is currently output and doesn't give the analyst an opportunity to find out what additional data an organisation might need or what data the organisation does not need. This information can be found out by following up document analysis with interviews.

The content of specifications

There are three types of specification used within the life cycle. These can be summarised as shown in Table 15.01.

Requirements specification	Design specification	System specification
Created by the analyst.	Created by the designer.	Created by the designer.
Contract between developer and client.	Shows what the system will look like.	Identifies the software and hardware needed to run the system.
Identifies what the system must do.	Describes how the system should work.	Identifies the minimum hardware needed to run the system.
	Specifies the data structure to be used.	

Table 15.01 - The different types of specification.

Requirements specification

A requirements specification is a contract between the developer and the client. It will specify exactly what the client needs the system to do so that the developer can produce a system that meets the client's needs. The analyst will usually write the requirements specification in consultation with the client who will approve it.

A requirements specification should include:

- the purpose of the system
- the main objectives of the system
- data that must be output from the system (e.g. invoices, sales reports)
- data that needs to be input to the system to generate the outputs, including any screens or data collection forms
- validation and verification that is needed for input data
- processes that need to take place to convert inputs into outputs or to store data
- data that need to be stored
- functional requirements such as performance measures
- deadlines for each milestone within the project.

EXAMPLE

Here is an extract from a requirements specification for a new town council website. The extract shows specific data that is required on the home page in addition to that which will have been specified for all pages:

- Quick links
  - Show list of links editable by content manager
  - Initially to be:
    - How can I get involved? (go to Consultations)
    - How can I stand for council? (go to Elections arrangements)
    - When is the next steering group meeting? (go to Meetings)
    - When will I be able to vote for councillors? (go to Key dates)
    - What powers does the Town Council have?
    - How do I report a problem? (go to City Council sub-page)
    - When can I vote for councillors? (go to Elections 2016 arrangements)
- News list
  - Picture, news title, date (taken from list of news)
  - Button: view all news
  - To show latest four news articles
- What's on list
  - Picture, event title with hyperlink, date and time (taken from List of events, Key dates and Meetings)
  - Button: view all events
  - Button: view all key dates
  - To show next four events.

System specification

A **system specification** lists all the software and hardware that is needed for the new system. The software needs to be identified first as the hardware will depend upon what software is needed. Only software that is needed to run the system should be specified. There may be different software identified for different types of users and for servers.

Once the software is known, the minimum hardware required to run that software can be identified. In addition to this, the analyst needs to consider how much storage space is going to be required for the data being used by the system. The analyst will probably also recommend higher than minimum specifications so that the system functions at a reasonable speed. These specifications will include the processing power and the amount of memory required. External hardware components that are needed should also be specified and these should be based upon the requirements of the user.

Design specification

The **design specification** is produced by the designer and is an illustration of how the system will look, what the

data structures will be and how the system will work. It is intended to give the user an idea of what the system will look like before it is developed so that the user's feedback can be incorporated into the final designs. The developer will then follow the designs.

Later in this chapter you will learn how to design:

- flowcharts
- data flow diagrams
- data collection forms
- screen layouts
- validation routines
- data dictionary.

In addition to this, a design specification will include:

- house style (logos, colours, fonts, styles, sizes)
- screen sizes
- connectivity diagram to show links between screens
- purpose of calculations.

QUESTIONS

1. Identify five stages in the system life cycle.
2. Explain why interviews are better than questionnaires for smaller groups of users.
3. State the purpose of the system specification.

15.02 Design

KEY TERMS

DFD: data flow diagram which shows how data moves around a system

System flowchart: an overview of how a system works in a diagrammatic format

Diagrams can be used to describe how a current system works (during analysis) or they can also be used to demonstrate how a new system will work (during design).

Data flow diagram

A data flow diagram (**DFD**) shows how data flows throughout a system. It is not about the order of processes, it is purely about the data flows. The elements shown in Table 15.02 are used within a DFD.

Element	Purpose	Symbol
Data flow	This is the data that is flowing throughout the system.	→ Figure 15.02 - **Data flow symbol.**
Process	This is an action that uses or manipulates data.	Figure 15.03 - **Process symbol.**
Data store	This is a place where data is stored. This could be a hard disk, cloud storage or a paper file, for example.	Figure 15.04 - **Data store symbol.**
External entity	This is where the data originates or is destined.	Figure 15.05 - **External entity symbol.**

Table 15.02 - DFD elements.

DFDs can exist at many levels. At level 0, or context level, the diagram will show the whole system and the data flows between the whole system and any external entities, such as customers, suppliers, members, guests etc.

To create a level 0 DFD, you should identify the external entities and the data flows between the external entities and the system. It is important to remember that it is the data flow that is being represented and not physical objects. Each data flow will be in one direction only.

54

EXAMPLE

A hotel accepts online bookings for its hotel rooms. Guests make a booking online and the booking is received by the hotel. When the customer arrives, they are given an electronic key which includes encrypted data that will unlock the door and allow purchases at the bar. At the end of the stay, the guest is presented with a bill which must be paid before leaving.

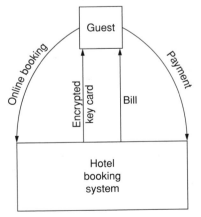

Figure 15.06 - Level 0 DFD.

This DFD shows the system as the hotel booking system. It shows the guest as an external entity. It then shows the four items of data that flow between the guest and the booking system.

DISCUSSION POINT

DFDs can also be considered to be one of the final stages of analysis as they can be used to record the data flows that are currently taking place within an existing system.

TASK

Create a level 0 DFD for the scenario below.

A car hire company accepts bookings of cars by telephone. A credit card payment for the deposit is taken from the customer at the time of booking. When the customer arrives to collect the car, they have to provide details of their driving licence, which are stored by the car hire company. The car hire company will provide the customer with details of the insurance and breakdown services for the car. The customer must pay the remainder of the hire cost before taking the car. The customer will be presented with an invoice showing the payments made.

The next level is a level 1 DFD. This shows the flow of data within part of a system, or if the system is small within the whole system. If the DFD is showing just part of a system, then other parts of the system are considered to be external entities. Each flow of data must be linked to a process, as something has to happen to the data before it can be stored or passed onto an external entity.

TASK

Create a level 1 DFD for the car hire company introduced in the previous task. Assume the DFD will be for the whole system.

EXAMPLE

Figure 15.07 is a level 1 DFD for the hotel booking system. Any other aspects of the hotel system are considered to be external entities.

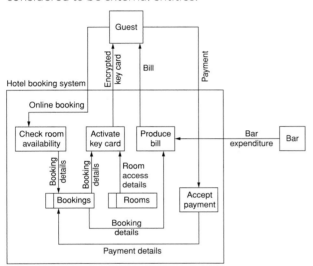

Figure 15.07 - Level 1 DFD.

When the guest sends their online booking, the room availability is checked and the booking details are stored. When the guest arrives, their key card is activated by retrieving the room access details. When the guest is ready to leave, a bill is produced by retrieving the booking details and any bar expenditure from the bar system. When payment is made, the booking details are updated to confirm that payment has been made.

To create a level 1 DFD, first identify any external entities and any other parts of the system that will be classed as external entities. Identify the data flows to and from those external entities. Each data flow must have a process attached to it. A data flow cannot move directly from one external entity to another or from one data store to another or between an external entity and a data store because a process is required to deal with the data. Ignore how the data will actually be processed and just focus on the data movements.

System flowchart

A **system flowchart** shows the processes that take place within the system and the decisions that are made. It focuses on the logic of the system, rather than the data within the system. A flow chart can represent a whole system or just part of a system. The elements shown in Table 15.03 are used within a flowchart.

Element	Purpose	Symbol
Terminator	The start and end of the flowchart.	Figure 15.08 - Start/end data flow symbol.
Arrow	Shows the direction of flow.	Figure 15.09 - Arrow data flow symbol.
Process	An activity within the system.	Figure 15.10 - Process data flow symbol.
Decision	A decision that has to be made with different output routes based on the result of the decision.	Figure 15.11 - Decision data flow symbol.
Input/ output	Input data or output data for the system.	Figure 15.12 - Input/ output data flow symbol.

Table 15.03 - Flow chart elements.

255

EXAMPLE

Figure 15.13 is a flowchart for taking a hotel booking online.

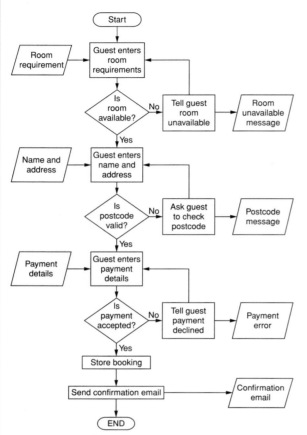

Figure 15.13 - Online hotel booking flowchart.

This part of the system starts by the guest entering their room requirements (type of room, number of guests and dates) into the online booking system. The system checks to see if a room is available. If it is not available, then the guest is informed the type of room is unavailable for the dates requested and the guest can try again by entering a different type of room or different dates. If the room is available, then the guest is asked for their name and address. The postcode is checked to ensure it is valid for the address entered. If it is not valid, then the guest is asked to check and re-enter the postcode or the address. If it is valid, then the user is asked for payment details. If the payment is accepted, then the booking is stored and a confirmation email is sent to the customer. If payment is not accepted, the guest is informed that payment has been declined and asked to re-enter payment details.

To create a flowchart, start by adding the terminator for the start. Always include both a start and finish terminator and never start with just a process. Then identify the first process that takes place. If user input is required or information is to be output, then add these symbols at the appropriate place. Be specific when identifying processes and outputs. For example, state 'Tell user payment declined' or 'Payment error' rather than 'Declined' or 'Error'. Continue to add processes until a decision is required. When a decision is required, ensure that there are both yes and no routes and consider where each route should go, and also be specific with decisions. For example, use a question like 'Is speed above 70 km/h', rather than 'Too fast'.

TASK

Create a flow chart for the scenario below.

A pizza delivery company accepts orders for pizzas by phone. The customer is asked for their address. If the address is not within the delivery area, then the order is stopped. If the address is within the delivery area, then the customer is asked for their order. The customer is offered the option to have garlic bread as a starter. If the customer accepts, then garlic bread is added to the order. If the customer does not accept, then the order continues to payment. If the customer chooses to pay by cash, then the order is complete. If the customer chooses to pay by credit or debit card, then the customer is asked for their card details. If the card details are accepted, then the order is complete. If the card details are not accepted, then the customer is asked to repeat the card details.

Data collection forms

Data collection forms are documents that are used to collect data without the use of a computer. These could include membership application forms, questionnaires, job applications or reply slips. It is important to design the form in such a way that the required data can be collected.

When designing a data collection form, it is good practice to follow the principles below:

- avoid colour as the document may not be printed in colour
- include instructions about how to complete the form
- give clear instructions about where the form should be returned

EXAMPLE

Membership Application

(PLEASE PRINT OR TYPE)

Company Name: ____________________

Primary Representative: ____________________ Title: __________

Address: ____________________

City: __________ State: __________ Zip Code: __________

Phone: (______) __________ Fax: (______) __________

Yes! Add me to your E-mail List: ____________________

Website Address (*Free Link under catagory listing*): http://www.__________

Yes! Website Advertising (*Subject to Annual Renewal*) $25 __________

(Please include camera ready company logo or email HI RES file to: marketing@cheektowaga.org)

Number of Employees: Full Time ________ Part Time ________

Business Category (choose from list above): ____________________

Signature: ____________________ Date: __________

Referring Member & Company: ____________________

METHOD OF PAYMENT

Dues Amount $ __________

Application Fee $ 40.00__

Website Advertising $ __________

Additional Reps. or Categories $ __________
($25 per each additional)

TOTAL $ __________

( ) Cash

( ) Check *Please make checks payable to: Cheektowaga Chamber of Commerce*

( ) MasterCard ( ) Visa

____
Name as it appears on credit card

____
Credit card account number

Exp. Date __________

AGREEMENT: I hereby authorize payment to be charged against the credit card listed above.

____
Authorized Cardholder Signature

____
Date

Cheektowaga Chamber of Commerce
2875 Union Road, Suite 50
Cheektowaga, NY 14227
Phone: 684-5838 Fax: 684-5571
www.cheektowaga.org

NOTICE
Membership dues in the Chamber of Commerce may be tax deductible as an ordinary and necessary business expense. Dues paid to the Chamber are not a charitable tax deduction for federal income tax purposes. The Chamber is not a charity, but serves as an advocate organization for area business.

ANNUAL MEMBERSHIP INVESTMENT

Membership Classifications
If Your Business Employs...
(Part-Time employees count as 1/2 an employee)

❑ **1-2** Employees **- $155** (includes **1** representative)

❑ **3-20** Employees **- $195** (includes **1** representative),

❑ **21-49** Employees **- $295** (includes up to **2** representatives)

❑ **50-99** Employees **- $395** (includes up to **3** representatives)

❑ **100 or more** Employees **- $495** (includes up to **4** representatives),

❑ **Individuals - $115** *(will be listed by name only, business name will not be listed),*

❑ **Community/Government Organization - $115**

❑ **Banking Institutions - $300**

❑ Additional Category Listings
$25 (per additional listing)
1) ____________________
2) ____________________

Please list any additional reps in this section if your company employs more than 20 employees or your Membership is at the $295-495 dues level OR
❑ ***Yes*** **— I would like to list additional representatives at $25 per rep/year**

Name: ____________ Title: ______
Email: ____________________
Name: ____________ Title: ______
Email: ____________________
Name: ____________ Title: ______
Email: ____________________

Membership rates subject to change.

Figure 15.14 - Data collection form.

- identify which questions must be answered and which are optional
- provide enough space for each answer
- use tick boxes for multiple choice lists
- make it clear how many options are allowed to be chosen from a multiple choice list
- ensure all fonts are consistently used
- avoid cluttering the form with too much information or too many questions
- ensure the font style and size are legible
- if the respondent needs to complete a scale (e.g. 1–10), then explain what the scale represents (e.g. 1 = very dissatisfied, 5 = neither satisfied or dissatisfied, 10 = very satisfied).

TASK

Explain how the application form in Figure 15.15 could be improved:

Membership Application Form

Name________

Address____________________

Gender____________________

Age____________________

Do you have any disabilities? Y/N

Which of the following types of movie do you watch? ❑ Horror ❑ Action
❑ Drama ❑ Comedy ❑ Other

Figure 15.15 - Poorly designed form.

Screen layouts

A screen can be used to ask the user for data to be input or to display information to the user or a mixture of both.

EXAMPLE

Figure 15.16 shows information about a property that is for sale. It also allows the user to change details about the property or add details about a new property.

Figure 15.16 - Screen example.

When designing a screen it is good practice to follow the principles below:

- use colour sparingly and appropriately; different colours could be used for questions and responses or for different types of data; colours that the user expects should be used, for example green is usually seen as a positive colour and red as a negative colour
- ensure all fonts are used with consistency
- avoid cluttering the screen with too much information, but at the same time try to fit all information that needs to be viewed at the same time on a single screen
- ensure the font style and size are legible
- if the screen requires user input:
  - include instructions about how to complete the form
  - identify which questions must be answered and which are optional
  - provide enough space for each answer
  - use tick boxes for multiple choice lists that can have more than one response
  - use drop-down boxes (combo boxes) or option buttons (radio buttons) for multiple choice lists that can only have one response.

When designing a screen or collection form, it is only necessary to indicate where questions and responses will go, the types of response options and the styles

to use. The layout of any information should also be indicated. The developer will then follow the design.

EXAMPLE

Figure 15.17 is a design for a screen.

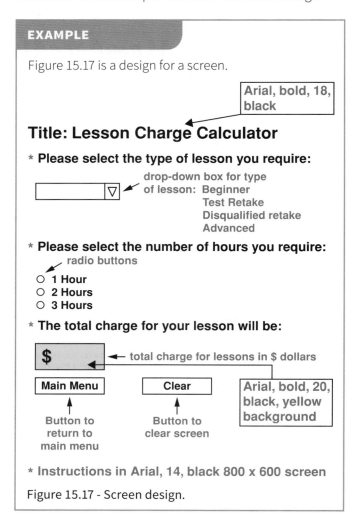

Figure 15.17 - Screen design.

Validation routines

TASK

Revise validation routines from Chapter 1. Complete the following table.

Validation type	Description	Example
Presence		
Range		
Type		
Length		
Format		

Validation rules should be used wherever possible and be appropriate in order to reduce the number of possible input errors. They only need to be used for input data so any calculations or output data do not require validating. Drop-down boxes should always be used instead of lookup validation checks. For example, if a category needs to be selected, then a drop-down box should be used to select that category rather than requiring the user to type in the category.

When designing a validation rule, identify the input data that is to be validated, the type of validation rule to be used, the rule that will be used and the error message that should appear if the data input is invalid. Error messages should be positive and guide the user as to what to do to correct the error.

EXAMPLE

Input data	Validation type	Validation rule	Error message
Surname	Presence	Surname must be entered	Please enter a surname
Date of birth	Range	Date of birth must be at least 18 years earlier than today	Applicant must be at least 18 years old
Application number	Type	Must be a whole number	The application number must contain only numbers
Telephone	Length	Must be between 3 and 15 digits	Telephone number must be between 3 and 15 digits
Product code	Format	XX999XX9	The product code must be in the format XX999XX9 where X is a letter from A to Z and 9 is a number from 0 to 9

Data dictionaries

TASK

Revise data dictionaries from Chapter 9. Complete the following data dictionary.

Attribute	Data type	Field size	Format
Vehicle registration			
Make			
Model			
Engine size (cc)			
Transmission			
Number of doors			
Date of registration			
Imported?			

Hardware and software for a new system

Earlier in this chapter you learned about the system specification. The designer will need to decide what hardware and software is required. If the application being designed is a small one, then it may be able to run on existing hardware and software within the organisation. The designer will need to determine the minimum hardware and software requirements and then find out if the hardware and software already exists and can be used.

In some circumstances, the application will need additional software in order to run. This is particularly the case if a database solution is being developed. The designer will therefore need to identify the new software that is required.

If the existing hardware within an organisation is not capable of running the software required or does not have enough storage space for the data, then upgrades to the existing hardware or new hardware will need to be specified.

TASK

An application that is to be designed will require Microsoft Access 2016 for Windows. List the minimum hardware specification that is needed to run this software.

QUESTIONS

4 Identify the purpose of a data flow diagram (DFD).

5 Identify one rule for data flows within a level 1 DFD.

6 Describe the difference between a tick box and an option button.

15.03 Development and testing

KEY TERMS

Test data: data that will be used for testing a system

Alpha testing: initial testing of the software by a limited group of people

Beta testing: a sample of users test a pre-release version of the software

Black box testing: testing of inputs and outputs to a system or part of a system with no consideration for the workings of the system

White box testing: testing the whole system in terms of structure and logic covering all paths through the system

The development stage is often referred to as the implementation stage where the design is implemented. Due to the confusion between implementation of the design and implementation of the system, development is now a more commonly recognised and understood term.

Test data

When a system has been developed, it needs to be tested. In order to test the system, data has to be created that will be used for the purpose of testing. This is known as **test data**. There will need to be enough test data generated to ensure that the system is able to cope under the pressures of large amounts of data in everyday use. There will also need to be specific types of data to test different scenarios within the software, including validation rules and queries.

When testing the input of data that is to be validated, Table 15.04 shows the types of data that should be included as test data:

Type of test data	Description
Valid (also called normal data)	Data that will be accepted by the validation rule.
Invalid (also called abnormal or erroneous data)	Data that will not be accepted by the validation rule.
Extreme valid (also called extreme data)	Data that will only just be accepted by the validation rule because it is at the limit of acceptability.
Extreme invalid	Data that will only just not be accepted by the validation rule because it is just beyond the limit of acceptability.

Table 15.04 - Types of test data.

EXAMPLE

To test the validation rule that gender must be 'M' or 'F', the following test data could be used.

Type of test data	Data
Valid (normal)	M, F
Invalid (abnormal or erroneous)	B

To test the validation rule that a date must be between 1/1/2017 and 31/12/2017, the following test data could be used.

Type of test data	Test data
Valid (normal)	12/5/2017
Invalid (abnormal or erroneous)	15/7/2012, 4/6/2019
Extreme valid (extreme)	1/1/2017, 31/12/2017
Extreme invalid	31/12/2016, 1/1/2018

TASK

Select test data to test the input of numbers in the range 2500 to 5000

Test data is also needed to test queries. Records will need to be created where there is data that meets the criteria of the query, does not meet the criteria of the query, only just meets the criteria of the query and only just fails to meet the criteria of the query. Where there is more than a single criterion, data should also be selected that only meets part of the criteria in case both parts have not been set up correctly.

EXAMPLE

The following data for records could be used to test the query for males over the age of 50 (including 50).

Record number	Gender	Age	Reason
1	M	65	Both criteria met
2	F	25	Both criteria not met
3	M	25	Gender part met, age part not met
4	F	65	Gender part not met, age part met
5	M	50	Age part only just met
6	M	49	Age part only just not met

The more criteria that are used and the more possibilities for extremes, then the more records that will be required to test the query fully.

TASK

Data is stored about cars, including their make, model, registration number, transmission (automatic or manual), colour, distance travelled and year of registration. Select test data that could be used to test the query to find all automatic transmission cars that were registered before 2016.

Alpha testing and beta testing

Alpha testing is carried out by the developers or a specialised team of testers before a system is delivered to the user. This usually takes place close to the end of the development stage when the application is nearly ready for the user. Alpha testing can take a long time because each time an error is found, testing has to be repeated when the error has been corrected and there may be knock-on effects to other parts of the system.

Beta testing is used when software is being made available to a large number of customers. Beta testers will be real customers who have been selected to test an early release of the application. Beta testing only takes place after alpha testing has been completed. Alpha testing is planned and structured using test data to follow all pathways through the software but beta testing involves customers using the software in a real world environment using real data. As bugs are found within a beta version, new beta versions will be released for further testing before a final version is released for sale.

Black box testing and white box testing

Black box testing involves selecting input data and checking that the expected output data matches the actual output data, with no knowledge or understanding of what happens inside the black box. The black box could be the whole system or part of a system. **White box testing** involves the same process of input and output data but the internal structure and logic of the program are known to the tester.

White box testing usually takes place with small program modules and is carried out by the software developers who coded the programs. They will do this to ensure that each module works in the way it was intended, and because they know the inner workings of the module they can test pathways that a black box tester would not know about. The testing will be focused on whether detailed designs, such as validation rules, have been developed correctly.

Black box testing usually involves testing the whole system or user testing. It can be carried out by specialist testers or, in the case of user testing, by the intended users. No knowledge of programming or the way the system works is required. The testing will be focused on ensuring the requirements specification has been met.

The importance of testing and having a test plan

Testing is necessary because no programmer or developer is perfect and errors are to be expected. These errors need to be found and rectified. It is important to

261

262

EXAMPLE

The extract below from a test plan, tests the input of data where the date must be between 1/1/17 and 31/12/17.

Number	Description	Type of test	Input data	Expected result	Pass/Fail
1a	Test the input of join date.	Valid	12/5/17	Accepted	Pass
1b		Extreme valid	1/1/17	Accepted	Pass
1c		Extreme valid	31/12/17	Accepted	Fail – error message
1d		Invalid	15/7/12	Error message: the join date must be in 2017.	Pass
1e		Invalid	4/6/19		Pass
1f		Extreme invalid	31/12/16		Fail – accepted
1g		Extreme invalid	1/1/18		Pass

The reason the test for 31/12/17 failed to be accepted may be because <31/12/17 was used in the validation rule rather than <=31/12/17. Similarly, the reason 31/12/16 failed to generate an error message may be because >= 31/12/16 was used in the validation rule rather than >31/12/16.

ensure that the system is error free so that the users can use the system knowing that it will work reliably and behave as expected. Although it's almost impossible to ensure a system is completely free of errors, a test plan can help to minimise the number of errors by ensuring that all pathways through a system and types of data have been tested.

A test plan will identify all the tests that are needed for every input, every button, every link, every report, every screen and all other elements of a system. The test plan will include different types of test data, including valid, invalid and extreme, so that inputs are tested to their limits. Without this planning, important parts of testing would be missed out and errors could be left undiscovered. The plan will also cover all the user's requirements and ensure that they are tested.

Test plans

A test plan will identify what is being tested, the type of test, the input data that should be used to test it, the expected result of the test and space to record the actual result. Each test will be numbered.

TASK

Create a test plan to test the input of data for a character code between the letters D and P.

As well as inputs, it is important to test that all calculations work as expected. Each input for a calculation will need to be identified and an expected result determined.

EXAMPLE

Number	Description	Type of test	Input data	Expected result	Pass/fail
2	Discount formula works for 2 hours	Calculation	Charge per hour = $13 on quote worksheet	Test retake = $25 in 2 hours column	Pass
3	Function for lesson charge	Calculation	Lesson type = advanced Number of hours = 2 on quote worksheet	Total charge = $19	Fail = $1.90

Any links or buttons also need testing.

Number	Description	Type of test	Input data	Expected result	Pass/fail
4	Main menu button	Button	Click on main menu button on quote worksheet	The main menu worksheet opens	Pass
5	Clear button works	Button	Lesson type = advanced, number of hours = 2 Click on the clear button on quote worksheet	Lesson type = (blank) Number of hours = (blank)	Fail – number of hours remained as 2

7 Describe the purpose of using extreme test data.
8 Describe two differences between alpha and beta testing.
9 Explain black box testing.
10 Explain the importance of having a test plan.

15.04 Installation

This section has the title 'installation', however, the term 'implementation' can also be used. Implementation can have two meanings within the system life cycle and is often understood to be the development stage where the design is implemented.

There are four different methods of installing (implementing) a new system which can be remembered as the 4 Ps:

- parallel
- plunge (direct)
- phased
- pilot.

Parallel running

Parallel running is when a new system and an old system are run at the same time. On an agreed date, the new system will become live but the old system will continue to run. Data will need to be duplicated from the old system to the new system. New data will need to be input into both systems and output will be produced from both systems. This will continue until the organisation is confident that the new system is running satisfactorily.

Direct changeover

Direct changeover is when a date is chosen for the old system to stop running and the new system to start running. The systems do not run at the same time and there is a clear break from the old system to the new system. Data will need to be transferred from the old system to the new system before the new system can be used.

Phased implementation

With phased implementation, parts of the new system will be introduced one at a time. This often takes place when there is a large system with lots of functionality that can be easily separated into sections. The old system will run until a date that has been agreed, at which point part of the old system will be retired and part of the new system will start running. After a while, another part of the old system will be retired and another part of the new system will start running. This will continue until the complete new system is fully running.

Pilot implementation

Pilot implementation takes place when part of an organisation starts to use the new system while the rest of the organisation continues to use the old system. The new system is effectively being beta tested by the pilot group who may also be able to deliver training to the rest of the organisation when the system goes fully live.

Implementation method

The most suitable changeover method will always be dependent upon the individual circumstances surrounding a new system. Factors that will need to be taken into account will include:

- how critical the system is to the running of the organisation
- cost
- number of users in the organisation
- the size of the new system.

The advantages and disadvantages of each method is shown in Table 15.05.

Installation method	Advantages	Disadvantages
Parallel	Less risky because if the new system fails the organisation can continue to run using the old system. The accuracy of the new system can be tested against the old system and any errors can be fixed.	Duplication of data input means additional staffing costs. There may need to be additional hardware installed at the same time as the old hardware is still being used, which will require physical space. Data may be input differently into the two systems, meaning that the data is not accurate in both.
Direct	This is cheap to implement because there is no duplication of work. The data being used will be consistent because it is only being used in one system at a time. There is no need for the new system to be compatible with the old system.	This is a risky method because any errors could lead to the system failing with no fallback. All the training will need to be done in advance of changeover and so if there are a lot of users this could result in some forgetting what they've learned by the time they start to use the new system.
Phased	If there are any errors, they will only affect the part of the system that has changed over rather than the whole system. End users can be trained how to use each phase of the new system and spend time using that phase before being trained in the next phase.	Delays can occur waiting for each phase to be running successfully before the next phase can start. Users will be using two different systems and they may get confused as to which system they should be using for which part of their work. This could lead to data being updated in the wrong system. Both the old and new system need to be compatible with each other in order for data to be used across both systems.
Pilot	If there are any errors, they will only affect the pilot group that are using the system. Any errors found by the pilot group can be fixed before the system is installed for all users. The pilot group can train other users on how to use the system because they will have experienced using it for real.	This is a slower method of changeover because the rest of the organisation has to wait until the pilot has been completed satisfactorily. Users in the pilot group might not be happy about using the new system while it may still have some errors in it and users not in the pilot group may be disgruntled that they have not been offered the opportunity to try the new software first. Both the old and new system need to be compatible with each other in order for data to be shared between the pilot group and the users still using the old system.

Table 15.05 - Advantages and disadvantages of implementation methods.

QUESTIONS

11 Identify four methods of changeover.

12 Describe one situation when direct changeover would be more appropriate than parallel changeover.

13 Describe one situation when pilot changeover would be more appropriate than phased changeover.

15.05 Documentation

Technical documentation

Technical documentation is an overview of the structure of the system, how it was put together and how it works. It will include a data dictionary to show how data has been structured within the system. Any programming code or macros will be annotated to explain their purpose and anything unusual. All validation rules will be listed with the criteria used for successful input and the error messages that they generate. The purpose of calculations within the system will be identified and an explanation given of how each calculation works. All buttons and links will be listed, including where they are located and what their function is. All files used by the system will be listed and their purpose identified. The technical documentation will also include flow charts to show how different parts of the system work and other diagrams that may have been used during design and development such as entity relationship diagrams and screen connectivity diagrams.

There will be an installation guide for the installation team and also in case the system has to be installed again in the future. All the results of testing will be recorded. Backup routines will be detailed to show where files are stored, how the routines were configured and how to restore from a backup. All security settings will be documented to show which groups have access to each part of the system and the permissions they have been granted. The software and hardware requirements will also be listed.

User documentation

User documentation is a user guide giving instructions to the user. It can be in electronic or printed format. A printed user guide should have a front cover that clearly identifies the name of the system and the whole guide should have a header or footer with page numbers. A contents page should be included with page numbers and an electronic version would include hyperlinks to those pages. An introduction to the purpose of the user guide should be included, but it only needs to be a few sentences. All the software and hardware requirements will be listed within the guide.

The main part of the user guide will be the instructions on how to use the system. This should include written instructions together with screenshots of the system or photographs of hardware. Arrows can be used to point to parts of screenshots or photographs. Bullets or numbering should be used to break instructions down into manageable tasks.

A glossary will show an alphabetical list of any technical terms that have been used within the user guide and a definition of each of those terms. There should be a troubleshooting section that includes a table of common problems (e.g. error messages) together with a description of what might have caused the problem and possible solutions for overcoming the problem. An index will be included at the end of the user guide with page numbers for each popular term.

EXAMPLE

This is an example of a troubleshooting guide for a printer.

Problem	Cause	Solution
Orange light displayed on printer.	No paper in feeder tray.	Add paper to the feeder tray.
Red light displayed on printer.	Paper is jammed in the printer.	Open the paper feeder tray and check there is no paper stuck there. Open the back door and check there is no paper stuck there. Open the toner door, remove the toner and check there is no paper stuck there. If any paper is found, gently pull any paper that is stuck.
Error message on computer says 'Printer Offline'.	Printer is turned off.	Turn on printer.
	Printer is not connected to the computer.	Ensure the USB cable is connected between the computer and the printer.

Below is an example of a troubleshooting guide for an order processing system.

Problem	Cause	Solution
Microsoft Access ✕ ⓘ Not enough items in stock OK Figure 15.18 - Error message 1.	On the New order form you have specified a quantity larger than the amount currently in stock.	Enter a smaller quantity.
Microsoft Access ✕ ⓘ Invoice cannot be paid if not dispatched OK Figure 15.19 - Error message 2.	On the Order details form you have ticked the Paid box before the Invoice has been dispatched.	Check the invoice has been dispatched. If it has, then tick the Invoice dispatched box.

TASK

Find a user manual for an electronic device or appliance at home. Identify the different sections that are used and compare them with those listed above.

QUESTIONS

14 Give three sections you would expect to find in user documentation.

15 Describe the purpose of a glossary in user documentation.

16 Give a situation when technical documentation would be needed.

Why technical and user documentation is needed

Technical documentation is required so that anybody carrying out future maintenance on the system will be able to understand how the system was developed and how it is configured. It is unlikely that the person carrying out future maintenance is part of the original development team and so will not be familiar with the system without the technical documentation. Even if it is the same person or team carrying out the maintenance, they will need the documentation to remember the structure of the system.

User documentation is needed so that the user can learn how to use the new system or look up how certain features are supposed to work. The troubleshooting section will be important for the user to understand what has caused an error to occur and what they need to do in order to stop the error from occurring.

15.06 Evaluation and maintenance

Evaluation

When a system has been developed and installed, the whole process will be evaluated. This is sometimes referred to as a review. The evaluation will consider how the project team and end users worked together so that lessons can be learned for future projects.

Users will be given questionnaires to find out what they think of the new system and how they feel it is improving their workflow (or not). Selected users will also be given specific tasks to complete that will be observed to see whether the new system is living up to its expectations. Some users will also be interviewed about their interaction with the new system.

The most important question to be asked will be whether the system meets the user requirements. Each requirement will be considered in turn to determine if it has been fulfilled. If it hasn't been fulfilled, then actions will be set to rectify the situation in the long run. The efficiency of the new system will also be discussed. Users will have been given an opportunity to feed back on how well the new system is working for them and if there are any problems. It is expected that the new system will work more efficiently than the old system. However, if there are problems that need addressing, then actions will be taken.

The requirements specification should have specified how easy the new system should be to use. This can be rather subjective and so it is difficult to measure. Again, feedback will have been gained from users as to how well they have adapted to the new system and how easy or not they find it to use now they are using it regularly. If there are issues regarding ease of use, then plans can be made to simplify any processes by adding additional features to the software if necessary.

There will also be an opportunity for users to make suggestions for future improvements or additions to the system.

Maintenance

Maintenance takes place after a system has been delivered to a customer and it is being used. There are four reasons why maintenance might be required, which are outlined below.

Perfective

The idea of perfective maintenance is to be always looking to improve a system. There may not be anything wrong with the system, but there may be ideas to make the system perform better or to do additional tasks. Sometimes improvements might be possible because of new technology that has become available. If a system remains in place for several years without any improvements, then it may become outdated and inefficient compared with other systems that are available. Users will also have new ideas and if they are likely to improve efficiency then they should be embraced.

EXAMPLE

An online accounts application sends out automatic reminders to customers when payments haven't been made. These reminders are sent to a single customer contact. The system only allows for the contact details of one person to be stored. Many users of the accounts application have requested that the system be adapted to store details of multiple contacts for each customer and that contacts who should receive invoice payment reminders are identified within the software so that they go to the right person.

Adaptive

Systems need to adapt to changes. There could be changes to internal procedures within an organisation or changes over which the organisation has no control. For example, new government legislation could be introduced to which the system has to adapt. It's necessary to adapt to changes so that the system continues to work effectively and doesn't produce incorrect outputs. It's important that the system enables an organisation to comply with new laws. There is also a need to adapt to new technology such as a new operating system or a new web browser.

EXAMPLE

The government introduced new requirements for organisations to provide pensions to all employees. The online accounts application needed to be updated to include a facility for checking that all employee payslips include pension payments unless they have opted out of the scheme. The accounting software was supposed to show a paper clip symbol to indicate that a receipt had been uploaded against a recorded expenditure. When a web browser was upgraded, this paper clip stopped being displayed. The software had to be adapted to work with the new web browser.

Preventative

Preventative maintenance is required to prevent problems arising within a system. This can apply to both hardware and software. Hardware should be regularly cleaned to stop dust from blocking any fans and regular scans of storage media should be carried out to ensure they are working properly. Heat should be monitored within systems for any abnormalities to prevent hardware failures. Data should be regularly checked for consistency and integrity. Performance of the system should be monitored to ensure that the processor, memory and storage are all working efficiently. By carrying out regular preventative maintenance, system downtime can be avoided.

Corrective

When errors or bugs are found within a system they need to be corrected. This will be the responsibility of the original developers, although it may be different people that carry out the maintenance. These errors need to be corrected so that the system can run efficiently and accurately and produce the results required by the organisation. Bugs that cause problems by making a system slow or by crashing a system can be very frustrating to users and reduce overall productivity.

> **EXAMPLE**
>
> A graphics application would intermittently stop responding for several seconds. This was not supposed to happen and so corrective maintenance was required.

> **QUESTIONS**
>
> 17 State three elements that might be evaluated after a system has been installed.
>
> 18 Give a situation when corrective maintenance would be required.

15.07 Summary

A new system evolves through the system life cycle. Requirements are specified by the client and recorded by the analyst. The designer will then follow the requirements specification in order to produce a design specification which will show the client what the new system is likely to look like. When the user is happy with the design specification, the system will be developed and then tested before being installed for the client. The client will be provided with user documentation. An evaluation will take place to review the system life cycle for the project. Any ongoing maintenance will be carried out by the maintenance team.

Review questions

Thornhill Estates runs several hotels. It would like a new software solution to manage room bookings, dinner reservations and purchases across all its hotels. It has asked a software developer to produce the software for them. The software developer will follow the system life cycle.

1a State one purpose of analysis in the system life cycle. [1]

1b Give two reasons why questionnaires would be appropriate for researching how bookings are currently managed at the hotel. [4]

1c State three other methods that could be used to research the current booking system. [3]

The analyst will interview a group of users to create a requirements specification.

2 State the purpose of a requirements specification. [1]

The designer will create a design specification based on the requirements specification.

3a Identify three factors that should be considered when designing a screen layout. [3]

3b Using an example, show how a validation rule could be designed for the hotel booking system. [3]

3c Apart from keyboards, mice and monitors, discuss three external hardware components that will be needed by the hotel system. [3]

Once the system has been developed, it will need to be tested.

4a Describe two differences between white box and black box testing. [4]

4b Explain one reason why beta testing might not be appropriate for the hotel system. [2]

4c Explain why invalid test data is used. [2]

The system will be installed in a pilot approach and user documentation will be provided to the hotel staff.

5a Give reasons for the pilot approach of installation for the hotel system. [4]

5b Explain why the user documentation should include troubleshooting and glossary sections. [4]

5c Give four reasons why the hotel system may require maintenance in the future. [4]

Chapter 16
Graphics creation

Learning objectives

By the end of this chapter, you will be able to:

- describe the difference between bitmap and vector graphics
- describe how typical features in bitmap and vector graphics are used in practice
- evaluate the impact of image editing on society
- create vector and bitmap images
- change the size and position of items in vector and bitmap images
- use tools to edit vector and bitmap images
- add text to vector and bitmap images
- save vector and bitmap images
- compress vector and bitmap images

KEY TERMS

Vector: an image that uses geometric points and shapes. Calculations are used to draw the image

Bitmap: an image made up of small squares, called pixels. Each individual pixel can only be one colour

Pixel: a small square of one colour. These are combined to create a bitmap image

16.01 Vector versus bitmap graphics

Remember

A **vector** image is created using shapes and coordinates. Mathematical formulae and calculations are used to draw the image and fill areas with colour. If you change the size of the image, the computer recalculates and redraws it. This means it does not go blurry (pixelate). The image itself is not saved. Only instructions on how to create the image are saved. For example, coordinates for a line and a calculation for drawing the line are stored, including the colour, width etc.

Figure 16.01 - A vector image.

Figure 16.02 - An enlarged vector image.

TIP

A **bitmap** image is made up of small squares called **pixels**. Each pixel can have one colour. If you change the size of the image, the pixels are enlarged or made smaller. By enlarging the pixels you pixelate an image, and it goes blurry.

Figure 16.03 - A bitmap image.

Figure 16.04 - A pixelated bitmap image.

The use of vector and bitmap images

The most common form of a bitmap image is a photograph. When you take a photo, the camera records the colours as pixels and the quality of an image depends on the resolution. Other common bitmap images including ones that have been scanned, or produced using painting software. Resolution is the number of pixels per measurement, for example dots per inch (DPI). The larger the DPI, the more pixels and therefore the more precise your image is.

Vector graphics are created using a computer, often with specialist drawing software, but word processors usually provide some vector tools, such as drawing shapes and

271

speech bubbles. They could be used, for example, to create a logo or an animation where characters can be drawn using a graphics tablet.

Figure 16.05 - Graphics tablet.

Deciding between vector or bitmap graphics

If you scan a document (e.g. a photo), then you will create a bitmap image. As increasing the size of this image may result in pixelation, you must be careful to ensure the resolution is high enough. These pictures cannot be created as vector images, so if you want to use a photo of you and your friends, it will be a bitmap graphic.

> **TASK**
>
> Open some of the images you have stored on your computer or on your account. Are they a bitmap or a vector image? Try enlarging them. Do they pixelate?

If you are creating a graphic using a computer, then you can choose between a bitmap and a vector image. If you produce a bitmap image, such as a photo, it may pixelate when enlarged. If you produce a vector graphic, it will not pixelate, but will require a lot of work to look realistic.

Software exists that can turn bitmaps into vectors, and vectors into bitmaps. For example, if you scan a document, you can vectorise it. Most image manipulation software has this option.

Use and impact of image editing on society

This section will explain some of the tools available to manipulate images. These tools can be used to edit

images to both improve the image and make the image look worse. For example, in magazines, photos may be edited (airbrushed) to make people appear thinner or to remove blemishes, such as wrinkles and spots.

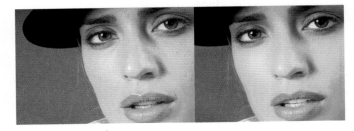

Figure 16.06 - Example of airbrushing.

Another way image manipulation software may be used is to put people in scenarios (e.g. memes) that have never actually happened. For example, using a selection tool to copy a person from one image and place them in another. The image of the person can be edited, and the colours manipulated, so they appear to belong in the new scene.

Figure 16.07 - Example of a meme.

Vector images can be used on their own or added to a bitmap image. For example in the meme shown in Figure 16.07, vector text has been added to the bitmap photo.

These are just two examples of how image manipulation can be used. Each have their positive and negative sides. In the first example in Figure 16.06, the company may increase sales by showing a perfect model. However, the image is not real and people may strive to achieve this impossible vision. This can contribute to mental health problems. Memes can be used to draw attention to an advert or create humorous effects, but they can also be used negatively, to make fun of people and situations and may be used without the consent of the person in the image.

DISCUSSION POINT

Look at a magazine, newspaper or book and the images inside it. How do you think the images might have been manipulated? Does this add to the publication? Why have they edited them?

Image editing can be used in politics both to promote a political agenda, for example enhancing images so they look more favourable, and to put people into situations where they have not actually been. A search for the use of image editing in North Korea will reveal multiple articles where Kim Jong-un is accused of using image editing software to present a false version of what is actually taking place.

Image editing can also be used in a negative way, to put opposing party members in unfortunate situations or to use memes to mock them, which can cause offence and influence people by creating images that are not real.

As well as being used for political purposes, it can also be used in the entertainment industry. Image editing is used to create posters, signs, CD and DVD covers, all of which are enhanced to increase their attractiveness and appeal. This can increase sales as the images are attractive, but it does not portray an image of real life.

QUESTIONS

1 What is a bitmap image?
2 What is a vector image?
3 Why might image manipulation be viewed as being a negative influence?

16.02 Vector images

Layers

Layers contain parts of an image, or an effect, that can be built up on top of each other to create the final image. By using layers you can move or edit elements of an image independently without affecting other elements of the image. You can also add effects, such as transparency, to one part of your image.

TASK

 CD 16.01 Background

Open CD 16.01 Background in your image manipulation software. You may need to convert this to a different file type depending on the software you are using. Add a new layer to this image and use the drawing tools to add shapes, lines etc. to the image. Use the drawing tools to draw a new tree or flower or other feature. Change the shapes, move them, delete them, and the background layer should not change. Add further layers with additional shapes or objects.

Grouping or merging

When creating an image, you may have multiple items (objects or shapes). These can all be moved individually, which can cause problems when you need them to stay together. You can group or merge items, which combines them into one item that can be moved and resized together.

You can ungroup or unmerge items to separate them again.

TASK

Using the image you manipulated in the previous task, select all the items you added in one layer (e.g. your drawing of a tree) and group or merge them. The item should now move as one, rather than as separate components.

Rotation and placing an item

To rotate an item, you will need to choose a rotate tool. This may be under a 'Transform' option. You can then place the cursor on the corner of an item and pull to rotate it. By using the cursor to select an item and then move it, you can drag it to a new location.

TASK

Rotate one of the items you have added in a layer, for example a tree. Move it to a new location.

Transform tools

Transform tools are used to change the size, rotation, distortion and skew of an item. There is often a 'Transform tools' tick box or option in the menu system to let you access these controls. You can then use the handles in the corner or edge of the item to change its size and orientation.

TASK

 CD 16.02 Bench

CD 16.01 Background

Insert the bench from CD 16.02 Bench into the background on CD 16.01 Background. Resize the bench and move it into a suitable position.

Selection tools

A selection tool lets you access, edit and manipulate just one part of an image. You can choose which parts to change. There may be a range of different tools that you can access depending on your software. For example:

- A lasso tool lets you draw freehand around the area of an image you want to select.
- A marquee tool provides you with a shape, such as a rectangle, that you can draw over your image to select a rectangular area.
- A magnetic lasso tool will stick to an edge within an image, for example a line or a specific colour, which means you don't need to follow the line precisely.

To select multiple areas, you usually need to hold down the Shift, or Ctrl key at the same time as making the selections.

When making your selection, make sure you are on the correct layer. If not, then you will be selecting that area of a different layer, which will not give you the image required.

TASK

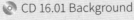 CD 16.01 Background

Use a selection tool on CD 16.01 Background. Select one of the trees. Create a new instance of this object (copy and paste it into a new layer), then use the transform tools to adjust its position and size. Repeat this with the bench.

Crop tools

Cropping lets you select only part of an image to keep and removes everything else. To do this, select the crop tool

(it may be in a toolbox or in a menu). It may look similar to the symbol in Figure 16.08.

Figure 16.08 - Crop symbol.

Highlight the area of the image that you want to keep. Press enter to complete the crop.

TASK

 CD 16.01 Background

Using CD 16.01 Background, crop the bottom layer of soil from the image and the top of the sky above the clouds. Make sure you have the correct layer selected before you begin, otherwise you will crop the wrong image.

Fill tools and colour gradients

A fill tool lets you select a colour, then fill a selected area with that colour. For example, if you select red, then the fill tool, then click inside a rectangle, it will change the rectangle to red. Some software may require you to select the fill tool, then the colour.

You may have further fill options, such as:

- Fill with gradient: choose two colours and the colour will gradually grade from the first to second.
- Fill with pattern: select from a range of patterns to fill a shape. You can usually choose a colour as well.

There may be a range of other fill tools, depending on your software, that you can experiment with to see what they do.

TASK

CD 16.01 Background

Use a fill tool to change the colour of the sky, trees and mountains in CD 16.01 Background. Make sure you have the correct layer selected first. Change the fill colour of the bench by use a fill pattern or gradient.

Node editing

Node editing lets you adjust a shape by manipulating the angles used to create it. Some software refers to nodes as paths. Figure 16.09 shows the node manipulation symbols that appear.

Figure 16.09 - Edit node.

The centre square allows you to move that point of a shape and the handles at the edge allow you to manipulate the shape. If you move the right-hand square up, that part of the image will follow, curving towards it.

In the software there will be a node select tool (or path selection). By clicking on an image it will provide you with points to manipulate.

TASK

 CD 16.01 Background

Select the nodes on one of the mountains on CD 16.01 Background. Manipulate the shape of the mountain. Make it higher and change the angles of each side. Repeat this with the copy of a tree you have made and change the shape of the trunk.

Fix text to a path

As well as adding text to an image, you can design a path for text to follow, so it can curve, spiral or do whatever you want it to do.

The path, or shape, for the text to follow needs to be drawn first. Make sure this path is selected and when you click on the text tool you should be able to click on the path. When you type, the text will follow the path.

TASK

 CD 16.01 Background

Draw a curved line, similar to that in Figure 16.10, above the trees in CD 16.01 Background. Give the image a title. Adjust the text size, colour etc. so it fits in with the scene.

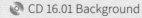

Figure 16.10 - Curved line.

Save and compress an image

There are a number of different file types for a vector image. The file types available to you will depend on the software you are using, for example Adobe Illustrator may provide a .ai extension and CorelDraw may provide a .cdr. These file types are not always compatible with other software.

To change the file format, you can either:

- Save As, and choose a different file type, or
- Export as a different file type.

File types may change the file size of your image, depending on the resolution and number of colours used. For example, you can save an image as a 256 colour bmp file, or as an eight-byte per pixel bmp file. The latter will have a much better colour depth (a larger range of colours used). However, the file size will be significantly larger. Some file types compress an image, either by lossy methods (removing aspects of the image so it will not be the same when decompressed) or lossless methods (the exact image will be reproduced). Reducing the number of colours is an example of lossy compression, because some of the colours will be lost and cannot be retrieved in that image. Some file types do not support layered graphics, so if you have created an image with layers, depending on the file type, the image may be flattened and the layers cannot be retrieved.

275

TASK

Look at the different file types available in your software. Research for what these are used. Save your image using different file types. Make sure you change the filename on each one so you do not accidentally overwrite your image. Compare the file sizes and the quality of the images you have saved.

TASK

A computer programmer has set up a company called Stars. They would like a logo created to put on their website, business cards and promotional material for the company. Design and create a vector logo for Stars.

QUESTIONS

4   What is a layer?

5   What are the three different selection tools?

6   What does grouping objects do?

16.03 Bitmap images

KEY TERM

Opacity: the lack of transparency in an image, or part of an image

Layers work in bitmap images in the same way as in vectors. You can add a layer to a bitmap image which contains another bitmap or add a vector drawing. You can edit each layer independently from the other aspects of the image. With a bitmap image, you can add further effects to a layer, because it can then be applied to a whole area of the image as opposed to individual objects within it.

> **TASK**
>
> 💿 CD 16.03 New York
>
> 💿 CD 16.04 Helicopter
>
> Open CD 16.03 New York. Add a new layer and add the image from CD 16.04 Helicopter.

Rotating and placing an item

The cursor is used to select and move an item placed into a layer and the transform tool 'Rotate' is used to turn an item. To select part of a bitmap image within a layer, you will need to use a selection tool (such as a marquee selection tool), to select the pixels that you want to manipulate.

> **TASK**
>
> 💿 CD 16.03 New York
>
> Move the helicopter to an appropriate position in the sky and rotate it so it fits into the skyline.

Grouping or merging

If you have multiple bitmap images in several layers you can merge them to move them together in one layer.

> **TASK**
>
> 💿 CD 16.03 New York
>
> 💿 CD 16.04 Helicopter
>
> Open CD 16.03 New York and CD 16.04 Helicopter. Add further copies of the helicopter onto the New York image in the same layer. Select all of these layers (you may need to use the Shift or Ctrl button to select more than one), then group or merge the layers into one layer. You should now be able to move them together.

Selection tools

The selection tools let you select only one part of an image. You need to use a marquee selection, a lasso or a magic wand to select the pixels that you want to manipulate.

> **TASK**
>
> 💿 CD 16.03 New York
>
> Use a selection tool (e.g. a magnetic lasso) to highlight one of the buildings in CD 16.03 New York. Copy this image and paste it into a new layer. Move the building so it looks as if it belongs in the city. Repeat this with other buildings to create your own version of New York.

Crop tools

The crop tool will let you select part of an image and delete the parts that are not selected.

> **TASK**
>
> 💿 CD 16.05 Frog
>
> Open CD 16.05 Frog. Crop the image so only the face and eyes of the frog are visible.

Masking tools

A mask lets you apply a technique (e.g. colour or transparency) to a small part of an image. This is a very powerful tool and can let you combine two images, by placing one image on top of a second, and then removing elements of it that you do not want to appear. To do this, you will need to add a mask to your top layer, by painting over the elements of the top layer (usually in black) you do not want to appear. They will become transparent.

> **TASK**
>
> 💿 CD 16.06 Doorway
>
> 💿 CD 16.07 Landscape
>
> Create a new bitmap image file and insert CD 16.06 Doorway and CD 16.07 Landscape. Place the CD 16.06 Doorway layer on top of CD 16.07 Landscape. Put a mask over the doorway opening, so the landscape is visible through the doorway (you can choose to leave or mask the wall).

Tools to improve parts of an image

There are a number of tools that you can use to edit parts of a bitmap image:

- Blend: using this you can blend different layers together by changing the **opacity** (transparency). If the foreground and background are different colours, the blend tool can create a gradient blend of these colours. There are a range of different blend techniques from which you can choose, for example a 'hard light' option will bring dark elements to prominence.
- Replicate: This may also be known as a clone tool. With this you can make an identical copy of part of an image. For example, if you have a tree that you would like to duplicate, by using this tool you can 'paint' a copy of the tree in a different place without having to trace the outline and copy it.
- Retouch: the clone tool can be included as a retouch tool, but there are often others such as a healing brush and patch tools. These apply the pixels from one area of an image to another area. For example, a smooth area of skin on a photo of a person can be used to cover blemishes by applying the pixels from the smooth area.

> **TASK**
>
> Find and save a photo of a person (it could be an image of yourself). Use the clone stamp tool to add more hair. Use the retouch to remove any flaws or remove items such as jewellery by using the skin to cover the area.

Remove red eye

The red eye tool will automatically remove a red eye effect caused by a photo flash. Once you have selected the red eye tool, simply draw a box across (or click on) the red pupil. You may need to do it more than once to get the whole area. The tools uses the other colours from the eye to fill in the pupil.

> **TASK**
>
> Take a photo of a person, using a flash, which results in a red eye effect or find a photo which is affected by red eye. Use the remove red eye tool to correct the image.

Filters

A filter can be used to add effects to an image or to change a small element of it. There are numerous filter tools you can use:

- Blur: this tool reduces the focus on areas of the image. You can adjust the strength of the blur, then drag the tool over the area of the image you want to blur.
- Distort: this tool allows you to change the perspective of an image, or part of an image. For example, if a photo has distorted perspective, using a lens correction distortion can realign the image.
- Sharpen: this tool improves, or increases, the contrast between colours. For example, an edge between a light and dark area can be sharpened to make it more defined.

> **TASK**
>
> CD 16.08 Fruit bowl
>
> Open CD 16.08 Fruit bowl. Use the sharpen, distort and blur tools to alter the image. For example, you could make the fruit the focus by increasing the contrast and blurring other elements. You could also use other tools mentioned above, for example the clone tool, to add more fruit to the image.

Adjusting colours

An entire image, or just part of one, can be converted from colour into black and white, or duotone. The colour is usually applied by adding a new layer on top of the image and this is then adjusted, for example by choosing a black and white, or more commonly, greyscale option.

Duotone involves selecting a colour, which is then applied to your image, again by adding it to a layer. To do this, choose a duotone option (this may be in the menu options). You can select two colours, for example black and red. You may then have an option to adjust the extent of each colour. The result will be the original image made up of just these two colours and their shades.

It is also possible to change an image to black and white, then add a duotone, which changes the impact because it is being applied to grey as opposed to a range of many colours.

Opacity means a lack of transparency, that is how solid and un-see-through the image is. Opacity is a percentage, which represents how transparent an image is. For example, 20% opacity means that the image is 80% transparent. This can be added as a mask to the entire image, or a small area of an image can be selected (using an appropriate selection tool) and then the opacity can be altered just in this area.

Transparency can also be increased by adjusting the alpha value. Alpha transparency, however, is not always maintained depending on the file type. See the section 'Save and compress an image' below for further information.

78

TASK

 CD 16.09 Village

Open CD 16.09 Village. Change the colour to black and white, duotone and a range of other colours. Compare turning an image to black and white then to duotone, rather than straight to duotone.

TASK

CD 16.03 New York

Open CD 16.03 New York. Add a layer and change the opacity of the helicopter.

Resizing

An image can be resized or scaled. Bitmap images may pixelate if they are increased too much in size. If part of an image needs to be resized, then you can use a selection tool to select the pixels you want to change and then a transform tool can be used to adjust the size. If the canvas needs to be enlarged, this can be done through the menu system by selecting canvas size and entering a new size. The canvas can also sometimes be increased in size by using the crop tool. Instead of removing parts of the image, move the edges out to increase their size.

The new background, outside the image, may appear as a checkerboard in grey and white. This means it is transparent. To change this, you will need to either fill the background with a colour, or colour gradient, or increase the size of the image to fill the new space.

Text tools

Text can be added to a bitmap image using the text tool. You will be able to change the font style, size and colour and make the text follow a path if needed. Select the text tool and click where you want to type your text. Adjust your settings from the menu. Using transform tools you will be able to move and adjust your text. Once you are happy with the position of your text, this will then be turned into a bitmap, and the text is no longer editable.

TASK

Add a suitable title to the images you have created. Use a range of styles and colours to edit your text.

Save and compress an image

There are a range of file types you can use to save your bitmap image. These can be selected by choosing an option when saving or exporting the image. Some of these include:

- BMP: There are a range of BMP formats, for example black and white, 256 colours, four-bit (16 colours), eight-bit (256 colours). The smaller the number of colours, the smaller the file size, but the quality also decreases.
- GIF: this is a compressed format that will reduce the file size and is commonly used for online images. This format allows for transparency, as long as it was not created using an alpha option, and is also restricted to 256 colours.
- JPEG: a common format that has a range of colour options to reduce file size. The image is compressed when saved, and decompressed when opened. The level of compression can often be altered to gain a balance of compression versus quality. A JPEG image does not allow for transparency. Any areas that are transparent will be stored as white or black.
- PNG: this format uses lossless compression to reduce the file size. It has a range of colour options, and it keeps transparency in all images, which is not so for all other options.
- TIFF: in this format the number of colours can be adjusted to reduce file size. This file type can save effects, such as the use of layers, if saving and reopening an image in the same software.

When choosing a file type, do not overwrite the original file as, if the compression reduces the quality, you may be unable to retrieve the original. Save it under a new name.

TASK

CD 16.03 New York

Using CD 16.03 New York, save the file under a range of file types and colour depths. Compare the differences between the image quality after saving, and the effects of the transparency of the helicopter.

TASK

Take a photo of yourself (or a friend). Create a set of images of you (or your friend), placed in a variety of famous places around the world. Make sure the image of the person fits into the scene and looks as though they belong there (if the colours are very different, try changing to a duotone).

QUESTIONS

7   What does a masking tool let you do?

8   What will happen if you duotone an image using red and blue?

9   What tool do you need to use to select part of a bitmap image?

16.04 Summary

A bitmap image is made of pixels while a vector image is made of shapes and coordinates (it stores how the image is created). A bitmap image pixelates when enlarged too much, but a vector does not.

Image editing software can be used to enhance images, for example changing photos for books, newspapers and magazines. Image editing has positive and negative effects: positive effects include removing flaws and improving the appearance of publications, while negative effects include creating unrealistic images to which people my aspire my try to emmulate.

There are a range of tools and methods that can be used on both vector and bitmap images (selection, grouping, layers, colour gradients, adding text). However, some tools can be used with bitmap images and not a vector (distortion, blend, replicate, remove red eye). Layers allow the components of an image to be kept separate and manipulated individually. Once images have been edited, bitmap and vector images can be saved as different file types and some images can be compressed, with different file types having different levels of compression.

Review questions

1   Describe the difference between a bitmap and a vector graphic. [4]

2   Explain why a bitmap image pixelates when increased in size. [2]

3   Explain why a vector image does not pixelate when increased in size. [1]

4   A fashion magazine is published, aimed at teenagers between the ages of 13 and 16. They are considering the use of image manipulation software to alter the appearance of the models and clothes in the magazine. Evaluate the use of image manipulation software in this magazine. [9]

Chapter 17
Animation

Learning objectives

By the end of this chapter, you will be able to:

- create an animation
- place objects and images
- use frames and key frames
- use timings and layers
- manipulate objects (show, hide, move and resize)
- understand and use tweening (motion and shape)
- understand and use morphing
- add text
- change the opacity of objects and text

KEY TERMS

Object: an image, or combination of images, that is manipulated as one item

Layer: an object or image given its own timeline for independent manipulation

Animation: a series of images that are played one after another to simulate movement

Key frame: a frame that has a change in the animation, for example a drawing has changed, or the start or end of a tween

Opacity: the lack of transparency

Tween: an animation where the start and end points are set. The computer generates the actual images to make the animation change

Frame: one screen, or page, where an image is drawn. A series of these frames are played one after the other to create the animation

Morphing: another term for shape tweening. One image changes into another image

17.01 Animation

Fundamentals

Objects and images

An **object** is a name for an item that is on the screen. Each object should, ideally, be in its own **layer** to allow for it to be manipulated independently. A single image, for example a tree, could be made up of many objects. Similarly, one object could be made up of many different components, that are then grouped together to act as one.

Objects can be drawn using the vector drawing tools in the software. Basic shapes such as rectangles, spheres etc. can be drawn and then manipulated (or transformed) into different shapes. There will also be the opportunity to use drawing tools such as a paintbrush, pencil etc. to draw freehand.

Images from other software can be either imported or copied and pasted into an **animation** file. These, again, should each have their own layer. An image that is imported will usually have to be treated as one object. It cannot be broken down into its subcomponents. This makes it difficult to manipulate.

Objects can be shown and hidden while working on the document, to allow you to view and manipulate other objects. This is often an option in the layer where the object occurs, allowing you to make the entire layer hidden.

The size of an object can be changed. If this is done in a **key frame**, then the new size will exist from that point onwards. Resizing may come under a transform option, which also lets you rotate objects.

The stage

The area in animation software where you draw and create your animation is called the 'stage'. The size of this stage is measured in pixels. You can change the size of the stage to meet your needs by increasing or decreasing the number of pixels in the width and height.

The stage has a set of x- and y-coordinates that you can use to position objects with more accuracy. The top-left corner has the coordinates (0, 0) and these then increase as you move down and across the image. Figure 17.01 shows an example stage with two coordinates.

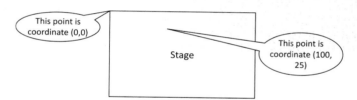

Figure 17.01 - An example stage.

Opacity

The lack of transparency of an object or a piece of text can be changed. In the software this may be referred to as the **opacity** or the alpha style. This is measured as a percentage. For example, 0% will have a fully transparent, invisible image. At 100%, the image is fully visible.

The visibility of an object can be set when it is created, and it can also be manipulated during an animation to make objects appear and disappear.

Text

Text can be added to the stage using the text tool. You will be able to edit the style, size and colour. Text is treated in the same way as objects, so you can use layers, **tweens**, change the opacity and manipulate text in the same way.

Frames, timeline, layers and timings

Frame

Take a blank notepad and draw a shape in the bottom right-hand corner, then draw the same shape but in a slightly different position on the next page. Repeat this on a number of pages. You can then create a basic animation by flicking through the page of the book, as shown in Figure 17.02.

Figure 17.02 - A book with the pages being flicked.

Each of these pages, or individual images, is called a **frame**. A computer animation is made up of a series of frames, which are played very quickly to give the illusion of movement. In reality, it is a sequence of individual images. Figure 17.03 shows a series of frames for a rabbit jumping.

Figure 17.03 - Frames of a mouse jumping animation.

Timeline

A timeline is made up of frames, in chronological order from left to right. An example of how a timeline may appear is shown in Figure 17.04.

	1	2	3	4	5	6	7	8	9	10	11	12	13	14	15	16	17	18
Tree 1	•	→	•															
Flower 1	•	•	•		•			•										

Figure 17.04 - Example timeline.

The numbers on the top row in Figure 17.04 represent the frame numbers. A frame that is grey, for example frame 1 for Tree, has an image in it for that layer. A frame that is white, for example frame 8 for Tree, does not have an image in it for that layer.

Key frame

A key frame identifies a change in an image. In Figure 17.04, these changes are represented by a • in the frame.

For example, Flower 1 first appears in Frame 1, it changes in Frame 2 and Frame 3. It does not change in Frame 4, but it still displayed. It changes in Frame 5, then stays the same in Frames 6 and 7.

An arrow in the timeline represents a tween, which you can find out more about later in this chapter.

To add frames and keyframes, you will first need to select the frame number where you want the frame or keyframe to appear, and then select the Insert or Add Frame or Key frame. This is usually by either right clicking or choosing it from the menu.

Layer

An animation is made up of layers which each has its own animation schedule. For example, in Figure 17.04, the Tree 1 and Flower 1 appear in frames 1 to 7, but frames 8 to 14 no longer have the Tree. By using layers, you can independently manipulate different parts of an image.

Each layer is shown on the left of the timeline. These should have an appropriate and descriptive name, for example in Figure 17.04 the Tree 1 layer contains the drawing of a tree.

It is important when designing an animation that all elements that need to move independently are in their own layer. You can create layer folders, which contain multiple layers. For example, if you are animating a person, then you may have a folder called Person 1, which contains layers:

- head
- body
- left arm
- right arm
- left leg
- right leg.

TASK

1 Using animation software, draw a stick person, as described above. Make sure each part of the person is in its own, appropriately named, layer.
2 Draw an underwater scene, with rocks, seaweed, fish etc. Make sure each component has its own layer.

282

Timings

A common misconception is that a frame represents a second, that is if there are ten frames, this takes ten seconds. This is not the case. The timing is measured in frames per second (fps), which can be changed, for example 10#fps, means that ten frames will be run each second; if you have 200 frames, the animation will last 20 seconds. The higher the fps rate, the quicker the frames change and the smoother the animation appears.

When designing an animation, you need to consider the fps, as this will affect the number of frames you need, and the extent to which you change the images in each frame. If you need an item to stay static for a set time, then it can be given frames (not key frames) where it exists, but does not change. When it needs to change or move, a key frame is then added.

TASK
1 Create an animation, using frames and key frames, to make a word appear letter by letter. For example, if the word was Animation, the 'A' would appear, then the 'n' etc.
2 Create an animation to make a flower grow. For example, start with a seed, the roots and stem grow from this and it eventually becomes a flower.
3 Create an animation for the stick person you drew previously. Make them walk across the screen. You could extend this and have two people who meet and perform other actions.
4 Change the fps for your animations by increasing and decreasing them. Discuss the effect this has on the animations.

Tweening

An animation created solely with frames and key frames can be quite robotic. By inserting a tween, the computer will generate the animation for you. For example, if you want to move a drawing of a fish across the screen, you can set the start location (A), the end location (B) and then the computer will work out how to get the fish from A to B.

When applying a tween to a layer, it will affect every item in that layer. It is important to make sure that each individual item has its own layer.

There are two types of tween you can use, motion and shape.

Motion tween

A motion tween only deals with the movement of an object, for example moving from one place to another, and rotation. If you use key frames, you have to position the object in each frame. Using a motion tween, the computer fills in the gaps in movement.

The item you tween needs to be set as an object or symbol before you start moving it.

The way in which a motion tween is created differs according to your software. Create the first key frame and position the symbol where you want the movement to begin. Select the next frame and either right click and choose create motion tween or select from the menu system to add the tween. Then add a key frame at the end and move the object to its new position.

To make an object move on a curved path, you can draw a motion path.

TASK
1 Using the underwater scene you created earlier, add motion tweens to make the fish move. Add bubbles floating to the surface. Each one will need its own layer and motion tween.
2 Draw a ball and make it move around the screen. Add stick people and get them to kick or throw the ball to each other.
3 Create a motion tween that incorporates a change in opacity, for example a fade in or fade out.

Shape tween (morphing)

A shape tween allows a shape to be changed into a new shape, for example a red square could be turned into a blue circle. The computer generates each step of the transformation.

The way in which a shape tween, or **morphing**, is created differs according to your software. Add the first key frame and the object as you want it to appear at the start. Select the next frame and either right click and choose create shape tween, or morph, or select it from the menu system. Then add a key frame in the frame where you want the transformation to finish. Either manipulate your existing object or delete it and add a new one. The computer will then change the object in the frames where the tween is placed.

A shape tween can also include movement, so the second object can be in a different location to the first.

TASK

1. Create a shape tween that changes a red square into a blue circle.
2. Create a shape tween that changes a rain cloud into a sun.
3. Draw a scene that shows the changes during a year, for example a river and forest showing a) lush green sunny days, b) leaves changing to red and orange and falling, c) a frozen river with barren trees, d) new growth emerging.

TASK

- Create an animated introduction to a TV show or film. Make sure you include images of the main characters and text introducing the title. Make use of opacity and tweens.
- Extend your underwater scene to include a range of sea life. Animate the background and plants to create a continuous, repeating scene.
- Create an animated cartoon that shows a day in the life of the central character. Use a range of techniques, including some key frame animation and tweens.

17.02 Summary

The numbers on the top row in Figure 17.04 represent the frame numbers. A frame that is grey, for example frame 1 for Tree, has an image in it for that layer. A frame that is white, for example frame 8 for Tree, does not have an image in it for that layer.

A tween creates a smoother animation as the computer calculates the changes. A motion tween is used to move objects. A shape tween, or morphing, allows an object to change into a different object. A shape tween can also allow colour change.

Opacity is the transparency of an image, this can be animated and may be called the alpha.

Review questions

1. Describe how layers are used in an animation. [2]
2. Explain the difference between a key frame animation and an animation using tweens. [4]
3. Define the term morphing. [1]

Chapter 18
Mail merge

Learning objectives

By the end of this chapter, you will be able to:

- create a master document
- create a source file
- link a master document to a source file
- set up mail merge fields
- create prompts for the user
- use filters to select records
- use a spell checker
- verify a mail merge master document
- perform a mail merge
- use mail merge rules to control record selection

KEY TERMS

Mail merge: the automatic addition of data, such as names and addresses, from a source file into a master document, such as a letter

Source file: the file containing the data that will be merged into the master document

Master document: the main document that will be used for all records

Field: a category of information

Prompt: a question asked to the user which requires a response

Filter: selecting records from the source file based on conditions

18.01 Mail merge

Remember

A **mail merge** is the automatic process of merging data, such as names and addresses, from a **source file** into a **master document**, such as a letter. The purpose is to save time having to write the same letter to lots of different people when their data already exists in a data source.

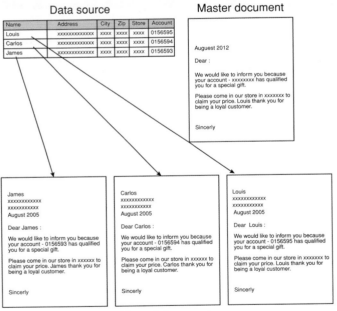

Figure 18.01 - Mail merge documents.

Create a master document structure

A master document is the main letter, email, memo, fax or other document that will be sent to all recipients from the data source.

EXAMPLE

 CD 18.01 Learner letter

CD 18.01 Learner letter is a master document. It is a letter written to learner drivers in a driving school. The words in italics are the data that needs to be inserted about each learner driver and will be obtained from the data source.

Pass 1st Driving School

Date will go here

Full name of recipient will go here
Full address of recipient will go here

Dear *forename*

We are conducting an annual check of our records. Could you please confirm that your telephone number is *telephone* and your mobile number is *mobile*.

We would be grateful if you could email us at info@pass1st.info with your email address.

Yours sincerely

Ben Dean
Senior Instructor

Figure 18.02 - Master document.

Notice how a standard letter includes the letterhead of the organisation sending the letter, the date of the letter and the full name and address of the recipient of the letter. When produced on a computer, a letter should always have all text (except the letterhead) aligned to the left.

TASK

Create a master document that will be used to write to customers of IT Distribution Inc. The letter should be in a standard letter format including space for the recipient's name and address. The letter should invite the customer to participate in a survey with the opportunity to win one of ten prizes each worth $250. The survey is available online and is available for two months from the date of the letter.

Create a source file

A source file contains the data that will be included in each mail merged document. It usually consists of names and addresses and other information about the people to whom a letter will be written.

EXAMPLE

CD 18.02 Driving school.mdb

CD 18.02 Driving school.mdb contains a table called Learner which includes the names, addresses, telephone numbers and mobile numbers of learner drivers in a driving school.

Forename	Surname	Address 1	Address 2	Post Code	Gend	Telephone	Mobile
Patricia	Thomas	896 Windsor Street	Birmingham	B21 4BR	F	0555 555 555	0777 777 726
Wendy	Carolan	22 Gate Way	York	HH6 Y72	F	0555 555 556	0777 777 725
Roger	Harrison	12 Deefrod Lane	Holyhead	HH7 6YT	M	0555 555 557	0777 777 724
Sally	Smythe	23 Hapstead Grove	Stevenage	HR5 3RD	F	0555 555 558	0777 777 723
Claire	Charkley	14 Green Lane	Stowbridge	HT6 8TN	F	0555 555 559	0777 777 722

Figure 18.03 - Source file.

Source files can be in a variety of formats including:

- database table
- database query
- spreadsheet
- word processed table
- variable length text file (e.g. comma separated values)
- fixed length text file
- email contacts.

TASK

CD 18.03 Student.csv

CD 18.04 Student.rtf

CD 18.05 Student.txt

CD 18.06 Student.xls

CD 18.07 Student.mdb

Examine the structure of the following data sources and identify which of the above formats they are in:

- CD 18.03 Student
- CD 18.04 Student
- CD 18.05 Student
- CD 18.06 Student
- CD 18.07 Student.mdb (Student table)
- CD 18.07 Student.mdb (query).

Create a data source using a table in a word processor that will include the following **fields**:

- forename
- surname
- email address.

Create three records in the data source.

Link a master document to a source file

The master document needs to know from where it will get its data. Therefore, the master document needs to be linked to the data source.

EXAMPLE

CD 18.01 Learner letter

CD 18.02 Driving school

CD 18.01 Learner letter has been linked to the Learner table in CD 18.02 Driving school.

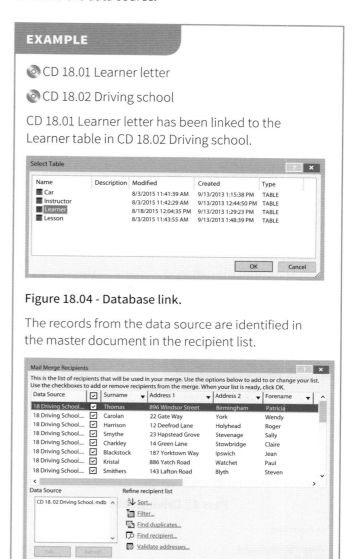

Figure 18.04 - Database link.

The records from the data source are identified in the master document in the recipient list.

Figure 18.05 - Recipients.

TASK

CD 18.08 New class

CD 18.03 Student

CD 18.04 Student

CD 18.05 Student

CD 18.06 Student

28

CD 18.07 Student.mdb

CD 18.09 Sales processing.mdb

Open the master document CD 18.08 New class and link it to each of the following data sources one at a time. Finish by linking it to the query from the database.

- CD 18.03 Student
- CD 18.04 Student
- CD 18.05 Student
- CD 18.06 Student
- CD 18.07 Student.mdb (Student table)
- CD 18.07 Student.mdb (query).

Open the letter that you wrote for IT Distribution Inc. Use it as a master document and link it to the table Customer in CD 18.09 Sales processing.mdb.

Set up fields

Having a link from the master document to the source file only tells the master document which file to use. The master document also needs to know which fields to put into the document and where to place them.

> ### EXAMPLE
>
> CD 18.10 Learner letter with fields
>
> CD 18.02 Driving school.mdb
>
> CD 18.10 Learner letter with fields includes the fields from the Learner table in CD 18.02 Driving school.mdb. The fields are highlighted in yellow in Figure 18.06.
>
> ### Pass 1st Driving School
>
> 18 August 2015
>
> «Forename» «Surname»
> «Address_1»
> «Address_2»
> «Post_Code»
>
> Dear «Forename»
>
> We are conducting an annual check of our records. Could you please confirm that your telephone number is «Telephone» and your mobile number is «Mobile».
>
> We would be grateful if you could email us at info@pass1st.info with your email address.
>
> Yours sincerely
>
> Ben Dean
> Senior Instructor
>
> Figure 18.06 - Merge Fields.
>
> When the merge is eventually run, the fields will be replaced with data from the Learner table.

TASK

CD 18.08 New class

CD 18.07 Student.mdb

CD 18.09 Sales processing.mdb

Use the master document CD 18.08 New class that you linked to the query in the database CD 18.07 Student. mdb. Insert merge fields for forename, surname and class.

Open the letter that you wrote for IT Distribution Inc. and linked to CD 18.09 Sales processing.mdb. Insert merge fields in the appropriate places.

Perform mail merge using the master document and data sources

Now that the fields have been entered, the mail merge can be completed. This involves telling the software to carry out the merge process. It is usually possible to preview the results of the mail merge prior to printing or creating a new document with the merged letters. It is also possible to merge the letters to an email address for each recipient.

> ### EXAMPLE
>
> CD 18.10 Learner letter with fields
>
> CD 18.02 Driving school.mdb
>
> CD 18.10 Learner letter with fields can be previewed. The data from the first record of the data source CD 18.02 Driving school.mdb is highlighted in yellow in Figure 18.07.
>
> ### Pass 1st Driving School
>
> 18 August 2015
>
> Patricia Thomas
> 896 Windsor Street
> Birmingham
> B21 4BR
>
> Dear Patricia
>
> We are conducting an annual check of our records. Could you please confirm that your telephone number is 0555 555 555 and your mobile number is 0777 777 726.
>
> We would be grateful if you could email us at info@pass1st.info with your email address.
>
> Yours sincerely
>
> Ben Dean
> Senior Instructor
>
> Figure 18.07 - Merge preview.

TASK

💿 CD 18.10 Learner letter with fields

💿 CD 18.08 New class

Open CD 18.10 Learner letter with fields and merge to a new document. Notice how all the records have been included so that there is one letter for every learner.

Use the master document CD 18.08 New class to which you have added merge fields and merge to a new document.

Open the letter that you wrote for IT Distribution Inc. Merge the letters to send as emails to the email address field in the Customer table.

Create prompts

Master documents are often used several times and on many different occasions. There may be some data that needs to be included within the master document that is not part of the data source but will change each time the mail merge is run. A **prompt** can be given to the user that asks the user what that data should be.

EXAMPLE

💿 CD 18.11 Learner letter with fill-in prompt

CD 18.11 Learner letter with fill-in prompt asks the user to enter the name of the senior instructor who will sign the letter.

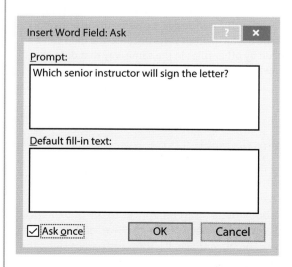

Figure 18.08 - Fill-In.

The Fill-In prompt rule can be viewed as a merge field code.

We would be grateful if you could email us at info@pass1st.info with your email address.

Yours sincerely

{ FILLIN "Which senior instructor will sign the letter?" \o }
Senior Instructor

Figure 18.09 - Fill-In code.

When the mail merge is processed, the user is prompted for the name of the senior instructor.

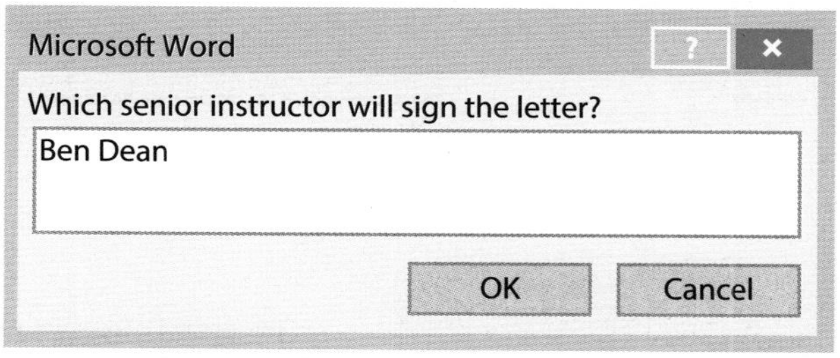

Figure 18.10 - Prompt.

DISCUSSION POINT

Microsoft Word uses rules to control the way the mail merge works. Fill-In is one of these rules. It is most commonly used to ask for one item of data that will be the same for every letter. However, by deselecting 'Ask once', it is possible to have a different response for every recipient.

TASK

💿 CD 18.08 New class

Open the master document CD 18.08 New class to which you have added merge fields. Add a Fill-In prompt for the name of the Head of Year.

Open the letter that you wrote for IT Distribution Inc. before you completed the mail merge process. Add a Fill-In prompt for the date until which the survey will be available.

There are occasions when the same data needs to be included more than once within a document. In these situations, an Ask prompt can be used instead of a Fill-In prompt. The Ask prompt stores the response in a bookmark which can be placed in more than one location in a document.

289

EXAMPLE

⊙ CD 18.12 Learner letter with ask prompt

CD 18.12 Learner letter with ask prompt asks the user to enter the date by which the information should be returned. You will notice that the difference from the Fill-In prompt is that the Ask prompt needs a bookmark to be defined. This has been defined as 'ActionBy'. You will also notice that the default text has been completed. This is necessary in order to be able to reference the bookmark.

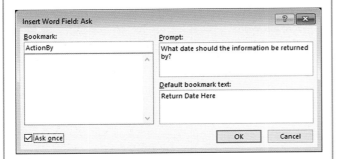

Figure 18.11 - Ask.

The Ask prompt rule can be viewed as a merge field code, but its location is not important due to the fact that the bookmark will be referenced in the required locations.

Yours sincerely

{ FILLIN "Which senior instructor will sign the letter?" \o }
Senior Instructor
{ ASK ActionBy "What date should the information be returned by?" \d "Return Date Here" \o }

Figure 18.12 - Ask code.

The bookmark now needs to be referenced in the document. In order to do this, a reference point is inserted.

Figure 18.13 - Reference point.

Figure 18.14 shows the two reference points highlighted in yellow that have been inserted.

Dear «Forename»

Action Required by Return Date Here

We are conducting an annual check of our records. Could you please confirm that your telephone number is «Telephone» and your mobile number is «Mobile».

We would be grateful if you could email us at info@pass1st.info with your email address by Return Date Here.

Figure 18.14 - Reference point text.

These can also be viewed as merge field codes.

Dear { MERGEFIELD Forename }

Action Required by { REF ActionBy * MERGEFORMAT }

We are conducting an annual check of our records. Could you please confirm that your telephone number is { MERGEFIELD Telephone } and your mobile number is { MERGEFIELD Mobile }.

We would be grateful if you could email us at info@pass1st.info with your email address by { REF ActionBy * MERGEFORMAT }.

Figure 18.15 - Reference code.

When the mail merge is processed, the user is prompted for the date by which the information should be returned.

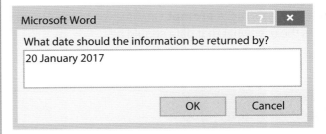

Figure 18.16 - Prompt.

DISCUSSION POINT

If you look carefully at the field code for the Ask prompt you will notice that it includes the name of the bookmark. This can be useful in other ways because the data can be referenced by other rules in the same way that data in fields can be referenced.

TASK

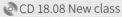 CD 18.08 New class

Open the master document CD 18.08 New class to which you have added merge fields. Instead of a Fill-In prompt, add an Ask prompt for the name of the Head of Year and assign a bookmark. Insert references to the bookmark at the end of the document where the Head of Year will sign and a new sentence that will inform the parents who the Head of Year will be.

Automatically select the required records

Data sources can often have thousands of records. The document that is being produced may not need to be merged with every record. It is therefore possible to select which records will be included in the mail merge by using a **filter**.

EXAMPLE

CD 18.13 Learner letter with filter

CD 18.13 Learner letter with filter has filtered the records so that the letter will only be sent to male learners whose records haven't been updated since 1 January 2015.

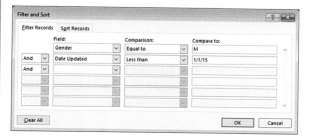

Figure 18.17 - Filter.

The recipient list now only includes the filtered records, meaning the letter will only be sent to those recipients.

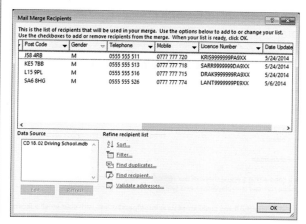

Figure 18.18 - Filter records.

TASK

CD 18.08 New class

Open the master document CD 18.08 New class that you have added merge fields. Set the filter so that the letter is only sent to pupils in class 9F.

Change the filter so that the letter is sent to pupils in classes 9F or 9B.

Open the letter that you wrote for IT Distribution Inc. Set the filter so that the merged email is only sent to customers who have agreed to receive marketing and live in the state of California (CA).

Conditional operators

DISCUSSION POINT

The conditional operator referred to by Cambridge International Examinations is different from that used in programming. In this situation, conditional operators are referring to a conditional function.

Data sources are often fixed and cannot be changed. Therefore, any data manipulation may need to take place in the merge master document. The IF...THEN...ELSE rule can be used to insert text conditionally based upon data within the data source.

EXAMPLE

CD 18.14 Learner letter with condition

CD 18.14 Learner letter with condition is to have a new sentence that asks users to confirm their gender has been stored correctly. Figure 18.19 shows how the IF statement was set up.

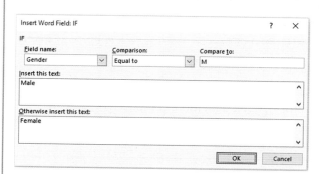

Figure 18.19 - IF...THEN...ELSE.

This can be seen in field code view as shown in Figure 18.20.

Our records show that your gender is { IF { MERGEFIELD Gender } = "M" "Male" "Female" }.

Figure 18.20 - IF...THEN...ELSE code.

This will work fine for situations where there are only two alternatives. However, when more than two alternatives are required, a different method needs to be used. One option is to use a series of IF...THEN...ELSE rules to cover each eventuality.

EXAMPLE

Some records may not have the gender recorded. In this situation, the letter should state 'your gender is not recorded in our records - please confirm your gender'. There are now three options: F, M or [blank] in CD 18.15 Learner letter with three conditions. ELSE cannot be used because it would apply the second outcome to both of options two and three. In Figure 18.21, three separate IF...THEN...ELSE rules have been used without defining the ELSE part.

Our records show that your gender is { IF { MERGEFIELD Gender } = "M" "Male"}{ IF { MERGEFIELD Gender } = "F" "Female"}{ IF { MERGEFIELD Gender } = "" "not recorded in our records - please confirm your gender"}.

Figure 18.21 - Separate IFs.

The other option is to use a nested IF...THEN...ELSE rule. This involves using another IF...THEN...ELSE rule as the ELSE part of the original IF...THEN...ELSE rule. This can only be manipulated in field code view.

EXAMPLE

 CD 18.16 Learner letter with nested conditions

CD 18.16 Learner letter with nested conditions has used a NESTED IF by entering the IF...THEN...ELSE rules within the ELSE parts of previous rules.

Our records show that your gender is { IF { MERGEFIELD Gender } = "M" "Male" "{ IF { MERGEFIELD Gender } = "F" "Female" "not recorded in our records - please confirm your gender" }"}.

Figure 18.22 - Nested IF.

It achieves the same outcome as the previous example, but is a bit more complex. The speech marks need to be in exactly the right places, as do the curly brackets.

DISCUSSION POINT

It's possible to use AND or OR operators within the IF...THEN...ELSE rule. It's also possible to include text from files as the outcome or pictures as the outcome. You may want to research how these can be achieved.

Error-free accuracy

There are a number of checks that should be carried out before completing a mail merge:

- run a spell checker and grammar checker on the master document
- visually check for any errors on the master document
- visually check for any errors on the preview or merged documents
- check that the correct records have been included in the filter.

Even if a spell checker has been run, there are errors that will not be spotted. These can include words that sound the same but are spelt differently, for example stationery and stationary. The spell checker will not be able to identify problems with layout, such as spaces that are missing or have been added by mistake. Errors in names are not spotted by a spell checker and field codes will not be checked by the spell checker. A visual check will also be required to see if all merge fields have been included.

EXAMPLE

CD 18.17 Learner letter with errors

CD 18.17 Learner letter with errors includes several errors.

Pass 1st Driving School

19 August 2015

«Forename»«Surname»
«Address_1»
«Address_2»
«Post_Code»

Dear «Forename»

We are conducting a anual check of our record. Could you please confirm that you're telephone number is «Telephone» and you're mobile number is «Mobile» .

We wood be greatful if you could email us at info@pass1st.info with your email address.

Yours sincerely

Ben Deane
Senior Instructor

Figure 18.23 - Errors.

Some errors have been spotted by the grammar and spell checkers: 'a anual' should be 'an annual', 'wood' should be 'would' and 'greatful' should be 'grateful'.

The errors highlighted in yellow require visual checking as they have not been identified by the grammar or spell checkers: 'record' should be 'records', 'you're' should be 'your' and 'Deane' should be 'Dean'.

The errors highlighted in blue also require visual checking but these may not be spotted until data is actually merged. Figure 18.24 shows what the data would look like when merged.

PaulKristal
886 Yatch Road
Watchet
JS8 4RB

Dear Paul

We are conducting a anual check of our record. Could you please confirm that you're telephone number is 0555 555 511 and you're mobile number is 0777 777 720 .

Figure 18.24 - Merge errors.

There is no space between the forename and surname and there is an additional space after the mobile number.

The criteria for the filter are that letters should be sent to male learners whose records haven't been updated since 1 August 2015. This should mean letters going to 11 learners. However, only four letters will be produced.

Gender	Telephone	Mobile	Licence number	Date updated
M	0555 555 511	0777 777 720	KRIS9999999PA9XX	5/24/2014
M	0555 555 513	0777 777 718	SARR9999999DA9XX	5/24/2014
M	0555 555 516	0777 777 715	DRAK9999999RA9XX	5/24/2014
M	0555 555 526	0777 777 774	LANT9999999PE9XX	5/6/2014

Figure 18.25 - Filter errors.

This has been spotted using a visual check. The error was due to the filter requiring an American layout of date which should be 8/1/15, rather than 1/8/15 that had been used. When corrected, the 11 learners are included.

Gender	Telephone	Mobile	Licence number	Date updated
M	0555 555 557	0777 777 724	HARI9999999RA9XX	6/8/2015
M	0555 555 511	0777 777 720	KRIS9999999PA9XX	5/24/2014
M	0555 555 512	0777 777 719	SMIT9999999SA9XX	6/8/2014
M	0555 555 513	0777 777 718	SARR9999999DA9XX	5/24/2014
M	0555 555 516	0777 777 715	DRAK9999999RA9XX	5/24/2014
M	0555 555 517	0777 777 714	BLAC9999999SA9XX	6/8/2014
M	0555 555 518	0777 777 713	DREW9999999JA9XX	6/8/2014
M	0555 555 519	0777 777 712	BROW9999999DA9XX	6/8/2014
M	0555 555 523	0777 777 777	PETE9999999PA9XX	6/8/2014
M	0555 555 525	0777 777 775	HARR9999999PA9XX	6/8/2014
M	0555 555 526	0777 777 774	LANT9999999PE9XX	5/6/2014

Figure 18.26 - Filter correction.

TASK

CD 18.18 New class errors

Open the master document CD 18.18 New class errors. Check the master document and merged letters for accuracy. The merged letters should be sent to pupils in classes 9F or 9B.

Change the filter so that the letter is sent to pupils in classes 9F or 9B.

Variable fields

One method of deciding which records will be included from the data source is to use a filter. Another method is to use a rule, which is a merge field code that will control which records will be omitted. The rule is called Skip If and this will omit the record from the mail merge if the conditions are met.

EXAMPLE

CD 18.19 Learner letter with selection codes

CD 18.19 Learner letter with selection codes includes a Skip If rule that states that if the gender field is equal to "M" then the record should be skipped.

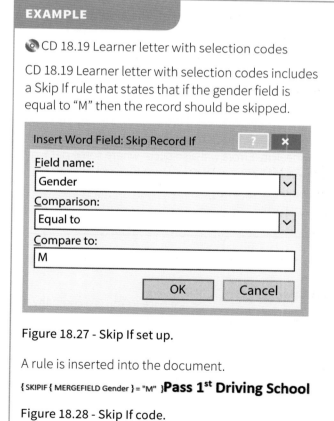

Figure 18.27 - Skip If set up.

A rule is inserted into the document.

{ SKIPIF { MERGEFIELD Gender } = "M" }**Pass 1ˢᵗ Driving School**

Figure 18.28 - Skip If code.

The rule should always be inserted at the beginning of the document. When using Microsoft Word, you will need to complete the merge to see which records have been skipped as they will still show when previewing the merge.

TASK

💿 CD 18.08 New class

Open the master document CD 18.08 New class.

1 Add a rule to skip records for class 9B.

2 Add a second rule to also skip records for class 9F.

Open the letter that you wrote for IT Distribution Inc. and remove any filters that you have applied.

- Add a rule to skip records for customers who have chosen not to receive marketing (this is a Boolean field that can be TRUE or FALSE).

- Add additional rules to skip records for customers who are based in New York (NY), California (CA) or Texas (TX).

Why mail merge documents are created

Mail merge documents are created to save time and improve accuracy. The main reasons include:

- Source data may already exist. Therefore it is not necessary to re-enter the source data for each letter, which is very time consuming, but instead use the data that is already within a file

- Accuracy is improved. As the source data will have probably been validated and verified, it is likely to be very accurate, whereas if the data on a letter has to be changed for each recipient, then errors are likely to sneak in. Errors will also occur where some data in a non-mail merge letter may not be changed when it should be.

- Each letter will be personalised to the recipient rather than being generic.

- It is quicker to proof read one master document than to proof read thousands of letters.

- The same master document can be reused in the future.

- Filters can be applied so that letters are only sent to recipients that meet specified criteria.

18.02 Summary

A master document is usually a letter that is sent to multiple recipients. A source file is a text document, spreadsheet, database or other data source that contains data about the recipients to whom the letter will be sent. The source file needs to be connected to the master document in order to send the letter to the recipients.

Merge fields are used to identify where in the document information about the recipient should be included. Prompts can be set up that ask the user to enter additional information when the mail merge is performed. Conditional functions (IF...THEN...ELSE) can be set up to include different information in the merged document based upon information stored in the data source. Filters can be applied within the master document to the data source to select which records will be included in the mail merge. Mail merge rules such as Skip If can also be used to determine which records should be excluded from the mail merge. A spell checker should always be used to check the spelling within a master document and the accuracy should also be checked visually.

Review questions

Service to You is a company that carries out car servicing at the customer's home address. They store details in a database of the services they have carried out and when the next service is due. When a customer's car is due a service, Service to You use mail merge to write a letter to the customer to let them know.

1a Describe the term mail merge. [2]

1b Describe the steps involved in creating a set of mail merged letters. [6]

Service to You sends out letters once a month.

2 Explain how Service to You can use mail merge facilities to only send letters to customers whose cars are due a service in the next month. [4]

3 Explain why Service to You uses mail merge instead of writing individual letters. [6]

Chapter 19
Programming for the web

Learning objectives

By the end of this chapter, you will be able to:

- explain the use of JavaScript to add interactivity to web pages
- use JavaScript to add interactivity to web pages

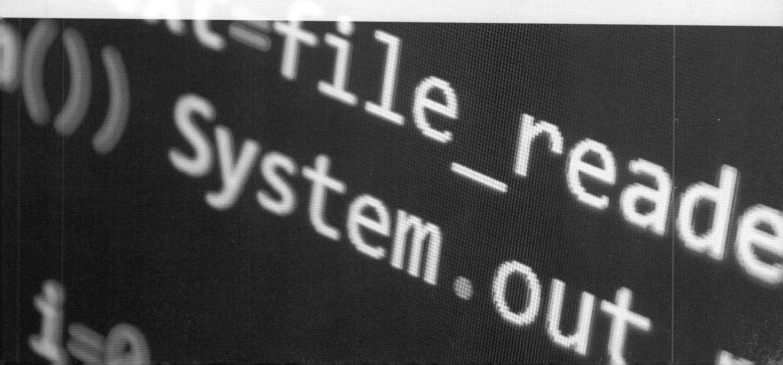

KEY TERMS

Variable: a space in memory that is given an identifier where data can be stored and changed

Identifier: a name given to a variable or function

Data type: the type of data being stored, for example a number, string (text)

Array: a data structure that can store multiple items under one identifier

Condition: a statement that can be evaluated as true or false, for example 5 > 6

Construct: a control structure, such as a loop or a conditional statement

Function: a separate piece of code that has an identifier and performs a task, it can be called from elsewhere in the code and returns a value

Iteration: a loop, to repeat

19.01 JavaScript

Remember

JavaScript is a programming language that can be used to add interactivity to web pages. Its code can be integrated into a HTML file to: create buttons, create text boxes, change content etc. It can be integrated with a range of other web-based programming languages such as PHP. JavaScript is often use with HTML forms, where it can validate data or perform actions such as when a button is pressed.

TASK

Find a website that has functionality (such as a form with a button). What tasks does this button perform?

JavaScript can be added to a HTML document. It is recognised by starting and ending the JavaScript code with a script tag. For example,

```
<script>
    Your JavaScript code would go here
</script>
```

Outputting data

To write an output to a text page, you can use the code document.write(*theOutput*). For example,

```
<script>
    document.write("Hello world");
</script>
```

You may need to write code in a set place or in an object that you have created. To do this, you need to give the area you want the output displayed an ID. For example,

```
<p ID = "paragraph1"></p>
```

In your script tag, you instruct JavaScript to add the text to the document, in the element with the ID 'paragraph1'. For example,

```
<script>
    document.
    getElementById("paragraph1").
    innerHTML = "Hello World";
</script>
```

TASK

CD 19.01 Task 1

CD 19.02 Task 2

- Open CD 19.01 Task 1 using a basic text editor such as notepad. Inside the script tags add code to output "Hello World" onto the web page using document.write.
- Open CD 19.02 Task 2 using a basic text editor. A paragraph has been given the ID 'paragraph1'. Inside the script tags add code to output "Hello World" into paragraph1.
- Add further paragraphs, change the text format for these in HTML and use JavaScript to write sentences in each paragraph.

Working with variables

A **variable** is:

- a space in memory
- given a name
- where you can store data
- where you can change that data.

For example, you could create a space in memory called 'name' and you could store the name 'Luca' in there. You could later change it and store 'Katerina'. You can check what is stored there by asking what is stored in 'name'. The computer would tell you 'Katerina'.

Declaration

A variable declaration tells the program that you need a space in memory and what its **identifier** will be. An example variable declaration in JavaScript is:

```
var name;
```

'`var`' tells JavaScript that you are creating a variable. '`name`' is the name of this variable.

Assignment

Assignment means adding a value to that variable. For example,

```
name = "Luca";
```

The name of the variable comes first and '=' can be read as the word '**becomes**'. This is the assignment operator. **"Luca"** is what is being stored. Luca is in speech marks (**" "**) because it is a string (see the section 'Data types'). For example,

```
age = 18;
```

This time the variable is called age, and the number 18 has been put into it.

You can change the value in the variable. For example,

```
name = "Katerina";
```

```
age = 21;
```

These values have overwritten their previous data.

Data types

The data stored in a variable will be of a set **data type**. Table 19.01 shows the main data types used in JavaScript.

Data type	Description	Example
Number	A numeric value	age = 16 score = 12.4
String	Letters, characters and numbers. Any text string must start and end with either single or double quotation marks, for example '...' or "...".	name = "Katerina" address = '24 Main Street' message = "Hello World"
Boolean	True or False	correct = true correct = false
Array	A series of values of the same data type (see section 'Arrays').	numbers = [1,2,3]
Object	A series of named values of the variable.	film = {title:"The House", genre:"Drama", length:96, releaseYear:2013}

Table 19.01 - Data types.

Data types are not declared when declaring a variable, it is assumed when a value is given to the variable. For example,

```
var name;
```

name could be of any data type. But if instead we put,

```
var name = "";
```

name is now a string.

For example in

```
var age;
```

age could be of any data type. But if instead we put,

```
var age = 0;
```

age is now a number.

> **TASK 4**
>
> Declare variables to store a person's first name, surname and age. Add data to these variables. Output the data onto a web page.

Operators

An operator is a symbol, or set of symbols, that perform an action. There are a number of these used in JavaScript. These are categorised as arithmetic, comparison and logical.

Table 19.02 shows the arithmetic operators.

Operator	Function	Example
+	Addition	x = 1 + 2; x is now 3
-	Subtraction	x = 5 - 1; x is now 4
*	Multiplication	x = 2 * 3; x is now 6
/	Division	x = 10 / 3; x is now 3.33
++	Increment (increase by 1)	x++;
--	Decrement (decrease by 1)	x--;
%	Modulus (return the whole part of a division	x = 11 % 5; x is now 1

Table 19.02 - Arithmetic operators.

In an arithmetic calculation, you do not need to deal with numbers, you can use variables instead. For example,

```
var firstNumber = 10;
var secondNumber = 20;
var result = firstNumber +
        secondNumber;
```

Table 19.03 - shows the comparison operators.

Operator	Function	Example
>	Greater than	5 > 6; This is false.
<	Less than	5 < 6; This is true.
>=	Greater than or equal to	5 >= 6; This is false.
<=	Less than or equal to	5 <= 5;)1 This is true.
==	Equal to	5 == 6; This is false.
===	Equal to and of the same data type	5 === "5"; This is false because the first is a number, the second a string.
!=	Not equal to	5 != 6; This is true.
!===	Not equal to or not of the same data type	5 !=== "5"; This is true, because they are not the same data type.

Table 19.03 - **Comparison operators.**

Table 19.04 shows the logical operators.

Operator	Function	Explanation	Example
&&	AND	Is true if the condition before and after are both true. If one is false, then it is false.	(5 < 6) && (7 < 10) Both are true, so the result is true. (5 > 6) && (7 < 10) The first statement is false, so the result is false.
||	OR	Is true if one or both of the conditions are true. If both are false, it is false.	(5 < 6) || (7 < 10) Both are true, so the result is true. (5 > 6) || (7 < 10) The second is true, so the result is true.
!	NOT	Replaces a true with false, or a false with true.	!(5 < 6) This is false because 5<6 is true, but the ! will change this to false.

Table 19.04 - **Logical operators.**

Logical and comparison operators are used in conjunction with a conditional statement or a loop.

To output the result of a logical or comparison operator, insert the operation into an output statement. For example,

```
document.write(10 < 6);
```

You will learn more about these in later sections.

TASK
1 Create two variables and add a number to each, for example `num1 = 10` and `num2 = 5`. Output the result of addition, subtraction, multiplication, division and modulus division using these number.
2 Create a program to output the result of each of the following logical operations:
- 5 > 6
- 20 === 20.0
- 10 <= 10.1
- Kristoff == Fredrick

String manipulation

A string manipulator allows you to perform actions on a string and extract information from it. When counting letters in a string, the first letter is letter 0, the second letter 1 etc. Spaces and all symbols all count as letters.

Table 19.05 shows the most common string manipulation methods you may need.

Operator	Description	Example
substring (*startLetter*, *endLetter*);	Return the letters from the position of *startLetter* to *endLetter*.	word = "Hello World"; subword = word.substring(7,11); subword will now hold "World" The variable, **word**, is used together with the operator, that is **word.substring**
substr(*start*, *noOf*);	Starting at the *start* letter, return the *noOf* (number of) letters.	word = "Hello World"; subword = word.substr(2,4); subword will now hold "llo"
replace("*string*", "*string*");	Finds the first string and replaces it with the second string.	word = "Hello World"; newW = word. replace("World","Friends"); newW will now hold "Hello Friends"
concat("*string1*", "*string2*")	Concatenate will join **string1** and **string2** together. You can have more than two strings.	word1 = "Hello"'; space = " "'; word2 = "World"'; final = word1.concat(word1, space, word2)'; final will now store "Hello World"
String1 + *String2*	+ works in the same way as **concat** on a string and joins two strings together.	word1 = "Hello"; space = " "; word2 = "World"; final = word1 + space + word2; final will now store "Hello World"
toUpperCase()	Converts the string to uppercase.	word = "Hello"; final = word.toUpperCase(); final will now store "HELLO"
toLowerCase()	Converts the string to lowercase.	word = "Hello"; final = word.toLowerCase(); final will now store "hello"
charAt(*number*)	Returns the character in the string at location *number*.	word = "Hello"; letter = word.charAt(4); letter will now store "o"

Table 19.05 - String manipulation.

DISCUSSION POINT

When might you need to alter words in a program? Have you ever needed to capitalise text? Have you ever had to extract some letters or parts of a word? Why was this needed?

Comments

A comment is text that you add to your code, which the interpreter (the software that runs your program) does not run. Comments can be used to make notes about how your code works so other developers can understand what you have done. To add a comment, write //, then anything after will be a comment. For example,

```
var count = 0; //number to act as
    //counter in loop

while(count <= 12){ //loop 0 to 12
    //displaying square numbers

    document.write(count * count);
    //output square numbers

    count++; //increment counter

}
```

299

TASK

1 Create a program that stores the first name, second name and age of a person. Output these in a sentence, for example Roberto Mantovani you are 20 years old.
2 Create a program that stores the first name and second name of a person in variables. Combine and output the first two letters of their first name with the first two letters of their second name.

Arrays

An **array** is a data structure that allows you to store multiple values under one name. It is often represented as a table, with each value given a number with which to access it (known as the array index). For example,

```
var colours = ["orange", "purple",
    "green", "yellow", "grey"];
```

This code declares an array, called `colours`, with five elements. These are shown as a table in Table 19.06.

Index	0	1	2	3	4
Value	orange	purple	green	yellow	grey

Table 19.06 – An array.

Elements can be extracted from this array. For example, the code below would store purple in `myFavColour`:

```
var myFavcolour = colours[1];
```

Elements can be replaced in this array. For example, the code below will replace 'yellow' with 'pink':

```
colours[3] = "pink";
```

Elements can be added to this array. For example, the code below will make a new index, 5, and put 'blue' in it:

```
colours.push("blue");
```

The length of the array can be found. For example, the code below will return 5:

```
var arrayLength = colours.length;
```

TASK

Create an array that stores the names of ten different films. Output each of these films, in turn, on a web page. Each film should be on a new line.

Conditional statements

A conditional statement lets you specify which, if any, statements are to be run.

If

`If` checks a **condition**. If it is true, the first block of code is run:

```
if (5 < 6) {
        message = "Yes it is!";
}
```

The code allocating text to `message` is only carried out if 5 is less than 6.

Else

An `else` gives you an option to run code if the condition is false:

```
if (5 < 6) {
        message = "Yes it is!";
}else{
        message = "No it isn't!";
}
```

If 5 is not less than 6, then the second block of code will be run and the message will be `"No it isn't!"`.

Else if

`Else if` allows you to have multiple conditions that you set to different outcomes. You can have as many else if conditions as you need, and can also combine them with an `else`:

```
if (5 < 6) {
        message = "Yes it is!";
}else if (5==6){
        message = "They're the same";
}else{
        message = "It's smaller";
}
```

Switch

Combining multiple `if`s can get difficult to manage. A `switch` statement is more efficient as it does not perform all of the conditions every time. It can take a variable (or expression) and then check its value against a series of options. These options can be values, as in the example below, or variables:

```
number = 5;

switch(number) {

  case 4;

        message = "It's 4";

        break;

  case 5;

        message = "It's 5";

        break;

  case 6;

        message = "It's 6";

        break;

  default;

        message = "It was none of
        these";

}
```

This statement will take the value stored in the variable **number** and compare it to the first **case** statement, in this code, **case 4**. If it is equal to it, it will write "**It's 4**" into the variable **message**, then run the **break** statement which forces it to break out of the switch statement (i.e. it will not then compare the value with the next **case**).

The **default** catches a value that is not caught by any of the previous **case** statements.

> **TASK**
> 1 Create a web page that has a person's age stored in a variable. Using an **If** statement, output a different message, depending on their age. For example, if they are between 13 and 19: **"You are a teenager"**.
> 2 Change the web page you created in the previous task and this time use a **switch** statement.

Loops

A loop is a **construct** that repeats a set number of times, usually based on a condition.

EXAMPLE

You may want to output a number ten times. Instead of writing the same line of code ten times, you can put it in a loop, which reduces the amount of code.

You may not know how many times some code needs to be run. For example, you want to multiply a number by itself until it is greater than 1000. You will not know, at the start, how many times this code needs to be run.

For

In a **for** loop, you need to know the number of times the loop is to run. The code below adds the value of **total** to itself ten times:

```
for (count = 0; count < 10; count++){
    total = total + total;
}
```

count is a variable that is declared for the loop. It usually counts the number of times a loop is run, although it can be used in other ways. This statement can be excluded if, for example, you want to use a variable that already exists.

The second element, **count < 10**, is the condition. As long as this is true, the loop will run. This code can be excluded, but the **for** loop will run continually unless you include a **break;** within the loop to make it stop.

The third element is what happens at the end of the loop. In this case the variable **count** increments. This statement can be excluded if, for example, you want to change the variable elsewhere within the loop.

The **for** loop shown below will write the first 12 square numbers:

```
for (count = 1; count <= 12; count++){
    document.write(count * count);
}
```

For/in

If you have an object that you need to loop through each element, for example to output them all, you can use a **for/in** loop:

```
var film = {title:"The House",
    genre:"Drama", length:96,
    releaseYear:2013};
```

```
var count;

for (count in film){

        document.write(film[count]);

}
```

This code will output each of the elements within the object `film`.

While

A `while` loop runs the code while a condition is true:

```
var count = 0;

while(count <= 12){

    document.write(count * count);

    count++;

}
```

This loop will display the first 12 square numbers. A counter (`count`) is declared before the loop. The value of this is checked in the condition to see if it is less than or equal to 12. If it is, it enters the loop, otherwise it skips it and jumps to the code below the closing. Within the loop this counter is incremented.

A `while` loop does not need to use a counter. For example,

```
var check = true;

while(check = true){

        document.write("It's true");

}
```

At the moment this loop will run infinitely. While the variable `check` is `true`, it will continue to run. This is a common programming error. The variable would need to change within the loop so that at some stage it is no longer true.

Do/while

In this loop the condition is checked at the end of the loop, which means the loop will always run at least once:

```
var count = 0;

    do{

        document.write(count * count);

        count++;

    }

    while(count <= 12);
```

In this example, `0*0` will always be output, then the value of `count` is checked and it decides if the loop will run again.

TASK
1 Create a web page that has a series of colours stored in an array. Use a loop to go through each element in the array and output it on a new line on the web page.
2 Create a web page that stores a number in a variable. Use a loop to output the 12 times table for this number.
3 Create a web page that stores a number in a variable. Output that number of asterisks (*) on a web page.

Functions

A **function** is a set of instructions that perform a specific task. It is given a name and can take values (parameters), and return values:

```
function addNums(num1, num2){

    return num1 + num2;

}
```

This function:

- has the name `addNums`
- it takes two numbers, `num1` and `num2`
- it adds these together
- it returns the result.

The add function can now be used within the code:

```
var result = addNums (2,3);
```

`num1` is given the value 2, `num2` is given the value 3. The function `addNums` adds these together (5) and returns the result. 5 is now stored in `result`.

A function does not have to take parameters and it does not have to have a return value. For example,

```
function outputNums(){

    document.write(0);

    document.write(1);

}
```

This function can be called with:

```
outputNums();
```

Functions are very useful for removing repeated code, especially when it may need to be repeated at different positions in the program. Rather than rewriting the code (which gives more opportunity for errors), just call the function.

TASK

1 Create a function for each of the three tasks you created at the end of the 'Conditional statements' section. Make sure each one has its own function, then call these functions.
2 Create a function that takes four numbers as parameters. Find the largest of these numbers and output it in an appropriate sentence.
3 Edit the function you created for task 2 and make it find the smallest number.

Iterative methods

An iterative method is a function (or task) that is repeated, for example applied to each element in an array.

Every

This iterative method will check every element in an array against a condition. It will return true if every item meets the condition or false if at least one element does not meet it.

The code below creates a function called `isTen`. Inside the function declaration is (`item, index, array`). These apply to the array being used and provide the value (e.g. 10), the index (e.g. 0) and the array (e.g. numbers) to the function:

```
function isTen(item, index, array){
    return (item == 10);
};
```

An array (`numbers`) is declared, and then the function `isTen` is applied to the array using the **every** method:

```
var numbers = [10, 20, 30, 40, 50, 60];
var everyCheck = numbers.
  every(isTen);
```

This code:

- declares an array called `numbers`
- calls an **every** method and sends the array elements using the code `function(item, index, array)`
- the condition is `item == 10`
- the result of this is returned and stored in the variable `everyCheck`.

It will return false, because not all elements in `numbers` are equal to 10.

EXAMPLE

Write code that checks if every number stored in an array is greater than 0:

```
function isGreaterThan0(item,
index, array){
    return (item > 0);
};
var numbers = [-1, 0, 5, 10];
var everyCheck = numbers.
every(isGreaterThan0);
```

Some

The **some** method checks if at least one item meets the condition:

```
function equalTen(item, index,
array){
    return (item == 10);
};
var numbers = [10, 20, 30, 40, 50,
60];
var someCheck = numbers.
some(equalTen);
```

This time, the method will return true, because at least one of the elements is equal to 10.

Filter

The `filter` method will return an array with all the elements that meet the criteria:

```
function lessThirtyFive(item, index,
array){
    return (item <= 35);
};
var numbers = [10, 20, 30, 40, 50,
60];
var filterArray = numbers.
filter(lessThirtyFive);
```

This time, the method will return [10, 20, 30] because these are all the elements that are less than, or equal to, 35.

303

ForEach

forEach runs a task, or command, on every element within the array. It does not return any value:

```
function addOne(item, index, array){

  item = item + 1;

  document.write(item);

}

var numbers = [10, 20, 30, 40,
50, 60];

numbers.forEach(addOne);
```

This time, the method will take each item, add 1 to it, then output the new value. The actual value stored in the array is not changed.

Map

map runs a task, or command, on every element within the array and returns the new, edited array:

```
function mapOne(item, index, array){

  item = item + 1;

}

var numbers = [10, 20, 30, 40,
50, 60];

var mapArray = numbers.map(mapOne);
```

This time, the method will take each item and add 1 to it. It will return the following edited values that are now stored in mapArray: 11, 21, 31, 41, 51, 61.

04

TASK

1 Create an array with a series of numbers.
   a Create a function that will multiply each number in the array by two and output the result, but do not store the result.
   b Create a function that will multiply each number in an array by ten, store the results and output them.
   c Create a function that will check if any of the numbers are greater than 20.
   d Create a function that will check if all the numbers are greater than 20.
   e Create a function that will return an array with all elements in that are greater than or equal to ten.

Trap errors

Errors can occur in a variety of places in a program and for a variety of reasons. For example, a user may have input invalid data, a calculation may not be possible or on the wrong data type, or the programmer may have made an error themselves.

To trap these errors, try and catch code is used. Within the try block are the statements that are attempting to run. You can throw a specific error message to be output after each statement. The catch block states what to do with the error message if generated:

```
var x = 21;

try{

  if(x>20) throw "over 20";

  if(x<=10) throw "less than 11";

}

catch(e){

  message.innerHTML= e;

}
```

This code checks if the value of x is greater than 20. If it is, it sets the error (e) to be "over 20". If not, it compares it to <= 10. If it is, it sets the error (e) to "less than 11". The catch takes this error, if it is generated, and then displays it. This code can be used to validate data on entry. Using ifs in this way will ensure all conditions are met, whereas a case statement may not catch all possible errors.

Hypertext Markup Language forms and control events

A Hypertext Markup Language (HTML) form lets you combine multiple objects and receive input from the user.

You need to tell HTML that you are creating a form using the <form></form> tag. All the code to display buttons, drop-down boxes etc. then comes within these tags.

An event can occur within the HTML code that can be acted upon by JavaScript, for example a button is pressed. Within the HTML code for these objects, a JavaScript function can be called to perform an action.

Button

The HTML code below will create a button that says "Press me":

```
<button onclick="outputMessage()">Press
me</button>
```

The code states that when the button is clicked, the JavaScript function `outputMessage()` will be called.

This function is then written in JavaScript:

```
function outputMessage(){
    document.write("Hello World");
}
```

When the button is clicked, the message `"Hello World"` will be displayed on the page.

Text box

The HTML code below will create a text box:

```
<input type="text" id="enterColour">
```

In the JavaScript, a function needs to be written to access the text in the text box. In this case it will write it back to the page:

```
function getColour(){
    var colourEntered = document.getElementById("enterColour");
    document.write(colourEntered.value);
}
```

`document.getElementById` refers to an HTML script that has been given a name. In this case the HTML code created a text box named `"enterColour"`.

`.value` will access the data that is currently in the object named `colourEntered`.

Drop-down box

The HTML code below will create a drop-down box called `colours`. It will create a number of options. Each `<option>` will be a new choice in the drop-down box:

```
<select id = "colours">
    <option>purple</option>
    <option>orange</option>
    <option>blue</option>
</select>
```

In the JavaScript, a function needs to be written to access the text in the drop-down box and write it to a set place in the HTML document:

```
function getColour(){
    var obj = document.getElementById("colours");
```

```
    document.write(obj.options[obj.selectedIndex].text);
}
```

The first line in the function takes the name of the element `colours` and stores it in the `obj` variable:

```
var obj = document.getElementById("colours");
```

This saves you typing the text to access the name each time you need it (it would make the line of code very long).

The second line in the function selects the item in the drop-down box that you have selected:

```
obj.options[obj.selectedIndex].text
```

It then displays this in the HTML.

`obj.selectedIndex` accesses the drop-down option you have chosen by a number (the first will be option 0, the second option 1 etc.). `obj.options` returns the full set of options in a drop-down box. Combined, these statements access the selected drop-down option.

Radio button

The HTML code below will create a radio button for each of the colours:

```
<input type="radio" name="colours" id="purple">Purple<br>

<input type="radio" name="colours" id="orange">Orange<br>

<input type="radio" name="colours" id="blue">Blue<br>
```

In the JavaScript, a function needs to be written to access which radio button has been clicked and write it in the document. This function needs to check each of the radio buttons you have created, in turn, to find out which one has been checked. This is done using a loop:

```
function checkColours(){
    var colour = document.forms[0];
    for(i=0; i<3; i++){ //loop through
    //all radio buttons
        if(colour[i].checked){ //check if
        //the current button is selected
```

```
        document.write(colour[i].value);
        //If true, display the id of the
        //button

      }

    }

  }
```

`var colour = document.forms[0]` sets the variable colour to hold the radio buttons.

`colour[i].checked` accesses the `i` radio button (first time through this is 0, then 1) and finds out if it has been selected.

`colour[i].value` gets the ID of the radio button `colour[i]`.

19.02 Pop-up boxes

A pop-up box can be used to display text or information. There are three types of pop-up box: Alert, Confirm and Prompt.

Alert

An alert box only displays text.

```
    e.g. alert("Hello World");
```

Confirm

A confirm box has two options, ok and cancel. The option chosen by the user is returned as a value that can then be used to decide what to do.

e.g.

```
    var answer = confirm ("Ok to proceed?");

    if (answer == true) {

        alert("Ok")

    }else{

        alert("Cancelling")

    }
```

Prompt

A prompt box allows a user to enter some text, and gives them the option of ok and cancel. If ok is selected, then the text input is stored into a variable.

e.g.

```
    var answer = prompt("What day is it?")
```

TASK

1   Create a form that takes a person's first name, second name and favourite number. Create a username for them in a function, using the first letter of their first name, their second name and their favourite number. Output their username in a sentence.

2   Create a web page that stores a number in a variable and asks the user to guess the number. Count how many guesses the person has attempted, and output this after each guess along with whether they were right or wrong.

3   Adapt the code you wrote for task 2 and tell them if their guess was too high or too low.

4   Adapt the code you wrote for task 2 or task 3 and trap errors such as guessing outside bounds that you set, making sure they use a number etc.

5   Create a form that lets the user enter their personal details including name, address and date of birth. Check that the data they have entered is reasonable and catch any errors they may input.

6   Create a form that lets the user choose from a series of options in a drop-down box. Change the text displayed in the web page depending on the option they have chosen.

7   Adapt the code you wrote for task 6, this time letting them choose using a radio button.

19.03 Summary

JavaScript is a programming language that is used in web pages. It can add functionality and interactivity to a web page. A function can be written to perform a task. This can then be called from elsewhere in a program and it can be used multiple times. JavaScript can be used to validate data entry using trap errors.

The code is written in a script tag. Variables can store data and you can change what is in them. A conditional statement, such as `if` or `switch`, lets you decide which code is to be run dependent on a condition. A loop, or **iteration**, will repeat a set of statements a number of times.

Remember

When creating web pages, there are a range of tools and protocols that can be used to add any required interactivity. When deciding which tool, or protocol, you are going to use, consider the appropriateness to the context and the users.

Review questions

1 Izabella is creating a web page for her business. She has been told to use JavaScript to make her web page better. Explain, using an example, how she could make use of JavaScript and the benefits it could have. [**4**]

2 Describe what an array is. [**3**]

3 Explain the benefits of using a function. [**3**]

4 Describe how JavaScript can validate data entry. [**3**]

Glossary

Actuator: this is a type of motor that controls a mechanism or system

Alignment: positioning text so that it is in line, for example on the left, right or centre

Alpha testing: initial testing of the software by a limited group of people

Analogue: this is the smooth stream of data that we process on a daily basis

Animation: a series of images played one after another to simulate movement

Array: a data structure that can store multiple items under one identifier

Artificial intelligence: computer systems that perform tasks that normally require human intelligence

Assignment: providing a value to a variable

Attribute: a category of information within an entity

Bandwidth: the range of frequencies available for a communication method which determines the transmission rate; the amount of data that can be transmitted at one time

Beta testing: a sample of users test a pre-release version of the software

Biometrics: the measurement of a person's physical characteristics; unique physical characteristic of a person that can be used by a computer for identification purposes

Bitmap: an image made up of small squares, called pixels. Each individual pixel can only be one colour

Bit rate: the number of bits that can be transferred per second

Black box testing: testing of inputs and outputs to a system or part of a system with no consideration for the workings of the system

Bluetooth: a short range wireless communication standard

Bridge: connects two LANs

Broadband: a method of faster data transmission that can carry several channels of data at once

CAD: computer-aided design

CAM: computer-aided manufacture

Cell: a rectangle within a spreadsheet where data can be positioned; the geographical area covered by a radio transmitter

Chaining: combining together instructions

Circuit switching: a single communication path is opened for the duration of data transmission

Client: a computer that is connected to a server

Closure: completion of a project

Cloud computing: using remote servers hosted on the internet to store data

Coding: representing data by assigning a code to it for classification or identification

Collaboration: working together

Compiler: translates high-level programming language into an executable file in machine code

Composite key: two or more fields that form the primary key

Conception: start of a project

Condition: a statement that can be evaluated as true or false, for example 5 > 6

Confidential: needs to be kept secret

Construct: a control structure, such as a loop or a conditional statement

Critical path: the tasks which must be completed on time for a project to complete on time

Custom-written: software that is written especially to meet the requirements of a client

Data: raw numbers, letters, symbols, sounds or images without meaning

Database: a structured method of storing data

Database management system: software used to manage a database

Data dictionary: metadata (information) about the database

Data type: the type of data being stored, for example a number, string (text)

Demographic: a particular section of a population

Design specification: illustration of how the system will look, what the data structures will be and how the system will work

Device: a hardware component of a computer system consisting of electronic components

DFD: data flow diagram which shows how data moves around a system

Diagnosis: identifying a problem or illness by analysis of the symptoms

Digital divide: the separation between those that have access to technologies and the internet and those that do not

Direct data source: data that is collected for the purpose for which it will be used

DPI/dots per inch: the resolution of an image

Dynamic data: data that changes automatically without user intervention

Ecommerce: business that is conducted electronically

Economic: relating to a country in terms of their production and consumption of goods and services

Encoding: storing data in a specific format

Encryption: scrambling data so it cannot be understood without a decryption key so that it is unreadable if intercepted

Entity: a set of data about one thing (person, place, object or event)

Entity relationship diagram: a diagram that represents the relationships between entities

Execution: the development stage of a project

Export: to prepare data for use in another application

Fibre optic: a fine strand of glass that transmits data as light beams

Field: a category of information; a common word for attribute; an individual item of data in a database, for example forename

Filter: selecting records from the source file based on conditions; an effect, often colour related, that can be applied to a clip

Firewall: prevents external users gaining unauthorised access to a computer system

Flat file: a database stored in a single table

Foreign key: a field in a table that refers to the primary key in another table

Formula: a mathematical calculation using $+$, $-$, $\times$ or $\div$

Frame: one screen, or page, where an image is drawn. A series of these frames are played one after the other to create the animation

Function: a separate piece of code that has an identifier and performs a task, it can be called from elsewhere in the code and returns a value; a ready-made formula representing a complex calculation

Gantt chart: a chart used for planning a project

Gateway: connects two different types of networks

GPS: global positioning system which uses satellites to determine the current location

Hardware: a physical component of a computer system

Heuristic: discovering knowledge through experience

HTTPS: hypertext transfer protocol secure

Hub: connects devices on a network in a passive manner

Humidity: the amount of water in the atmosphere

Hyperlink: a link that can be clicked to locate to another place in a document, or a different document entirely

Identifier: a name given to a variable or function

Import: to bring in data from another application

Indirect data source: data that was collected for a different purpose (secondary source)

Information: data with context and meaning

Infrared/IR: a wave of light that is invisible to the naked human eye, emitted by an object; used by remote controls

Infrastructure: the physical structures that are needed for a service or operation

Input device: a device that allows data to be entered into a computer system

Internet service provider/ISP: A company that provides access to the internet

Interpreter: translates high-level programming language into machine code one line of source code at a time

Iteration: a loop, to repeat

Key: a sequence or algorithm used to encrypt or decrypt data

Key frame: a frame that has a change in the animation, for example a drawing has changed, or the start or end of a tween

Knowledge: information to which human experience has been applied

LAN: local area network which connects devices in a single building or area

Laser: an intense beam of light used for transmitting data

Layer: an object or image given its own timeline for independent manipulation

Legitimate: looks like the real standard a document would have

Mail merge: the automatic addition of data, such as names and addresses, from a source file into a master document, such as a letter

Maintenance: changes made to a system after its implementation

Malicious code: code that is intended to harm a computer

Malware: malicious software

Management information system: a system that provides summary data for management to enable them to make decisions

Master document: the main document that will be used for all records

Message switching: a method of transmitting data through intelligent nodes

Microprocessor: an integrated circuit used in monitoring and control technologies

Microwave: an electromagnetic wave of energy

Model: a representation of a process

Morphing: another term for shape tweening. One image changes into another image

Network: a set of computers and devices connected together so they can communicate and share resources

Network architecture: the design of a network

NFC: near field communication

NIC: network interface card which connects the motherboard of a device to a network cable

Non-volatile: data remains when there is no power

Normal form: the extent to which a database has been normalised

Normalisation: process of structuring data in a database

Object: an image, or combination of images, that is manipulated as one item

Off-the-shelf: general purpose software available to a large market

Opacity: the lack of transparency in an image, or part of an image

Operating system: software that manages the hardware within a computer system

Operator: a symbol, or set of symbols that performs an image

Orientation: the direction of text, for example horizontal or vertical

Output device: a device used to communicate data or information from a computer system

Packet: a set of bits which represent data to be transmitted

Packet switching: data that is broken down into packets are sent through different routes and reassembled by the recipient

Parameter: data used within the criteria for a query

Peer: a computer in a network that is not connected to a server and does not control another computer

Photoresistor: this is a light controlled resistor

Piezoresistance: a specific level of electrical charge that is linked to a specific level of resistance or pressure

Pitch: the highness or lowness of a tone

Pixel: a very small square of one colour that is illuminated on a display screen. These are combined to create a bitmap image

Pixelate: when a bitmap image is enlarged, the pixels are enlarged and become visible causing the image to appear blurry

Predecessor: a task in a project that must be completed before another task can start

Primary key: a field that contains the unique identifier for a record

Private key: used in encryption to decrypt data

Prompt: a question asked to the user which requires a response

Proof reading: checking information manually

Protocol: a set of rules that ensure data is transferred between devices correctly

Prototype: a 'mock-up' of a software or manufactured solution

Public key: used in encryption to encrypt data

Query: a question used to retrieve data from a database

RAD: rapid application development

Record: a common word for entity

Referential integrity: data in the foreign key of the table on the many side of a relationship must exist in the primary key of the table on the one side of a relationship

Relationship: the way in which two entities in two different tables are connected

Rendering: combining the effects created in a video file to create an output video file

Repeater: amplifies the signal on a network cable

Requirements specification: what a user needs a new system to do

Resolution: the number of pixels per measurement of the image, for example DPI

RFID: radio-frequency identification

Router: a switch which can forward data to the correct location in the most efficient manner

Satellite: an object in space that follows an orbital path

Sensor: a device that records data about the surrounding physical environment

Server: a computer on a network which provides resources that can be used by client devices

Simulation: using a model to predict real-life behaviour

Software: programs which give instructions to the computer

Source file: the file containing the data that will be merged into the master document

Spyware: malicious software that records what a user is doing on a computer system

Static data: data that does not normally change

Storage device: a device used to store data onto a storage medium

Storage medium: the medium on which data is stored

Streaming: a method of displaying sound or video without waiting for the whole file to be downloaded

Switch: connects devices on a network in an active manner

System flowchart: an overview of how a system works in a diagrammatic format

System specification: the hardware and software needed to run the system

Table: a set of similar data (about people, places, objects or events)

TCP/IP: a communication protocol used by the internet

Teleworking: working from home using technologies to keep in contact with an employer

Test data: data that will be used for testing a system

Track: a single audio section in a sound or video file

Transaction: a collection of data that is exchanged; the action of buying or selling an item or service

Transition: the movement from one clip to the next

Tunnelling protocol: a tunnel between two points on a network that is governed by a set of rules

Tween: an animation where the start and end points are set. The computer generates the actual changes to make the animation smooth

User interface: communication between the user and the computer system

Utility software: software that performs some sort of maintenance on the computer system

Validation: the process of checking data matches acceptable rules

Variable: a space in memory that is given an identifier where data can be stored and changed

Vector: an image that uses geometric points and shapes. Calculations are used to draw the image

Verification: ensuring data entered into the system matches the original source

Verify: to check that data matches the original data

Virus: software that replicates itself between computer systems and is designed to cause disruption to a computer system

Volatile: data is lost when there is no power

WAN: wide area network which connects devices that are geographically remote

Web browser: a software application for retrieving and presenting information on the World Wide Web

White box testing: testing the whole system in terms of structure and logic covering all paths through the system

Wi-Fi: wireless Ethernet which allows devices on a LAN to connect wirelessly

Wireless access point: connects Wi-Fi enabled devices to a network

WNIC: wireless network interface card which enables a device to use Wi-Fi

Chapter 1 - Data, information, knowledge and processing

1 For example 000000 (there must be no explanation, just the data).

2 For example, context is added to 000000 because we are told it is a colour code. Meaning is added by telling us it is the colour code for black.

3 Knowledge is applying experience to information so that the information can be interpreted.

4 Area calculator, Length =, Width=, Area=, m, m2 (not 3, 5 or 15).

5 15 (not 3, 5).

6 Measure it himself.

7 Accept measurements given by the customer.

8 He can rely on the measurements he has taken himself to be accurate.

9 Accuracy, relevance, age, level of detail, completeness.

10 The user guide could be written for an old operating system that has since been updated.

11 Saving storage space, enables validation, can help with presentation of lists, speed of input, speed of processing, confidentiality.

12 Computers can only understand on and off (1 and 0), so text needs to be encoded into a standard character set that uses numbers represented by binary.

13 Sample rate, bit depth, number of channels.

14 WELL DONE.

15 To ensure data that is input matches the source data.

16 Presence, range, type, length, format, check digit, lookup.

17 Data can match the rules but still be incorrect (e.g. date of birth of 29/1/13 matches the rule of a data type but it may be that the date should have been 29/1/03). Data can be checked against the source, but the source maybe incorrect (e.g. the name 'Siohan' is written on the original source and is visually checked to have been entered as 'Siohan', but the actual spelling should have been 'Siobhan').

Review questions

1 E.g. 573dds [1]. If further explanation given then 0 marks.

2 Either of the following [1]: Understanding information [1] a person's experience/learning [1].

3a Any combination of the following [4]: Static data does not change [1] whereas dynamic data changes automatically [1].

Static data can get out of date [1] whereas dynamic data updates when the data source is updated [1].

Static data can be viewed offline [1] whereas dynamic data requires network connectivity [1].

Static data is more likely to be accurate [1] whereas dynamic data may contain errors if produced quickly [1].

3b Any two of the following [4]: accuracy [1] data that contains errors is not of good quality [1].

Relevance [1] data must be useful for the purpose it will be used [1].

Age [1] data must be up to date [1].

Level of detail [1] too much detail makes it difficult to find the required information [1].

Completeness [1] missing data such as a postcode for an address [1].

3c E.g. FT for full-time [1].

3d The video will be downloaded over the internet [1] so file size needs to be reduced as bandwidth will be limited [2].

3e Any three from the following [1]: Width/height/resolution; frame rate; audio sample rate; audio bit depth; audio channels; compression.

3f Any of the following [4]: Image size, the wider and taller the image the higher the file size.

4a Any combination of the following [4]: Credit card information is sensitive [1] because it could be used for fraud [1] HTTPS is an encrypted method of passing information over the web [1] which will mean the credit card information will be scrambled [1] and unusable by anybody without a key [1].

4b The sender and receiver use the same encryption/decryption key [1].

4c Any two of the following [2]: The sender uses the public key of the recipient to encrypt the message [1] The message is sent in an encrypted format [1] The recipient uses their private key to decrypt the message [1] The sender and recipient need to exchange digital certificates [1].

4d Either of the following [1]: The user could be asked to enter their password twice [1] the user could type their password and then visually check it [1].

5a To ensure that data matches a given set of rules [1].

5b Any of the following [3]: E.g. presence check [1] to ensure news story [1] is present [1]. E.g. format check [1] to ensure email address [1] contains @ symbol [1].

Chapter 2 - Hardware and Software

1 A physical component of a computer system.

2 Carries out calculations/logical operations; executes instructions; processes data.

3 Generates signals needed to display output to a monitor.

4 RAM is volatile meaning that data is lost when power is disconnected, whereas storage is non-volatile so data is retained when power is disconnected. RAM stores currently active programs and data, whereas storage stores both active and non-active programs and data. RAM is much faster than storage devices; storage devices can store more data than RAM.

5 Both a digital camera and a scanner can take pictures of objects and turn them into a digital picture. A digital camera is mainly used to take photographs, whereas a scanner is mainly used to digitise 2D documents. A digital camera can zoom into objects, whereas a scanner can only take images at a set distance. A digital camera uses a focal point, whereas a scanner takes an even focus across the whole document. A digital camera captures an image in one go, whereas a scanner has to digitise an image by moving across it.

6 An OMR will be able to read multiple choice answers that have been completed in specified positions and will read them accurately with very little margin of error. An OCR would also be able to read multiple choice answers, but the process would be slower using a conventional scanner. An OMR would not be able to read written answers to questions as it relies on marks being given. An OCR could read written answers to questions and turn them into text, but poor handwriting could be illegible and the OCR would not be able to interpret the answers.

In conclusion, a specially designed scanner that can detect when it needs to read lozenge marks for multiple choice answers combined with more detailed scanning for OCR of text would be suitable.

7 System software maintains or operates the computer system whereas application software carries out tasks for the user.

8 Allocating memory to software; sending data and instructions to output devices; responding to input devices such as when a key is pressed; opening and closing files on storage devices; giving each running task a fair share of processor time; sending error messages or status messages to applications or users; dealing with user logins and security.

9 Users are usually already familiar with word processing software so they can create a website quickly using tools with which they have experience. However, some tools required for website features will not be available, for example forms validation, and so the web page will be limited to the capability of the word processor. Web authoring software can be quite complex to use but there are plenty of user friendly applications available to use now. Web authoring software will include specialist tools such as setting up the website structure and creating a navigation bar automatically, whereas using a word processor will require a lot of work to set up all the navigation on each page. Web authoring software will include a file transfer feature to publish and update the information, whereas in a word processor this would have to be done using separate file transfer software. In conclusion, although web authoring software can take a while to master, it is the only suitable tool for creating a full website because of the specialist features it includes.

10 To carry out additional tasks that the original software is not capable of doing, to simplify tasks that are complex using the original software.

11 Light text on a dark background or vice versa, such as white on dark blue, should be used so that users can easily read the text against the background; bright colours can be used to highlight important information so that the user's attention is drawn to it; colours in the user's mental model should be used appropriately, such as green for go or yellow for warning, so that the user is not confused by colours they expect to mean something different.

12 Anti-virus; backup; data compression; disk defragmentation; format; file-copying; deleting.

13 To stop viruses or malware from being executed and causing damage to files and programs.

14 Software that already exists and is readily available to be purchased.

15 The client has to wait a long time for it to be developed; it is expensive because the client has to cover the whole development cost; the software won't have been used by other customers before so bugs are likely to be found when the software is used; the only support available will be from the company that developed the software.

16 To translate source code into object code ready for execution.

17 When testing a program, an interpreter can translate just the code that is being tested which saves translation time; source code can be translated into object code for more than one operating system.

Review questions

1a Connects the main components of the computer together [1].

1b HDD or SSD [1].

1c Any from [2]: So she can connect a monitor to the computer [1] in order to see the display output that is generated from the computer [1].

2 Any combination of the following [4]: She can purchase as little or as much backup storage as necessary [1] based on the amount of data she has stored [1]; the back-up process can be automated [1] as long as she is always connected to the internet [1]; she will not need to transport data off-site [1] because it will already be off-site in the cloud [1].

3 Any combination of the following [6]: Magnetic tape can store several terabytes of data [1] which is required for all the servers [1] and user data from 500 employees [1]. Magnetic tape is small and lightweight which means it is portable [1] so it can be taken off-site [1] so it is not at the same location as the original data [1]. Magnetic tape is the cheapest storage medium [1] meaning that several tapes can be used [1] to backup data using a tape rotation system [1].

4 Any combination of the following [4]: The surveys could use multiple choice questions [1] which can be read by an optical mark reader by identifying the dark areas [1]. There will be lots of surveys [1] and an OMR will have an automatic document feeder to input all the surveys in one go [1].

5 Any combination of the following [6]: Custom-written software will meet all of the requirements for waste management [1] because it is written especially for the council [1]. Custom software can be designed especially to be compatible with existing systems [1] such as the web interface used by residents [1]. Custom-written software will be very expensive [1] compared with off-the-shelf software [1]. The council will have to wait a few months [1] for the system to be developed for them [1]. There may be very good alternative off-the-shelf solutions [1] which would be able to be used instantly [1] at a much lower cost [1] and with a lot of support available [1]. In conclusion, the council should investigate existing off-the-shelf solutions before committing to the cost and development time of a custom written solution [1].

6a Both of the following [2]: Videos can be clipped [1]; Titles can be added [1].

6b Both of the following [2]: The council could remove parts of the raw footage that contained mistakes [1]; The council could put a title of the information video at the beginning [1].

Chapter 3 - Monitoring and control

Review questions

1 Any combination of the following [2]:

- An input device that records data about the environment or surroundings.
- Automatically inputs the data into a computer system to be processed.
- Can monitor a range of aspects such as light, temperature, pressure, moisture and humidity.

2 Any two of the following [4]:
- An infrared (motion) sensor can be used …
- … monitors infrared energy emitted and can detected an increase from an intruder.
- A pressure sensor (switch) can be used …
- … can sense a change in weight of an intruder entering a building.

3 Any two from the following [4]:

- Sensors can be placed in areas that are dangerous for a human to enter …
- … this means that crucial elements of the system, such as areas of radiation, can be measured and controlled from a safe distance.
- Sensors can take readings 24/7 …
- … this means that humans do not need to be present in the plant at all time to monitor processes and can just be alerted to a crisis situation, should one arise.
- Sensor readings will have a higher level of accuracy and consistency …
- … in an environment where the accuracy of readings is paramount due to safety, this is vital.

4 Level of response:

Level 3 [5–6 marks]

Candidates will address a range of household appliances and evaluate their use in terms of monitoring and controls systems. The points raised will be justified. There will be a reasoned conclusion.

The information will be relevant, clear, organised and presented in a structured and coherent format.

Level 2 [3–4 marks]

Candidates will address a limited range of household appliances and look at their use in terms of monitoring and controls systems, although development of some of the points will be limited. There will be a conclusion. For the most part the information will be relevant and presented in a structured and coherent format.

Level 1 [1–2 marks]

Candidates may only give reference to a single household appliance, with limited reference to monitoring and control systems. Answers may be simplistic with little or no relevance.

0 marks for a response with no valid comments.

Possible points:

- Increased safety for appliances.
- Appliances can be made more efficient.
- It may be possible to remotely control devices.

5 Any combination of the following [4]:

- Motion sensors could be used to control light systems …
- … this would mean that lights would turn off automatically when a room is unused, making it more energy efficient.
- Temperature sensors could be used to control the air conditioning system …
- … the system could be turned off when the room reaches the desired temperate and turned back on again when it falls outside of this, making it more energy efficient.
- Pressure sensors could be used on windows …
- … this would detect if a window is open and turn off an air conditioning system to save energy if it is.

Chapter 4 - E-safety and health and safety

Review questions

1. Mention six points from the following (maximum four marks for each term) [6]:

Phishing

- A legitimate-looking email is sent to the user.
- The email contains a link for the user to click.
- The link will redirect the user to a legitimate-looking website.
- The website will request personal data that will be stolen when entered.

Pharming

- Malicious code is installed on the user's hard drive or server.
- A user will type in a common web address, but will be redirected to a fake website instead.
- Unaware, the user enters their personal details in the fake website and the details are stolen.

2. Any two of the following two points [2]:

- It restricts a user's access to the files on their computer.
- It restricts the files access to the files either by locking the system or encrypting the files.
- A ransom message will appear when access is attempted requesting payment for access.

3. Answer must include the following points [3]:

- It is a bot that is automated to carry out a simple or repetitive task.
- The tasks it carries out will be party to criminal activity, such as bombarding mail boxes with SPAM email.

4. Level of response:

Level 3 [5–6 marks]

Candidates will discuss in detail the need to keep personal data safe. The points raised will be justified. There will be a reasoned conclusion. The information will be relevant, clear, organised and presented in a structured and coherent format.

Level 2 [3–4 marks]

Candidates will provide limited discussion of points about keeping personal data safe, the development of some of the points will be limited. There will be a conclusion. For the most part the information will be relevant and presented in a structured and coherent format.

Level 1 [1–2 marks]

Candidates may only give reference to a single aspect of safety. Answers may be simplistic with little or no relevance.

0 marks for a response with no valid comments.

Possible points:

- Personal data is very valuable and for this reason people will put a lot of effort into stealing it.
- A perpetrator can steal a person's identity through collecting their personal data/identify fraud.
- A person could also suffer personal attacks such as blackmail or cyberbullying if they reveal, or have stolen, certain personal information that could be used against them.
- Even small amounts of data released on social media over a period of time can be pieced together for criminal activity.

5. Any two of the following injuries and prevention methods [4]:

- Repetitive strain injury can occur from repetitive moments such as clicking a mouse …
- … this can be prevented through the use of support devices such as wrist rests.
- Carpel tunnel syndrome can occur through repetitive or continual movements …
- … this can be prevented by taking regular breaks in work sessions/varying the position used for work.
- Back ache can occur from poor posture …
- … this can be prevented by sitting on an adjustable chair with added support.
- Eye strain can occur as a result of looking at a monitor for long periods of time …
- … this can be prevented by using any settings a monitor has to aid prevention/focussing on points away from the screen periodically.
- Deep vein thrombosis can occur when pressure is put on the legs from sitting for long periods …
- … this can be prevented by standing regularly and moving around periodically.

6. Any two of the following safety issues and prevention methods [4]:

- Fire can occur from equipment overheating/overloaded socket …

317

- ... this can be prevented by keeping the room well ventilated.
- ... this can be prevented by not plugging in too many devices to a socket, especially those that require lots of power.
- Trailing wire can cause injury to a person who trips over them ...
- ... this can be prevented by securing wires in a cable management system.
- Electric shock can occur from spilt drinks/ touching wires together ...
- ... this can be prevented by not eating or drinking at a computer.
- ... this can be prevented by an inexperienced user not handling wires.
- ... this can be prevented by having regular electrical safety checks carried out.

Chapter 5 - The Digital divide

Review questions

1. Answer must include the following points [3]:
   - The technology divide between countries, demographic groups and areas.
   - It concerns the availability of modern technology.
   - It can include the divide caused by age, status and location.

2. Level of response:

   Level 3 [6–8 marks]

   Candidates will discuss in detail a range of points describing how a country can be affected by the digital divide. The points raised will be justified. There will be a reasoned conclusion. The information will be relevant, clear, organised and presented in a structured and coherent format.

   Level 2 [3–5 marks]

   Candidates will provide limited discussion of points describing how a country can be affected by the digital divide, the development of some of the points will be limited. There will be a conclusion. For the most part the information will be relevant and presented in a structured and coherent format.

Level 1 [1–2 marks]

Candidates may only give reference to a single aspect of the digital divide. Answers may be simplistic with little or no relevance.

0 marks for a response with no valid comments.

Possible points:

- Can prevent access to further education such as online courses and training.
- Can affect entertainment experiences if connections are too slow.
- Can prevent effective communication.
- Can prevent the ability to be competitive in trading and ecommerce.

3. Any two of the following strategies with explanation [4]:
   - Improving the infrastructure that is currently in place ...
   - ... this will provide better access for more people and improve the level of aspects, such as using technology for entertainment.
   - Getting the technologies of those upgrading recycled for use by those who do not have access ...
   - ... this will improve the access to online services such as education and training.
   - Setting up cyber cafes in both urban and more remote areas ...
   - ... this can provide some access to those who cannot afford regular access to the benefits of technology, such as online learning.
   - Setting up community teach programs ...
   - ... this can help those who do not know how to use the technology gain an understanding in a friendly environment.

Chapter 6 - Using networks

Review questions

1. Any four of the following points [4]:
   - LAN covers a small geographical area ...
   - ... WAN covers a large geographical area.
   - LAN normally uses infrastructure owned by the individual or organisation ...
   - ... WAN can often use infrastructure owned by a third party.
   - LAN will normally have a faster data transfer rate, up to 16Gb ...

- … WAN normally has a lower rate of data transfer, up to 200Mb.

2. Any four of the following points [4]:

   - It is a privately owned network that uses internet technologies.
   - It is used internally within an organisation.
   - It often accessed using a webpage.
   - It can provide services such as news updates, file sharing and instant messaging.
   - It can provide access to training materials for employees.

3. Choose four of the following points (at least one advantage and one disadvantage) [4]:

   - Uses an additional level of security when transmitting data …
   - … this means that the user can feel their personal data is safer when being transmitted.
   - They use the infrastructure that is already in place …
   - … this means that there is little additional cost to setting up a VPN.
   - … this can mean that the performance of the infrastructure is outside the control of the individual or organisation.
   - They require a higher level of expertise to set up …
   - … if this expertise is not present it may need to be purchased.

4. Answer must include both of the following [2]:

   - The internet is the physical infrastructure of the largest WAN.
   - The WWW is a collection of webpages that contain text, images, videos and sounds.

5. Any combination of four from the following [4]:

   - Desktop computer/laptop/mobile device
   - Webcam
   - Microphone
   - Monitor
   - Speakers
   - Network infrastructure.

6. Level of response:

   Level 3 [5–6 marks]

   Candidates will discuss in detail a range of points about the impact of video conferencing on education. The points raised will be justified. There will be a reasoned conclusion. The information will be relevant, clear, organised and presented in a structured and coherent format.

   Level 2 [3–4 marks]

   Candidates will provide limited discussion of points about the impact of video conferencing on education. The development of some of the points will be limited. There will be a conclusion. For the most part the information will be relevant and presented in a structured and coherent format.

   Level 1 [1–2 marks]

   Candidates may only give reference to a single aspect of video conferencing and its use in education. Answers may be simplistic with little or no relevance.

   0 marks for a response with no valid comments.

   Possible points:

   - Learners can participate in conversation with other learners world wide.
   - learners can speak to and listen to industry experts without the need for travel.
   - Learners can benefit from watching international lectures to experience a range of teaching methods.
   - Experts can instruct those in training in important educational training, such as medical procedures.

Chapter 7 - Expert systems

Review questions

1. Any six points from the following (2 marks maximum per component) [6]:

   - The knowledge base …
   - … a database that allows the storage and retrieval of the knowledge gathered from experts.
   - … contains both factual knowledge and heuristic knowledge.
   - The inference engine …
   - … the component that makes judgements and carries out reasoning.

- … based upon a set of rules and follows a line of logic.
- … chains together IF-THEN rules to form a line of reasoning.
- … can use either forward chaining or backwards chaining to draw a conclusion.
- The user interface …
- … is the method used by the user to interact with the system.

2. Two expert systems and its use from the following [4]:

- As a medical diagnosis tool …
- … it can help a doctor narrow down a diagnosis by providing a list of possible diagnoses from the symptoms.
- As a car mechanical diagnosis tool …
- … a car mechanic can connect a car electronically to the system and all elements of the car can be tested to find the fault.
- As a telephone helpdesk …
- … to help narrow down the reason for a customer's call to direct them to the right person.
- As a troubleshooting tool …
- … can obtain a description of a fault that has occurred with hardware, such as a printer, and provide a diagnosis and information on how to fix the error.

3. Any combination of four from the following (advantages) [4]:

- They can help provide information that is outside a user's knowledge and experience …
- … this can help a user solve a problem that they may not have the knowledge to do so otherwise.
- They will not forget to ask question or be subject to other human errors …
- … this means that all the data required to draw a conclusion can be obtained and will be consistent.
- They do not require a human to be present to answer questions …
- … this means they can be made available to use 24/7.

Any combination of two from the following (disadvantages) [2]:

- They are not able to use common sense …

- … this means they can only provide a logical answer to a question and not a creative one.
- Errors may be present in the knowledge bases …
- … this can result in incorrect conclusions being drawn.

4. Choose four from the following points [4]:

- An online processing system processes data in transactions …
- … whereas a real-time processing system process data as soon as it is input.
- Online processing systems are often used in booking systems, where all the data for the transaction can be collected and then processed …
- … whereas real-time processing systems are used when the immediacy of the data is vital, such as air traffic control systems.

5. Any combination of two from the following points [2]:

- A collection of fields about a main element of a data system.
- Stores all of the more permanent data about the customer/employee.
- A transaction file is normally used to update a master file.

Chapter 8 - Spreadsheets

1. The named range can be referenced directly by name instead of by cell references; it can be used as an absolute reference when replicating a lookup function.

2. A formula is a simple calculation using basic arithmetic of $+, -, \times, \div$, whereas a function is a predefined complex calculation that can be called by name and includes a series of formulae of which the user is unaware.

3. The user could read each cell in a row and compare each cell with the source data. When finished reading the row, the user would move to the next row and repeat the process.

4. When formulae and functions are replicated, absolute cell references remain the same, whereas relative cell references change in relation to the row or column.

5 A tax rate could be stored in a single cell. A set of prices would be stored in a column. When calculating the tax to be applied to the first price in the column, the price would be a relative reference (e.g. B3) and the tax rate would be an absolute reference (e.g. F1). These two references would be multiplied together and then replicated down the spreadsheet. B3 would change to B4, B5 and so on as it is replicated to each row below, but F1 would remain the same.

6 Line, because it shows how data has changed over a period of time.

7 Pie, because it is showing each piece of data in proportion to the rest of the data.

8 The ability to change variables within the software; asking what-if questions to see what the result of changing variables might be; formulae and functions to carry out the mathematical calculations that form the basis of the model; automatic recalculation of formulae and functions; rules that define how the model behaves; layers of abstraction so that different parts of the model can be viewed and analysed separately.

9 Variables can be used to change the rental costs; formulae and functions can be used to calculate the total cost of each of the premises; graphs can be used to show the distances from important locations for each of the premises; goal-seek can be used to find out what the rental cost would need to be to match the current costs; conditional formatting could be used to show the cheapest and most expensive options.

10 Fuel costs can be saved by not having to fly real aircraft; wear and tear of aircraft does not take place during training which saves on maintenance costs; instructors do not need to be present for all training sessions; unforeseen or dangerous circumstances can be invoked to test the pilot's reaction without experiencing the real danger.

11 The learner driver does not get to experience the real reaction of a car; the simulator is only as good as the model it is based upon meaning that the simulator will not react exactly the same as a car would.

Review questions

1a Horizontal set of cells [1] e.g. for one car [1].

1bi Either of the following [1]: Arithmetic calculation [1] plus, minus, divide, multiply [1].

1bii E2*4.55 [1].

1biii Any of the following [1]: Complex calculation [1] reserved word in spreadsheet [1] ready-made formula [1].

1biv Lookup or vlookup or hlookup or index [1].

2a Two of the following [2]: Select column D [1] apply a filter [1] of fuel type = petrol [1].

2b Any two of the following [2]: Apply conditional formatting [1] to fuel type column [1] where diesel, petrol and lpg are each set to a different colour [1].

3 Any combination of the following [4]: Relative referencing used for cost per gallon [1] so when the formula is replicated [1] it refers to the cost per litre on the next row down [1]. Absolute referencing used for the fuel type table [1] within the lookup function for cost per litre [1] so that when replicated down the lookup function keeps referencing the fuel type table [1].

4a Any three of the following [3]: Variables can be used to change the distances travelled [1] what-if questions can be asked such as "what will be the cost if the car travels 300 miles?" [1] formulae and functions can be used to calculate the total cost [1] graphs and charts can be used to compare the costs of each car [1] formulae and functions will automatically recalculate so results can be seen instantly [1] conditional formatting can be used to show cars that cost a specific amount [1] goal-seek can be used to find out the optimum speed to travel at [1].

4b Any one of the following [1]: The model will only be as good as the rules [1] the speed the car is travelling at will need to be taken into account [1] unforeseen circumstances such as traffic jams will affect the costs [1].

5 Any combination of the following [4]: Dangers such as hazards, other cars, pedestrians etc can be avoided [1] because the simulator can model these instead of using the real road [1]. Learners do not always need to have an instructor present [1] because the simulator does not pose any danger [1]. Learners can experience circumstances they may not normally encounter [1] such as a child running into the road [1] because these can be modelled [1]. The learner can practice complex manoeuvers without holding up other road users [1] because the simulator can model the presence of other traffic [1].

Chapter 9 - Database and file concepts

1 A field that is a unique identifier for each record.

2 Simple query uses one criterion, whereas a complex query can use multiple criteria.

3 To allow the user to decide the parameter value of the query, such as choosing the class for which to display student records.

4 Decide the file format; decide whether to use fixed length or variable length fields; decide whether to include field names; decide where to save the file.

5 Referential integrity is a form of lookup validation that ensures data exists in a related table. It is important because it prevents data from being entered that is not valid and that does not have any related data, so it ensures data is linked. For example, an order must have a customer. If a customer that does not exist is entered, then this can create mismatched orders which can be lost because they are not linked to the customer.

6 Non-atomic data; no repeating groups of data; unique primary key.

7 No attributes can be dependent on a non-key attribute.

8 Duplicate data is removed from a database, which reduces the database size and removes the potential for errors and inconsistencies; the database will perform better because searches can be carried out on indexed fields; maintenance tasks such as rebuilding indexes can be completed more quickly because there is no longer any redundant data; the database is more flexible because it is easy to add new fields to tables without affecting other columns and new tables can be added without affecting existing tables.

9 Any three data dictionary components listed with related description e.g. field size is the maximum length of data for a field.

10 Text

Date/Time

Date/Time

Text

Integer

Text

Boolean/Logical.

11 Starts with zeros and numbers can't start with zero; may contain spaces, which requires a text data type which allows spaces; may contain hyphens or brackets, which can't be stored as a number data.

12 Different software applications store files in different ways and so generic file types are needed to transfer data between software applications.

13 Read through the index until the required data is found in the key column; identify the corresponding storage address; go directly to the storage address; read sequentially until the record is found.

14 Sequential access requires the data to be stored in order, which is a problem when new records need to be added and old records are deleted, whereas direct access does not require a sequential order and so new records can be added using a hashing algorithm and found again using the same hashing algorithm.

15 Collates data from databases and other sources; interconnects data from different sources; analyses data to provide the data that is required by management; produces summary reports and charts for managers that will help with decision making.

Review questions

1a All of the following [3]: Charity [1]; Donor [1]; Donation [1].

1b Both of the following [2]: One charity has many donations [1]; One donor makes many donations [1].

1c Both of the following [2]: Each donation will need to be for a charity that already exists and from a customer that already exists [1]. This will prevent donations from unknown donors or to unknown charities and therefore ensure the money gets to where it needs to go [1].

2a Both of the following [2]: Apartment ID [1] ; Customer ID [1].

2bi Alphanumeric or text or string [1].

2bii Boolean [1].

2biii Integer [1].

2c Any combination of the following [4]: Query would include all three tables [1]; dynamic parameter would be used for the Apartment ID or Apartment Name [1]; dynamic parameters would be used to compare the start date and end date [1]; the names of the customers would be included as fields in the query [1].

2d Both of the following [2]: Complex queries have two or more criteria [1]; there are three criteria for Apartment ID, start date and end date [1].

2e Any three of the following [6]: Field names [1] to identify each field [1]; validation rules [1] to restrict data entry for each field [1]; relationships [1] between each table [1]; primary keys [1] which are unique to each table [1]; data types [1] to define the type of data that is stored in each field eg alphanumeric [1].

3 All of the following [4]: STUDENT (Student ID, Forename, Surname, Address 1, Address 2, Address 3, ZIP, Telephone, Tutor Group) [1].

TUTOR (Tutor Group, Forename, Surname) [1]

LOAN (Book ID, Student ID, Return Date) [1]

BOOK (Book ID, Title) [1].

4 Both of the following [2]: Proprietary formats are used by manufacturers of software applications for their applications only [1] whereas open-source file formats can be used by any application that supports them [1].

Chapter 10 - Sound and video editing

Review questions

1. Choose any four of the following [4]:
   - If the time of the video is sped up, this can create a rushed effect …
   - … this can be used to pass time quickly in a scene.
   - … it can add a comedy effect to certain actions.
   - If the timing of the video is slowed down, this can add a calming effect …
   - … this can be used to enhance and show the beauty of an action scene.
   - … this can also be used to create a solemn feeling, creating almost a tedious effect.

2. Answer must include both of the following explanations [2]:
   - a single still image.
   - the individual parts of a video that are joined together to create the video.

3. Answer must include both of the following explanations:
   - a single audio section in a sound file.
   - they can be layered together to create a more complex/interesting sound file.

4. Any four of the following points [4]:
   - It provides a voice over …
   - … without removing the noise or sound in the clip that is already present.
   - The voice over is recorded as a spate track …
   - … it is then layered over the original sound clip.

5. Answer must include all four of the following points [4]:
   - The number of samples taken of recorded sound …
   - … normally per second.
   - It is measured in Hz or kHz.
   - A sample rate of 20 Hz means that 20,000 samples were taken in a second.

Chapter 11 - Emerging technologies

Review questions

1. Level of response:

   Level 3 [6–8 marks]

   Candidates will discuss in detail a range of points relevant to the impact 3D printing has had on medicine. The points raised will be justified. There will be a reasoned conclusion. The information will be relevant, clear, organised and presented in a structured and coherent format.

Level 2 [3–5 marks]

Candidates will provide limited discussion of points relevant to the impact 3D printing has had on medicine, the development of some of the points will be limited. There will be a conclusion. For the most part the information will be relevant and presented in a structured and coherent format.

Level 1 [1–2 marks]

Candidates may only give reference to a single aspect of 3D printing in medicine. Answers may be simplistic with little or no relevance.

0 marks for a response with no valid comments.

Possible points:

- Used to create casts for broken bones that are a lot more flexible that conventional casts.
- Used to create complex and intricate prosthetic limbs that have improved the mobility of the user.
- Used to create artificial organs and blood vessels allowing access to replacements without the need for others to have suffered loss.
- The artificial organs created are not subject to life expectancy or blood type.

2. Level of response:

Level 3 [6–8 marks]

Candidates will discuss in detail a range of points about the impact of artificial intelligence being used to create self-driving cars. The points raised will be justified. There will be a reasoned conclusion. The information will be relevant, clear, organised and presented in a structured and coherent format.

Level 2 [3–5 marks]

Candidates will provide limited discussion of points about the impact of artificial intelligence being used to create self-driving cars, the development of some of the points will be limited. There will be a conclusion. For the most part the information will be relevant and presented in a structured and coherent format.

Level 1 [1–2 marks]

Candidates may only give reference to a single aspect of artificial intelligence and self-driving cars. Answers may be simplistic with little or no relevance.

0 marks for a response with no valid comments.

Possible points:

- It can make the experience of travelling from one place to another a more pleasurable experience.
- It can increase the level of safety on the roads because a computer can have a faster reaction time to safety issues that may occur.
- It can affect the current legislation and insurance process in place for driving a car on the road.
- More powerful algorithms will cost more to develop, so this could add to the digital divide.
- Some decisions can be more ethical rather than logical, such as would a person swerve to avoid a pedestrian if it meant putting themselves in danger, in comparison to how a computer would react to this.

3. Level of response:

Level 3 [6–8 marks]

Candidates will discuss in detail a range of points about the impact of emerging technologies on our personal entertainment. The points raised will be justified. There will be a reasoned conclusion. The information will be relevant, clear, organised and presented in a structured and coherent format.

Level 2 [3–5 marks]

Candidates will provide limited discussion of points about the impact of emerging technologies on our personal entertainment, the development of some of the points will be limited. There will be a conclusion. For the most part the information will be relevant and presented in a structured and coherent format.

Level 1 [1–2 marks}

Candidates may only give reference to a single aspect of emerging technologies and personal entertainment. Answers may be simplistic with little or no relevance.

0 marks for a response with no valid comments.

Possible points:

- Virtual reality can give users an experience of a situation that they may not able to do otherwise, such as flying a plane.
- Ultra-high definition can enhance the user experience of watching movies.
- It is difficult to be able to stream data at ultra-high definition, so this may prevent users being able to take advantage of the technology.
- Wearable technology has allowed an element of gamification to everyday tasks or exercises, people can compete against each other or their own previous records.

Chapter 12 - Role and impact

Review questions

1. Choose from any three of the following points [3]:

    - It is an internet based form of money.
    - It is a currency that can be used internationally …
    - … without the need for exchange rates.
    - A good example would be bitcoin/litecoin.
    - They are often anonymous in their use, so cannot be tracked.

2. Level of response:

    Level 3 [5–6 marks]

    Candidates will discuss in detail the impact of online shopping for the customer. The points raised will be justified. There will be a reasoned conclusion. The information will be relevant, clear, organised and presented in a structured and coherent format.

    Level 2 [3–4 marks]

    Candidates will provide limited discussion of points about online shopping, the development of some of the points will be limited. There will be a conclusion. For the most part the information will be relevant and presented in a structured and coherent format.

    Level 1 [1–2 marks]

    Candidates may only give reference to a single aspect of online shopping. Answers may be simplistic with little or no relevance.

    0 marks for a response with no valid comments.

Possible points:

- It can be much more convenient for both the customer and the trader.
- Customers can shop on the go with their mobile device and an internet connection.
- It is easier for a customer to see the range of choices offered to compare products.
- Customers who do not enjoy public places are able to enjoy shopping for products from the comfort of their home.
- Customers can shop around different companies more easily to get the best price for their product.

3. Level of response:

    Level 3 [5–6 marks]

    Candidates will discuss in detail the effect that social networking has on our social patterns. The points raised will be justified. There will be a reasoned conclusion. The information will be relevant, clear, organised and presented in a structured and coherent format.

    Level 2 [3–4 marks]

    Candidates will provide limited discussion of points about the effect that social networking has on our social patterns, the development of some of the points will be limited. There will be a conclusion. For the most part the information will be relevant and presented in a structured and coherent format.

    Level 1 [1–2 marks]

    Candidates may only give reference to a single aspect of social networking. Answers may be simplistic with little or no relevance.

    0 marks for a response with no valid comments.

Possible points:

- Many forms of social networking now exist to suit the individual.
- They have allowed many people to stay in touch over long distances, with greater ease.
- Some argue they can help develop greater social skills through encouraging communication.
- Some argue they have a negative effect on social skills as people do not act as they should in many situations.

- There is concern that young people may see the way many act on social media and believe this is normal behaviour.
- Some believe this had led to greater issues such as online bullying.

4. Any combination of four from the following points [4]:

  - Sorting through large sets of data …
  - … to identify patterns and trends.
  - … to establish relationships between the data.
  - Extracting information from sets of data to inform and instruct future decisions.
  - Can involve three stages, exploration, validation and deployment.
  - Used to try and predict changes before they occur.

5. Any combination of four from the following points [4]:

  - Learners can learn at their own pace …
  - … this means that they may have more confidence and can revisit areas with which they struggle.
  - Training can be given in many forms, such as text based, videos and podcasts …
  - … this can help allow for different learning styles between people.
  - A bespoke course can be created depending on a learner's needs …
  - … this can be automated by the software adapting the training to weaknesses highlighted by the learner.
  - Software can be designed to automatically mark any assessment …
  - … this can provide the learners with instant feedback.

Chapter 13 - Networks

1. It boosts a signal along a network cable by receiving data packets and then retransmitting them.

2. File server; print server; mail server; application server; proxy server.

3. Bandwidth measures the frequencies available on a communications channel in Hz, whereas bit rate measures the amount of data that can be transferred in bps.

4. A buffer is used to keep a video running smoothly. Without a buffer, any data congestion would be noticed by the video pausing, missing out frames or pixelating until the full transmission rate is available again, even if it was only for a split second. A buffer downloads parts of the video in advance of it being watched so the user is always watching video that has already been downloaded while the next part of the video is added to the buffer.

5. Packet switching; message switching; circuit switching.

6. Fibre optic strands are very fine so lots can be fitted into a small space to enable more data to be transmitted at once; fibre optics carry data at the speed of light, meaning there is negligible latency; light signals in fibre optics are not susceptible to interference or hacking.

7. Hands-free operation in a car/headset; linking to a smartwatch; linking to biometric devices; streaming videos to a display; streaming music to speakers; transferring files.

8. Wi-Fi is susceptible to interference from other radio devices and microwaves; Wi-Fi signals deteriorate over distance, especially when transmitting through walls and other obstacles; Wi-Fi can be easily intercepted and hacked if encryption is not set up correctly.

9. A video conference is a live transmission of data and so it is critical that the data arrives in real time. The bandwidth needs to be sufficient to provide a transmission rate capable of transmitting the video and audio immediately. If the transmission rate is insufficient, then there will be delays in the delivery of the video and audio, or parts of video and audio will be missing.

10. Both IMAP and POP allow emails to be downloaded to client email software; POP removes the email from the server by default when it has been downloaded, whereas IMAP leaves a copy of the email on the server; IMAP supports multiple folders on the server, whereas POP only supports one folder on the server.

11. Unauthorised access; DoS attack; malware.

12. The user would be expected to log on using their username/banking number and password/PIN; the user could provide additional personal information such as specific characters from their mother's maiden name; the user could be asked to put their debit card into a card reader and provide a code issued by the card reader;

a Short Message Service (SMS) text message that contains a number the user enters into the bank account website could be sent to the user's mobile phone.

13 Backups are a second copy of data and are only needed if the original data is damaged. The original data will still be available and hackers could still gain unauthorised access.

14 Data must be used fairly and lawfully; used for limited, specifically stated purposes; used in a way that is adequate, relevant and not excessive; accurate; kept for no longer than is absolutely necessary; handled according to people's data protection rights; kept safe and secure; not transferred outside the European Economic Area without adequate protection.

15 Information about salary scales must be accurate so that the employee gets paid the correct amount; information about next of kin details must be up to date in case of an injury.

16 Subscription costs are expensive compared with other broadband options; there is a latency so it is not suitable for real-time applications; bandwidth is lower than other broadband options; the equipment is costly to set up.

17 Some channels will be subscription only and so the satellite television networks will want to ensure that only those viewers that have paid for a subscription are able to access those channels.

18 GPS can provide an exact location on earth which can be useful for identifying where the nearest emergency vehicle is to an emergency; GPS can identify an exact location in order to automatically add geotagging information to a photograph; GPS can identify an exact location on a map so a driver is always aware of their current position when driving to a destination.

Review questions

1a Either of the following [1]: Router [1] or Gateway [1].

1b Any three of the following [3]: Switch or Hub to connect the devices together using cables [1]; wireless access point to provide a wireless connection for the laptop and mobile phone [1]; NIC to connect the desktop PC to the network [1]; wireless NIC to enable the laptop and mobile phone to connect wirelessly [1].

2 Any combination of the following [4]: Levi will need sufficient bandwidth to stream the music and video without it being interrupted. [1] If there is insufficient bandwidth then there will be gaps in the music or videos or distortion [1] that will ruin his listening or viewing experience [1]. For the video conferencing, he needs enough bandwidth to receive both the audio and video streams synchronised together [1] and live so that he can participate in real-time [1]. If there isn't sufficient bandwidth then he will receive the audio and video after it happened [1] and if he tries to respond it will not be at the right time [1].

3 All of the following [4]: If Levi wants to use a wired connection then his desktop computer will have to be near the switch [1] which is probably part of the router and must be by the telephone connection [1]. This may not be a suitable location. If he uses it somewhere else then a long cable will be required [1] which could be unsightly, could be a trip hazard and he may not be allowed to fix cables to the walls of the apartment [1].

4a A set of rules used for communication in networks [1].

4b Both of the following [2]: It sends requests to a web server to view a page [1] and sends that page back to the browser [1].

4c Either of the following [1]: IMAP or POP [1].

5a All of the following [4]: Levi should check the legitimacy of the site and download links [1] to check that they are genuine [1]. Levi should have anti-malware software installed [1] that will prevent any malware from infecting his computer [1].

5b Any two of the following [2]: Malware could be attached to a file on a USB stick or other portable memory that Levi uses [1]. Levi could open an infected attachment from an email [1]. Levi could open a macro that is infected with malware [1].

6a Two of the following [2]: Levi could have full create, read, update and delete access to his own user documents because they belong to him [1]. Levi could have read-only access to documents provided by his lecturers so he can view them but not change them [1]. Levi could have create, read and update access to files for a project he is working on with a group of other students so they can collaborate together [1]. Levi might have no access permissions to printers while working from home so that he doesn't send lots of documents to be printed [1].

6b Both of the following [2]: Levi's finger print will be unique so it will identify who he is to give him access rights [1] and it will confirm that it is Levi because he is the only person with his finger print [1].

7a Any two of the following [4]: Levi will have access to more channels [1] because there is a higher bandwidth available with satellite television [1]. Levi will be able to access subscription channels [1] because he will have a set-top-box capable of decrypting the signal [1].

7b Any one of the following [1]: The satellite dish will need to be installed [1] and he may not have permission to install it in his apartment [1]. If weather conditions are bad then the broadcast may be interrupted [1] meaning he cannot watch the television channels properly [1].

Chapter 14 - Project management

1 During monitoring and control of the execution, resources may become unavailable, timescales may not be met and the budget may be exceeded. If this happens, plans will need to be revised to allocate different resources, adjust timescales and adjust expenditure.

2 Web-based software can be used by multiple users at once, whereas single-user desktop software is only available to one user; web-based software can be used by any device, whereas desktop software can only be used by the device(s) on which it is installed; web-based software can be used for collaboration, whereas single-user desktop software can only be used by one person.

3 Resources will have been defined within the software, including their availability and costs. The project manager can then select available resources and allocate them to tasks where they are required. Allocation of already assigned resources at specified times will be prevented by the software. The project manager will be able to assign an amount of time to each resource for each task. The project manager will be able to see the costs involved for each resource and how much each task will cost.

4 Power cut; fire; flood; denial of access to premises; malware; unauthorised access to data; theft of data; corruption to data; loss of key personnel.

5 Recovery procedures are not used very often, if at all, so they need to be tested to ensure they work; if they don't work, then disaster recovery won't work and that could shut down an organisation.

6 Evolutionary prototyping develops each prototype further, whereas throwaway prototyping involves disposing of the prototype. Evolutionary prototyping involves refining user requirements after each evolution of the prototype and throwaway prototyping also involves refining requirements after the prototype is developed. Both methods involve producing a basic version of what the user interface will look like. Both methods involve getting feedback from the user early during the project.

7 JAD involves both users and developers working together to develop a working prototype, with the user being able to refine the design and layout as development progresses. Software application frameworks are used to develop the prototype and end solution.

8 A library of objects (e.g. walls, windows) could be used to design the model; 3D views could be used to see what the extension will look like from a variety of angles; windows and doors can be added to the design and their size and position altered; the colour of walls can be experimented with until the right one is found; different lighting options can be experimented with to give the right amount of light.

9 Loss of jobs; imperfect testing; not the same as a prototype; highly trained staff required; initial costs of purchasing software; still prone to human error; limited to vector objects.

Review questions

1 Conception/initiation; planning; execution; monitoring/control. [4]

2a A large team is likely to require sub-project managers who will need to update different parts of the plan at different stages of the project; members of the team will be able to use a web interface to update their progress; access will be available from any computer which is important for a large team who may be working in different places; team members can collaborate on documents throughout the project; each team member will be using the same version of the software so there won't be compatibility issues.

2b Personal; desktop; single-user. [1]

3 The software will provide an option to define resources; availability of each resource can be identified; costs can be assigned to each resource; resources can be allocated to individual tasks; resource conflicts and overload can be highlighted. [3]

4a Both charts can show the critical path; both charts show the length of time each task takes; both charts show predecessors/dependencies. [2]

4b Resource allocation; start/finish dates; task progress. [2]

5a A 'mock-up' of a software solution; partially completed product used for evaluation/ feedback. [1]

5b Evolutionary prototyping develops each prototype further whereas throw-away prototyping involves disposing of the prototype so the prototype can grow rather than having to start again. Evolutionary prototyping involves refining user requirements after each evolution of the prototype which will enable the landscape gardening company to better understand their own requirements as the prototype develops. The landscape gardening company can canvass opinion from customers on what the user interface will look like. The project team can get feedback from the landscape gardening company early during the project. [4]

6 Paving slabs; shed; borders; flowers; trees; shrubs; garden furniture; soil; grass; hedge; wall. [3]

Chapter 15 - System life cycle

1 Feasibility; analysis; design; implementation/ development/coding/programming; testing; installation/changeover/implementation; maintenance.

2 The analyst can expand upon questions that have been asked during the interview to gain further information from the user; questionnaires take time to create and are unnecessary when a small group of users can all be interviewed.

3 To identify the hardware and software required to operate the developed system.

4 To show the data flows within a system.

5 Each data flow must have a process attached to it. A data flow cannot move directly from one external entity to another or from one data store to another or between an external entity and a data store.

6 A tick box allows more than one response, whereas an option button only allows one response.

7 To test that a validation rule accepts data that is only just acceptable and to test that it produces an error message for data that is only just unacceptable.

8 Alpha testing is carried out by the development team, whereas beta testing is carried out by users; alpha testing is planned and structured, whereas beta testing is ordinary everyday use; alpha testing uses test data, whereas beta testing uses real data.

9 Tester will use input data to test part of a system or a whole system and check the expected results against actual results without knowing or understanding the code inside the black box.

10 A test plan will identify all the tests that are needed for every input, every button, every link, every report, every screen and all other elements of a system. The test plan will include DIFFERENT types of test data including valid, invalid and extreme so that inputs are tested to their limits. Without this planning, important parts of testing would be missed out and errors could be left undiscovered. The plan will also cover all the user's requirements and ensure that they are tested.

11 Parallel; direct; phased; pilot.

12 If it would be too costly or take too long to input data into both systems, then direct would be more appropriate.

13 If there are a lot of users, then pilot changeover will enable training to take place in stages rather than all at once; if the new system is not very big and doesn't have features that can be separated, then pilot could be used instead of trying to phase something that can't be broken into parts.

14 Cover, contents, introduction, hardware/software requirements, instructions, glossary, troubleshooting, index.

15 To give definitions of any technical terms used in the user documentation.

16 When a system requires maintenance.

17 Working relationship; efficiency of system; bugs or errors in the system; ease of use of the system; possible improvements to the system.

18 If a bug or error is found within a system.

Review questions

1a To find out how the current system works; to find out the requirements of the client. [1]

1b There will be lots of staff in several hotels so there won't be time to interview them all but questionnaires can get information from all staff; the data will need analysing and so the questions can be written in a way that will gather responses in a structured manner. [4]

1c Interviews; observation; document analysis. [3]

2 To identify what the client needs the new system to do. [1]

3a Use of colour; consistent use of fonts; avoiding clutter; legibility of fonts; instructions to the user; optional vs compulsory questions; sufficient space for answers; tick boxes or drop down boxes or option buttons for multiple choice lists. [3]

3b Example should identify the input data, type of validation, rule and error message. For example, Number of nights, Type check, Must be numeric, Please enter a numeric value. [3]

3c Printer to print invoices for the customer; barcode scanner to read barcodes on customer booking printout or mobile phone display; magnetic stripe / smart card reader/writer to initiate room keys; touch screen for the point of sale terminal in the bar and restaurant. [3]

4a White box testing requires understanding of the module or system being tested whereas black box testing only requires input data and output data to be used; white box testing is usually carried out by the developer whereas black box testing is usually carried out by the user or specialist testers. [4]

4b Beta testing requires a very large user base and usually applies to off-the-shelf software whereas the hotel system will need to be used consistently by all staff within all the hotels. [2]

4c It's needed to check that the system can cope with invalid data and reject it appropriately without system errors occurring. [2]

5a There are lots of hotels so one hotel could pilot the system and identify any problems which could be rectified before the system is installed in other hotels. Only a small group of staff need to be trained in how to use the system initially at the one hotel. The hotel that pilots the system could be used to train staff from the other hotels how to use the new system. [4]

5b Troubleshooting will show common errors and how to solve them so if the staff come across one of these errors they can find out what to do. Glossary will include definitions of technical terms used in the documentation so if staff don't understand a term in the documentation they can look it up. [4]

5c Errors may need correcting; the system may need to be adapted due to organisational or external changes; to prevent problems from occurring; to improve on the software. [4]

Chapter 16 - Graphics creation

1 An image made up of pixels. It pixelates when it is enlarged too much.

2 An image stored as coordinates and equations. It is recalculated then displayed. It does not pixelate.

3 Image manipulation can be used to make people look worse, make fun of people, be negative or give false impressions that people believe.

4 Parts of an image, or an object, that can be built up on top of each other to create the final image.

5 Lasso, marquee, magnetic lasso.

6 Combines the objects into one object that can then be manipulated.

7 It lets you apply a technique to just part of an image.

8 The colours in the image will be replaced with shades of red and blue.

9 A selection tool (lasso, magic wand, magnetic lasso).

Review questions

1 Two marks from Bitmap and two from Vector [4]

Bitmap
- Made of pixels (small squares).
- Each pixel has a colour.

Vector
- Stored as points/coordinates and calculations.
- The image is recalculated when loaded.

2 Both of the following [2]:
- The pixels are increased in size/the squares of colour are enlarged.
- This makes the pixels more visible/the squares that make the image are more visible.

3 The following [2]:
- The image is recalculated when enlarged.

4 Maximum four marks for benefits (two for benefits, two for expansions) [4].

- Flaws in the images can be removed.
- Result in better appearance/more professional images/magazine.
- Magazine may have more sales.
- If the clothes look better … more companies may want to advertise in the magazine.

Maximum four marks for drawbacks (two for benefits, two for expansions) [4].

- The clothes/models are not 'real life'/fake.
- Deceiving the audience … as the clothes may not look the same in real life.
- Self-esteem issues …. models are too 'perfect'/unrealistic …. teenagers may try and achieve their looks/size.

Maximum two marks for a reasonable, justified conclusion. Accept a conclusion going either way, or compromising [1].

- The magazine should allow for some manipulation but this should not change the actual people or clothes.
- The magazine should not allow for manipulation because they should not be deceiving the audience.
- The magazine should allow for manipulation because they need to create sales and the images need to look good to do this.

Chapter 17 - Animation

Review questions

1 Any combination of the following [2]:

- Each layer can be manipulated independently
- Each element of an image that needs to be manipulated ….
- … must have its own layer.

2 Maximum four marks. (two from Key frame, two from tween) [4].

Key frame

- Each Key frame is a change in an image.
- The animation is jerky (depending on the fps).

Tween

- The start and end points are created.
- The computer generates what happens in between.
- It is a smoother animation.

3 Changing an object into a different object [1].

Chapter 18 - Mail merge

Review questions

1a Both of the following [2]: Mail merge is the automatic addition of data from a source file [1] such as names and addresses into a master document such as a letter [1].

1b Any combination of the following [6]: Create the master document [1]; link the master document to the data source[1]; insert merge field codes[1]; spell check the master document[1]; visually inspect the master document to check for accuracy[1]; set up any filters that are required[1]; preview the mail merge[1]; check the preview for accuracy including the correct records and layout[1]; run the mail merge to produce the letters [1].

2 All of the following [4]: Filter will be required [1] that compares the date of service [1] from the source file [1] with the date specified by the user [1].

3 Any combination of the following [6]: Service to You already has a source file [1] so using mail merge saves having to enter all the data again [1] as it would take a long time to change each letter for each service [1]; errors are likely to occur when changing data [1] whereas the data in the database is more likely to be

331

accurate [1]; filters can be used [1] so that the letters are only sent to customers who have a car due for service [1]; the same master document can be used every month [1] and only the date specified in the filter needs changing [1]; Service to You will only need to proof read one master document [1] rather than every single letter they send out [1]; customers will know the letter is specifically for their car [1] and that a service is genuinely due rather than it being merely marketing [1].

Chapter 19 - Programming for the web

Review questions

1   Maximum two marks for Uses and two marks for Benefits [4].

Uses:

- Add interactivity and/or functionality.
- Relevant example, e.g. choosing an option and displaying text for it.
- Add validation to data entry.

- Relevant example, e.g. stopping words being entered where a number is required, or restricting the range of numbers.

Benefits:

- Allow users to change content so it is relevant to their needs.
- Validate to restrict/prevent data entry errors.

2   All of the following [3]:

- It stores multiple pieces of data.
- Of the same data type.
- Under the same identifier.

3   All of the following [3]:

- Code is independent of the main code.
- It can be called multiple times.
- Saves the code being repeated.

4   Any combination of the following [3]:

- Check the data being input…
- …against restrictions.
- Trap errors.
- Report the error to the user.

The authors and publishers acknowledge the following sources of copyright material and are grateful for the permissions granted. While every effort has been made, it has not always been possible to identify the sources of all the material used, or to trace all copyright holders. If any omissions are brought to our notice, we will be happy to include the appropriate acknowledgements on reprinting.

Cover image: wu kailiang/Alamy Stock Photo; Chapter Opener 1 agsandrew/ Shutterstock; Fig.1.01 MBI/Alamy Stock Photo; Fig.1.03 CBW/Alamy Stock Photo; Fig.1.04 Met Office © Crown copyright; Fig.1.05 Montgomery Martin/ Alamy Stock Photo; Fig.1.06 Anatolii Babii/Alamy Stock Photo; Fig.1.13 RT Image/Alamy Stock Photo; Fig.1.21 AngelSID/Shutterstock; Chapter Opener 2 Sergey Nivens/ Shutterstock; Fig.2.01 Robert Lucian Crusitu/Shutterstock; Fig.2.02 BonD80/ Shutterstock; Fig.2.03 vetkit/ Shutterstock; Fig.2.04 hadescom/ Shutterstock; Fig.2.05 nistor razvan/Getty Images; Fig.2.06 yclinf/Getty Images; Fig.2.07 Moreno Soppelsa/ Shutterstock; Fig.2.08 pryzmat/ Shutterstock; Fig.2.09 Steven Puetzer/Getty Images; Fig.2.10 Pakawat Suwannaket/Shutterstock; Chapter Opener 3 lucapierro/ Getty Images; Fig.3.01 Federico Rostagno/Getty Images; Fig.3.02 Oli Scarff/Getty Images; Fig.3.03 Balancici/Getty Images; Fig.3.04 Bloomberg/ Getty Images; Fig.3.05 Goodshoot/Getty Images; Fig.3.06 TORU YAMANAKA/Getty Images; Chapter Opener 4 wk1003mike/Shutterstock; Fig.4.04 Science Photo Library/ Getty Images; Chapter Opener 5 Aeriform/Getty Images; Fig.5.01 Kheng Guan Toh/Shutterstock; Fig.5.02 created by Jeff Ogden (W163) for Wikipedia, using dated by the International Telecommunications Union (ITU); Chapter Opener 6 KTDESIGN/ SCIENCE PHOTO LIBRARY/Getty Images; Fig.6.05 Rawpixel Ltd/Getty Images; Fig.6.06 Lewis Mulatero/Getty Images; Fig.6.07 Dan Kitwood/Getty Images; Fig.6.08 John Fedele/Getty Images; Fig.6.09 Brian Brainerd/Getty Images; Fig.6.10 Monty Rakusen/Getty Images; Chapter Opener 7 KrulUA/Getty Images; Fig.7.01 © NHS Choices; Chapter Opener 8 Gregor Schuster/ Getty Images; Fig.8.52 PhotoCuisine RM/Alamy Stock Photo; Fig.8.62 ORLANDO SIERRA/Getty Images; Chapter Opener 9 Sergey Nivens/ Shutterstock; Chapter Opener10 Don Farrall/Getty Images; Chapter Opener 11 Anthony Harvie/Getty Images; Fig.11.01 Trevor Williams/Getty Images; Fig.11.02 Bloomberg/Getty Images; Fig.11.03 Sean Gallup/Getty Images; Fig.11.04 ERIC PIERMONT/ Getty Images; Fig.11.05 Aaltazar/Getty Images; Fig.11.06 YASUYOSHI CHIBA/Getty Images; Fig.11.07 Bloomberg/ Getty Images; Fig.11.08 Neilson Barnard/Getty Images; Chapter Opener 12 violetkaipa/Getty Images; Fig.12.01 KTSDESIGN/Getty Images; Fig.12.02 Ramón Espelt Photography/ Getty Images; Fig.12.03 LaraBelova/Getty Images; Fig.12.04 Monty Rakusen/Getty Images; Chapter Opener 13 Mina De La O/Getty Images; Fig.13.01 vtls/ Shutterstock; Fig.13.02 Jelena83/Getty Images; Fig.13.04 luxxtek/Getty Images; Fig.13.06 Noraznen Azit/Getty Images; Fig.13.07 umbertoleporini/Getty Images, Fig.13.11 asharkyu/Shutterstock; Fig.13.13 Alexandr Spatari/Getty Images; Fig 13.14 Editorial Image, LLC/Alamy Stock Photo; Fig.13.16 Peshkova/ Shutterstock; Chapter Opener 14 Hero Images/Getty Images; Fig.14.18 Mikhail Bakunovich/ Shutterstock; Chapter Opener 15 MimaCZ/Getty Images; Fig.15.01 Plinthpics/Alamy Stock Photo; Chapter Opener 16 artishokcs/Getty Images; Fig.16.01 lilu330/ Shutterstock; Fig.16.03 Yadid Levy/ Alamy Stock Photo; Fig.16.04 Dincer Dokumcu/Shutterstock; Fig.16.05 Wavebreakmedia Ltd/ Alamy Stock Photo; Fig.16.06 kris mercer/Alamy Stock Photo; Fig.16.07 petoei/Shutterstock; Fig.16.08 Creative Stall/Shutterstock; Fig.16.09 DesignPrax/ Shutterstock; Chapter Opener 17 Shivendu Jauhari/Getty Images; Fig.17.02 Brian A Jackson/Shutterstock; Fig.17.03 Karl Van Ginderdeuren/Buiten-beeld/Minden Pictures/Getty Images; Chapter Opener 18 Yagi Studio/Getty Images; Chapter Opener 19 Mclek/Shutterstock

On CD-ROM (landscape) lilu330/Shutterstock; (bench) NokHoOkNoi/Shutterstock; (New York City) Songquan Deng/Shutterstock; (helicopter) Zooner GmbH/Alamy Stock Photo; (frog) David Cook/blueshiftstudios/Alamy Stock Photo; (doorway) Valery Sidelnykov/ Shutterstock; (mountains) Peter Haigh/Alamy Stock Photo; (fruit) pilipphoto/Shutterstock; (houses) JeniFoto/Shutterstock.